THE WAR BETWEEN THE TURKS
AND THE PERSIANS

THE WAR BETWEEN THE TURKS AND THE PERSIANS: CONFLICT AND RELIGION IN THE SAFAVID AND OTTOMAN WORLDS

Giovanni-Tommaso Minadoi

Translated by Abraham Hartwell

I.B. TAURIS
LONDON • NEW YORK • OXFORD • NEW DELHI • SYDNEY

I.B. TAURIS
Bloomsbury Publishing Plc
50 Bedford Square, London, WC1B 3DP, UK
1385 Broadway, New York, NY 10018, USA
29 Earlsfort Terrace, Dublin 2, Ireland

BLOOMSBURY, I.B. TAURIS and the I.B. Tauris logo
are trademarks of Bloomsbury Publishing Plc

Original translation imprinted at London by Iohn Wolfe 1595
This edition first published in Great Britain 2019
Paperback edition first published 2021

Introduction copyright © Rudi Matthee, 2019

Rudi Matthee has asserted his right under the Copyright,
Designs and Patents Act, 1988, to be identified as Author of the Introduction.

All rights reserved. No part of this publication may be reproduced or
transmitted in any form or by any means, electronic or mechanical,
including photocopying, recording, or any information storage or retrieval
system, without prior permission in writing from the publishers.

Bloomsbury Publishing Plc does not have any control over, or responsibility for,
any third-party websites referred to or in this book. All internet addresses given
in this book were correct at the time of going to press. The author and publisher
regret any inconvenience caused if addresses have changed or sites have
ceased to exist, but can accept no responsibility for any such changes.

A catalogue record for this book is available from the British Library.

A catalog record for this book is available from the Library of Congress.

ISBN: HB: 978-1-7807-6952-3
PB: 978-0-7556-4275-5
ePDF: 978-1-7867-3584-3
eBook: 978-1-7867-2584-4

Typeset by Newgen KnowledgeWorks Pvt. Ltd., Chennai, India

To find out more about our authors and books visit
www.bloomsbury.com and sign up for our newsletters.

CONTENTS

Introduction by Rudi Matthee	vii
The Epistle Dedicatorie	xv
The Authors Epistle to the Reader	xvii
The First Booke	1
The Second Booke	25
The Third Booke	53
The Fourth Booke	81
The Fifth Booke	113
The Sixt Booke	137
The Seauenth Booke	179
The Eight Booke	203
The Ninth Booke	227
A Letter to the VVorshipful Signor Mario Corrado	249
A Table, conteyning the *declaration of the Names and wordes, vsed* in this Historie, aswell Auncient, as Barbarous	259

INTRODUCTION

Between 1501, the year when the Safavid dynasty established a state in Persia, and 1639, the year when the Persians and the Ottomans gave up fighting each other by concluding a peace accord that proved to be definitive, these two states were engaged in no less than six major wars. All of these stretched out over multiple years and involved numerous campaigns and battles as well as the repeated invasion and conquest of the frontier zones lying astride the territory of the two states – Armenia and Georgia – located in the piedmont of the Elbruz mountain range, the mountainous terrain of eastern Anatolia and the lowlands of Mesopotamia.

Launched and fought over the types of interests that have ignited wars since the dawn of time – territory, resources, kingly glory – the various instalments of the protracted Ottoman–Safavid conflict were articulated in religious terms, in a way that bears more than a little resemblance to the wars of religion that raged in contemporary Europe. The Ottomans saw themselves as the champions of Sunni Islam; the Safavids went into battle under the banner of Islam's Shi'i variant; and each party vilified the other as heretical, the representative of irredeemable evil and utter depravity.

For the interaction between the Ottomans and the Safavids, including their military engagement, we have a plethora of Persian- and Turkish-language sources, some of which narrate entire campaigns in considerable detail. Yet all are rather stylized accounts, true to the genre of Persianate chronicle writing in being somewhat formulaic in their approach, aside from offering only the viewpoint of the side their authors represent. Western accounts of these conflicts, in turn, are rather few in number – even though the European nations at the time had a keen interest in the conflict and its outcome – mostly because few Western observers witnessed the events with their own eyes. Their observations, nevertheless, are extremely useful for complementing the information offered by the Safavid and Ottoman chroniclers, whose concerns were naturally very different from those of outside visitors.

Surely the most detailed account of the sixteenth-century Ottoman–Safavid military encounter is the monographic work of Giovanni Tommaso (Thomaso) Minadoi. Minadoi was a renowned Italian physician who in the 1570s spent some seven years in Aleppo and Istanbul serving the consuls of Venice and who in this period collected a great deal of material on what would be the longest of the conflicts between Muslim powers: the war that broke out in 1578 and that would continue until 1590, when Shah 'Abbas I (r. 1587–1629) decided to accept the humiliating terms of a peace proposal offered to him by his opponent, Sultan Murad III (r. 1574–95).

Minadoi's family originally hailed from Sicily and had reached northern Italy either via Manfredonia on the Gargano Peninsula in Puglia or via Naples.[1] His father, Giovanni Battista, was born in 1501 in Ferrara and served as a medic in Rovigo, a town located halfway between Padua and Ferrara, in the northern region of Veneto. The precise year of Giovanni Tommaso's own birth is not known. He probably came into the world in 1548–9, the third of four brothers. Giovanni Battista, who had moved to Rovigo before his third son was born, died in 1574, stabbed on a public street while Giovanni Tommaso and his older brother Aurelio were studying philosophy and medicine at the University of Padua. Giovanni Tommaso Minadoi graduated from the University of Padua in 1574. Two years later, he went to Syria as resident physician to the Venetian legation, to serve Teodoro Balbi (1542–1619), the newly appointed consul to Aleppo (served 1578–81).

Minadoi remained in Ottoman territory, mostly in Aleppo, with various stays in Istanbul, for a full decade. In this period he went back to Italy only once. Upon his return to the Levant, he was asked to enter the service of Balbi's successor, Giovanni Michele (Michiel) (served c.1582–4). Following his definitive return to Italy in 1586, he became *medico condotto* (i.e. community physician) in the town of Udine, the capital of Friuli, located some hundred kilometres northeast of Venice. After a falling-out with the town's authorities, he was appointed professor of *medicina practica* at the renowned faculty of medicine of the University of Padua, a position he would retain for almost two decades. In this period, Minadoi wrote a number of treatises mixing medicine with theology on such topics as obesity and hair loss.

To most historians, Minadoi is best known as the author of a substantial work on the Ottoman–Safavid conflict that had broken out while he resided in Ottoman territory. Minadoi published the result of his research on this conflict shortly after his definitive return to Italy, having spent a brief two months preparing the manuscript. In 1587 the first edition, consisting of four 'books' or chapters, appeared under the title *Historia della guerra fra Turchi et Persiani, descritta in quattro libri* in Venice published by Andrea Muschio and Barezzo Barezzi, and in Rome published by I. Tornerio and B. Donangeli. In spite of the hasty final preparation, the book must have been years in the making, since as early as 1583 the Italian Pietro Bizarri appended part of a manuscript version of the work to his own *Persicarum rerum historia*, the first comprehensive history of Persia to appear in Europe.[2] Minadoi, now having access to proper libraries, kept adding material to his research, as a result of which a new, expanded version of his book saw the light of day in 1588. Titled *Historia della guerra fra Turchi et Persiani di G. T. Minadoi … dall'istesso riformata, e aggiuntivi i successi dell'anno 1586*, this second edition was published in Venice by Andrea Muschio and Barezzo Barezzi, and in Turin by Giovanni Battista Bevilacqua. The account had been updated to 1586, ending with a report on the murder of Hamza Mirza, son of Shah Khodabanda and heir apparent, in December 1586; the four 'books' had been rearranged and expanded to nine, and the work now included a chapter on the Safavid administrative system. The work also contained a lovely map, presented as a double-page hand-coloured spread. In 1594 Andrea Muschio and Barezzo Barezzi reprinted this edition. In the intervening time, Minadoi had become the private physician of the Duke of Mantua, a position he retained until 1593.

Minadoi's work was quickly translated into various languages. The Spanish rendering, titled *Historia de la guerra entre turcos y persianos de Juan Tomas Minadoy, en quatro libros, començando de año de 1576, que fueron los primeros motivos della, hasta el año de 1585*, was published in Madrid in 1588 (repr. Valencia: Universidad de Valencia, 2010). While evidently based on the original Italian edition, this translation was different in that it lacked the map and that each of the four 'books' was now divided into chapters. The sympathy that existed at this point among the Spanish political elite for Persia, as a country that might be enlisted in the struggle against the Ottomans, accounts for the timing of this translation, which really served as a piece of propaganda. The translator, Antonio de Herrera, a historian from Tordesillas, dedicated the work to the royal secretary, Juan de Idiáquez, one of Philip II's most trusted officials.[3] In 1592 a German translation appeared in Frankfurt am Main as *Persische Historia, Das ist: Warhaffte und Ausführliche Beschreibung von dem alangwirigien und erschrockligen Krieg, der Turcken, wider die Perseier, welcher sich im Jahr nach Christi Geburt 1577 anngesponnen und bisanhero mit vielem Blutvergissen verhalten hat*. In 1601 a Latin translation came out, also in Frankfurt, as part of a reprint of Bizarri's *Rerum Persicarum Historia, initia gentis, mores, institute, resque gestas ad haec usque tempora complectens*.

The English translation, *The Historie of Warres between the Turkes and the Persians*, which is here presented in a new edition, was originally published in 1595 in London by the printing house of John Wolfe, a key figure in the expanding foreign news market at the time. It is a faithful rendering of the expanded Italian edition of 1588. Yet it, too, lacks some of the features of the Italian original. Thus both the decorative borders at the top of the page and the illustrated squares enclosing the drop capital letter that opens each 'book' are hand-coloured in the original. The handsome map, presented in the Italian text in colour, appears in black and white in the translation.

The English translation remains better known than any other version of Minadoi's work, including the Italian original, mainly because it was reissued in a facsimile edition in Tehran in 1976, as part of the Pahlavi Memorial Series. The translator, Abraham Hartwell (1553/4–1607), was a member of the Society of Antiquaries, a society founded by Archbishop Parker in 1572. In his capacity as secretary to Archbishop Whitgift of Canterbury (1530–1604), a favourite of Queen Elizabeth I, Hartwell also served as a most active ecclesiastical censor, licensing a number of books on Turkish history for publication. Operating in an environment of heightened interest in Turkish affairs following the Ottoman conquest of Cyprus and the ensuing battle of Lepanto of 1571, as well as the launching of the English Levant Company a decade later, he also translated Lazaro Soranzo's *L'Ottomanno* into English.[4]

Minadoi's work consists of nine books, followed by a letter to Mario Corrado, in which the author voices his opinion about whether or not Tabriz corresponds with the classical Ecbatana, and a glossary of geographical names and terms. The first book, which covers the period between the late reign of Shah Tahmasb (1524–76) and the accession of Shah 'Abbas I in 1587, focuses on the reign of the two protagonists of the Ottoman–Safavid war: Sultan

Murad III, who had come to power in 1574, and Shah Mohammad Khodabanda, who in early 1578 succeeded the sanguine Shah Esma'il II. Books two to nine narrate the war between its outbreak in 1578 and the occupation of Georgia by the Ottomans some two years later.

Minadoi's account has to be read in the context of the conflict between the Ottoman Empire and Europe, and by extension between Islam and Christendom. The author makes it clear that the research he conducted for his work did not just receive encouragement but had actual material support from the Venetian authorities. In collecting the information that he used for his account, he stood in a century-old Venetian tradition of gathering intelligence about the Ottomans and their enemies, especially those who might become allies with the Christian nations in a common anti-Turkish front. Like Balbi and Michele, as well as the well-known (Flemish) Austrian ambassador Oghir Ghiselin de Busbecq, Minadoi never visited Persia itself. This tradition goes back at least as far as the days of Uzun Hasan (r. 1453–78), the ruler of the west-Persian Aq-Qoyunlu (White Sheep) dynasty, who in the mid-fifteenth century had requested assistance from the Venetians in his own struggle against the Turks. The Aq-Qoyunlu were defeated by the Ottomans in 1473 and faded soon after Uzun Hasan's death five years later. Less than a quarter of a century later, the rise to political power of a new dynasty – the Safavids – rekindled hopes that relief from the Turkish scourge might finally be at hand. The *Diarii* of the panoptic Venetian annalist Marin Sanudo and the account of Giovanni Rota, a physician stationed in Aleppo, which came out in 1508 in the form of a letter to the doge, portray the phenomenal rise of Shah Esma'il Safavi in 1501 as the *parousia* of a messianic saviour.[5]

Minadoi himself was a Christian, or at least viewed the conflict between Ottomans and Safavids through Christian eyes. Indeed, like most of his Renaissance peers, Minadoi clearly saw the Ottoman–Safavid conflict as potentially beneficial to Christian-European interests. As a good Venetian, he dreaded the Ottomans and the chance that 'each campaigning season might bring a renewal of Ottoman attacks on the West'. Minadoi even went so far as to accept 'as true whatever misfortune the Turks might plausibly have suffered'.

For a more sympathetic view of the Ottomans, one has to look for countries that were not directly at war with them or that competed with the Hispano-Portuguese Empire, such as France and England. Whereas Minadoi had dedicated his work to Pope Sixtus V (r. 1585–90), Hartwell in turn dedicated his translation to the Archbishop of Canterbury. England at this point occupied a peculiar position in this struggle. Not directly involved, it was relatively favourably inclined to the Ottomans, seeking their support, if only because its own arch-enemy, Spain, was a sworn enemy of the Turks. The English Levant Company understandably also had considerable interest in maintaining good relations with Istanbul. This may have been the reason why Hartwell cryptically refers to the secrecy he chose to keep with regard to some of the reasons why he had decided to undertake the translation of Minadoi's work.

Minadoi, meanwhile, shows some sympathy for the Safavids – whom various European nations had continued to court as potential allies against the bellicose Ottomans. Indeed, following a venerable Western tradition, he views Persians as a sophisticated and cultured people, as opposed to the Turks, whose reputation was that of primitive and predatory brutes.

Yet Minadoi's work is no ode to the Persians. Unlike Hartwell, who had a mostly negative view of Persia, Minadoi was ambivalent about the Safavid realm. If in many passages in his work he seems to tilt towards Persia, this is less from a love for the Safavid state than from fear of the greater evil: the Turks. At the same time, he voices the stereotypical views of Persia and Persians expressed by many before and after him, conflating, in the antiquarian fashion current at the time, the ancient inhabitants of the country and the modern ones, calling the Persians 'great deceivers, full of craftie Stratagemes, unconstant, and breakers of their word'. Yet, referring to a perceived anarchic disposition, he also claimed that they were 'never content with any mans governement'. Alluding to a presumed creative spirit, he further insisted that they were 'lovers of novelties' (p. 74). Yet on balance, not yet seduced by the wonders of Isfahan as fashioned and embellished by Shah 'Abbas I a generation later, and not having set foot in Persia and thus unable to report on the cultural sophistication and hospitality of its people from first-hand experience, Minadoi classified the Persians as barbarians, just like the Turks.

Superimposing the Catholic–Protestant rivalry onto the Sunni–Shi'i conflict that suffused the enmity between the Ottomans and the Safavids, Minadoi ultimately argued that they were both believers in the same prophet, that the Persians were just as inveterately inimical to Christianity as the Turks. In his account, the conflict between these two states thus becomes part of a providential plan designed to weaken the major Muslim powers and, therefore, Islam. In keeping with a sentiment that would long persist, the war, in his words, although 'long and bloudie', was also 'very commodious and of great opportunitie to the Christian Common-wealth'. Minadoi hoped that his book would 'animate Christian princes to take up arms against barbarians under whose rule famous and once powerful nations are reduced' (pp. 1–3). He thus advocated a strategy that today we would call 'dual containment'.[6]

What is perhaps most striking about Minadoi's work is its break with past custom. Histories of Persia written by Europeans, before and after him, tended to make connections between Persians in the present with their forebears in antiquity in ways that Persians themselves came to do only in the late nineteenth century and under the influence of European practice. His work is pragmatic in character and purpose: rather than engaging in historical digressions about the presumed origins of the Persians and the Turks, Minadoi keeps the war he describes in focus, providing a wealth of detail about its origins, its landmark events, battles and skirmishes. He also pays much attention to the terrain, the topography and especially place names, seeking to give their accurate rendering. In this, he represented a new trend among scholars, who relied less on ancient nomenclature than their forebears in their attempt to find accurate current names for topographical places. In the process, Minadoi also provides a great deal of information about other aspects of the Safavid polity, much of it remarkably accurate, given his lack of direct access to the country. He thus touches on the formidable Pari Khan Khanom, Shah Tahmasb's daughter, her role in the successive enthronement of her two brothers, Isma'il II in 1576 and Mohammad Khodabanda two years later, and how she was sidelined and killed by the Qezelbash shortly thereafter. Further, he was the first European to give a detailed and informed overview of the Sunni–Shi'i divide in Islam.

Minadoi's narrative was not above controversy. He made the mistake of identifying Tabriz with Ecbatana, the capital of the Medes, most likely present-day Hamadan, and got into a dispute with Paulo Giovio, a contemporary Italian historian who had written on the Turks, concerning Giovio's argument that Tabriz was to be equated with ancient Terva (Yerevan in

Armenian) – hence the letter to Mario Corrado.[7] Minadoi became involved in a similar discussion with the Austrian humanist scholar Hans Löwenklau (Johannes Leunclavius), a specialist of Byzantine as well as Turkish history, who resided in Istanbul in 1585–7 and subsequently published various books about the Ottoman Empire, beginning with *Annales Sultanorum Othmanidarum usque ad annum 1588*.[8] In 1595 the Venetian publisher Nicolao Morettum brought out the controversy between the two scholars under the title *Thomae Minadoi pro sua de bello Persico Historia adversus ea quae illi a Ioanne Leunclavio obijciuntur. Disputatio. Ad Aloysium Foscarenum Senatorem Illustrissimum*. This book was edited by Aurelio Minadoi, Giovanni Tommaso's brother, who dedicated it to the Venetian senator Luigi Foscarini (dedicatory letter by 'Aurelius Minadous' on the first pages).

What is especially important for the modern reader is that neither Minadoi's anti-Turkish bias nor his qualified sympathy for the Persians stands in the way of his search for the 'truth'. He goes to great lengths emphasizing that he has made great efforts to find the truth behind the story he is telling. This is a trope, to be sure, but in Minadoi's case, it is more than that: as he himself states, he interviewed many people and double- and triple-checked facts in the face of many inconsistencies with regard to place names. In his preface, Minadoi insists that he has done everything possible to collect and collate information from various sources, most notably by consulting eyewitnesses, 'men of great authority who were present for the most part at these actions' (author's epistle to the reader). He mentions how his medical knowledge has helped him gather his information. In this he was heir to another tradition with a long pedigree: in Islamic lands, Westerners were (until quite recently) often automatically credited with medical knowledge, and their (presumed) knowledge of illnesses and curative skills literally opened doors for European physicians, even to the inner sanctum of the homes of the elite. Their access to the royal palace was one of the reasons why Jewish doctors serving the bailo in Constantinople were highly prized by the Venetians.

Aleppo, the terminus for a branch of the silk trade originating in Persia, was an ideal venue to collect information on the Safavid state. Minadoi in particular invokes as informants the two successive Venetian consuls to Aleppo under whom he served, Teodoro Balbi and Giovanni Michele, calling them 'two most noble, prudent and valorouse subiectes of the State of Venice', and who 'most magnificently without sparing of any costes did favour me herein' (author's epistle to the reader). Balbi in turn benefited from Minadoi's knowledge. Upon his return to Venice in 1582, Balbi gave testimony on Persia to the Venetian Senate, and the similarities between his text and that of Minadoi makes it likely that the latter actually wrote Balbi's report to the Senate.[9] Minadoi also mentions a Venetian named Cristoforo de Boni, who served as interpreter to these diplomats.

Most valuable for the information Minadoi offers on the Safavids, especially on their administrative system, must have been his other, 'native', informants. One was the renegade Scipione, the son of a nobleman from Genoa who had fought as a corsair until he was captured by the Ottomans, at which point he had converted to Islam. Upon his release, now known as Sinan Pasha, he had made a career for himself in the Ottoman army, to the point of assuming the function of commander-in-chief in the war against the Safavids. Eventually, suspected of plotting against the sultan, he had been dismissed and sent into exile. Minadoi mentions how he had treated him, curing him of a 'certain illness', most likely venereal disease. Equally important as a source of information was an official named Maqsud Khan, who came to the Ottoman Empire as an envoy from Shah Mohammad Khodabanda seeking peace, and who upon his return was made governor of Tabriz. He next had a falling-out with the shah, causing him to take refuge with the Ottomans, to be appointed governor of Aleppo. Minadoi specifically notes how he met with Maqsud Khan's son after the latter's father had been made governor of Aleppo.

Minadoi's work, in its original version as well as its various translations, would have considerable influence on the image of Persia, its political system and its confrontation with the Ottomans in seventeenth-century Europe. The best illustration of such influence is Oruch Beg, better known as Don Juan of Persia, the secretary of an embassy sent to Spain by Shah 'Abbas I who, having arrived in Valladolid in 1601, converted to Christianity and chose to remain in Spain. He, or rather his Spanish mentor and translator, Alfonso Remón, followed Minadoi's account of events and made extensive use of his work.[10] Another example is the English historian Richard Knolles (c.1545–1610), who copied the parts of Minadoi's work that deal with the Sunni–Shi'i schism verbatim for his own acclaimed work, *Generall Historie of the Turkes* (1603–4). The information contained in Knolles's book, the first major work in English on the Ottoman Empire, was further publicized by Paul Rycaut's highly influential *The Present State of the Ottoman Empire* (1665), which rivalled Knolles's account as the standard work on the Ottomans in Europe well into the eighteenth century. The information Minadoi provided shows up as well in the works of John Cartwright and Samuel Purchas, two authors who reached a mass audience in seventeenth-century Europe by being included in the exceedingly popular Hakluyt series. Some of the various anonymous manuscripts on the Persian-Turkish wars that appeared at the turn of the seventeenth century are undoubtedly based in part on his work as well. The information offered by Minadoi thus long reverberated, helping to shape and solidify opinions about Persia and its inhabitants, separately and in relation with the Ottomans, that would have enormous staying power.

Rudi Matthee
University of Delaware

NOTES

1. This biographical information is largely based on John R. Walsh, 'Giovanni Tommaso Minadoi's History of the Turko-Persian Wars of the Reign of Murād III', in Bobodžan G. Gafurov (ed.), *Trudy dvadcat' pjatogo Mezdunarodnogo Kongressa Moskva 9–16 avgusta 1960: Obščaja čast', zasedanija sekcij I – V* (Moskva: Izdat. Vostočnoj Literatury, 1963), vol. 2, pp. 448–9; Lucia Samaden, 'Giovanni Tommaso Minadoi (1548–1615). Dal medico della «nazione» veneziana a professore universitario a Padova', *Quaderni per la Storia dell'Università di Padova* 31 (1998), pp. 91–164; and Nancy G. Siraisi, *History, Medicine and the Traditions of Renaissance Learning* (Ann Arbor: University of Michigan Press, 2007), pp. 246–60.
2. Pietro Bizarri, *Persicarum rerum historia in XII libros descripta, totius gentis initia, mores, instituta, et rerum domi forisque gestarum e narrationem continens* (Antwerp: Plantin, 1583).
3. Enrique García Hernán, 'The Holy See, the Spanish Monarchy and Safavid Persia in the Sixteenth Century: Some Aspects of the Involvement of the Society of Jesus', in Willem Floor and Edmund Herzig (eds), *Iran and the World in the Safavid Age* (London: I.B. Tauris, 2012), p. 190.

4. V. J. Parry, *Richard Knolles' History of the Turks*, ed. Salih Özbaran (Istanbul: ISIS, 2003), p. 13; and Anders Ingram, *Writing the Ottomans: Turkish History in Early Modern England* (New York: Palgrave Macmillan, 2015), pp. 38–9, 48–9.
5. The specific references to Persia in Sanudo's encyclopedic work have been brought together by Biancamaria Scarcia Amoretti, ed., *Šhāh Ismā'īl I nei «Diarii» di Marin Sanudo* (Rome: Istituto per l'Oriente, 1979; index, ed. by Laura Bottini, 2005). See also Giovanni Rota, *La vita, costume e natura de' Sofi re di Persia e di Media* … (Rome: Eucharius Silber, 1508); and Pierre Dodogne, 'La «Vita del Sofi» di Giovanni Rota. Edizione critica', in *Studi in onore di Raffaele Spongano* (Bologna: Boni, 1980), pp. 215–33.
6. This is a mirror image of the Iranian perspective and perception. The Safavids were quite happy to see the Ottomans and the Europeans engaged in war since, so long as the Ottomans were involved on their western front, they would not have the resources to take on Iran.
7. *Thomæ Minadoi Rhodigini Pro quadam sua sententia Disputatio*, Patavii: Apud Franciscum Bolzettam, 1604.
8. Frankfurt am Main, 1588. For Löwenklau, see Pál Ács, 'Pro Turcis and contra Turcos: Curiosity, Scholarship and Spiritualism in Turkish Histories by Johannes Löwenklau (1541–1594)', *Acta Comeniana* 25 (2011), pp. 1–22.
9. See Gugliemo Berchet (ed.), *La Repubblica di Venezia e la Persia* (Turin: Tipografia G. B. Paravia e Comp., 1865; repr. Tehran: Offset Press, 1976), pp. 276–89.
10. Don Juan of Persia, *Don Juan of Persia: A Shi'ah Catholic 1560–1604*, trans. and ed. G. Le Strange (London: Routledge, 1926; repr. 2005), introduction, p. 19.

The Epistle Dedicatorie

To the most Gracious and Reuerend Father in God, IOHN by the prouidence of God, Lord Archbishop of Canterbury, Primate and Metropolitane of all England, and one of the Lords of her Maiesties most honorable Priuie Councell.

Most Reuerend and my singular good Lorde, May it please your Grace with honorable fauour to accept of this paper-Present, which by starts I haue drawne out of Italian into English. Sondry reasons there were that at the first, about three yeares agoe, moued me to begin the translation thereof, but because they are such as concerne matter of estate, where withall I list not to meddle for feare of burning my fingers, I thought it good rather to conceale them, then in printe to publish them. The onely occasion, that caused mee after so long time hauing layed it aside, to take it vp againe and finish the same, was the graue iudgement of S^r. Moile Finche a right worshipfull knight in Kent, who this last Sommer beeing with you at your Maner of Beakesbourne, vpon speech then had about the great preparations of the Turke agaynst Christendome, and the huge victories that he had atchieued vpon his enemies that sought to weaken him, did verie highly commende this booke, and the Author thereof: whose eloquence although my english pen cannot possibly reache and expresse, yet is it trulie and faithfully doone in as plaine and significant Termes as I could: whereuntoo I was once minded to haue added certain aduertisementes and collections, as well out of the old auncient writers both sacred and prophane, that haue written of the most stately & magnificent Empire of the Medes and Persians in times past, as also out of Leunclaius & others, that haue lately written of the moderne and present estate thereof, which hath scarse a shaddow of the antique gouernement, wherewith it was then ruled & gouerned. But that matter grew to be so long, that I gaue ouer my purpose therein, least the volume should haue waxen too great. I was also minded to haue inserted into this Treatise, a certaine Prophesie touching the Catastrophe of the Turkish kingdom, which Antonius Torquatus of Ferrara did deliuer to Matthias king of Hungary in the yeare of our Lord 1480. De Regnorum Europae Mutationibus. But because he doth peremptorily set downe, that the Turkes shall fall into the handes of the Christians about the yeares 1594. & 1595. and that the house of the Ottomans shall vtterly decay in their thirteenth or fourteenth king, and that it shall not exceede that nomber, nor passe the yeare of our Lord 1596: He shall pardon me, if I do not beleeue him, nor commend his credit to future posteritie. For (with great griefe it must bee vttered) wee see all thinges go so quite contrarie to this prognosticon, and the power of the Turkes growe so huge and infinite; and their enemies so diuided and weakened, that vnlesse God come downe as it were out of an Engine, to protect the Gospell of his Sonne Iesus Christ, and the Professors thereof, I feare greatly that the halfe Moone which now ruleth & raigneth almost ouer all the East, wil grow to the full, and breede such an Inundation as will vtterly drowne al Christendome in the West. God for his mercies sake rebate her Hornes with the glorious shine of his brightest Sonne. The houres, that I haue employed in writing this translation, were stollen from your Graces grauer businesses whereon I should haue attended: And therfore no man can by any right chalenge the same from you, nor I in duetie offer it to any other but to your Grace, whose wholy I am and must be, & of whom I may truely and iustly say as Oedipus saith in Sophocles. […].

The Lord God long maintaine your Grace in all honor and health vnder the most blessed gouernement of our most happy & renowmed Queen ELIZABETH, for the continuance of the peace of this Church of England, and comfort of all those that are bound to honor and loue you. At Lambehith, this New-yeares-day 1595.

Your Graces most humble Seruant at commaundement, Abraham Hartwell.

The Authors Epistle to the Reader

Although Strabo doo write, that the writinges touching matters of Persia, had alwaies but small credit euen vntill his time: and therefore it may seeme likely, that I, who haue taken vpon me to wryte such thinges as haue happened in those cuntries within the space of nyne yeares, ought greatly to feare lest these my writinges should haue the very same successe, that they had: yet I haue thought it necessary to aduertise the reader, that for that respect I did not surcease, or refuse to publish this my history, (though indeed for dyuers other wantes and defectes it may seeme peraduenture not soe worthy to appeere before the learned persons of this present age:) But rather, euen for the selfe same cause, it may rest assured, that without manifest wrong & iniury it cānot be despised or discredited. For if those former Historiographers (if algates they were euer worthy of that name) haue deserued, that little credit should be yelded vnto them: this default was imputed vnto them not for any despite or reproch, but in iustice and in reason: because (as Strabo himselfe saith) they louing more to delight then to profit, inserted many fictions & many fables in the truth & purity of the History. And so the things that happened in deed, being mingled and confused with such as were cogged and fained, they that read them, could not be so truly enformed of those aduentures and actions, as they desyred, and peraduenture as they had great neede at that time to be instructed in. But I haue written this history, with a full and sound resolution, neuer to decline from the truth, & not to suffer, that vpon any occasion whatsoeuer, any thing should bee discoursed therein, but that which eyther I my selfe haue seene, or possibly could vnderstand to be true. Wherein, although I haue found many difficulties and vsed great labours, (aswell through the ignorance of the people, who being not able to tell me any other name of the Cittyes, of the cuntries, of the fieldes, of the Riuers, & of the hilles, but onely the barbarous names of them, they made the certaine knowledge of those places, wherein these battells were foughten, to be very difficult vnto me: As also because it was very requisite, that I should haue an eie to the seuer all qualities of dyuers nations, who are sometimes giuen to lying, and by whom many thinges are wont to bee spoken, and many thinges concealed, for their owne particular respectes.) Notwithstanding I haue endeuored by all the best meanes I possibly could, to discharge my duty therein, ouercomming these & such other difficulties, with continuall conference among dyuers men in dyuers places, to the end I might find them agree together in their reportes, and expecting withall, that Tyme it selfe would at last bring forth the truth. Neither did I euer content my selfe with the first or second aduertisement deliuered vnto me, but alwaies iustified the first with the last, by conferring together the testimonies of both sides. And lastly, without regard of danger, of expenses, or of labour, I haue enformed my self of euery particularity, that possibly I could, by such men, as were esteemed no liers, but men of great authority, who were present for the most part at al these actions. Which purpose and resolution of myne, was greatly fauoured and assisted by three priuate & extraordinary meanes. First, by the credit and authoritie of Theodoro Balbj, and Giouanni Michele, being then the right honorable Consulles in Soria for the Venetian Senate, two most noble, prudent, and valorouse subiectes of the State of Venice: who most magnificently without sparing of any costes did fauour me herein, & in all my other studies, where, vnto I applyed my selfe in those countries. Secondly by the familiar conuersation which I had with one Christoforo de Buonj, cheefe Interpreter to the said most honorable Lordes, a person of great valour, well frended and beloued among those nations, and aboue all, of singular faith and dexterity. Thirdly, by my knowledge in Phisicke, which I was not squemish to practise among those people, to the end I might the better, & without ministring any suspition to any man, enter into their most secret & important aduertisementes: and so by this meanes to purchase familiarity in the principall howses of those Cities, wherein for the space of almost seuen whole yeares together, I liued and was entertayned. And of thus much it shall be euen sufficient to haue aduertised the readers, who without any other Apologie or iustification of mine, mayrest contented and satisfied with my desyre, which hath beene to represent vnto the world Accidentes, that haue happened so far off, so strange, and so important, that thereby they may reape great profit both in peace and warre. Which satisfaction if I shall obtaine of their gratitude, I shall thinke my selfe to haue gayned enough, in lieu of all the trauelles, of all the dangers, & of all the expences, that I haue susteyned, & I shall rest assured that I haue not beene an vnfruitfull labourer herein.

The First Booke

The Argument.
The causes that moued the Author to write this Historie.
The Originall of this warre.
The causes of the same warre.
Aidere beheaded.
Ismahel the king vseth great cruelties, publisheth a new Religion, and spreadeth ab […]ad a speech that he would passe into Babylonia.
Amurath resolueth to moue warre against Persia.
Periaconcona beheaded.
New stirres in Persia, wherof Vctres Bassa aduertiseth Amurath: who therby is confirmed in his opinion to make this warre.
Consultations at Constantinople, of the maner how to manage this warre.
Amurath will not in person go with the Armie: but choseth Mustaffa Bassa to be his Generall: who passeth to Chalcedon, and from thence to Erzirum, where he mustereth and surueigheth his Armie, and then departeth for Siruan.
Mustaffa arriueth at Chars: goeth vnder the Mountaines of Chielder, and there encampeth himselfe artificially.
The King of Persia sendeth Souldiers against the Turkes: and ouer them he maketh Tocomac the Sultan his Generall.
Tocomac cometh toward Chars; he findeth out his Spies, and being deceiued by his Spies, he doth confidently assault the Turkes.
At the first, Tocomac doth happely ouercome the Turkes, but afterwardes he was discomfited, and saued himselfe by the oportunitie of the night.
The particular of the Victorie.

Manucchiar the Georgian yeeldeth himselfe to Mustaffa, and is interteined by him.

THE WARRES BETWEENE THE TURKES AND PERSIANS

<small>The warre in Persia commodious for the state of Christendom.</small>

I write the sondry successes of the warre betweene Amurat king of Turkie, & Mahamet by surname caled Codabanda king of Persia, both of them among the Barbarians beeing most mightie & most warlike Princes. A warre not onely long & bloudie, but also very commodious and of great oportunitie to the Christian Common-wealth: for that it hath granted leisure to the Champions of Christ to refresh and encrease their forces, being now much weakened by warres both Forreine and Ciuill. A matter in truth rather diuine then humane, there being now newly arisen among the Turkes, fresh hopes of victories, by meanes whereof (contrary to the custome of such contentions) the wrath of these two Princes was drawne in length, which if they had bene conuerted against Europe, might haue made our state most troublesome and turbulent. These successes and all the rest, that together with the like motions haue come to passe, sometimes intermingling among them the priuy treacheries of the Tartarians, sometimes the oppressions of the people of Drusia, and sometimes also the insolencies of the Arabians, I here take in hand to describe, being therunto moued, principally vpon two occasions. The one is, for that they all seeme to me of themselues very worthy to be knowne both of the men that liue at this day, & also of those that shall come after vs: neither haue I as yet seene any man that hath made any full or true report thereof Which notwithstanding I hope shalbe herein performed by my myselfe who haue bene entertained almost seauen whole yeares (during the said warres) partly in Soria, partly in Constantinople, and by occasion of my practise in Phisicke, haue bene familiarly conuersant with many Bassaes, Embassadours, and other great men, aswel Persians as Turkes, that haue beene agentes and dealers in these affaires. The other is, for that I doe verily persuade my selfe, that I shall breede great profite and delight to all nations Christian by the reading of this history, wherein they shall vnderstand how mighty the forces are of these two enimies of the name of Christ; and in what termes they stand euen at this day: by meanes of which knowledge it may peraduenture fall out, that our Christian Princes will bee encouraged to take vp armes against the Barbarians, vnder whose gouernement so many famous and potent nations are already reduced. A losse (to say the trueth) very great, and not to be thought-of without shedding of teares, that whereas a people so renowmed for their Nobilitie, & glorious in all ages for wisedome

<small>The causes that moue the author to wryte this historie.</small>

THE FIRST BOOKE

and science, did in times past gouerne so many nations, as though they were Lordes of the whole world: Now being either driuen from their proper Colonies, from their owne houses, from their domesticall confines, they goe wandring vp and downe poore, & needy of other mens helpe: Orels being brought into a most vile kind of seruitude, some serue as sclaues, & some yeeld obedience to the enimies of Christ in such sorte, that euen in Greece it selfe, the very name of Greece is quite extinguished, and al because it was departed from the bosome of the Catholike Church. But let not this my history take his beginning at these quarrels and complaintes, which peraduenture to some mens humors would seeme the more vnpleasant, in that they would proue more necessary to be set downe in this respect: And therefore my conceit is rather, that in mentioning such thinges as are neerer to our remembrance, I should beginne at the death of olde Tamas the most famous king of Persia, and withall discourse vpon the state and condition of that kingdome whilest it remained in the successors of the said Tamas, videlicet Ismahel and Mahamet, his sonnes: for that by this very briefe narration, euery man shall manifestly see the true occasions of this warre, and so we shall auoide the inserting of any superfluous replication in the contexture of this our history.

 I say then, that Tamas after the warres, which he valorously waged with Soliman the first of that name, and the eleuenth Emperour of the Turkes, at such time as the said Tamas did driue Soliman out of Tauris (being of old called Ecbathana, the very same, wherein Herodotus writeth, that the kings richesses & treasures were then kept, & not Terua as P. Giouius would haue it) a Citty which the same Turkish Emperour had sacked, and hauing concluded a peace, wherein it was agreed that the Castell Cheiseri, by the Turkes called Chars, & by Ptolomee (as a man may resonably coniecture) Corso, being in this great change reduced by Soliman, into a fort, should be razed: he withdrew himselfe to the gouerment of his own kingdome. Vnder whome the Persian Empire flourished in sacred & redoubted lawes, the people demeaned themselues after the best manner they could, abundance of collections came plentifully in, the Rentes of his chambers increased wonderfully, Armes, Artes & Sciences did happely prosper, and were highly esteemed: neither was there any more feare that Soliman would renew the warres, as one that had altogether bent his thoughtes another way. When as after a few yeares, wherein both Soliman and his sonne Selim, which after him had enioyed that damned foelicity of his Empire, departed out of this lyfe, Tamas also himself died in the yeare 1576, the xj. day of May, hauing left behind him eleuen children, one called Mahamet the eldest, who passed his life a while in Heri, (in times past called Aria,) and afterwardes in Siras, (of old called

A peace betweene Tamas & Soliman, & the conditions thereof.

Soliman & Selim dead. Tamas dyeth. Tamas leaueth eleuen children.

Persepolis) by the appointment of his father, being nowe waxen proud for his issue of many sonnes. Another named Ismahel his second sonne, who for the fiercenesse of his courage was banished into a Castell, called by the Persians Cahaca, situate betweene Casbin (otherwise called Arsacia) & Tauris. The third, who had to name Aidere, was kept in the custody of Zalchan, Piry Mahamet, Acta Hussain, and other of his kinsfolkes, by occasion of the mother of the said Aidere, all being cheefe Capitaines in the coast of Istigelù. Other eight children there were partly by the same mother partly by other women, whose names were Mamut, Solimano, Mustaffa, Emanguli, Alichan, Amet, Abrahin, & Ismahel the yonger.

Tamas his last will. This Tamas, before he dyed, did solemnely appoynt by his will, that his sonne Ismahel the elder should bee set in the kingdome: who although, because he was yonger then Mahamet, could not bee his lawfull successor, yet did he yeeld great hope of his most excellent wit, and singular vertues: insomuch that he seemed to promise euery man an happy gouernment, & sufficient habilitie to defend himselfe against his enemies, were they neuer so fierce and warlike. Ismahel, after that he was confined by his father Tamas into the eastel of Cahaca, had euer sought to shew himselfe superior to his brother in the Arte milirarie: and although he gaue himselfe by secret industrie to learne the preceptes of the Turkish law (a thing which if it had beene publikely knowen, would alone haue beene enough to haue barred him from succession of *The simulation of Ismahel.* the kingdome:) yet had he alwayes endeuored himselfe to be an open enemy to the Turkes, and thereupon with his often inuasions (which was the cause of his imprisonment) whiles the peace held betweene Tamas and Soliman, he was so bould as now & then, contrary to his fathers commandement to assault the Territorie of Erzirum and beyond all honestie to spoile the townes & castelles of that region withhis sodaine incursions. By meanes whereof he made shew of his great valour to all people, but principally to his father Tamas, who although in outward shew he seemed greatly to mislike those his youthful heates, yet was he dayly confirmed in the opinion, that he carried of him, to name him his successor, thinking verily that of soe great a dignity he would proue himselfe either altogether, or at lest more worthy then his brother Mahamet. Which Mahamet (to speake the truth) aswel for the *Why Mahamet was called by surname Codabanda.* disease of his eyes, whereby for his surname he was called Codabanda, as also for the manner of his life altogether giuen to that ease, which is proper to such as are studious and quietly mynded, neuer shewed himselfe sufficient to sway the burden of the Empire,, and to brydle *Mahamet loueth not the charge of a king.* the fiercenesse of his enemies: yea and he protested himselfe that hee did vtterly abhorre so great a weight, and those so many cares, as are wont to follow so ample and soe many-partied a kingdome. And yet for all that did not Mahamet remaine altogether depryued of all the whole fauour of his father: forsomuch as Abas Mirize, the middlemost i of his sonnes, was confirmed in the Citty of Heri, (where he was before borne,) and honored with the tytle of the Visier of that remote and abundant Cuntry: yea and Tamas himselfe had established Emir Hamze, the eldest of Mahamets sonnes, in some great dignitie, if death, though some what tardee, yet not altogether vnlooked for, had not by preuenting him, bereaued him of his lyfe, and taken from them all hope of greater matters.

Abas Mirize Mahamets sonne, in Her

Emir Hamze Mahamets sonne.

King Tamas then being thus dead, the said Ismahel was called by the Sultans, for the execution of his fathers will, to Casbin, that he might (as he ought) be saluted & proclaymed king. But while the Postes (whome the Turkes call Volacchi) ran with these great aduertysementes to Ismahel, there arose a stirre within the Citty of Casbin, or rather within the pallace of the king, where remayned at that tyme Periaconcona, a woman in yeares elder then all those her brethren, the sonnes of Tamas, who was niece to Sahamal the Georgian on her mothers side, being sister to Sahamal, & wife to the said Tamas, of whom also was borne the yong Mustaffa, being one of the eyght sons aboue named. She hauing the care committed to her, and other Sultan Councellers of estate, to see the last will and testament of the dead king put in execution, was by sondry deuises dyuersly attempted, that the place might not be preserued for Ismahel, but vnlawfully yeelded to Aidere: who whiles Tamas was sorest aflicted with his sicknes, boldly entring into the chamber, where he lay, had adorned his forehead with his fathers Crowne, and in the sight of his old and weake parent, with an action more rash then became his honestie, shewed himselfe desirous of this ambitiouse succession. And besides this errour, (for the which he was presently & sharpely rebuked) after the death of Tamas, he with drew himselfe to his sister, most instantly beseeching soe desyred a dignitie at her handes: with whome, as also with the rest of the Counsellors of estate he had vsed so many prayers & fauours, that the enheritaunce could not be any longer kept from him, but by the helpe of some secret deceit. His sister durst not be so bould, as to moue any important mittigatiō of these matters before the Counsellors, neither would her hart suffer her to set forward any action, that might be preiudicial to her brother Aidere: neither could she tell how to permit so great an iniury to be done to Ismahel, who was chosen by his father into the succession. And therefore in this perplexity she sought meanes to satisfy the ambitiouse youth being present, the right and reasons of Ismahel being absent, the honour of her dead fathers will and testament, and the proffit of the kingdome. For hauing consulted with all the Sultans, she resolued to yeeld, that Aidere, being inuested

Ismahel called to Casbin to be crowned king of Persia.

Stirres in Casbin.

Periaconcona, sister to Mahamet, Aidere & Ismahel, yet elder in yeares then they.

The singular boldnesse of Aidere.

Aidere procureth to bee made king before Ismahel.

The subtilty of Periaconcona to entertayne Aidere.

in his regall apparell, and setled in the great gallerie, should attend the acclamation of the people, and be publikely installed, as though he were elected king. And euen thus did this vnwise & bould youth suffer himselfe to be led by the blind desires of gluttonous glory: who being set in his maiestie perswaded himselfe, that he should now see his frendes and foes obedient vnto him, and himselfe reuerenced of all men, as king of the Empire. But to these designementes so hasty and so prosperous, the successes that sprong from the subtilty of those Counsellors, and his dissembling Sister, were nothing conformable: for that by their aduise she tooke order, for the gates of the Pallace to be presently locked, leauing at euery passage asure guarde, and permitting that one narrow wicket onely should remayne open, and safely warded with a company of most faithfull and valourose Captaines, wholly deuoted to Tamas & Ismahel, who had strait charge also giuen them to suffer euery man to enter in, sauing onely the followers and keepers of Aidere. In this sort did she thinke to entertaine the young man, vntill such time as the nominated king should arriue from Cahaca, and so put in execution what he thought best, for the honour of himselfe, for the custodye of the kingdome, which fell to him by inheritance, and for the generall quiet of all Persia.

Aidere stalled king in Casbin.

Thus then sate the young man Aidere, replenished with vnwonted ioyes, receauing honour from al the people of Casbin, sauing onely from his frendes and keepers. By meanes whereof, perceauing now the prohibition of them, and the great stirre of Zalchan his chiefest fauorite, (who discouering the prepensed deceit, and crying vpon king Aidere, threatned the lady, the Sultans, & all the rest that waited vpon this fained succession, which was indeed ordayned but for a scorne & despight of him) he acknowledged this publicke derision, and secretly together with all his misfortune, he abandoned his fresh-begun honors, and of a king (as he presumed to be) he had the grace to make himselfe a fugitiue, and being become all fearefull and sorrowfull, with all the force he could he withdrew himselfe closely among certayne women of the pallace, hoping so to find some way to escape with his lyfe.

Aidere acknoledging his publike derision, flieth all fearefull among certaine women.

In the meane tyme so greatly encreased the cryes and threatnings of the frendly company of Istigelu (and now all of them had prepared themselues for some dangerous & pernitious attempt against Persia) that the counsellors, with consent of the lady were enforced to take order, that to bereaue these tumultuous and seditious people of all their hope and courage, Aidere should be depriued of his lyfe. And so Sahamal the Georgian vncle to the young man, after long search made for him, at last found him hidden among the weomen, and without any stay, taking his head by the lockes, cut it quite from his carcase: and in the place, where Zalchan with the rest of vnfortunate

Aidere beheadded by Sahamal his vncle.

THE FIRST BOOKE

Aidere his fauorites stoode crying and threatning, among the greatest medley & thickest presse of the proude conspirators, he flong the head all blouddy, & as it were breathing for heate, crying out vnto them, Behould there your king, enioy him at your pleasure. At this sudden and horrible spectacle euery man burned in rage and anger: neither did there want for the present time many a rash head, that meditated most cruel reueng, & turbulent stirres: Yet in the end when they perceiued that the neere succession of Ismahel was ineuitable, and the death of Aidere (that followed) irreuocable, euery one betooke himselfe to his owne priuate affayres, & at last deuyded themselues one from another, and seuerally departing from the pallace, some saued themselues here, and some there, leauinge those courtes and lodginges all in quyet.

The head of Aidere throwne among the conspirators.

In the meane tyme was Tamas buried acording to their prophane rites, and Ismahel the successor arriued from Cahaca, who without any stirre at all was embraced by his sister, saluted by the Sultans, and reuerenced of all men, as the lawfull heire of so great an Empire. But he, assoone as he began to sway the regall scepter, and sawe himselfe superior to all men in liberty & authority, without any pitty at all (swaruing therein from the Persian custome, and imitating the Turkish maner) caused the heades of all his eyght yonger breethren to be cut off, and with all vsed such f [...]nder diligence, that not onely all those which were neere vnto them in bloud or affinity were bereaued of their liues, but also all the fauourites of the late slaine Aidere, were vnhappely destroyed in that publike slaughter, so that the streetes of Casbin were defyled with bloud, and all the City resounded with mourninges & complaints. Which vnexpected cruelty, being altogether vnworthy of so worthy-a-thought king, did in such sort encrease that opinion of great successes, which all the Persians had conceaued of the person of Ismahel, that there was not a man to be found, which changed not his former hopes into new fears, & bitterly sorrowing for the calling of such a Lord to rule ouer them, did not hate this new fiercenes of his mind, & bewayle so vntymely & miserable a massacre. But much greater and farre more lamentable did these miseries growe, assoone as certayne speeches were published and spred of the king, That hee would change the religion, (if we may so call it:) & assoone as he commanded openly, that whosoeuer desyred to liue vnder his standard, & loued to obey his lawes, should detest the superstitious worships of Aly, the foolish and false prophet of the Persians, & according to the impious custome of the Ottomans, obserue and mayntaine the impure and wicked rytes of Abubac, Osman, and others, that were reuerenced & honoured by the Turkes with a profane worship. So that by this great nouelty, quite contrary to the late publike and famous actes of Ismahel, and altogether repugnant to their hope, whereby they expected glorious matters from

Ismahel putteth to death many kinsfolkes and frendes of his dead brother Aidere.

Euery man bewaileth the cruelty of the new king Ismahel.

Ismahel publisheth a new superstition.

him, to the generall benefite of Persia, the myndes of all men were so afflicted, that the country neuer felt greater trouble, nor euer indured a more dangerous & vncouth a change: by meanes whereof, & by force of this publike Edict of the new king, (whether he did it because he was in loue with this wicked worship, and had learned this abomination rather then any other, as we sayd before: or whether he did it to reuoke his neighboures the Mesopotamians, the Babilonians, and Assyrians, vnder his banners:) many of his prophane priestes, many of the Gouernors of his frendly and subiect Citties, being too much inflamed with the former superstition, were dryuen into exile, many put in prison, some had their eyes pluckt out, (among whome was the Califfe of Casbin) and not a few others in sondry sortes depriued of their liues: yea many Ladyes, ioyned in bloud with Ismahel himselfe, & dyuers others of his kinsfolkes, to whom neither sex, nor age, nor innocency could be a sufficient defence, did endure sondry tormentes and strange calamities.

New publike griefes & new deathes happening by occasion of Ismahel.

The Califfe of Casbin depryued of his eyes by the commandement of Ismahel.

In this so great an innouation, and among these tumultes, there went abrode with all, an vniuersall rumor, not onely among the Citties of Persia, but in the regions of the Turkes also, (Fame the publisher of euill, rather then of good newer, arriuing euen to the City of Constantinople) that with all these disorders, Ismahel sought to put in order a great number of such soldiers, as fauoured this new proclaimed vanity, & passing with them to the city of Babylon, now called Bagdat, there, to the imitation of Soliman, would receaue the Crowne of the Empire at the hand of him, that (whosoeuer he was) he should find to be the successor of their great Califfe, and in the cheefest place among theyr vncleane priestes. In this dyuers variety of matters, and in so great nouelty of euentes, beyond all common expectatiō, whiles there encreased rather feares of newe motions, then ensued hopes of auncient quyetnesse, by the helpe of the aforenamed Lady Periaconcona, (who as the kinges greatest fauorite suruiued all the rest) he was sodainely bereaued of his lyfe: whether it were that this his death happened by occasion of certaine amorous practises of Ismahel himselfe, or whether his sister had cuningly conueighed poyson into some electuary prepared for him: or (as some more probably do affirme) that his sayd sister hauing priuately conspyred with Calil-chan, Emir-chan, Piry Mahamet, Curchi Bassi, being al at that time captaines of great accompt, & as it were Presidentes of the kingdome, had brought them in, apparelled in womens weedes & gowns, & that they strangled him, at such time as Ismahel had priuately withdrawen himselfe among his paramoures. Howsoeuer it was, sufficient it is, that by the helpe of the saide Periaconcona, the 24. day of Nouember being S. Katherins euen, in the yeare of our saluation 1577. this king, being generally tearmed

A rumor spread that Ismahel would passe to Babilon with an army.

King Ismahel suddenly perished, & the manner of his death.

by his people a seditious man & a contemner of the lawe, was suddenly taken out of this world, to the exceeding ioy of all those Nations, that by his death thought they should remaine freede from great and manifold troubles.

Ismahel being thus dead, the Lady began presently to parlee with al those Sultans, that were the ministers of this fraudulent death, & told them, that as they had giuen aduise, for the greater benefit of all Persia, that Ismahel should be depryued both of his kingdome & lyfe: and that as yet it was not knowen, who should worthely succeed in that Crowne, which now remayned in their handes, forasmuch as the king, that dead is, hath left no issue behind him: so it touched them verye neere to take vpon them the protection thereof, and preseruing the maiestie of the Scepter, the liberties of the people, and the peace of the subiect Citties, strongly to defend and deepely to settle the safety of that nation, which onely possesseth the true orders of the elect disciples of crafty and wicked Mahamet. There were at that tyme many gouernours and Capitaines assembled in Casbin: and euery one of them had withdrawen himselfe thether, for the accomplishment of his owne priuate designementes, these gaping after the mutations of the world. Emir-Chan he burned in ambitious desires, and hoped by the meanes of a match, to be concluded with a sister of Periaconcona, (who was already greatly inclyning to him) that he should be exalted to the soueraigne degree of all Persia. Mirize Salinas, cheefe among the Sultans, of that court, he hoped on the other syde to aduance into the estate, eyther Mahamet brother to the dead king, or els Hamze the eldest son of the sayde Mahamet Codabanda: and by bestowing vpon him his daughter to be his wyfe, (as afterwarde hee did) so to encrease the glory of his house. Others there were that hoped they should be able to draw Abas out of Heri, and to create him king of the Empyre. There was also one of the Tutors of the infant Tamas, who waited likewise for some oportunity to settle Tamas in the kingdom, and so by meanes of his greatnes to exalt himselfe to the soueraigne Tytle of cheefe captaine among his fellowes. Neither did there want a number of others, that secretly watched to vsurpe any occasion that might be presented vnto them. How be it in this so great variety of thoughts, the Sultans aunswered the Lady with one consent, and promised her in most liberall termes all the protection, that their forces could afforde, or their wepons procure: and yet did euery one of them both in action and worde clerkly dissemble their seuerall imaginations where unto they myrid was as proue and deady, as their harte was cunning to conceale them closely. And in this sort were ended those great noueltyes which arose (I know not vppon what occasion) & were brought in by this ambitious king.

Periaconcona parleeth with the captaines of Persia.

The answere of the Captaynes to Periaconcona,

In the meane space, which was one yeare seuen monthes and six dayes of king Ismahels raigne, Amurat the new successor also of his father Selim, who was now wakened at the death of old renowmed Tamas, and at the rumor spred abroade of the desyre which Ismahel had to passe to Babilon, & at the fresh report of this new published superstition, & had throughly learned of all sides, what harme this late inconstant & variable king had wrought in Persia, what dissentions he had raysed, & how hardly all the Prouinces of the Persian Empire had endured those strange calamities, & so hoped in himselfe either in Ismahels lyfe tyme, or after his death to succeed him, for that heareby occasiō might be ministred vnto him to take vp armes against Persia, & matter suggested to put in execution his vnmeasurable desires of some new conquestes: which desires had alwaies made both him and other his predecessors not onely suspected, but also terrible & fearefull aswell to his frendes as to his enemies: for asmuch as there is an auncient custom, which is grown as it were to be a law among the Ottoman kings, that those Emperours cannot challenge their due honours in their life tyme, nor their proud monuments after their death, (which are so durable, as at this day they remayne equall with Aeternitie,) vnlesse they attempt some great and ambitious actions & enterpryses, and vnlesse they performe some exployte, that may be conformable to theyr maiesty. Amurat therefore bending all his cogitations to these great stirres, would not direct his mind any other way, or moue warre agaynst any other nation, vntill he might first see what issue these maruellous innouations would bringe foorth which in the succession that followed, & namely in the person of Mahamet now king, simed to be more pregnant and perseuerant, then euer they were before, and ministred to Amurat new occasions of victorious and strange hopes, for that assoone as Ismahel departed out of this lyfe, by the aforenamed Mirize Salmas, (being in dignitie the cheefe man among the Sultans, though in bloud and nobilitie inferior to them all) after many letters dispatched too and fro, Mahamet Codabanda was at last assured, how with all quietnes of mind and security of person he might come and take possession of the kingdome. He was also certyfied by the same Salmas of the whole conspiracy plotted agaynst his Brother to put him to death, and likewise made acquainted how the fraudulent lady with the Sultans had capitally consulted against him, & how she fauouring Emir-chan & Abas Mirize of Hert, her nephew and his son, more then became her, did little regard the due and rightfull succession of him being her brother. And for these causes did Mahamet greatly beare himselfe bold of the faith and diligence of Mirize Salmas: and had withall no small desyre to see his eldest son Hamze Mirize, advanced to some such soueraigne dignity, as he saw was due to the liuely hope,

Amurat at the stirres in Persia, entreth into mind to make warre vpon them.

An auncient custome of the Turkes.

Amurat intentiue to the matters of Persia.

that euery man perceaued to bein him, in regarde of his vertue & prudence, for managing the common wealth, and dispatch of matters of warre: wherein also he shewed himselfe to his father very iealous and suspicious, least some other man should vsurpe vpon him that honour and authority which so properly appertayned vnto him. And thereupon did Mahamet in the end resolue with himselfe, not to leaue the kingdome in the handes of priuate persons, not in the lightnes of an inconstat woman, who by the occurrents sent him from his counsellor, was detected to be an vnshamefaced queane, and are bellious conspirator against her owne bloud, where with she had now twise defiled her selfe, without any pitty or remorse of conscience. And therefore he wrote back againe, that he was mynded to take the rightfull succession vpon him: that (God so fauouring, ayding and assisting him) hee would enforce himselfe to profit Persia, to proue a more thankfull and commodious a member to the common wealth, then his dead brother: & that for the same purpose he was putting himselfe on his iourney: with straite charge notwithstanding, that Mirize Salmas, to make his comming seeme the more acceptable, should before his entrance within the gates of Casbin present him with the mischeeuous head of Periaconcona, a woman (in respect of the scorne exercysed agaynst yong Aidere, and of the treacherous death practised and executed vpon his brother, and of the perucise imaginations which she conceaued to cause the succession to fall into other mennes handes, and of the prodigall familiarity which she had with some of the Sultans,) well worthy of a thousande deathes. Secreatly did Mirize Salmas put in execution whatsoeuer Mahamet had priuately enioyned him, so that by his meanes he was presently & solemnely proclaimed king of Persia. And afterwardes hauing gathered togeather many squadrons of men, wholly deuoted to the bloud and name of Mahamet, the same Mirize Salmas put himselfe on his way to meete him, carying the head of that audacious & manlike virago vpon the top of a lance with her hayre dispersed, and some other vncouth behauiours that moued terror to the beholders. From which nouelties (one mischeife as it were hudling vpō the neck of another) there sprongvp dyuers inward hatreds, sundry tumultuous seditions, and many ciuill warres, insomuch that the king for his parte being continually solicited by Mirize Salmas, (the cheefest and deerest fauorite he had,) sought by all meanes to take reuenge of those treacherous companions and complices of his brothers death, who on the other syde did euen burne in immoderate desyres to aduance their owne priuate estates, and withall their might opposed themselues against his power and authority, whereby the state of Persia began to fall into greater inconueniences, and of these nouelties to reape new losses. Sahamal the Georgian, (he that by the appointment

Mahamet Codabanda resolueth to come and be crowned King.

Periaconcona beheadded.

New stirres and mischeefes in Persia.

Sahamal the Georgian flyeth from Casbin into the mountaynes.

Leuentogli desyrous of innouation.

The people of Seruan euill affected towardes the new king.

Vstress the Bassa of Van aduertyseth Amurat of the stirres in Persia.

of his neece Periaconcona, and of the conspiring Sultans, was the minister of Aidere his death,) assoone as he heard of the misfortune of his neece, fled to his places of rest in his mountaine of Bruz, fearing greatly the wrath of this new Lord. Leuentogli likewise one of the Lordes of Georgia, who by reason of these accidentes, which happened to his brother at his owne perill, did reposesmall confidence in the Persian protection, vnderstanding the flight of Sahamal, being very neere vnto him both in countrey and bloud, estranged himselfe so farre from his old loue and auncient deuotion, that he seemed to desire some new innouation. The Nations also that were neighbours to the Turkes, and the people of Media Atropatia, where Seruan is at this day, remayned malcontent at the same of this new king, & in the end it appeared that Persia vnder this fresh successour, through many murations, was fallen into a most notable misery, & the state thereof more weakened then euer it was wont to be.

Of all these late successes, aswell as of the former intelligences, was Amurat aduertysed from dyuers partes, but specially and particularly Vstref the Bassa of the Citty of Van, a city according to Strabo situate in Armenia the greater, vpon the Lake Actamar (sometymes called Palus Mantiana,) sent him most perfect information of all these stirres in Persia, discoursing vnto him of the death of Ismahel, the consultations of the Sultans, the treacheries & death of Periaconcona, the broyles betweene the king and the Sultans, the nature of the new king being diseased in his eyes, little esteemed by his subiectes, besotted in his affections towades his three sonnes, (at whose handes he foresaw notwithstanding, that hee should receaue many iniuries and troubles,) the facility to ouer-rule the cheefe Gouernours of the Georgiani, and the people of Atropatia, otherwyse called Seruan, which were euill affected towardes the new king: and to be briefe whatsoeuer had in truth succeeded in Persia, and might inflame the mynd of Ottoman to conuert his forces agaynst an enemy of small counsell and much cnofusion: adding thereunto, that neuer was there greater opportunity to ouercome that kyng then now was offered, and that in any case hee should not let slip such an occasion, as the Ottoman kings neuer had before to obtayne so certayne and so famous victoryes, with so great glory and felicity in these enterpryses.

Amurat, whose eares had along time beene filled with those stirres, that Ismahel had raysed, and whose cogitations were wholly bent to marke what wold be the issues thereof, liued with a mynd altogether inflamed with an vnmeasurable desire of the newes, and assoone as to his owne naturall inclynation, and to other mens reportes, there was added also this information of Vstres, (who peraduenture had that charge particularly enioined him) he setled himselfe more deeply in his former conceytes, vz: to proue his forces in subduing a king of an ancient time, dissenting and estraunged from the lawe of Mahamet, a contemner of his maiesty, and to be short, his onely corriuall and odious competitor in all the East: and therewithall began to call to his remembarnce, how Selim father to his grandfather, and Soliman his grandsyre would haue taken this enterprise to hart, recording priuately to himselfe how they being captains of most mighty armies, went themselues in person, fought with the Persian kings, sacked and tooke many of their Citties, and reduced their bordering enemyes into very strait termes. But no one thing did more enflame the Turkish Emperour, then did so rare an occasion which he thought was now offered vnto him, to haue for his enemy a king not well practysed in feats of war, besotted & confounded in affection & conceyt towardes his children, and weakened through the dissention of his subiectes: he measured and weighed his owne forces, he considered the peace which his people had enioyed from the taking of Goletta, euen vntill this tyme: he collected the infinite number of his vassalles aswell horsemen as footemen, he surueighed the rentes of his customes, his meanes to fynd money, his engynes of war (wherein he did far surpasse the Persians,) the citties of his enemy layde all open, and without any defence of fyre or by such lyke instruments of death: and in breefe when he had called to mind whatsoeuer he durst attempt and promisse to himselfe, he did more and more resolue with himselfe to take the occasion that was now offered him to begin this warre. For the compassing of which his purpose he was greatly fauoured by the present state of Christendome, at that tyme being wholly in league & amity with him: and the peace yet continuing that the Emperour had made with him: and the rather, because he was verily perswaded that he should not haue any disturbance by the Catholike king, who no doubt would graunt him a truce by reason of his warres in Flanders, wherewith hee perceiued hee was shrewdly occupied, (which truce afterward ensued by occasion of the kingdome of Portugall.) The State of Venice also obseruing that faith and promise, which with publike capitulations, they had faithfully established in concluding a peace, after that singular victory, which they had obtayned neere to the Islandes Echinades against the Turkish Fleete. And to be shorte the Turke assured himselfe that he should not any way suffer any annoiance or impedimenr by any prince of Europe.

In this generall tranquillity & common peace with the Potentates of Christendome, did Amurat with more security and bouldnes discourse with him selfe about the broaching of this warre in Persia: and at last not fynding any thing contrary to his designementes, he resohied to haue a treaty with those chief Bassaes called Visiers that vse to sit at the Court gate, & to take sound aduise with those that had the

Amurat is confirmed in his opinion to make warre.

Amurat in peace with the Christian Princes.

Amurat in peace with the Christian Princes.

Amurat taketh counsell of his Visiers.

vniuersall gouernement of the whole Empyre in their handes, whether it were better vpon this present occasion to begin the prepensed warre, or if they thought this oportunity not to be so fit, then to lay it aside, & to conuert their forces and counselles against the common wealth of Christendome. So impiously and so barbarously is this Empyre managed; that whensoeuer there is any treaty to attempt any enterpryse for the aduauncing thereof, it is lawfull to violate any truce and to breake promisse: whereupon although this warre could not bee moued eyther agaynst the Persians, or agaynst the Princes Catholike, without breach of theyr promised sayth, (altogether counterfetting and pretending capitulations of peace, leagues & oathes that ought to be inuiolable:) yet in the manifold consultations, that passed among these Visiers, there was not a man found that had any consideration or made any accompt of that defect: but euery one of them (as their manner is in all thinges) preferring violence before reason, thought it conuenient to set forward the wicked desyre of their Lord, without any godly or honest respect at all. And among the rest, Mahamet the Visier, being cheefest in authority, experience, and yeares of gouernement, was of aduice that it would proue a more easy and lesse dangerous attempt to warre with the Persians, then with the christian princes: aswel for that the ciuil dissentions lately sprong vp in the kingdome of Persia, and the condition of the new successor of the Persian Empyre in his gouerment and warre, promised all fortunate victory: as also for that to wage battell agaynst the Christian Princes, was not to make that Prince onely his enemie against whom he should fight, (whose forces notwithstanding, bee what Prince soeuer he may bee, haue euer beene most terrible, some by sea & some by land) but it was to bid battell to all the Potentates of Christendome at once; those potentates (I say) that not many yeares before had discomfited a fleete of 300. Gallies & mo, & awhile after that, had put to flight another fleet either as great as it, or not much inferior, & peraduenture was still able to performe, whatsoeuer they desyred. In these consultations & other like discourses, in the end they al agreed, that it would be much better to make war in Asia against dartes, agaynst swordes, agaynst Citties eyther lying open or slenderly fenced, then in Europe, agaynst lightninges and fyres, against bowes and arrowes, agaynst deuouring flames, agaynst strong places fortifyed with munition and instrumentes of death. And if there were any difficultie at all therein, there were but two onely that seemed to be of any weight: one was the great distance and rough passage of those places, through which they were to leade their horses, their Cammells, their artillery and their men, euery man knowing that the Country of Georgia is compassed rounde about with verie roughe mountaines and thick woods, where the enemy vseth

Turkes make no accompt of breaking Promisse.

Mahamet the Visier aduiseth to make warre.

The generall conclusion of them all.

Two difficulties found in the resolution to make warre.

THE FIRST BOOKE 15

all good oportunity to lay ambushes, and to worke treason against such as passe that way: another difficulty was money, Sinan Bassa among the rest offering to their considerations, that if a man would conquere a new countrey, it was necessary for the mayntenaunce of the conquest to erect Castelles and Fortresses, which being leaft to the defence of valiant souldiers would require large stipends, without which euery souldyer willingly forsaketh his charge. Sauing these two difficulties (which notwithstanding were not greatly debated, but in answere thereof as much spoken by the king himselfe as was thought sufficient) euery man thought the conquest of the kingdome of the Cheselbas to bee the playnest & easyest, & promised to themselues vndoubted victory of it. But aboue all other Mustaffa Bassa, he that reduced the Ile of Cyprus vnder the Ottoman power, infamous for the cruell, barbarous & vniust death of Marcantonio Bragadino the stoute and valorous Captayne of Famagosta, whose name shall neuer dye in the tongues and myndes of all ages, hee (I say) with exceeding audacitie set out great hopes of glorious conquestes not concealing the vertues of the Latines, & the perilles passed in the wars of the said Islande, and particularly in the expugnation of the Citty, preferring the armes, forces, and valour of the Latines before the valour, forces, and armes of the Georgiani and the Persians: and in breefe assuring more certayne hope of this warre in Asia, then of any other that could possibly be raised in Europe. And in this sort were the first discourses and originalles of these motions in the East, begun and practised: whereby all men may see that neither zeale of religion, nor any iniury receaued from the Persian Kinges, but onely the ambitious desyre of Amurat to subdue a kingdome, both in his owne conceyte and also by other mens relation ill gouerned by an effeminate and sottish king, and through ciuill dissention brought into great danger, was the first prouocation of making this warre: and thereby may all Catholikes learne, that there is nothing more pernitions to the Christian Common wealth, then ciuill discord.

 When they had thus concluded vpon this resolution to make warre in Persia, there arose new consultations touching the manner thereof, and vpon what coast they should begin their iourney, that so they might expect the more honorable successe: which poynt Amurat did greatly vrge, protesting before al his Visiers, that he would not enter into a warre, vnlesse he were in great hope to beare away the promised victory. Many were the propositions and opinions of the Visiers: and many questions did the king propound, whereunto hee himselfe did readily answere. On the one side some thought, that it wold be very conuenient to send the Army to Babilon, and from thence to Syras, (in old tyme called Persepolis) famous for the praye that Alexander tooke

The difficulties aunswered.

Mustaffa Bassa the infamous, hath great hope in this warre.

Mustaffa preferreth the valour of the Latines before the valour of the Georgians & Persians.

Discord dangerous to a common wealth.

Amurat protesteth to the Visiers, that of this warre he would both reape profit and honour.

The opinion of some touching the manner of the warre.

there, (as Q. Curtius wryteth,) and by that way to attempt the conquest of all Persia. Others were of a contrary mind, & did giue aduice, that the Army should bee sent by direct course to Tauris, there to erect strong fortresses, and to take possession of all the country subiect round about. It is reported also, that some there were that thought it better to send two seuerall Armyes from both the places aboue mentioned, that so bringing the enemy into a straite, they might inforce him to retire, and to yeeld vnto them whatsoeuer they should demand. But Amurat durst not repose such confidence in his owne forces, as to thinke that with his battells deuided & so weakened, he should be able to ouercome that enemy, who had alwaies fought most valiantly agaynst the monstrous and couragious Armyes of his forefathers, not without some feare also of the auncyent vertue of the Persian people, whereof Fame hath euer resounded an immortall and glorious report. Neyther did he make slender accompt of the Georgiani, the most antique tributaries and confederates of the Persians, by whose onely assaultes his Army could not but suffer many inconueniences and sundry trauelles: forsomuch as if they should assaile his battels behind or on both sides, & the Persians should set vpon his forefront, though they were many in number and fenced with artillery, yet being ill planted, and in such difficulty as they could not vse their Artillery, it would be a very easy matter to defeate them. And therefore he did firmely resolue with himselfe to send one onely Army, and with vnited forces to seeke the ouerthrow of his enemy. And thus preferring his strong hope to conquere the countrey of Siruan in Georgia, and the chiefe Citties of Media the Great, before the difficultie of making warre vpon the coast of Siras, reposing great confidence in the notable helpe that was promised him by the Cumani in Tartaria called Precopenfes, he confirmed his counsellors the Bassaes in the same opinion: and withall discouered a matter, which to all of them but especially to Sinan seemed most strange, namely that he was determined not to go in person with his Army about this enterpryse, but was minded to send one of his worthiest Captaines in his steed. The respectes that held Amurat from going himselfe with the Armye, were many: but principally the Falling sicknesse, wherewith hee was troubled: the zeale hee did beare to the kingdome, fearing greatly (and that not without good cause) least his sonne being in fauour with the people might peraduenture vntimely be aduaunced before him: and the danger that he suspected at the handes of the Christian Potentates.

While they were thus in parlee about this expedition, and Sinan, Mustaffa, and some other Visiers made meanes to bee sent as Vicegerentes and soueraigne ministers of their Lordes designement, he dispatched away sondry postes and light-horsemen with order to the Bassaes, Gouernours, of Van, of Babilan, of Erzirum, in the borders

The opinion of others.

A third opinion.

The deliberation of Amurat.

Amurat goeth not in person to this warre, and the reasons why.

of Cappadocia & Armenia the greatter, that they should by often inroades spoyle the townes and castelles of the Cheselbas, and euery way doo them what harme they could, Which was presently put in execution by them all, and specially by the aboue named Vstref Bassa of Van, who besydes the burning of dyuerse townes, brought many a soule into slauery, and in the countryes aswell Tributary as subiecte to the Persians, made many incursions, and wrought much annoyance.

Through these and other lyke iniuries theyr myndes were greatly incensed with anger, and theyr wrathfull hartes filled with a most ardent desyre of reuenge: and whiles with shame enough they romed vp and downe dayly, sharpening their hatred as it were agaynst a whetstone, in the yeare 1577. the abouenamed Mustaffa was elected Generall of the Turkish Campe, prouision was made ready for him, and authority giuen him to prepare whatsoeuer was needefull. So messages were sent, and commandement giuen, ouer all the countreyes heareafter named, that all the Bassaes, Sangiacchi, Agaes, Spahini, Gianissaries, and souldiers of all sortes, that were bound by their perpetuall annuitees to go to warre, should take their iourney in the beginning of the spring to the City of Erzirum, (which if it be any of the old cities, it is very likely to be Simbra mentioned by Ptolomee) there to bee ready for the charge that should be enioyned them by their new Generall: who hauing his dispatch from Constantinople, & passing to Chalcedon (which Herodotus in respect of the founders errour calleth Blynde and now is named Scutari,) through the countryes of Amasia and of Siuas, (the one being the natiue soyle of Strabo, and the other in old tyme called Sebastopolis), hee arriued in Erzirum in the very beginning of Sommer, and there stayed till such tyme as all his people, corne, artillery and other necessarye prouision were gathered together, and at last departed for Struan, hauing first taken an vniuersall and diligent surueigh of all his Army: whereby distinguishing the sound & strong from the sicke & feeble, the armed from the vnarmed, & the couragious from the cowards, weighing in equall ballance his owne forces, hee might assuredly know what to looke for at their handes. Then he deuided his troupes: and first in order were mustred the people of Mesopotamia, to the number of xij. thousand, (their Captayne being well checked by the Generall for bringing so few this yeare) all of them for the most parte Archers, not of any great courage, and accustomed to the vse of the Scimitarre. The second were the Assyrians and Babilonians, watered with Euphrates & Tigris, coming from the very confines of Balsara, (in old tyme called Teredon,) in number no more then xiiij. thousand horsemen, yet all armed with sword and darte, after the manner of their neighbours the Mesopotamians. The third in order were the Sorians, a people more riche in apparell then

Order giuen by Amurat to the borderers to annoy Persia.

Vstref doth much harme to the borderers.

Mustaffa elected Generall of the Turkish Campe against the Persians. A. 1577.

Mustaffa at Chalcedon.

Mustaffa at Erzirum.

The muster of the army in Erzirum.

The Mesopotamians.

The Assyrians and Babilonians.

The Sorians.

stout in armour, & rather alluring their enemies with the goodly shew of their spoiles then terrible to them, being ij. thousand in number, all of them being very cunning to vault and turne themselues round about in fighting. Then were mustred the men of Siuas, of Amasia, of Maras, of Bursia, of Angori, and other places comprehended vnder the name of Natolia, (where in tymes past were the Magnesians, the Bithynians, the Phrygians, those of Pontus & Lydia,) to the nomber of x. thousand, hardy people and well armed, but for the most part archers on horsbacke. There came next after them those of Iury, and Palestina, vpon swift coursers, continuall darters & archers, more ready for flight and spoyle, then for fight and foyle, poore in apparel and vertue, to the nomber of one thousande. The Cilicians succeeded them, now inhabiting Caramania, to the nomber of iiij. thousand, armed with Scimitarre, battell axe, and bow, a harde and rough nation, giuen to spoyle and robbery. Then followed the glory and hope of all the Campe, the people of Grecia, souldiers full of franke courage, armed with arcubush and sworde, mounted vpon good and valiant horses to the number of 10000. And after them the familiar & faithfull garde of the Generall, iij. thousand Gianissaries of Constantinople with arcubush on the shoulder and sword by the syde. Vnder the standard of Beyran Bassa, were lykewise mustred the people of the Citty and iurisdiction of Erzirum leuied out of those places, where in tymes past the Cappadoces bordering vpon the Armenians did inhabite, to the nomber of iiij. thousand: souldiers accustomed to braules and battelles, and first in the field to meete their enemies, armed with sword and arcubush, dartes or Indian Canes, and yet all of them on horsebacke. Euery troupe had their seuerall Captaynes, who notwithstanding were changed at the Generalles pleasure: whose names seruing to no purpose we will quite leaue out, the rather to auoyde the tediousnes of the reader, being not acquaynted with barbarous tearmes.

These were then the squadrons of such souldiers as were stipendiaries to the Turkish king, to the number of whom those which went as voluntarie aduenturers were little inferior, yet better armed peraduenture and more hardy to fight: so that there were found in this surueigh about a hundred and ten thousand horsemen. Neither was there any stirred out of Arabia Felix, out of AEgipt, out of Hungarie, out of Africa, or out of other places remore, or situate vpon the sea coastes: as also those Prouinces, that had sent the squadrons afore mentioned, were not leaft destitute of their ordinary guards and garnisons, no nor without a great multitude of idle persons: yea & Damasco, which in old tyme carried the name and pryce for matters of warre, kept backe their band of Gianissaries being Arcubusiers, to take their ease at home vnder the standerds of their owne captaines. Mustaffa brought with

Marginalia:
- The Natolians.
- The Iewes & Philistims.
- The Caramanians.
- The Grecians.
- The Constantinopolites.
- The men of Erzirum.
- Voluntary men little inferior to the number of stipendaries but better armed.
- Places that sent no souldiers this yeare to the warres of Persia.
- 500. peeces of small artillary with Mustaffa

500. peeces of small Artillary with Mustaffa. him fiue hundred peeces of small Shotte, aswell for safety of his army, as also for seruice in defending such fortresses and castelles, as he should be enforced to erect in the new-conquered countries. He had also of the king many loades of money for his souldiers pay: with furder order and direction to vse the chamber of Aleppo and of other Citties, if he should stand in neede. He caused likewyse to be brought from the prouinces aforenamed, by imposition of Tenthes for graine, and taskes for cariage of camells (which they call Nosul and Auaris) an exceeding great quantity of corne: which he made to bee transported in Gallies by the great sea (in tymes past called Pontus Euxinus) to the hauen of Trapezuntia, or Trabizonda, vnder the generall conduct of Aly-Vcchiali, that for the ease of the army it might so be conueighed from Trabizonda; to Erzirum, being but onely foure dayes iourney distant from thence. He had also gathered together a great number of Pioners and Myners: and to be short hauing taken order for all things that he thought might be necessary for the warre, he departed in comely manner & seemely a […]ray from Erzirum, and in the end of eyght dayes arriued at the ruines of Chars, where among good pasture and abundance of come frute and wa […] herested himselfe. And being surprised with an excessiue raine, which falling in great quantity made newe pooles and brookes, and being mixed with stormes, and tempesturous winds rent his tents asunder, & wrought great harme both to men & cattell, he was compelled to stay in that place three whole dayes together not without some inconuenience, by meanes whereof many fell sicke & were constrayned to abandon the army. From Chars he departed with al his people that were not hindred with sicknes, and tooke vp his lodging that eueninge vnder certayne mountanes (now called Chielder) being in myne opinion the hilles of Periardo, and because he was aduertised, that the Persians were in the field to make battell with him, being now passed beyond their own borders, which were so set out by Soliman in the peace concluded with Tamas, (as before we haue said,) & doubting least peraduenture they might encounter him, where he little looked for them: he thought it best for the more security of his hoast to pitch his Tentes in such a place as he might well discouer them, and yet not be assaulted at vnawares. And therefore he planted himselfe in the plaine, and gaue order, that Beyran the Bassa of Erzirum should take possession of a certaine hill that was on the right hand, & Dreuis the Bassa of Caraemit should keepe another hill that stood on the left hand and with them Osman Bassa, Mahamet Bassa, Mutassade Bassa being aduenturers, with many others aswell of the kinges stipendiaries as voluntary men, should like wyse pitch their Tentes vpon the same hilles, in such sorte as they making as it were two Cornettes or winges to the

Many loades of money.

Taxes and Tenthes for corne and cariage.

Trabizonda but 4. small daies iourney distant from Erzirum.

Mustaffa departeth from Erzirum to the ruines of Chars.

An excessiue raine.

Some fall sicke.

Mustaffa departeth from Chars. The mountaines of Chielder.

The artificiall manner of encamping, which Mustaffa vsed.

campe, might discouer the comming of euery man, and he himselfe being shadowed with the two hilles might be perceaued of no man.

But whiles all these thinges with such military preparations were made ready by Amurat: the new king of Persia, who was yet scarce setled in his kingdome, being stirred vp by the same of these motions, resolued with himselfe to send men against the Turkes for defence of his state, and was content for the tyme to dissemble his conceaued and hatred, which he bare to some of the Captaines of Persia and of Georgia, & to make some apparant shew that he was reconciled with them, for that without them he could not promisse himselfe any forme of an army or defence: and for all the hurley-burley, wherwith his kingdome was troubled, & for all the disorders whereintoo both the Sultans & people were fallen, yet he wrought so throughly, that all the Captaines of accompt tooke vpon them the protection of his honour & kingdome. And so Tocomac a Sultan; the Chan and gouernour of Reiuan, being elected generall of this expedition, a souldier very famous and well knowen to the Turkes for the many embassades, wherein he serued often tymes to Selim and Amurat, and in Persia deemed to be a man of singular vertue, he gaue him in charge, that gathering together the greatest number of men he could out of Atropatia, out of Media the greater, and other places neere to the Turkes, he should seeke all the meanes he was able to stop their passage into Georgia & Media Atropatia, And thereupon Edictes and preceptes were sent out to all the cities of the kingdome, and principally to Amadan, to Genge, to Taiuris, to Nassiuan, to Marant, to Ardeuil, to Soffian, to Carachach, to Turcomania, to Giaunt, & to many other places on this syde and beyond Casbin, that all the Chans, Sultans, and souldiers whatsoeuer, should come ready prest to follow the commandementes of their new Generall. Many there came that were obedient to the kinges proclamation, but many there were that would not stirre a foote, for their obstinacy in the broiles begun, and for the suspition which they had of vnlooked-for mischeefes: wherefore the king remayned greatly discontented, and much greeued at this first disobedience of his subiectes, and cleerely perceaued how much better it had beene for him to haue liued in peace and amity with Amurat: how be it to make the best of the matter he was inforced to take this defence vpon him, as also for the satisfaction of the subiectes of Georgia, (which desyred the same with earnest request by certain embassadors sent particularly from Daut-Chan for that purpose) to salue his owne honour and the succession of Emir Hamze his eldest sonne. And therefore with those fewe, which for the loue of iustice were met together in those partes, being not aboue twenty thousande, Tocomac was dispatched about his busines, hoping that the enemyes army (wherein he heard say the king in person was not) might be such, as with these his smal forces it were not impossible for him to oppresse them in some narrow straites, where the multitude commonly vseth rather to be: in confusion & perplexity, then ready and able to helpe one another. These xx. thousand were all horsemen, armed with Scimitarre and bow with some Arcubuses among and (which is wont to stand this nation in great steed) they were furnished with very syne and well tempeted Armour, but specially couragious they were and resolute, and made more hardy by the vertue and valour of their Captayne. And therefore with all their prouision necessary for victuall and fight, keeping the way of Tauris and Genge, they came to the turning of Chars, where they were aduertysed that their enemyes army was passed.

The manner how the Persians are armed & their conditions.

Tocomac with his host commeth toward Chars.

They were now arriued within a daies iourney neere to Chielder, when they were resolued to send quicke and faithfull spies that might bring them certayne newes of the armes, condition, and number of the Turkish souldiers: who came thether euen at the very tyme that the Turkes were encamping themselues betweene the two hilles, whereupon the two Bassaes Beyran and Dreuis with their people had already pitched their Tentes. The Persian spyes discouered the Turkish hoast aloft, and perswaded themselues that there were not any other battell then those which they saw vpon the two high hills: whereof with all the speede they could they returned news to Tocomac, who at ease had followed these his spies a farre off. When Tocomac vnderstoode theyr information; agreeing with his former conceit, which he brought from Casbin of the nomber of his enemyes: peraduenture also perswading himselfe, that if a greater army were to come out of the borders, the same might now bee at Chars, and these onely troupes sent before to discouer the cuntrey: he became very bould & foole-hardy through too much desyre of glorie, and determined with himselfe to go and assault them: and hauing discouered his enemyes tentes, he was throughly confirmed in his former opinion, and the spyes relation, and with so much the more confidence went forward to assayle them. But Beyran and Dreuis, who quickly from the hill had perceaued the Persians comming in the plaine against them, although they knew them to be full of courage, yet reposing great confidence in their fellow battell, (which did not shew it selfe,) with all speed mounted vpon their horses, and ranne to meet them: and in the foresaid plaines vnder Chielder within one houre after noone, they ioined a most bloudy battell: wherein there were slayne at last seuen Turkish Sangiacchi, with a very great number of souldiers, both stipendiaries & voluntary, without any apparant losse at all among the Persians, who closing themselues together, in great heat and all bee-bloudied in the battel, did prosecute their happy and fortunate victory.

Tocomac sendeth spyes,

The errour of the Persian spyes.

Tocomac falleth into the same errour that the spyes did.

Tocomac commeth boldly to assaile his enemies.

The Persians obtaine a happy and fortunate victory.

But Generall Mustaffa, who perceyued all that had passed, and stayed waiting till the fight was at hottest and the medley at the thickest, that so the flight of his enemies might breed the greater disorder: & seeing at length that his people could no longer endure the fury of their enemies rage, (euen as though it had lightned and thondred, and as though the earth had beene shaken,) with such cries and exclamations, as the Turkes vse in their assaults for the more terror of the enemy, exciting his army, he ran as it were headlong vpon his aduersaries, and with greater cruelty renued the terrible battell. The Persians did couragiously sustaine this vnexpected & fearefull assault, and seeing the night now very neere approching, rather then they would suffer the disgrace of a shamefull and ignominious discomfiture, with vnexplicable signes of valour, in that little tyme of day-light that was leaft them, they continued their manifold slaughters, vntill at last being fauoured with the darkenes of the night, they resolued to withdraw themselues with as little losse as possibly they might. Mustaffa neither could nor durst any longer pursue them, but was constrayned by night to returne to his pauiglions. The Persians for their partes did with all diligence dispatch men in post, to the King being at Casbin, aduertysing him aswell of the successe of the battell, as also of the greatnes of the Turkish army, and likewise what they were determined to do that they might annoy it: By the Turkes also there were presented to Mustaffa (who had already sent away Postes to Amurat,) fiue thousand heades, which by their colour, countenaunce, and beardes bewrayed themselues to bee Persians, and 3000. Persians aliue. Mustaffa did greatly reioyce at the victory, and to make it seeme the greater, (seeking by all meanes to conceale his owne losses, and mynding to make the issue more dreadfull, that so he might rayse a greater terrour by the fame that should thereof arriue to the enemy,) he caused the heads of those three thousand that were brought before him aliue, to bee presently cut from their shoulders, and vsing a most straunge Arte to breede terrour in the Persian, he gaue order, that of those heades there should be framed a bulwarke in those fields, for a most horrible and vncouth spectacle.

The same day, that Mustaffa the Turkish Capitayne employed himselfe about this barbarous & cruell worke, there came vnto him certaine messengers frō Manucchiar the yonger son of the Georgian widdow, called Dedesmit, who being brought into his pauigliō, told him, that with his good fauour and licence Manucchiar their Lord and maister came to salute him, & to offer himselfe vnto him as his obedient and deuored seruant. At which newes Mustaffa redoubling his ioy, gaue commandement, that all the Bassaes & Capitaines of the hoast, with all solemne pompe, with trumpettes, drommes, peales of Artillery, and with all other signes of magnificall and ioyfull entertainement should go forth to meet the said Manucchiar, and to accompany him to his presence: which they did accordingly, and encountring him with all signes of honour, conducted him with an infinite traine to the great pauiglion of Mustaffa, who also caused him to bee saluted againe with an other peale of ordinance and Arquebuseshot, and with a second reply of trumpets and drummes. Manucchiar dismounted from his horse, and (although against his will) he beheald the strange and vncouth pile of heades all pale and filthy to looke on, and indeed imagined what the matter meant, all which Mustaffa himselfe discoursed at large vnto him from poynt to poynt: notwithstanding before all other thinges, hauing done his due reuerence to the said Mustaffa, and according to his degree placed himselfe next to his syde, after he had presented him with such giftes as his countrey yeelded, 'hee gaue him to vnderstand, That for the honour and estimation which he bare to the Turkish valour, he was alwaies deuoted to the house of the Ottomans: and as he had oftentymes desyred to spend his goodes and lyfe in their seruice, so at this present being moued by his auncient desyre, allured by the strange fame of this victorious and wonderfull army, and stirred vp by a particular fantasy to learne the paynefull and harde preceptes of Arte Military vnder such a Captayne, being a maister of other captaynes, hee offred him all deuotion and seruice, more then euer he had done heretofore: and himselfe, hauing nothing in the world more deere vnto him, consecrated his owne lyfe to his commandementes, desyring that the same might be emploied in the conflictes of warre, vnder his banners, among warriers and souldiers of same and renowne, & therefore he besought, him, that hee would accept of him in the name of Amurat, whose obedient vassal he vowed himselfe to remaine for euer.' Mustaffa did gratiously receaue all this discourse of Manucchiar, and hauing shewed him againe the pyle of heades, together with his battelles, armour and prouision of war, told him, That as 'all these forces are the gift of god, who alwaies fauoured the righteous counselles of the Ottoman kinges (an impudent speech too bould & vnbrydeled) in such sort, that they lord it ouer all the world, euen to the astonishment of all that liue in the world at this day: so had he for his parte chosen the better parte in comming now to yeelde himselfe & to submit his obedience to his king although it had beene good if he had do one it before.' And as concerning the desyre which hee had to bee his companion & fellow in these warlicke affayres, he did very frendly accept of his comming, & promised him all good entertainment and assured safety. And so in exchange of the presentes which he brought him, hee apparelled him in cloth of gold, honored him with a battell-axe and target, wrought with gold & ammell: & neuer permitted him to go from his pauiglion without a traine of his slaues.

Manucchiar honorably receaued by Mustaffa.

The speech of Manucchiar.

The aunswere of Mustaffa.

But to the end that from thinges vnknowen, and principles not vnderstood, the course of my history proceed no furder, for that in certaine strange and important successes, the readers will be desirous to know the seuerall nations, scituations, Citties, riuers, mountaines, counties, Dukedomes, kingdomes and prouinces: it shall not be amisse in a distinct booke by it selfe to declare, what these enemies are, against whome the Turkes make warre, and to describe what and how great forces they haue, what kingdome they possesse, what prouinces are subiect vnto thē, their worship or religion, their kind of gouernment, their wepons, their manner of fight, their forme of battell, their reuenues, their expenses, and to be short whatsoeuer els shall bee necessarie to bee knowen, and so with greater perspicuity to proceed in the continuation of our interrupted history.

The end of the first booke.

The Second Booke

The Argument.
The birth of Mahamet and his proceedinges.
The Testament and Death of Mahamet.
The Originall of the Persian and Turkish Sectes.
The errors of Iouius and others, touching the Originall of the Name of Soffito or Soffi.
The encrease of the Persian kingdome.
The Geographicall description of the kingdome of the Persians, first vniuersally and then particularly.
The Geographicall description of Georgia.
The Historiography of them both.
The Orders of Dignities or Offices in the Persian Religion.
The Orders of Dignities or Offices in the Persian gouernement.
The Persian Souldiers.
The Armes and weapons of the Persian Souldiers.
Their horses: and the manner of Ordering their Armies.
The Surueigh of the Persian Armies.
The reuenues of that kingdome.
The Expenses of the same.
The causes of the declination of that Empyre.
Certaine aduertisementes of the Author to the Readers.

Mahamet, or (as some call him) Mahomet was borne in the yeare of our saluation 593. or (as others write) 567. of Abdalla, the son of Abdel Mutalep, who had also an other son called Abutalep, father to Aly, all of them among the Arabians of a very base and poore estate: which Mahamet by good hap being married to Cadige, (or as some terme her) Hadige, a woman of noble parentage and notable wealth, & by

Cadige the wife of Mahamet.

her hauing had a daughter called Fattime, who afterward was the wyfe of the aforesayd Aly, departed into Egypt, with rich wares and important merchandises, where withall his wife had furnished him. And being ambitious to know many thinges, and to fit his humour, which he perceaued in himselfe to bee giuen to matters of fame and of glorious report, hee entred into strict familiarity with one Sergio, a fugitiue of Christendome, of whome learning many particulars of the holy testament, he disgested them in his mind, & was in good hope by meanes of the great authority, that he had already purchased at home with his fortunate mariage, to cause the simple people there to belieue him of his owne credite, and thereupon perswaded himselfe, or rather was confirmed in the wicked opinion which he had conceaued, that he might vsurpe the name of a Prophet or Diuine. And so being assisted by dyuerse lewd and vngodly persons, he began to giue out the report that he was a worker of miracles and a fauourite of God himselfe, and besides the counterfeting of a cloude, which (as Sergio & other fautors of his shamelesse lyes most falsly feyned) did continually couer him, he made a shew to the world of dissembled abstinence, hipocriticall solitarines, & ambitious contempt of wordly riches, inuenting also certaine superstitious prayers, and false visitations of an Angell, and to be short a number of other lying and enormous miracles. By meanes of all which thinges hauing gotten the credite to be a deuout person, a Saynt, a Prophete, (being assisted by the temporall authority which he had obteyned with his riches and his wiues kinred) he made that fickle & miserable nation subiect to his wicked law: and among other filthy and vnrighteous orders, which are scattered in the Alcoran, and other bookes of treacherous inu [...]ntion, this was most singular, which he imposed vnto them touching the manner of praying, couering all his wickednes with an honorable kynd of prayer, made to that one God, whom this people being but lately reuolted to these idolles and monstrous lyes did little vnderstand. This prayer he appointed should bee thus. *In the name of the religious & mercifull God. Praised be the soueraign Lord of the worlds, the pittifull, the mercifull, the Lord of the day of iudgement. Thee we serue: from thee we looke for helpe: shew vnto vs the right way, that which thou hast shewed to the prophets, not that, for which thou art angry with the wicked, Amen.* And cōmanded that it should be said fiue tymes a day, namely, in the morning, at noone, at Euening, at night, and at two of the clocke after midnight: & that in saying thereof this order following should be precisely obserued. The Fachi, that is to say, he that hath the charge of the ceremonies, being somewhat before all the rest, when they are assembled together, prescribeth vnto them all, the manner and pronuntiation of the praier, not only by falling downe flat vpon the ground with his face and

---

Marginalia:

Sergio a fugitiue of Christendome.

The suttlenes of Mahamet to cause himselfe to be held a Saint.

Certaine Iniunctions genen by Mahamet, as it were for a law.

A prayer inuented by Mahamet, common both to the Persians and to the Turks, and to all those that professe Mahamet.

raysing himselfe vp againe, but also by singing and crying out himselfe, causing all the rest euen as it were in the same moment to doo the like. Mahamet was the man, that where soeuer he was himselfe, performed the office of Fachi: & all those that in other places did order the praiers did represent Mahamet, though indeed they were farre inferiour vnto him. For he was the cheefe man not onely in the Church (which they call Moschea,) but also in the Court of iudgement: so that he had both temporall & spirituall authority, (as we may say,) if so be it be lawfull to such impure and fifthy institutions to apply the religious and holy tearmes which are proper to our most pure & sacred profession. The others were cheefe in the Moschea, but yet were subiect and obedient to their Gouernor and king: so that at this day besides the king, the Bassa, and the Sangiaceo, which are the Temporall Magistrates in the court, there are the Musti, the Fachi, & such like, which are the principall ministers in the Moschea, and in the law.

> *Mahamet was priest & Prince.*

By meanes of these leaud Institutions, the filthy and leacherous wretch, hauing obtained the name of a Wise man and a Prophet, persuaded his wife Cadige, by whome he had gotten all his state and wealth, that by the commaundement of God, it was necessary for him to marry with eight other women, meaning vnder the colour of a diuine Oracle to satisfy his beastly lustes. His credulous wife graunted vnto him that which hee required at her handes, and so in profane uptialles hee satisfied his vncleane desires with eight other wiues or Concubines: among whom of greatest accompt were Aisse the daughter of Abubacher, Ofesa the daughter of Omar, and Fara the daughter of Ottom [...] by whose meanes he assured his temporall authority ouer the people, and soundly rooted his new inuentions in their minds. But (as it is the property of all flesh) at the last he was brought to his end in the sixty & third yeare, or (as some say) in the sixtieth yeare of his age, hauing raigned about thirty, or (as others write,) about fiue and twenty yeares: and whiles he was sicke, to the end that his treacherous orders should not cease, but specially that his new-deuised maner of prayer should not be left, he appointed Abubacher his second father in law, for him and in his steed to keepe the first and chiefe place in the Moschea at Mecca. With great silence although with as great maruell, was this determination of Mahamet tolerated: but particularly as great griefe had Aly and his hinse folkes to heare these newes, supposing that the succession should rather haue belonged to Aly, beeing both Nephew & Son [...]e in Law to Mahamet. Yet did Abubacher excercise the dignity appointed vnto him, without any strife or contention for the same, vntill the death of Mahamet: and then Aly with his kinred, no longer fearing the false Prophet deceased openly made challenge thereunto. At whose first demaund it seemed that Abubacher was

> *Mahamet is married to 8. other concubines.*

> *The death of Mahamet.*

> *Abubacher left successor to Mahamet.*

> *Aly would dryue out Abubacher.*

somewhat willing to haue yeelded, making a shew that he would do it to gratify such persons, as sued for Aly (being a man more worthy, for his neerenesse in bloud for his agility in body, & for his valour in Armes) rather then for that hee was resolued to surrender to another the honor, that Mahamet had graunted to him. But afterwardes hauing secretely vnderstood the mindes of some that were more mighty then his aduersaries, who counsailed him in any case not to spoyle himselfe of the honor which he had obtayned, he began openly to resist Aly, and to vse not onely reasons, but force also against him: so that he established himself in the said Succession. Which Aly, for that he would not disturbe the new-deuised sect, did brooke better then it was thought hee could, although at last in recompence of this his tolleration, being forsaken of all his freendes and fautors, hee and hys wife Fattime were also spoyled of all the substaunce that was left vnto them by his Vncle: Abubacher vouching for a reason of this his cruelty, That the enheritance of riches belongeth vnto him, to whome the Charge of the Law and of Wisedome belongeth: and That he being adiudged lawfull heire of the Wisedome, ought also to inherite the riches. Leauing it (as it were) for an Ordinaunce to the people, That a Prophet cannot separate his substance from his dignities and knowledge: but whosoeuer is left heire of a mans wisedome, is also to be taken for the heire of a mans wealth. Wherevpon diuers wise men of that age tooke occasion to write bookes, and therein disputed, whether a Prophet might haue authority to make one and the selfe same person, the heire of his learning and of hys riches. Howbeit this Aly liued so long, that he saw the death of his predecessors Abubacher, Omar, and Ottoman, and after their decease he himselfe also succeeded in the Dignity, which till then they had vsurped vpon him. For conseruation whereof he was compelled to make battell with Maui Lord of Damafco, ouer whome with great glory he gayned the victory, and so euer after to his immortall praise and commendation hee exercised that Office. At the last he died also, (leauing behind him the report of a magnanimous, variant and iust Prince,) and was buried with two of his Sonnes Hassan and Ossain, in Cafe, a place within two dayes iourney neere vnto Babylon: among whose Successors was allwayes thoroughly obserued, whatsoeuer Mahamet had commaunded to be obserued for a Law.

And although the East was diuided into diuers and sondry States and Gouernementes of many persons, yet notwithstanding the superstition of Mahamet, was with all conformity maintained by them all neither was there heard either of any schisme, or insurrection, or waighty dissention among that people: but for all the inequalitie of those countries and dominions this opinion continued equall and vniforme. At what time, euen on a sudden & beyond all expectation, there arose

Aly driuen out by Abubacher, and spoiled of all his substance.

Bookes written by those first wise men.

Aly succeedeth in the dignity of Mahamet.

Aly dyeth: leaueth behind him a good report.

Two sonnes of Aly buried in Cafe.

a superstition in the mindes of certaine Mahometanes, which in few yeares being sowen and scattred ouer all Asia, did breed a great contention and warre among those nations, that, beeing before vnited together by Mahometes deuise, seemed to be more then frendes and in league one with an other. Of this nouelty one Sexchiuni, or (more distinctly to expresse his name) one Siec Giunet was the author, who vnder the name of Sofi and of Siec, (that is to say, of a wiseman & an author of Religion,) or rather, vnder the pretence of holynesse began to persuade the people, being by nature inconstant & superstitious. That those three first Successors of Mahamet, were vniust and vnlawfull vsurpers of the dignitie, That modest & iust Ali onely ought to be named the lawfull Successor. That he alone ought to be called-vpon in their prayers for helpe, and that by all possible meanes all honors should be yeelded and rendred to him, and taken from those three first, as from persons that were vndoubtedly damned and altogether reprobate. With many argumentes did Giunet approoue his Inuention, & at last persuaded many therevnto that beganne very readily to follow him as the head and founder of so new a verity: Whereupon by the appointment of this new master they did all with one conformitie vse this forme of Prayer, *Cursed be Abubacher, Omar, and Ottoman, and God be fauourable to Aly, and well pleased with him.* From the time of this inuention forwardes, the Sepulcher of Aly and hys sonnes in Cafe grew in great credite, and the followers of this new superstition began euery yeare to visite it, in all respectes euen after the same sort, that the Turkes do visite the Sepulchre of the three first Successors: Yea the very kinges of Persia themselues vsed to be crowned and girte with their sword in Cafe neere vnto Babylon, (as it is sayde before,) where euer after, their great Calife was woont to keepe his residence, as being the mā that represented Aly, and occupied the chiefe roome of their filthy and damnable Priesthood.

 Vppon this occasion it is not amisse to aduertise the Reader, how false that rumor hath bene and is, whereby it is noysed abroad, that the kinges of Persia perfourmed these ceremonies in Babylon. The cause of which falshood was, for that Case lying neere vnto Babilon, and being a very little place, as resembling rather a village then a towne, or a Citty, the people reported that all these thinges were doone in Babilon that famous City: no otherwise then as Strabo writeth to haue happened about the ouerthrow that Darius had when he lost the Empyre. Which ouerthrow although it was at a little village called Gaugamela, (that is to say, the Cammelles house) yet the wryters and people do say, that it was at Arbella, a notable Citty neere to the said place called Gaugamela. Whereupon it is not much from the purpose to note also, how greatly they are deceaued, that thinke Arbella to

The author of the Persian superstition.

The new praier of the Persians.

The sepulchre of Aly held in great reuerence.

be that which is now called Tauris, whereas Strabo doth playnely say that Arbella lyeth in the Countrey of Babilon which is Assyria, and it is very manifest, that Tauris is in the Countrey of Media. By this briefe narration it appeereth that Paulus Giouius hath erred, where he writeth that the superstition of the Persians did begin in Persia at the very same tyme, that the heresy of Luther was sowen in Germany: and where he maketh one Arduelle, who was also called Aidere, to be the author of the Persian Faction: whereas he is notably deceaued both in respect of the tyme, and also of the person: of the tyme, for that it sprang vp before the publication of Luthers religion: and of the person lykewise, for that Arduelle was not the first inuentor thereof, (as hee saith) but Giunet Siec, called also the Sofi, as shalbe declared a little after. The Turkes in the meane tyme, by reason of this new deuysed nouelty, thinking themselues to be of a sound and sincere opinion, did alwayes call themselues Sunni, (that is to say, men of a good faith) and on the other syde they called the Persians Rafadi, that is to say, men of a false faith and going-astray, onely because they forsooke those first successors of Mahamet, Abubacher, Omar & Ottoman, whom they belieue to bee the lawfull heyres of that cheefe dignity. And in this sort began the Persian superstition, and not (as some thinke) from the dyuers interpretations of the Alcoran, much lesse from the execution of the law of Aly. For as touching the Alcoran, they doo all expound it after one and the selfe same manner: and as for Aly, hee neuer framed any lawe, but onely confirmed that which he found already ordayned by Mahamet their onely law-maker. Besydes that the Turkes doo reuerence Aly together with the other three Abubacher, Omar & Ottoman, as him that was also a successor to Mahamet: But the Persians, although indeed they worship Aly, yet for all that they doo not onely not reuerence the other three, but curse them & hate them as impious and damned persons.

Afterwardes the Persians were called Cheselbas, of a certaine red marke which they carried on their heades, by an ordinance that was instituted for the same by Arduelle, who was esteemed a very holy man. Which name was confirmed afterwardes in the succession of Ismahel, who renued the name of Sofi, being first vsurped by Giunet, for his inuention of the superstition that was spread abroad by him: and so continuing the said name of Sofi euen vntill our age, among the people of Asia, who by the forces of Alexander were in old tyme subdued with a number of other nations, that were famous in those dayes (if Quintus Curtius may be beleeued) for the value of their iewelles, for the beauty of their bodies, and for the excellency of their dogges. Of this name Sofi, and Sofiti many particularities we could rehearse, if we were not afraide to depart from our matter now in hand; and

The errour of P. Giouius.

The errour of many.

The Persians called Cheselbas.
The name of Sofi renewed in Ismahel.

The auncient Sofiti subdued by Alexander the great.

therefore differring them till some other occasions, it shal be sufficient to repeat, & with diligence to note, that the first man which merited this name was Giunet, who, because hee found out this notable sect, obtayned the name not onely of Siec, but also of Sofi, although in deed he had not gotten the name of Saha, and that because he gaue his mynd rather to matters of learning and studye, then to matters of Armes & gouernment. After whose example there succeeded three other, who were content to be called by the name of Siec, but not of Sofi, vntill that after thē there succeeded Ismahel, who contemning the name of Siec was called Saha, that is to say, King, & did in such sort enlarge the boundes of his kingdome, that, in respect of his greatnes, men will hardely beleeue at this day the intollerable oppressions, which those Prouinces in truth haue suffered and endured. And herein is Paulus Giouius found to haue erred also where he writeth, that this Ismahel was the first of all the Persian kinges that merited the name of Sofi, which indeed he did rather renewe in his owne person, hauing receaued the same from Giunet, the first authour of the damnable superstition, who first tooke that Tytle vpon him.

This Persian superstition was first brought in by Siec Giunet the Sofi, afterward maintayned by Siec Sederdin, and after him by Siec Giunet the seconde, then, by Siec Aider (called by Giouius, Arduelle,) and at last so encreased & emenlarged by Ismahel the Saha and Sofi, that vnder his gouernment Persia seemed to enuy the glory of Cyrus & Darius. After the death of Ismahel it descended to Tamas, who reygned with lesse felicity then his father did, being many a time and often greatly damnifyed by Soliman, and after Tamas succeeded Aidere the second, who raigned but for certaine dayes and houres, as the Historie setteth it downe: and then followed Ismahel, who troubled all the Citties of his kingdom with manifold hurley-burlies: & last of all the king that now is, being more vnfortunate and vnhappy then all the rest. And euen as Giunet, founder of this sect, being a man that was esteemed to be wise and holy, did renew the name of Sofiti, which for many ages past had beene extinguished in Asia, and in other his successors Sederdin, Giunet the second, & Aidere Sisopi, who were contented onely with the bare name of Siec: so was it agayne reuyued in the sprouting glory of Ismahel, who did so largely dilate the confines of his kingdome, that it seemed he had (as it were) founded it anew: and yet afterwardes, it was suppressed againe in his successors Tamas, Aidere, Ismahel & Mahamet, who leauinge the names of Sofiti and Siec retayned onely the Tytle of Saha. In this sort, began encreased and declined, the kingdome of the Persians, who were followers of the diuision and superstition of the false law of Mahamet.

The succession of the Persian Kings.

The errour of P. Giouius.

The names of the Successors in the kingdome of Persia.

What the occasions were, why in so shorte a space, so famous and redoubted a kingdome began to declyne, it shalbe declared hereafter: for that it is now tyme to proceed in the narration of more important matters, beginning at the Geographicall description of the kingdome it selfe: wherein it shall behoue the reader to walke with good circumspection, because the confynes thereof are set downe neyther so ample and large as they were in the tyme of Ismahel, nor lesse then they were at such tyme as these warres were moued. For Ismahel had in such sorte enlarged the limits of his Empire by his new deuised superstition, that hee had not onely stretched them on the East beyond Aria, and on the South vpon the red sea in the Golfe of Persia, but on the West also he had made the Georgiani tributaries, subdued the Armenians, the Mesopotamians, the Babilonians, the Assyrians, and threatned that he would Lorde it euen to the confynes of Europe. But this so notable felicity of his continued no long time, because both he himselfe was dispossessed by those that were mightier then he was, and after his death, Tamas was so straitly shut vp, euen into the innermost places of his kingdome, that it were but a small matter for wryters to describe the compasse and quantity of that which was left. For being depryued of Bithynia, of Mesopotamia, of Armenia, and of Assyria, the poore Persians had much adoo to retaine the people of Georgia and Atropatia at their commandement and deuotion: but auoyding the outrages and incursions of the Turkes, they were inforced to transport their Regall seat to Casbin, & to forsake Tauris the auncient Pallace not onely of these princes, but also of all the other kings of those prouinces.

And therefore setting asyde the first felicity, and large compasse of this kingdome, (the memory whereof can serue to no other purpose then to bewayle so great a decay, and to teach vs that we ought not to put too much confidence in wordly riches, nor wax proud in the great authority of rule and gouernement:) measuring the state of this realme, as it was when these warres began, we say, that for the North part, beginning at the very vttermost East of the sea of Baccu, and coasting all that Sea, and then entring into Seruan and Georgia euen vnto Mengrelli, and so a little lower vnto Chars, lying in the champaine country vnder the mountains of Periardi called Chielder, where also is erected a Castell called Childerum for defence of the borders, you haue the description of all that the Persians possesse on that syde. From thence drawing a lyne by the East, and rolling the same ouer the Lake Actamar, and ouer Coy in the champeine of Caldaran, & then carrying the same lyne towardes the South to the Citty of Salmas, and a little higher towards Seresul, euen to the channell of Euphrates, there is comprehended all the West parte of this kingdome. From the channell of the sayde riuer, where the Bassora lyeth, coasting all

The changes of the Persian state.

The North parte of the Persian kingdome.

The West.

The South.

along that syde of the sea, euen vntill the mountaines Techisnandan, and more towardes the East to the kingdome of Candahar, & there making an end of that compasse, all the South parte of this present Empire is figured. The East whereof is included betweene the borders of Corassan, and of the Tartarian Iesselbas, euen from the City of Samarcante on the east parte of the Casptan Sea, otherwise called the sea of Baccu.

The East.

The compasse appeareth to bee very great and of importance, comprehending in it many prouinces, not onely famous in our tymes, but also much more glorious in the daies of those Aunciers: for that in the West is included with the countrey of Georgia, parte of Turcomania, and of Cussestan: in the North, Seruania, the countrey of Gheilan; and Massandran: in the East, Candahar, Corassan, and Heri: and in the South, all the kingdome of Fars, (the cheefe Citty whereof is Siras,) with Caramania the Desert. In the very middle and Centre of this Circle are the Territories of Casbin, Cassan, and Hispahan. So that in the beginning of this warre, the King of Persia ruled ouer all these prouinces, Georgia sometyme called Iberia, Seruania, otherwise called Atropatia, Tauris with the territories belonging vnto it called in times past Media the Great, Gheilan or Gely, Masandran or Hircania: & more inward Parthia, Aria, Candahar or Peripaniso, Farsi or Persia, and parte of Cussestan in old tyme called Assyria. All these prouinces in times past subdued by the Macedonians, the Graecians, and Barbarians, wasted by so many mutations and States, and outrages of Armyes, haue also lost their auncient names, and according to the seuerall languages therein vsed, haue had dyuers and sondry appellations, which (as a man may probably coniecture) are in truth those, that are last named. Of all which prouinces, Anania, Pius the second of happy memory, Negro the Venetian, & some other late Geographers haue beene so bould as to wryte many thinges, rather fabulous then true; after the example and imitation of those that are so greatly reprehended by Strabo and Thucydides: & therefore avoyding the danger of lying, and laying also a side for this time, the History of thinges Naturall, Miraculous, and Poeticall, (for of Poeticall matters especially, the particular Geography of Danaeus reporteth) we will onely speake of such thinges, as will serue our turne for the better knowledge of the State and condition of this kingdome.

The prouinces of the Persian kingdome.

Tamas had vnder him, (and so he left the kingdome to Ismahel, in whose time and by whose meanes these warres were raised) threescore and tenne Gouernementes, all bearing the Titles of Sultans & Chan: so that in his whole Empire, he had seauentie Citties of such state and condition, as they deserued to haue a Gouernour of the same dignitie, that the Bassa is with the Turkes, as shall be declared in the exposition of Names. Now what they were, it would be a very hard matter precisely to know; yet some of them we haue learned; and the principall thereof peraduenture were, Sumachi, Sechi, Eres, Seruan, Derbent, Caracach, Ardouil, Tauris, Reiuan, Genge, Hispahan, Masandran, Gheilan, Heri, Cassam, Siras, Starabat, Chilmisnar, Candahar, Iesed, Sapanec, Sultania, Bargo, Cum, Coran, Seua, Casbin, and others, all which haue Iurisdiction ouer many Villages and Townes, from whence there are leauied many men of warre. Hispahan onely hath in her gouernement twelue Sultanes: Casbin three Sultanes & the king: Heri three also and Abas Mirize: Candahar three, and Rustan Mirize. Of all these places to make an exquisite description Geographicall, to tell the Mountaines, the Riuers, the Champaines, the Distances, the Situations, the Altitudes of the Pole, and such other particularities, it would not be an enterprise fit for our handling, except we would insert many lies therein, (as a number of writers haue heeretofore done:) & therefore, seeing neither the battels of the Turke haue entred into those partes, nor any thing happened in them that requireth any great diligēce of discourse, Let that little bee sufficient, which wee haue already touched in this History by occasion of Abas Mirize, and of the Turcomanni: and returning to Georgia, to Seruan, and to Media the Great, with a peece of Armenia, we will vse our best diligence, euen as neede shall require, and our informations will serue vs.

The Citties of the kingdome of Persia.

Georgia then is that prouince, which in auncient tyme was called Iberia, which on the West is bounded vpon Colchis, at this day called Mengrellia: on the East vpon Media Atropatia, at this day called (as we said afore) Seruan: on the North vpon Albania, now called Zuiria: and on the South vpon Armenia the Greater, now called Turcomania, whereof it doth also possesse a parte, so that Iberia and part of Armenia is comprehended vnder this name of Georgia. It is for the most part full of hills, woods, rockes, and ruynes: and hath abundance of silkes, fruites, wilde beastes, and Faulcons. It is watred with many famous riuers, (and so was euen in the tyme of Strabo) but principally with the riuer Cirus, whose gulfe openeth in that country, and is ioyned with Araxis. The riuer Araxis springeth out of the hill Taurus, in that parte, where Periardo is situate, on the syde of the hill Abo, and so running by East euen to the confynes of Seruan, windeth it selfe towardes the west by the North, where it is ioined with Cirus, and then passeth to Artaxata a cittie of the Armenians, right against a place, which is very famous in this warre, called Reiuan, and so watring Armenia, and coursing all along the playne of Araxis, (which peraduenture is the champaine called Caldarana,) dischargeth it selfe into the Caspian Sea, at this day called the sea of Corazun, and of Baccu, on the one syde by south leauing Armenia, and on the other syde by North leauing

The prouince of Georgia.

The riuer Araxis.

Seruania, whose cheefe Citty is Eres, which is so famous in this booke; as in fit place it shalbe shewed. It is a riuer very deepe and large: but yet at this present it contayneth not those meruails; that Herodotus reporteth of it, as also it is very hard to vnderstand that which Quintus Curtius wryteth touching the course thereof, and that which Natalis Comes hath left written of it in his history. Cirus likewyse springeth out of the same hill Taurus, and yet in Armenia, and so descending into the Champaines and plaines of Georgia, charging it selfe, and being greatly encreased with other riuers, it is ioyned with Araxis, and so maketh his issue also into the Caspian sea. This riuer the inhabitants of the countrey at this day call by the name of Ser in their owne language, but the Turkes call it Chiur: the other Riuer both the one nation and the other doo vniformely call Arasse. In that parte of the land, where Araxis insinuateth it selfe betweene Media Atropatia, and Armenia, it receaueth into it diuers Riuers that spring out of the hilles of the said region of Armenia, among which is Canac, very famous in this history, which making (as it were) almost an Island, a little on this syde of the Citty Eres, vniteth it selfe in the Channell with Araxis, as in his place shall be shewed. The riuer Cirus.

The riuer Canac.

This Prouince is in habited by sundry Earles, Dukes, & Lordes, aswell in the plaine and champaine, as also in the rough and mountaine cuntrey; and these inhabitants are for the most part Christians, (& yet obseruers of the rytes and schismes of the Graecians,) stout people, stronge of complexion, and obstinate in their opinions. The principall Potentates of this Prouince, (besides many others that enioy whole Counties and diuers Lordships) are the Widow and her Sonnes, Manucchiar and Alessandro: the Sonnes of Lauassap deceased, Dauid and Simon: Leuentogli, who by his countrymen is called Schender, and by vs Alessandro, surnamed the Great: Giusuf the Sonne of Gori: old Sahamal, of whome wee made mention afore, when we wrote of the death of Aidere: and the sixt is Basacchiuc.

Sahamal keepeth his gouernement betweene the territorie of Siruan, and of Alessandro, by nation rather an Alano, then a Georgiano, and hath one Sonne, which succeeded after him, when Osman Bassa depriued him of his life for his treason that was discouered, whereof shall be spoken in place conuenient. He dwelleth in a rough & high mountaine, by the Turkes called Brus, whose top is couered continually with white and hoarie snowes: he is in religion, by his owne choice, a Soffian, although by nature a Georgian: hee is in money poore, but in shaking a launce and shooting a darte very valorouse: few cities, or rather no one place woorthy the name of a citie doth hee possesse, but certaine Villages and some base Townes hee hath: and the people that is subiect to him is altogether a fauage people, and giuen to robbery and flight. *Sahamal the Georgian and his state.* *The mountaine Brus.*

Giusuf the Georgian and his state.

Giusuf is in deede by countrey, by nation, and by religion a Georgian, although touching his religion hee hath alltogether abandoned the name of Christ, and hauing voluntarily reuolted to the Turkes, hath chaunged his Grecian Faith into another religion, that among all wicked religions is most impiouse. He hath his place at Gori, and his territorie lieth on the West bordering vppon Basacchiuc, diuided from him by the Lake of Esecchia, and on the East vpon the Countie of Derbent. He being brought into a narrow streight by Osman Bassa on the one side, and by the whole Campe on Teflis side, resolued himselfe to yeeld to the Turkes, as in fitte oportunitie shall be declared.

The widdow of Georgia and her state.

The Widowes yonger Sonne called Manucchiar, is he that came to yeeld his obedience to Mustaffa, as wee haue tolde you before, and the elder is named Alessandro, of whome we shall speake sufficiently when we come to describe his misery. She holdeth many [...]ownes, but hath put her elder Sonne in possession, and left vnto him the vniuersall care and charge of her whole estate, which afterward was fraudulently taken from him by Amurat and by his yonger brother Manucchiar. Her territory lieth in the confines of Chars on the West, & the State of the two brothers Simon and Dauid on the East, watred with a Riuer by the Turkes called Chiur, which perhaps may bee some braunch of Cirus: The pallace of this Dominion is Altunchala, so called in Turkish, and in our language may bee interpreted the Golden-Castell: there is besides, a very commodious and remarkeable place called Clisca, and also Carachala, so tearmed by the Turkes, and signifying in our tounge the Obscure or Blacke-Castell: and diuerse other Iurisdictions both of Townes and Castels. This pallace aswell on the side of Teflis, as on the side of Chars is compassed with the rough mountaines of Periardo, and with horrible thicke woodes, very fit for treacherous ambushes, and in all respectes most daungerous for an Army: But Altunchala it selfe lieth in the middest, being (as it were) most cunningly defended by nature.

Lauassap the Georgian and his state.

Simon and Dauid.

There follow, as ye go towards the East, rather in Armenia then in Iberia, the places that sometimes belōged to Lauassap, but now enioyed by the two brethren Dauid & Simon, of their fathers valour and of their fathers estate, both by nature & by vertue the rightfull heires, although in truth they had greatly defyled themselues with a beastly change of their religion, whereby they did wonderfully obscure their glory, being otherwise worthy of singular commendation: and principally Simon, who by his knowledge in Arte military, and by his learning in matters of Poesie and Philosophie had merited the grace and familiarity of Ismahel the Sonne of Tamas, whiles he was in captiuitie in Persia, of whome we shall haue occasion to speake hereafter in due time. But what vertue could there be in them glorious and renowmed, which was not obscured by this soule fault committed by them both? it being the occasion why the one and the other were not onely depriued of their goods, their State, and their honour, but also that they abandoned wholy the most sacred and glorious name of Christ. For Lauassap their father beeing dead, who by his last will and testament left Simon his Sonne to be his Successor in the kingdome, not onely because he was the elder in yeares but also because he excelled his brother in valour, Dauid, being of an intollerable nature, greatly enuying his brothers succession, & ouergreedie of glory and rule, began to seeke meanes how to driue Simon out of his State, & with force and Armes to arriue to that place, wherunto neither the will of his father, nor the lawes of nature could bring him. And therfore withdrawing himselfe into the field, being followed by a kind of people desirous of Nouelties, and rather louing seditions and tumultes, then easie peace and quiet rest, he began to take vp those rentes; which his brother did yearely expect from such places as lawfully were subiect vnto him, conuerting to his owne vse whatsoeuer he could by any meanes most vnhonestly vsurpe: and by these spoiles making his followers and souldiers more bounden vnto him, he did in such sort increase his squadrous, that being waxen very terrible to all Georgia, hee put his brother Simon also in a marueilous great feare: who hauing vnderstood his malignant and mischieuous intent, and hauing none other meanes to mainetaine & defend himselfe, fled for helpe to Tamas king of Persia, & opening vnto him his great necessitie, requested succours at his handes. Tamas was nothing slow to gratifie Simon herein, but dispatching foure thousand horsemen vnder the conduct of one of his owne captaines, sent him into Georgia, with speciall order, that he should take Dauid aliue, and bring him into Persia, in case hee would not chaunge his religion, and so bee setled in that State as his lawfull subiect, and not as a francke tributarie, such as hee was before. Which if he would be content to doe, then the king commaunded his Captaine to seise vpon Simon, and in case he would not chaunge his faith, to bring him away with him, and substitute Dauid in his place: but in case Simon should be readie and willing to do as his brother had done, then should he be caused to put the matter in execution, and so be confirmed in his possession, & Dauid should be brought, as wee haue said before, to Casbin. The Persian Captaine departed into Georgia, and without any stirre, or any delay he tooke Dauid, & in the name of Tamas made vnto him the former offer, whervnto he did straight way consent, and so forsaking his religion, and chaunging holy Baptisme for Circumcision, he did most impiously consecrate himself a voluntarie sacrifice to false Mahomet, & (which is most horrible & fearfull to write) renounced the Sauiour of the world. Then did the Persian Captaine seise also vpon Simon, & tould him, that to gratify him, he was come into Georgia at

The history of the two breethren Simon and Dauid.

Dauid denyeth Christ & becometh a Persian.

the commandement of Tamas, that all thinges were performed which he required, and that he had taken his enemy-brother prisoner. Howbeit that he must not thinke to enioy that kingdome vnder the protection of Tamas, vnlesse he would change his faith, and become an obseruant of the same prophet and of the same lawe, whereof king Tamas is a champion and defender: & therefore he must resolue himselfe so to doo, otherwyse his brother Dauid should be setled in his place, who had already very voluntarily chosen that parte,

Most bitterly did Simon bewail the fal of his brother, & being now more setled & constant, then euer hee was, in the most sacred & holy faith of Christ, he surrendered vp his earthly kingdome, because hee would not loose the kingdome of heauen, which he hoped for, and of a King became a prisoner, being betrayed by those very persons, whom he had called to be his defenders. After that Daut-Chan (for so was Dauid now called) had mumbled vp with his vncleane mouth, the wonted and vsuall blasphemies of the Persians, being circumcised, and apparrelled in the habite of a Barbarian, he was in the name of Tamas enstalled, not by the terme of King or Duke, but of the Chan of Teflis, and all the other places, heareafter mentioned: And poore Simon was carried away to Tamas, by whom, for all the many instances and earnest requestes, that were made vnto him to become a Persian, yet could he not be remoued from the foundation of his natiue faith, & therfore was sent into the Castell or Rocke of Cahaea, wherein banished Ismahel, the sonne of Tamas liued, who afterward was king, as before is declared. And so contented himselfe rather to remaine in temporall prison, then to change his first Christian religion (wherein notwithstanding he was a Schismatike,) and to prepare for himselfe perpetuall chaines, and blind & eternall captiuity in hell for euer. By this successe of Simon we may easyly learne how dangerous a thing it is, to draw the Barbarians into our states and gouernements for our defence and helpe: for that wee see most manifestly, there is no one thinge more doubtfull, more vncertaine, or more impious, then their faith or promises, and that to spoyle other men of their states, they will not sticke most impudently to venture vpon any wicked enterprise.

An aduertisment not to trust the promises & helps of the Barbarians.

The promises of the Barbarians deceauable.

The places subiect to Lauassap.

But following the description of those places, that belonged to the father of these two vnhappy heires, we say, that the Citties subiect vnto him, were principally Teflis, Lory, Tomanis, Chieres, Giurgi-Chala & many other townes & villages. But the cheefe pallace of all was euer at Teflis, and neere therunto euen at this day are to be seene the sepulchers of the kinges of this parte of Georgia. It is a place very strong by situation, watred with a small riuer, which descending from certaine hils neere thereaboutes rometh along this coast and entreth into his neighbour Araxis. This small riuer the Turkes call Chiur, supposing peraduenture that it is some braunche of the Riuer Cirus, the graund waterer of all this region. On the syde of Armenia, towardes the South coast, where Tomanis standeth, there are many very narrow lanes in the mountaines, & very deepe valleys, wherein the foresaid riuer Araxis with most outragious turninges and windinges, and his many rushing downefals among the rockes doth euen be-deafe a mans eares, & with his most violent roming in and out doth drowne and ouerwhelme, whosoeuer by miserable chance falleth downe head-long from the toppes of those narrow passages which are vpon the mountaines. And vpon the creastes of the said mountaines, on the syde of the sayde narrowe passage, there growe most hideous woodes and antique forrests full of Beeches and Pynetrees, where the horrour of darkenes, and silence which is oftentymes interrupted, onely by the whistlinge of windes, or by the cry of some wilde beast, doo make the poore passengers most terribly afraide. On the Weste syde there are most difficult passages on the rocks of Periardo, which maketh both the borders of this countrey, and the borders of the Widowes countrey also most dangerous and full of a thousand annoyances: and there likewise the riuer Araxis with his crooked courses in the low and deepe valleyes, maketh a most narrow and perrillous passage for any man. On the North syde is the roughe and noysome mountaine of Caucasus: and by that coaste the Turkes could not possibly get any entrance into this Region, vntill they had conquered the Cittie of Derbent. So that on all these three sydes, by which the Ottomans might make their way into that countrey, that is to say, by Colchos, by Periardo, and by Armenia, Nature defended the land from forraine and strange nations, as though she had foreseene this calamity and tempest of the Turkish fury, and of her owne bounty and benignity supplyed those wantes of Arte, which were in that people, who was vtterly ignorant in casting of Gunnes; and in the vse of such lyke engines. Of these straites of Georgia as also of the fower entrances before named, it seemeth that Strabo maketh manifest mention in his seconde booke, where he also writeth, that Pompeius, & Canidius, did vse two of these passages to enter with their Armies into this prouince. But in this present warre the Turkes sought to vse them all fower at one tyme: by the way of Colchos, sending their fleete on the great sea into the Channell of the riuer Fasis: by the coast of the Albanians leading Abdilcherai the Tartarian into Seruan: and by these two straites carrying all their Army, as in fit places it shall be set downe.

    As ye walke towards the North, on this syde of the lake Essecchia, (which perhaps is the marish called Lychnitis) there standeth the Cittie Basacchiuc, with certaine other Townes and Cities, for a long time subiect to Basacchiuc being a Lord of that name. Who was allwaies

Vallies and narrow cuttes in the mountaines of Tomanis.

Woodes and old darke Forrestes.
Cerri: trees lyke Poplers carrying mast fit for hogges.

Hard passages.

Strabo maketh mention of the passages into Georgia.

Pompeius & Canidius vsed these straites. The Turkes sought to occupy all the 4. entrances into Georgia.

Basacchiuc the Georgian and his state.

more rusticall and vnciuill then all the rest, as one that dwelt far out of the ordinarie waies, by which the Turkish Armie made their iourney, and by that meanes neuer endured the like troubles and inconueniences that others did: so that in all these stirres and hurly-burlies among his neighbours, withdrawing himselfe into these fortes made and framed by nature, he sat as it were in a watch-tower to behold the accidents of this doubtfull warre. Which rest certainely he had not so quietly enioyed, if the Tartarians had not fayled in their promises made to Amurat: whose breach of promise did in deede frustrate and thwart many important enterprises and singular conquestes, that Ofman the Bassa had plotted in those quarters.

Breach of promise in the Tartariās, dammageable to the Turke.

Now the Sonne of Leuent, called by the inhabitantes there, Schender, and by vs Alessandro surnamed the Great, and brother of Ixis, hath his state betweene Reiuan & Siruan, wide of Tomanis, and though it be accounted among the Georgian States, yet is it situate rather in Armenia the Greater in the borders of Atropatia, then in Iberia. This man in steed of armes hath continually vsed prayers and presentes, and as he that more then all the rest lay open to the passage through Siruan, and dwelt neere to Reiuan and Teflis, he was likewyse subiect to the Persian fury: yet for all that he handled the matter so well with the Turkes on the other syde, that by his rich and liberall gifts, in steed of armes and wepons, euen in the greatest heates of this warre, he kept himselfe equally vntouched and free from the violence both of his foes and frends. His cheefe pallace is Zaghen, fruitfull of silkes, he hath also Grin, and diuers other villages & townes: he surpasseth at this day all the rest of his neighbour Georgians in riches & money, & enioyeth withall greater tranquilitie and quiet then they all. He was in tymes past greatest affected to the Crowne of Persia, but since the tyme, that Tamas sought by vniust and vnlawfull meanes to depryue him of his state, and in his rowme to substitute his brother Ixis, (who being become a Persian, and hauing giuen himselfe to Tamas and to Satan, like a wicked wretch, gaped after it aboue all things in the world,) he then began to repose small confidence in the Persian succours, and resoluing with himselfe to remaine a Neuter, he followed the campes of the conquerours, and fauoured the Ensignes and name of those that were mightiest. And in this case standeth the state of Georgia at this day.

Leuentogli the Georgian and his State.

The Citties of Leuentogli.

But the countrey of Siruan, which on the West is ioyned with this Prouince, (whereof wee will make but a briefe discourse,) hath also on the North syde the Albanians, and a little beyond them some wandring and vagabound Tartarians called Pericorschi, betweene Caueasus & the riuer Volga, whereupon it may be that the Tartarians are comprehended vnder the name of the Volcenses: on the East it hath the lake (if with

The countrey of Siruan.

Polycletes we may so terme it,) or rather (as other call it) the sea of Corazan: on the South syde Armenia, and more toward the South and southeast Media the greater. The Metropoliticall city of Siruan is Sumachia, situate betweene Derbent and Eres: and as Derbent lyeth in the way for the Scythians, so doth Eres make way for the Armenians and Medes to enter into the country that is subiect to the said Citty. All Atropatia, was subiect to the Persian King, and was obedient to him, being induced thereunto first by Aydere, and afterward by Ismahel Sofi, sauing onely that it seemed the people of Derbent did ordinarily loue rather the fame and renowne of the Turkes, then the gouernement of their natiue Prince, sticking also to the auncient religion which Aidere shooke, and Ismahel subuerted. The whole countrey is fruitefull, and watred with Araxis and Cirus, and other riuers that are famous euen in antique writers: and principally Eres, which yeelded in tymes past great store of those fine white silkes, commonly tearmed by the marchantes Mamodean silkes, whereof at this day there is not to be found, no not a very small quantity, by reason of the monstrous ruines and ouerthrowes, that haue happened in those countreys. The king of Persia maintained in Derbent and Eres, after the naturall Lord was driuen out of them by Ismahel, certaine gouernours with the tytle of Sultans: and in the Citty of Sumachia one onely Gouernour with the tytle of Chan, who ruled both ouer Sechi, & also ouer the other Cities that were subiect to that iurisdiction. But Derbent, as we haue already written, euē as it was the last city on that side which was subdued by the Sofi, & made more resistance, then all the rest, in receauing the superstition of the Sofiti or Cheselbas, insomuch that Aidere left his carcase vnder her walles: euen so, though at the last it was ouercome, yet did it always remaine most affectionate to the first faith & opinion that it held, when the law of Mahomet had not yet tasted of the Schisme of the Sofians: howbeit, it could neuer fynd opportunity to receaue the Turkish captaines into her, and so vtterly shake-of all obedience to the Cheselbas.

Betweene Seruan and Tauris is situate the countrey of Caracach, fertile and rich in corne and cattell, very commodious for the feeding of Beastes, in situation not greatly subiect to windes, by reason that it lyeth rather alow then aloft, but yet pleasant and temperate: and it seemeth that this countrey on that side, bordereth vpon the Atropatians and the Medians, where the Cittie of Tauris standeth, euen at the rootes of the mountaine Orontes, which according to Straboes opinion is a portion of Taurus. Of this Cittie we haue sufficiently spoken in this History, & much more largely in the Letter, which in manner of an Appendix wee haue added in the end of this worke, for the more manifest declaration of our opinion touching the recognition of this place: the reading wherof may peraduenture more distinctly expresse the Geography of

Polycletes callesh the Caspian sea by the name of a lake.

Sumachia. Derbent. Eres.

Atropatia is fruitefull.

Eres made Mamodean Silkes.

Sechi a city of Siruan.

Caracach.

The mountaine Orontes, The mountaine Taurus

these countries. And now taking this Cittie of Tauris for the middell, or (as it were) the Center in a circle, wee will also vse it for an obiect in all the considerations, which very briefly wee shall heere ser downe. All those that come from Van or from the Lake of Vastan, and make their voyage towardes Media, doo arriue at Tauris, trauelling alwaies by East, or by East & by North, being nyne dayes iourney or thereabouts, and leauing Coy, Merent, and Soffian. And this was the way that Osman Bassa, and Ferat Bassa kept when they went with their Army to this citty, and which Angiolello also held, when he was in Persia,, as is manifest to be read in Ramusius. Besydes this way, there is also another comming from Reiuan, from whence as ye trauell by a direct line (as it were) by East, leauing Nassiuan and Chiulfall, you shall arriue at Tauris, within the space of nyne or tenne daies iourney of an ordinarie carriers pace: and therefore Ferat Bassa, the first time that he was generall, attempted this way beginning at Reiuan, which he made a Fortresse. Aboue Nassiuan, & Chiulfall is Seruan, and the countrey of Caracach which (I know not whether it be true or no) they say the Turke goeth about to strengthen with fortes, and to subdue, as he hath begun. From Tauris towardes the south by west standeth Salmas, and on the south Siras in Persia, and on the South by east Casbin, distant from Tauris about eight or nyne dayes iourney, (as saith Barbaro and Angiolello) with certaine other cities amōg, wherof there is sufficient mention made by vs in the history, & therefore we will not stand here to repeat them. More towards the East is Cassan, and further beyond is Hispahan, foure and twenty dayes iourney distant from Tauris. Then followeth Heri, and Corazan, & the Ieselbas, who were so troublesome to Ismahel, that by their meanes he was ouercome and put to flight by Selim.

In Armenia the Great there are dyuers Lakes, whereof the greatest according to Strabo his opinion, is the lake Martiano, called by the inhabitantes there Actamar, and by vs the sea of Vastan. Next to this is the Lake Arasseno, called Tospite & Toeti, which breaketh and teareth apparrell asunder, as Strabo wryteth: and through this riuer doth Tigris runne with such violence and swiftnes, that it doth not mingle his waters with the lake. Aboue the lake of Actamar are the champaines of Caldaran, famous for the battelles beteweene Selim & Ismahel. But not to stand long in repeating such thinges as are written by vs and others vpon other occasions, it shall bee well to descend to those particulars, which as they haue not beene hitherto precisely described by any man that I know, so may they bring vnto vs more certaine knowledge of this Empyre.

There is resident in Casbin their prophane Priest called Mustaed-Dini, that is to say, the chiefe of the law, who is as the Mufti among

THE SECOND BOOKE   43

the Turkes: and in the other subiect Cities are certaine peculiar Heades, obedient to this cheefe Priest: who notwithstanding are not chosen or displaced at his pleasure, as our Bishops and prelates are by our most holy Pope, the true Viccar of God and pastor of the holy Catholike Church; but by the King himselfe, who, (as we haue said before) should be not onely a king, but also a Priest, euen as Aly and Mahamet were. Howbeit for avoyding of greater trouble, he graunteth that fauour and putteth ouer that burden from himselfe vnto others, to whose iudgementes hee also referreth himselfe; whensoeuer there is any consultation or treatie touching their law and obstinate religion. Vnder the Mustaed-Dini are the Califes, and these are they that execute their dayly seruice in their Moschees or Temples. The chiefe of these Califes is he that putteth the Horne vpon the kinges head, when he is first inthronized: A ceremonie now perfourmed in Casbin, because the Turkes forbad it to be perfourmed in Cafe neere vnto Babylon, where also in times past (as we haue sayd before) the Persian kinges were wont to girde themselues with their sword. Those three Sultanes that remaine at Casbin for the generall gouernement of the whole Empire, haue their seuerall distinct charges. One hath the care of matters of warre ouer all the kingdome: and the other two gather vp all the reuenues, and keepe a diligent reckoning thereof: which two may be rather called Treasurers then any thing els, such as the Turkes call Deftardar. Next vnto them there are at Casbin two great Chauncellours, whome the Persians call Mordar, whose office is to write all the orders, Commaundementes, and letters concerning the gouernement of the kingdome: one of them keepeth the Seale, and the other the penne. There is also in Casbin the magistracie of Iudges, exercised by two persons, whome the Turkes call Caddi, and wherof in Constantinople there are wont to bee three, as also the nomber of Sultanes there is greater then in Casbin. And these two Iudges do make aunsweare and giue sentence in matters of controuersy and ciuill quarrels. For as touching criminall causes they haue no further authoritie, but onely to frame examinations of witnesses, & to make declaration thereof, which they call Sigil: and this Sigil they deliuer vp into the handes of the Sultane that is gouernour of the cittie or of the Empire, & he causeth execution to be done according to custome. And euen as the chiefe cittie is thus ordered, so likewise all the other Cities haue the selfe same magistrates, but yet all at the kings disposition & appointment: for in them also, besides the Chan, or Sultan, besides the Mustaed Dini, and the Calife, there are the Caddi, the M[...]rdari, and the Desiardari, which exercise the same authoritie within their priuate gouernementes, as the others do [...] ouer the whole state. This is then the order of the States of the kingdome: First the Saha, then the Miriza

The Califes,

The Sultans.

The Deftardari. The Mordari

The Caddi.

The order of the Persian dignities.

and Mirize, the Chan and Sultan, the Mordar, the Def [...]ardar, the Caddi, the Mustaed-Dini, and the Calife. The king keepeth also for the gard of his Palacegate certaine orders of souldiours: whereof the most noble and greatest in nomber are those that the Persians call Curchi, which are as it were the Kinges gentlemen, being six thousand, all of them diuided vnder seueral captaines: which Captaines also doo yeeld obedience to their generall Captaine called Curchi Bassa, a person alwaies of great authority. The other next vnto this is the order of the Esahul to the number of seuen hundred, distinguished also vnder particular Captaines, after the manner of the Curchi, and the captaine of those captaines is called Esahul Bassi. There want not diuers other seruices besydes these, which doo not deserue in this place to be nombred. And this is the state of Persia.

The kings Curchi.

The kinges Esahul.

But as concerning the state of their warres and warfare, it cannot bee precysely and particularly descrybed, neither in respect of their forces, nor of their weapons, nor of the manner of their fight: and yet will wee set downe that little which we know for certaine. The souldiers of this kingdome would in truth be very many and terrible, if al those places, which we haue comprised within the cōpasse therof, as they are accompted, so they were indeed obedient to this crowne, and if also all those fables could be verified of it, that are dyuersly reported by dyuers wryters, of so many horsemen & so many footemen. But for somuch as not onely the Tributaries, but also the very naturall subiects doo not send in their ordinary and due aydes and succours, hereupon it springeth that in all their occasions their forces prooue so weake, and their Armies of a very small nomber. Of the discordes and diuisions in Georgia, which haue now bene tried by long experience to haue bene no lesse hurtful to them selues, then to the Persians, we haue already spoken asmuch as may suffice: and now we will speake of some others, beginning with Amet-Chan, who hath a long time been Lord of Gheilan. This man, although he were of hability to haue yeelded singular aide to this crowne, (it being the generall opinion of all men, that he could gather together xx. thousand horse) yet could hee neuer be induced to serue in warre, but rather enioying a base and infamous lyfe, he is become both vyle to himselfe, and vnprofitable and hatefull euen to his neighbours & kinsfolkes. For which cause king Tamas, when hee was free from the Turkish warres, employed all his forces against him, and followed him so hardly, that in the end hee tooke him prisoner, & so kept him till he dyed, which was for the space of xv. yeares. But assoone as the now king Mahamet was inthronized in his kingdome, being carried away with a vaine and foolish pittie, hee deliuered him out of prison, hoping (lyke an vnwyse man as he was) that this most couetous and suspicious wretch would haue proued

The state of the men of warre in Persia.

Amet-Chan.

Amet-Chan imprisoned by Tamas & enlarged by Mahamet.

curteous, and kynd towardes him, which was a thing quyte contrary to his nature and disposition. And behold, neither thoseuerity of Tamas, nor the lenity of Codabanda, could euer perswade him to change his mynd: for in the greatest daungers of this present warre hee could neuer tynde in his hart to apply himselfe to the performance of any noble acte, that was not only worthy of his great forces, but also especially required by the present necessities.

The like treacherie shewed Rustan Mirize, the king of Candahar, and sonne to a brother of king Tamas, who neither for neerenesse of bloud, nor for common honour, nor for the estimation and reputation of his owne superstition, could euer be wrought to pitty the calamities of Persian: and yet the kingdome of Candahar was very well hable to gather about xxv. thousand horse: Neither may his excuses auaile him, that he alleadged touching the far distance of his countrey: For if distaunce of place was no hinderaunce to the enimie to bring his Armies euen to Tauris, to annoy the Persians: Lesse reason had Rustan Mirize to withdraw his ready forces frō defending his frends, the iourney from Constantinople to Tauris beeing no shorter, then it is thither from Candahar. Rustan Mirize.

Like vnto these was, and still is Emir-Miran the Lord of Iest, a hard man, and very obstinate in coueteousnesse, who doth not onely not send any voluntarie aide, but also refuseth to pay those tributes which by couenant & composition he is bound to send: And yet is he able to yeeld foure or fiue thousand horse of great valour in warre. Emir-Miran.

The Lord of Lar also, called Ebrain-Chan, famous for his mightinesse, although in times past hee hath alwayes helped the common forces with his priuate succours, yet at this day he vtterly denieth both the one and the other, and threateneth rather to suppresse all Estates, then to aduaunce and encrease any that belong to this crowne. Ebrain-Chan.

But aboue al the rest, me thinketh that Abas Mirize this kinges sonne is most impious and wicked, who not onely would neuer fauour his fathers enterprises against the cruell enimies of the common libertie, but also hath sought by all meanes possible to driue both his brethren and his father out of the State, and to enter himselfe into the succession and gouernement of this diuided and troubled kingdome. So that vnder his Iurisdiction there are idlely fed eighteene thousand horse, which would prooue very stout and strong in warre, if they wanted not discipline. Abas Mirize.

In Cussestan, those Arabians that were wont to be ready for any seruice to the Persian kinges, haue yeelded thē selues to the Turkes, and often times worke great annoyances to the Persians by their suddaine incursions. But within the very bowels of the kingdome, the Turcoman nation, that would haue beene a great strength to these forces, if they Cussestan. Turcomania.

would haue ioyned with them, Behold, how it hath not failed to procure many ouerthrowes to this kingdome: a great parte whereof we haue described in the fourth booke of this history. The kingdome of Seruan also is in such sort spoyled and decayed, that the cities of Sumachia, Eres, Sechi, Derbent and others, out of which there was wont to bee leuied a good reasonable nomber of people, as also Reiuan, Teflis, and other countries of Georgia and Armenia, are not able to yeeld any succours in the time of warre: so that the Crowne of Persia beeing depriued of such and so many helpes, is at this day constrayned to wage warre with very slender forces, which very briefly shall be heere set downe.

Seruan.

Out of Hispahan, and the territorie thereof, (to reckon their Stipendiaries to the vttermost) they leauie eight thousand souldiers on horseback: out of Bargo, two thousand: out of Cassan, foure thousand: out of Seua, one thousand: out of Sultania, one thousand: out of Casbin, twelue thousand: out of Ardouil, one thousand: out of Siras eight thousand: out of Tauris foure thousand: out of Cum and Cuohiue-Tauris two thousand: out of Genge & the rest of Georgia, foure thousand. Besides these they may hire others, when their occasions do so require, and they haue alwaies volūtary souldiers, & that in som good nomber so that the greatest Armie that they can possibly gather, will hardly amount to threescore thousand horse: (alwayes prouided that euery cittie aforenamed do send in their Stipendiarie Souldiers according to their duety.) Whereas if all the other Capitaines, that are noted aboue to be obstinate and rebellious, would agree and concurre in one vnitie, they might make an hoast of an hundred & thirty or an hundred and forty thousand persons or thereaboutes.

The forces of the Persian kingdome, whose seruice may be vsed.

Their Souldiers are armed for the most parte with Scimitarre, Launce, and Darte, but specially, the Scimitarre is most familiar vnto them, and all the Persians do make a singular profession and vse of it: although there want not among them some that can handle the Arcubuse also, the exercise whereof hath of late yeares growen more familiar and vsuall, then it was in the time of Ismahel, and in the first yeares of the raigne of king Tamas. For their owne defence they are armed with good Corselets, and strong helmets, many of them able to keepe out an Arcubuseshot, much more to daunt the force of a Darte: Some of their horses also are armed with very good Armour, most finely and soundly tempered. And these their horses are of a singular vertue, equall with those of the old time, which (as Strabo writeth) were accustomed to be fed and brought vp in Armenia for their kings vse. Swift in course, fierce in battell, long breathed and very docible. When they are vns […]dled, gentle and milde, but when they are armed, warlike, hardie, and manageable, euen at the pleasure of

The weapons of the Persian souldiers.

The Persian horses very good.

the Ryder: so that it is no meruaile, if one of them haue bene sold for a thousand or a thousand & three hundred *Duckates.

*Cocchini.

Those that follow & attend the exercises of warre are for the most part men of noble me […], and therevpon it cōmeth, that they are more hardy and valiant to foyle then to flie. And beeing compared with the Turkish people, (who for the most part are very rascalles, of vile race, ready to fly and to rauine) they are by good right very worthie to be highly esteemed. The Persians are great deceiuers, full of craftie Stratagemes, vnconstant, and breakers of their word: (a vice that seemeth to haue beene alwaies proper to the Barbarians.) Neuer content with any mans gouernement, and louers of nouelties, wherein Persia was alwaies noted particularly & specially to haue offended. For testimony whereof we may vouch those ancient poysoninges and wicked treacheries, which were plotted not onely by Subiectes against their kinges, but also by children against their naturall father: which name (as Iustinus writeth) was in so small estimation with those fiftie sonnes of Artaxerxes, that with one consent they all conspired vpon a most wicked pretence to murther their father, without that any one of them, either in regard of his Fatherly Maiestie, or reuerence to his age, or naturall pietie, did attempt to prohibite so great an iniquitie. An Acte (as it seemeth) very well marked by the Sofian kings, who as we may read of Vngher, Mahamut and others, and (as it is written in this Historie) the Children with the Father, the Father with the Children, and the Children one with an other, haue learned it by course, and dayly doe practise it to destroy one another: and so weakening their owne forces, do make themselues spectacles of infamy to all the world.

The Persians valorous and noble souldiers.

The Persians giuen to noueltie.

The impiety of the sonnes of Artaxerxes the Persian king.

The people of Persia are afrayde of Artillery beyond measure, and yet sometimes they haue not beene afraide with suddaine assaultes to assaile their enimies trenches, & lodginges in their Campes. And although they be so timorous and fearefull of that Engine, and know of what moment it is in a battell: yet haue they not hetherto receiued the vse thereof, being rather obstinate in their blind ambitious conceite, that it is a sinne and shame to exercise so cruell a weapon against mankinde, then ignorant how to make it, or destitute of matter to cast it.

The reason why the Persians do not use Artillary or Canons.

The manner of ordering their battell is after the fashion of a horne or of the Moone, as a man may call it, and in open battell their Squadrons are ordered on this sort. In the right horne or wing, by auncient custome were placed those troupes that were guyded by the captaynes of Istigelu, which is now called the Traytors lyne, by reason of Zalchan and the rest, that were so ready & resolute in the conspiracy, which was made in the fauour of Aidere, whereof we haue already written in this history. In the left cornet or wing were placed

The order o their battell.

The right wing.

the people that were led by the captaines Zambeluzes, who vaunt of their auncient discent from Damasco, and from the Tacaluzes, a nation neuer greatly esteemed for any valour or knowledge that they had in warfare. In the body of the battel was appointed the kings guard, who was alwaies accustomed to be present at warre with his Armies, although this king partly by reason of the infirmity of his eies, and partly for the dissentions in his kingdome durst not venture to goe in person, but in his steed sent Prince Amze, a valorous & good warrier. In the middest of the battell also, about the King, went the people of Ausares, which are pressed out of Persia, all of them accounted very warrelike, and more valiant then all the rest. Neyther would it bee greatly amisse to thinke that from hence were those troupes fetched in tymes past, which Xerxes was wont to terme by that proude tytle Immortall, the immortall souldiers. The Rere-ward was kept by those that descended from Calirchan, which were neuer as yet depryued of that honour, for the good desertes that Calirchan shewed to Ismahel, when he strained himselfe, to passe with a mighty Army euen into Cafe, to performe the Regall Ceremonies at his Coronation, and yet for all that neuer stirred the ordinary guarde of Casbin. The people of Caribdiler and Chiaperis made-vp the Vaunt-Guarde, accompted also to be men of good sort and very warlike, because they haue alwaies shewed themselues ready in any occasions or troubles of warre, and performed their partes very valiantly. And this was the manner of ordering their battelles in late tymes.

Touching the reuenues of this kingdome, the common opinion is, that in the dayes of Kinge Tamas the crowne did yearely receaue into the Chamber of Casbin, foure or fiue millions of gold, which afterward he caused to be worth eight millions, by a sudden enhaunsing of the value of his coyne, geuing in commandment by most seuere Edictes, that ouer all his Empyre, for a certayne space, all the money that he had receaued, should bee taken and accompted for asmuch more as it was worth, and accordingly made pay to his souldiers and Sultans, & all other that were in his pay. Which example (meethinkes) was well followed by Amurat the now-king of the Turkes, who receauing at the Citty of Cairo the Cechino of gold for xliii. Maidini, he put it out againe in Constantinople, to pay his Capigi and Ianissaries withal for lxxxv. Maidini, commanding that it should be of that value ouer all the Citty, and countryes subiect vnto it. But in the dayes of this king of Persia, the reuenues of this crowne are thought to be so much diminished, that it is the opinion of all men, they amount to little more then two millions in all. Neither is there to be found in him that industry & prouidence which was in Tamas, and though it were, yet peraduenture it would not be regarded by his subiects: & it seemeth that the occasion of this decay is the losse of so many countries as Soliman conquered, and particularly Mesopotamia, and Assyria, besydes Erzirum and the Tributes that are denyed by the people of Georgia, and by other nations of this kingdome. Next after this kinde of reuenue, which is payed in ready money, and collected into the Chamber of Casbin from among the Citties that are subiect vnto it: (although all the countrey, that was possessed by these kinges, were not appoynted by diuision to the payment of a certayne nomber of souldiers, as the Turke vseth to doo in those Countries that he subdueth:) yet is there a great sort of towns and villages which are very Feudataries to the croune of Persia, & are so many that they supply a part of the pay that is due to the horsemen aboue mentioned, to foure thousande of the Curchi of Casbin, and to the Esahul aforenamed. Among all the reuenues that are gathered out of the Citties subiect to Casbin, the greatest were alwaies payed out of Tauris, Cassan, & Hispahan, all Citties of great traffike, where the marchandise of Europe & all Asia doo arriue. And these are the reuenues of this Crowne.

Certain lands assigned for the payment of the Persian souldiers.

The greatest reuenues com out of Tauris, Cassan and Hispahan.

The expenses briefely are these. The threescore and ten Sultanes, that serue in the gouernement of the subiect Citties, are payed in ready money out of the Chamber of Casbin, with a stipend of three thousand, foure thousand, or fiue thousand Cecchins a peece. The two thousand Curchi, that remaine to be paide for their attendance, (who haue no landes assigned to them for their pay, as the foure thousand abouenamed haue) doe also receiue their ordinary wages out of the kinges Chamber, from a hundred & threescore, to two hundred Cecchins a man. From thence also are defraied the stipends for the magistracyes of the Iudges, not onely of Casbin but of all the whole empire, & all the Treasurers likewise. Wherof some haue a thousand, some fiue hundred, and some a thousand and fiue hundred Cecchins yearely. The Garnisons of certayne Fortes, as of Elegie neere to Nassiuan, Guuergi-Chalassi, Cahaca-Calassi and such like, consisting some of a thousand and fiue hundred persons, some of a thousand, and some of fiue hundred, are payed with these Reuenewes, and euery Souldier of them receiues for his pay fiue Cecchins a moneth little more or lesse. I do not heere reckon the expenses that go out for the pay of other base Offices, of his household, of the Queene, of the Prince, of his Children, of the Temples called their Moschees, of the buildinges, of the gardens, and such like: and so I leaue you to make an accompt, how much remaineth ouer and aboue, for the king to put vp in his purse yearely.

The expenses of the Persian kingdome.

Fortes that haue neede of ordinary Garrisons.

And now hauing respect to the order of those thinges, which I propounded to my selfe to treate-of, there resteth nothing els, but onely briefely to consider the occasions, whereby it is come to passe, that a kingdom so meruelously encreased is so suddenly decreased and decaied. And we think the principall occasions therof were three. The first, because the enemy did in very short space waxe verie strong and mightie, by the great conquestes that he made both by sea and by land: by meanes whereof it fell out that those calamities and assaultes, wherewith Persia was at sondry tymes dyuersly afflicted and trauelled, did alwaies proue very grieuous and mortall vnto it. The second because the empyre of Persia had no fenced citties, that were able to hold out or maintaine themselues: and if there were any, as Van was one, it was because they knew not how to fynd the meanes, either to maintayne, or to recouer themselues: And who knoweth not, that the country lying open, without any resistance, not onely the huge forces of the Turke, but also farre lesse forces had beene able to worke these mischeefes, yea and farre greater then these are. The third, is the conquest of all Artes that the Turke hath made in the winning and subduing of so many christian cities, which are replenished with al kind of diligent study & arte. By which conquests the Turke hath not onely learned to vse his wonted and natiue weapons after a more mortall and deadly manner: but also hath inuented new, to the great astonishment & terrour of his enemy, who hath not onely neglected to make vse of forraine instructions, and to learne the true meanes, to encrease his owne forces, but (as it were) contemning all other mens wittes; hath thought himselfe alone able to teach and instruct others. And this is that haultinesse and ambitious conceite of the Persian, who in this present misery of his owne, vaunteth & braggeth of great matters, though all the world can see nothing but most vnhappy euentes in all his warres. The fourth is the concord and celerity of the Turke, whereby he hath attempted whatsoeuer he would, and hath obtayned whatsoeuer he attempted: yea and oftentimes, before the Persians could take their Armour, he hath taken their countryes. The fifte, which is the roote and fosterer of all the rest, hath always beene the discord and dissention in the kingdom of Persia, and the keeping aliue of so many brethren or nephewes of the king at once: and not onely the keping of them aliue, but also the maintaining of them in authority, in gouernement, and in maiesty. For hereby it came to passe that all counselles and execution of counsailes were diuided, Armies weakened, Captaines minds suspended, and inclyning to dyuers parties, & to be briefe there followed a meere confusion of all thinges. It is in deed a barbarous and inhumaine thing for one brother to dye his crowne & Scepter with the bloud of another, and oftentymes of so many of his breethren, and out of all doubt it is a very harde and cruell position, that a man shall not be able to rule without the making away of his deerest frendes: But yet on the other syde it cannot bee

The occasions of the declination of the Persian kingdome.

but too much negligence and lenity, to permit that breethren and children, being of speciall ambition waxen ouer proude in their owne conceytes by reason of their princely gouernementes and authorities, should stirre-vp armes one against another, and in the meane while scarce leaue any meanes for the poore king to scape with his life: who being by his owne bloud made (euen as it were) a rebell to the honour and quyet of the kingdome, must needes reduce his empire into a most vnhappy state. Both these kyndes of gouernementes, are in extremities, and therefore infected with vice and barbarisme, and not to be exercised by any man. And although Cornelius Tacitus saith, that Great enterpryses, which are recompensed with the proffit and safety of the Commonwealth, may haue some iniquity or vnlawfulnesse in them: notwithstanding euery Christian prince ought by all meanes to auoide them, and to establish the quyetnesse of his kingdome, neither with too great cruelty, nor with excessiue lenity, in which two poyntes all the Barbarian kinges doo ordniarily offend.

I had heere made an end of this booke, had there not beene brought vnto me certaine bookes, some written in French and some in the Latin tongue, some with the tytle of commentaries, and some of an History, vnder the names of dyuers Authours more Poeticall then Historicall, as far as I can gather: in which bookes hauing found many wantes, aswell concerning matters of the Persian and Turkish opinions about their lying religion, as also touching the recognition of certaine auncient cities, the tymes wherein things haue happened, the actions themselues, the voyages of the armies, and many other particularities, I thought it my dutye to admonishe all those, that after this our age shall happen to read those bookes and this history, that they walke verye circumspectly in reading such writings. And especially let them take great heed, that they doo not belieue these things following: namely, That the Turkes follow Aly, and the Persians follow Omar and Abubacher: for the matter is quite contrary. Likewise, that Scutar was in old tyme Chrysopolis, whereas it is a most cleere case that it was Chalcedon, the founders whereof were termed blynde, because they did not see what errour they committed in buylding a Citty there, and leauinge the place where Constantinople nowe standeth, as farre excelling the situation of Chalcedon, as gold excelleth leade. Also that Esrum or Erzirum, as it should be called, is a city of Assyria, whereas indeed it is not a city of Assyria, but of Cappadocia, if we speake properly. That Seruan is the auncient Media, it being in truth Atropatia. That Osman Bassa tooke Teflis, Mustaffa himself being there in person with all hys hoast, & not (as one of them saith) Citra memorabile damnum, without any memorable losse, no, not with any losse at all, because he found it emptie. That Mustaffa, poysoned himselfe voluntarily, which he did

An aduertisement to the reader.

not indeede, but fell into an Apoplexie. And many other such tales, wherof it is not now conuenient to make any particular confutation. And therefore passing them ouer, wee will prosecute our former order of this History.

The end of the second Booke.

The Third Booke

The Argument.
The Turkish Armie departeth for Teflis. and commeth to Archichelech.
A reuiew of the Armie, and the nomber of those that wanted in the Army.
It commeth to Triala. It winneth a Castell.
It taketh Teflis, and fortifieth it, and then departeth for Seruan.
The Sorians forsake the Armie of Mustaffa, and in their returne home to Aleppo they are assayled and discomfited by the Georgians.
The Ambassadours of Leuentogli entertayned by Mustaffa.
Leuentogli himselfe also entertained.
Seclis a Cittie vnder Seruania, yeelded to Mustaffa.
A Dearth in the Turkish Armie.
Victuallers go out for prouision of Corne and Victualles, but they are discomfited and vtterly destroyed by the Persians.
Mustaffa with all his Armie goeth to fight with his enimies, and foyleth them miserably.
Diuers disturbances and losses in the Turkish Armie, by passing ouer the Riuer Canac.
A wonderful kind of foorde found out.
The Turkes being refreshed frō diuers annoyances, arriue at Eres in Seruan.
Mustaffa fortifieth Eres, and leaueth Caitas Bassa in it.
Mustaffa departeth, and leaueth Osman Bassa, as Generall and Visier in Sumachia.
The people of Derbent yeeld themselues to Osman Bassa.
Mustaffa returneth home: is in the countrey of Leuent, commeth to Teflis, and there leaueth succours and a garrison.

Mustaffa departeth thence, in his iourney he endureth great cold, and losses in his Armie, through the cunning stratagemes of the Georgiani, and namely Hassain Bey discomfited.

Mustaffa at Altunchala receiueth the Widow and her other Sonne Alessandro.

He goeth to Clisca, and so to Erzirum.

He sendeth both the Sonnes of the Widow to Constantinople.

Abdilcherai the Tartarian Captaine commeth to succour Osman Bassa.

Ares-Chan withdraweth himselfe to the Riuer Canac, and is discomfited by Abdilcherai.

Genge sacked.

The Tartarians pitche their Tentes in certaine champeines and there take their ease.

Caitas Bassa and his people vtterly destroyed by the Persian Prince.

The Tartarians also destroyed by the same Prince.

Abdilcherai taken aliue and sent to Casbin.

Osman Bassa flyeth from Sumachia to Demir-Capi.

Sumachia destroyed by the Persian Prince, and the people of Sechi also chastised.

Abdilcherai at Casbin falleth in loue with the Queene: he is discouered, and both he and the Queene slaine by the Sultans.

Osman Bassa taketh to wise the daughter of Sahamal the Georgian. He discouereth the treacheries of his Father in Law: hee putteth him to death, and causeth his countrey to be destroyed.

Aly-Vechiali returneth from Mengrellia to Constantinople, and reporteth what he hath done in his Nauigation.

THE THIRDE BOOKE

After the solemne entertaynment of the Georgian Manucchiar, Generall Mustaffa had geuen order ouer all his Campe, that the next morning they should remoue from those mountaynes. And now was euery man bucklinge himselfe to accomplish the Captaines commandement, when as there happened very obscure and darke stormes that couered the heauens (as it were) with night and terrour, and being turned into raine and wind, casting out flashing fyres, & scouring the aire with terrible lightnings, did freshly afflict the Turkish armie. Which raine continued so vehement for the space of foure daies together, that it seemed the heauens were melted into waters: by meanes whereof it came to passe that out of the dead carcasses, & heads before mentioned, there issued a most horrible stinke, so that partely thereby, and partely by the myre,

A notable raine.

and other filth of the Cammells, Mules, and horses, they spoyled their armour, their apparrell, their deuises, their plumes, their pauillions, and all things els that was of any worth, yea all their brauery and beautie, and in the bodies of the people there arose dyuers diseases and infirmities, though not very pestilent, but breeding rather annoyance then death to the Turkes. But at last the heauens hauing ceased the raine, the lightning, the blustring and the stormes, and the Sunne hauing cleered all the ayre, Mustaffa raysed his campe to passe towardes Teflis: & because the ground was still very moyst and slabby, with the raine that had fallen in such aboundance, the Camells, that carried the heauiest burdens could not go onwardes, and the horses that drew the artillery, were subiect to the same difficulty, & so the army could not that daye passe any further then the plaines where the lake called Chielder Giol standeth, which (if the distance of places, & the nouelty of names do not deceiue vs) may wel be thought to be that, whēce Euphrates taketh his beginning. And there they stayed to drye and trim their apparrell, their weapons, and their harnesse, and to yeeld to their sick and wounded souldiers their due and deserued refreshing. *[The Turkish army remoueth towards Teflis. The Lake called Chielder-Giol.]*

 The Turkes remouing from thence the next day about noone arriued at a Castell called Archichelec, sometymes belonging to the Georgiani, but conquered by Soliman in his late warres against Tamas, and euer sithence possessed by the Turkes. Heere Mustaffa taking fit occasion of this frendly castell, and hauing commodity of pasture and opportunity of faire wether, (by reason of the losse which happened vnto him in the last battell, & the necessity of continuall trauelling through his enemyes cuntry) resolued to take a surueigh of all his army, wherein hauing ranged them in due order, & marshalled them with exquisite diligence, he found his nomber diminished, aswel by meanes of his late battel, as also of the forenamed infirmities, by forty thousand persons or there aboutes. Of which number, there was not a few that fled away from the hoast, and being wearie with following so rough and perrillous a iourney, closely and by night departed from the Campe, and returned into their owne cities, to take their ease at home. From hence the Army departed, and lodged the next night neere to a vile & filthy marish, called by the Turkes Peruana-Giol, which wee may well call, The Lake of Slaues: and the next day at Triala, where there are to be seene at this day the ruines of a great Citty and of many churches, whereof some being repayred and restored by godly men, are still maintained and kept by catholike priestes according to the holy customes of Rome. The reliques of those happy and religious forces, that with so great and faithfull zeale passed the seas and mountaines, and with the Sacred signe of the triumphant crosse, (being displaied in the winds vpon their victorious Ensignes,) perced through these

The Turkes at Archichelec.

A surueigh of the army.

40000, persons wanting in the Turkish Army.

The Turkes at the lake called Peruana Giol. The Turkes at Triala.

The praises of those Christian forces that tooke the holy Citty.

barbarous nations, euen to the borders of the Leuant. Blessed & happy soules, that prepared for your selues so fruytefull deathes, and with so great glory purchased at one tyme both kingdomes vpon earth, and the kingdom of heauen. Very well worthie are you, that as in the heauens you are entertained and praised by those soules that are Cittizens thereof, so here vpon earth you should bee commended and celebrated by the hautie verses of so graue & worthie a wryter. Reioice and liue in Gods name eternally, and pray vnto that soueraigne bounty, that into the hartes of his mighty champions he would inspire that enterprise, that is so greatly desyred of all men, & the longer it is delayed and slowed, the more difficult and perrillous it will proue.

The next day the Turkes ascended the high and craggy mountaine, that standeth vpon Teflis, from the toppe whereof descending the day following, the seised vpon a Castel of the Georgiani, called by the Turks Giurgi-Chala, & by vs the Georgian Castell: & departing from thence, & making their next abode in certaine plaines, the day following they came in good time nere to the riuer that runneth by Teflis. But in this iourny, frō the place, where the surueigh of the Campe was made, euen to this Riuer, there happened diuers and sundry slaughters of certaine souldiers, that separating themselues from the army, being dryuen thereuntoo by hunger, went to get some victualls, for themselues and their beastes: for that dyuers Captaines of Georgia, as Giusuf, Daut, and (as some saye) Alessandro the eldest sonne of the widdow, hauing gathered together a number of their owne countrey souldiers, had secretly followed the Turkish army, and as men that wer acquainted with al the waies of that regiō, they stood watching in such places as the victuallers should passethrough, and suddenly setting vpon them, spoyled them at once both of their goodes and lyfe. And this happened as often as there were either footemen or horsemen, (without any notice giuen thereof to their generall, who had graunted them certain sure souldiers to guide them,) that being perswaded thereuntoo by hunger, diuyded them selues from the custody and safe keeping of the rest of the hoast.

Mustaffa found the rocke or castell of Teflis empty, & without any inhabitant at all, for that Daut (of whome euen now we made mention) running away assone as he heard of the comming of the Turkes, and betaking himselfe to the fields, sought means to prouide better for himselfe that way, then he could haue doone, if he had stayed still in the Forte, & so should haue beene constrayned of necessitye to haue remayned prisoner. Whereupon Mustaffa, rather then he would vtrerly raze it, resolued to restore the old and weake walles thereof, and to make them stronger, that they might endure the sounde & shaking of the Artillary, wherewithall hee ment to strengthen it: which

The praise of Torquato. Tasso.

Giurgi Chala possessed by the Turkes.

The ambush of the Georgiani.

Mustaffa at Teflis.

Mustaffa fortifieth the walles of Teflis.

resolution he put in execution, and placed therein a hundred peeces of artillery, and appointed Generall Gouenor of that forte Mahamet Bassa, sonne of the late Ferat Bassa, one of the Aduenturers, with six thousand souldiers, partly stipendaries, and partly subjects to the said Mahamet: and after he had thus done, he departed towards Siruan.

But those that had bought the thousande loades of Corne from Aleppo, for the rent of their twelve thousand three hundred and nyne families, together with the people of Omps, (in tymes past called Hus, the Cittie of patient Iob) and other places of Soria, perceauing that Mustaffa, without giuing them licence to returne, followed on his iourney into farre countries, and being not willing to follow the hoast, as men that were rather bounde nor able to do it, they resolued to returne home into Soria. And so the people of Aleppo, being conducted by Nassardin Chielebi, mine acquaintaunce to whome the said corne & the charge also to conueigh the same was committed, did secretly and closely put their determination in execution. They were in all about a thousand persons, but indeed a vile people, and of small courage, there being in that number Scribes, Eunuchs, seruants and such kind of men to whom there were also joined certain other, of the like account, that had noted the resolution of the rest, and so made up the full number of a thousand and fiue hundred. And being thus all agreed, when Mustaffa departed towards Siruan, they turned towards Soria. But having passed through many great feares euen to the borders of the Widdows cuntrey, they repented themselves that they did not follow on the iourney with Mustaffa. For the three Georgian Captaines, of whom we have made mention afore, had gathered together about three thousand men, whereof some had followed and watched the army of Mustaffa, and some had betaken themselues to these borders, waiting for some good aduenture to happen vnto them, either of those that by some casualty could not overtake the Hoast. Or of those that meant to return to Erzirum. These Georgiani did the people of Soria light vpon, and were assaulted by them. They fought a long tyme, & endured the assault in the best maner they could: but when they perceaued the Georgiani to prove their good maisters, and that amonge their owne companies there remained no more strength, or force to rebate their enemies rage, they endeuored to saue themseules by flying, and committed their liues to the safeguard of their swift horses. But by this their flight, their losses were increased, and their slaughter augmented, In such sort that they were almost all of them slaine, sauing those few that being aided by the swift running of their valiant and good horses, escaped alyue. Among whome was Nassardin Chielebi abouenamed, who having fought very valiantly, vntill he had three fingers of his right hand quite cut-of, so that he could not vse his sword any longer, he was

The Sorians determine to forsake the Army. Nassardin Chielebi of Aleppo Captain of the Sorians.

Alessandro, Giusuf, and Dauid agreed together.

The Sorians assayled by the Georgiani at vnwares.

The Sorians flye from the battell begun with the Georgiani. Nassardin Chielebi wounded.

constrayned to turne his backe to the Georgiani, and saued himself by flight and having cured himself in those partes as well as he could, he arriued safe at Aleppo, where by Osman Bassa, with whome he was very familiar, he was appointed to be a vizier, & also rewarded by him with a good stipend, worthie of his great peril and danger.

Now Mustaffa, after he had passed the descent & steepness of the mountains of Teflis, the next day he encamped Among certain marishe and lowe champaines: and whiles he was there, the Embassadors of Leuentogli cane vnto him and tould him, that their Lord Alessandro, if it so pleased him, was ready to doo him reuerence, and by worde of mouth to promisse him that deuotion, which he had alwaies borne in his mind to the Ottoman kinges. With merry countenaunce did Mustaffa behould these Embassadors, and most cheerfully heard their offred obedience: and thereupon presently sent them backe & willed thē to cause Leuentogli to come, for that his frendship should be deere and acceptable to him. The Christian embassadours went to fetch their Lord, for whose welcome the Turkish Generall tooke order with all the Captaines of his army, that they should shew the greatest signes of ioy that might be: which was with all solemnity accordingly performed, & his coming celebrated with all tokens of fauour and kindnes. And after he had presented those precious & rare guifts that he brought with him, he offred his obedience to Capitaine Mustaffa, with the most earnest and liuely speeches that he could possibly deuise, calling Amurat his Lorde, and shewing that hee tooke it in ill parte, that Mustaffa passed not through his territory, where he might haue enioied all maner of commodities, abundance of corne, and other helps necessary for his army: yet for his better satisfaction, hee would looke for him at his returne from Siruan, being in the meane tyme most ready to bestow all that he had for the seruice of the Ottomans: telling him moreouer, that forsomuch as in many iust and lawfull respectes he could not possibly wait on him into Siruan, yet hee would accompany him alwaies in mind, & would pray to the creator of all things for his prosperity and all happy successe. And so eftsoons praying him to returne by his Citties, he tooke his leaue. Mustaffa receaued his presents curteously, & in exchange thereof bestowed vpon him a Battell-Axe, a Targat, and some apparell of cloth of gold, and gaue him his answeare in very magnificall and graue termes, and in the end promised the Christian Duke, that in his returne hee would passe through his countrey, and so dismissed him: with speciall commaundement, that his departure should bee honoured in the same sorte, as hee was entertained at his comming.

The Turkish Armie followed-on their begonne iourney towardes Siruan: and in the space of twelue dayes, after their departure from

Teflis, traueiling allwayes thorough low and moorish wayes, that were intricate by reason of reedes and myre, they arriued in the confines of the Medians, otherwise called the Siruanians, neere to the riuer of Canac, where of in the desoription of Georgia, Armenia, and Atropatia, we made but a short, & yet a plaine & manifest mention. Somewhat on this side of the same riuer, the Turkes ascended a little higher, being very weary with the long iourney that they had made, and rested themselues one whole day, in which time the Subiectes of the Cittie of Sechi bordering vppon the Siruanians and the Georgiani, foure dayes iourney distant from Sumachia, came to offer themselues to Mustaffa, as vassalles and subiectes to the Turke: All which were gladly entertayned, and some of the chiefe of them apparelled in silkes and gold, and honoured with great magnificence, and in the end had all protection promised vnto them.

Mustaffa and his host at the riuer Canac.

The subiectes of Sechi come to offer themselues to the captaine.

The Turkish Armie, as I haue told yee, was all foreweatied with the continuall iourney of twelue dayes together: but yet farre more afflicted with hunger, hauing not found in those parts so much as one wild beast, wherby they might quench their desire of meate; so that there was not a man among them, but sought meanes to get some store of victuaile, especially when they vnderstood, that Mustaffa was resolued to passe ouer Canac, and enter into a new countrey, vnknowne to them all, and where they knew not what hope to conceaue of finding any substance fitte for them. And whiles they were enquiring among themselues, who was able to conduct them into any place where they might finde reliefe, behold, there were certaine Persians taken, (whether they were there by chaunce, or brought thither for some Stratageme, I know not,) who beeing demaunded where they might haue corne and meate to slake the hunger of the Armie, after much resistaunce, and at the last told them, that not farre from the Campe, after they had passed certaine marishes, where Canac dischargeth it selfe, and runneth into Araxis, they should finde many fieldes, full of ryse and corne in the blade, and a little farther, certaine fat heardes of cattell feeding, that would bee sufficient to satisfie the appetites of all their people. Of this newes was Mustaffa certified, and although hee greatly doubted the treacheries of his enimies, and the subtleties of the Persians, yet to gratifie his souldiers, and to make them the more willing to follow him in his passage to Siruan, hee licensed euery man, that had any desire thereunto, to goe and prouide them selues of victuails, & so suffered all that would, to goe freely. When the Captaine had graunted them this licence, many Spahini, many Zaini, and some Sangiacchi also, sent diuers mē to fetch this prouision of corne and cattell. And there went for that purpose about tenne thousand seruile persons, with many Camels, horses, and mules to carry the pray.

The hunger of the Turkish Army.

The Persian spyes taken.

The intelligence that the spyes gaue for vittaile.

Mustaffa lycenceth euery man that would go for corne and other necessaries.

Ten thousand seruile persons go for victuaile.

But the successe fel out quite contrary to their designementes: for Tocomac, Alyculi-Chan, Emanguli-Chan, Serap-Chan, and all the rest of the Souldiers, that escaped out of the ouerthrow giuen them by Mustaffa in the plaines of Chielder, (after they had with all diligence made report to their king at Casbin of the issue of this battel in those champaines) hauing gathered together so many of their people, as were left them, able to endure the difficulties of warfare, & hauing recouered such places as they thought safe and frendly for them, did alwayes lie in awaite to know the marching and passing of the Turkish Armie. And at last, beeing certainely infourmed by the inhabitantes of Reiuan and Georgia, what way they kept, and that of necessitie they must needes arriue at the bankes of Canac, they beganne to deuise some notable Stratageme, whereby they might reuenge the great boldnesse of their enimies, and make this their entrie into Siruan very daungerous and dammageable to them. And yet hauing neyther courage nor force sufficient to assault the whole Armie, they resolued with themselues, (as men that had stomacke inough to attempt great matters,) to stay in priuie ambush at some fit place, till some bande of the Turkish Armie should arriue, where the pray of corne and cattell might allure some of them to descend into those fieldes to relieue their common necessities: and so they sent out diuers men, who fayning that they went about their owne businesses, made shew as though they had suddeinly and at vnwares lighted vpon the Turkish Campe, and reuealed vnto them, as a great secrete, what a good pray was hardby them. And so withdrawing themselues out of the way, they stayed priuily to watch, when the Turks would send their victuailers to fetch away the corne & cattell: when as, within the space of three onely dayes, it so fell out that the foresaide ten thousand seruile persons arriued at the place, where they had no sooner begun to charge themselues with their pray, but they were surprized by the Persians, and sauing a very few, that were nimble at flight, they were all slaine, and left both their pray and their liues behind them. The noise of their crie, and the thunder of their Gunnes was heard in the Turkish hoast, which made Mustaffa to imagine, that the matter was fallen out, euen as in deede it was, & therefore presently mounting on horsebacke, and raysing his whole Armie, euery man desirous of reuenge, ranne with bridle on the horse-necke to succour the poore people that were already slaine. And although the Turkes came not in so good time, as to yeeld them any aide, yet came they very fitly to surprise the Persians, who beyond all honesty and duetie were ouer-busie in loading themselues, and carrying away the pray that they had recouered.

The place, where the corne was gathered, was as it were almost an Islande, watered with two riuers, Araxis, and Canac, which with

The Persian Captaines take counsell how to annoy the Turkes.

The stratageme of the Persians.

The ten thousand victuailers shame by the Persians.

Mustaffa runneth with all his hoast to succour the victuailers.

a little compasse fetched-about, dischargeth it selfe with a very deepe channell into Araxis. On the side of Araxis, which was the left side of the Turkish hoast, Dreuis Bassa kept one wing: on the side of Canac, being the right side, did Beyran Bassa holde another wing: and Mustaffa himselfe led the middle of the battell. which if the Persians would not haue encountred, then should they haue beene constrayned to haue runne and drowned themselues either in Canac, or in Araxis. Assone then as the Persian Captaines had descried Mustaffa with all his forces making hast towardes them, and saw such a multitude of souldiers, of ensignes, of speares, and of fyreworkes, and with all remembred the late ouerthrow in the Champaines of Chielder, then beganne they to beethinke themselues how much better it had beene for them to haue vsed more speede in departing out of that Demy-Island, and so with suddaine dispatch avoiding their enimies forces to haue contented themselues with the late slaughter of those sclauish and seruile people, and not to haue stayed for so vnequall and importunate assault. And being excited thereunto by a certaine intrinsicall and natiue vertue, they discoursed among themselues, whether it were better for them to flie, or with so great disaduauntage to ioyne battell with them, and rather to die with an honorable death, then to liue with reproache of a shamefull flight. At the last, whiles euery man was thus tossed with the tempestes of thoughtes, they resolued vtterly to preserue themselues for the state of Persia, and to continue their liues for the great and waighty affaires of that kingdome: deeming it rather to be a point of high wisedome, then of shame, not to lay open their security and the honour of their publike and priuate causes, to most certaine and vndoubted losses, and miserable issues.

But in taking their prepensed flight they discouered new difficulties: for that they were in such sort straightened within the saide Demy-Island, as they had none other ground left, but onely that, which beyond their expectations the Turkes had already possessed, and so being greatly perplexed with these troubles, euery man began to betake themselues to their owne priuate conceites. Tocomac and Emir-Chan, with other Capitanes of the army were the first that tourned their backes, and some by wading, and some by swimming passed ouer Canac, beinge greatly holpen by the valour and agilitie of their aduenturous and gallant horses. The example of these Capitaines moued many other to doo the lyke, though with a contrary fortune: for that their horses being out of breath and windlesse, there remained a great number of them drowned in the waters. At which fearefull spectacle, others being amased, euen as it were in a headlong rage & fury, perceiuing that if they should fly, vnavoydeable death was present before their eies, setled all their trust in resisting, and reposing all their hope euen in despaire,

The order of Mustaffa his battaile.

The Persians repent their long aboade.

Great thoughtes that troubled the Persians. The Persians resolue to abandon the fight, and to flye.

Difficulties in taking their flight.

The Persian Capitaines saue themselues by passing the river

The Persians drowned in the Riuer.

they shewed vnspeakeable actes of valor in fighting. But what can one doo against a hundred? For they also without any great adoo were all destroyed, though with lucke and fame farre vnlike their fellowes. But what helpeth Fame in such a medley, where the names of those are not knowne, that either fight manfully or flie effeminately? Others at last resolued to yeeld thēselues without drawing sword or bending bowe, imagining that by so doing they might recouer themselues, together with such spoiles and riches, as they had, whatsoeuer they were. But what benefite can gold and precious stones be to a few in the tumult and confusion of many conquerours, who being geuen rather to vniust rauening then to vpright piety, doo but hardly make accompt of their promises, much lesse to be liberall of that which they haue not promised? In this sort did the Persian armie rest discomfited and destroied: & so this Demy-Island being first stayned with the bloud of the enemy, & afterward with the slaughter of the neighbour and proper inhabitant, was the perpetuall sepulcher of a couragious and warlike people.

> The Persians in fight shew great signes of valour.

> Conquerours doo but little regard their promises, being geuen to spoile. The Demye Island made the perpetual graue of a couragious & warlike people.

The Persian Capitaines fled away in great sorrow and affliction for their vnexpected ouerthrowe, and knowing now assuredly whether the designementes of the Turkes tended, who were already turned towardes Siruan, they resolued in as ill plight as they were, to retourne home to their places of aboad, which they had forsaken, and to certify the king in Casbin therof with all speed, to the end that (if he could) he should send such prouision as might bee sufficient to annoy the enemies army: whereof (as Emir Sultan a Marchant of Azemia, of great traffike, of a very sincere mynd and affection, and a man of free speech; being my very familiar frend, hath often tymes confessed vnto me in Aleppo) Tocomac fayled not to write vnto his king, that there was slaine of the Turkes a great number: and so meaning to excuse his late ouerthrow, & to make his losse to seme more tollerable, he made shew of a great slaughter of the Turks in this second battell also: although in very deed, with the miserable and totall destruction of his owne slender Armye, the losse of the Turkes in this fight did not exceede the number of three thousande besides the slaughter of ten thousand victuailers. And when this certificat was made to the King, euery one of the saide Persian Capitaines, with the lycence of Tocomac departed to their seuerall gouernementes, as Emanguli-Chan to Genge, Serap-Chan to Nassiuan, Tocomac himselfe to Reiuan, & all the rest to other Cities, to the gouerement whereof by the commandement of the king they were before appointed, & so remayned in expectation of new warrantes from Casbin.

> The losse of the Turkes in this battell.

> The Persians withdraw themselues to their seuerall gouernementes.

In the meane while the Turkes had retired themselues againe to their Tentes, from whence by occasion of this vnexpected battell they were sodenly raised, & now was Mustaffa with all his troupes arriued at the bankes of the riuer Canac on the same syde, where he must beginne to passe ouer, as before is mentioned. For being mynded to go vp to the Cittie of Eres, which first of all offreth it selfe to your sight, when ye trauell on that syde to Sumachia, there was no remedy but he must needes passe ouer the foresayde water of Canac: a thing very displeasant to the whole Army, and yet could not bee auoyded, if hee would execute the commandementes of his king. And therefore (fall out whatsoeuer could fall) making strayte proclamation ouer all the hoast, that euery man should bee ready the next day to wade ouer the riuer, he prepared himselfe for that passage. At this proclamation sodenly all his people arose in a tumult, with great pride ranne beefore the Generall, with iniurious termes reprooued his folly and inhumanity, protested vtter daunger to himselfe, and vniuersall confusion to the whole army, & to be briefe, praied him that he would surcease from proceeding any furder, vnlesse he would replenish the whole campe with carcasses & spoiles. But neither could their threatnings nor yet their entreaties any thing moue the resolute mynde of the Generall, who gaue them none other answere but this: That so had Amurat appointed: that if all the rest should shew themselues vnwilling to obey their soueraigne, he would not, and in duty thought hee could not doo the lyke, but in truth would be the first man to attempt and performe that which all they so abhorred and reproued: That not in Idlenes & ease, but in great paine and difficult enterprises true souldiers are discouered, who ought neuer to be afrayde of chaunging brittle lyfe with euerlasting honour, nor to auoide death, if it should happen, for the seruice of their King. And for his owne part he did most earnestly pray them, that after he had attempted the passage of the water, if any thing hapned to him otherwise thē well and to be alyue, then he might bee carried dead to the other syde of the riuer, to the end that if hee could not execute the commandement of his King, whiles he was alyue, yet he might performe the same at least, when he was but a speechlesse and a lyfelesse carcasse: and for making too great an accompt of his owne lyfe, the desyre of his King might not in any sorte be defrauded. Diuers and sundry murmurs and whisperings followed vpon this speech of the Generall, who notwithstanding the next morning (imitating therein the example of Alexander, in making his army to passe ouer Tigris, if wee may beleeue Quintus Curtius,) did first of all wade the deep and swift riuer himselfe, and presently after him waded ouer all the Bassaes of the Campe, and with them all their slaues: by whose example the rest also at the last were induced to doo the lyke, and so continued till

Mustaffa commandeth all his hoast to passe ouer the Riuer Canac.

The souldiers in a tumult threaten Generall Mustaffa.

The answere of Mustaffa to his soldiers

ouer Lib. 4. Mustaffa first of all wadeth ouer the deep Riuer Canac.

by the darkenesse of the night their passage was interrupted: which was the occasion, why more then halfe the army could not get ouer, besydes that their publike treasure & artillary were yet also on this side of the water. But this passage being attempted with very great tumult and disorder, & no regard had to the places that were wadeable, it came to passe, that about eight thousand persons, being carried away by the violēce of the riuer, were miserably drowned, with the great outcry of all the hoast. The lyke happened also to many mules, cammelles & Sumpter-horses, vpon whose backs diuers persons being mounted, because they were desyrous to passe dry ouer the water, were likewyse headlong ouerwhelmed therein.

With great complaintes and blasphemous cursinges was the whole night spent on this syde Canac, and euery man being euen desperate knew not what to doo to auoid that dangerous passage, whose feare and griefe the example of their vnfortunate fellowes that were drowned did greatly increase: And no doubt some pestilent sedition had ensued thereupon, that would haue bredde much harme to the Turkish affayres, if by the death and ouerthrow of those that were drowned, there had not beene discouered a shallow Forde, that assured safe passage to those that were left: wherin they were much more happy then their former fellowes, in that their delay had wrought them great ease. For in the passage, which the people made that followed Mustaffa, the grauel of the bottome of the riuer being raised and remoued by the heauy hooues of the cattell, was driuen downe along the saide water to a place, where by great good hap there was also a Foorde, and there gathering it selfe together in a heape, had in such sort raised the depth of the channell, that it made as it were a shelfe for their commodious passage, so that the remnant of the people, carriages, and artillary passing ouer the same, there was not so much as one man that perished. And in this manner did the Turkish people passe ouer Canac, and vpon the bankes thereof did they rest themselues that day, and the next, and there made stay till the whole army was mustred and set in order. From thence remouing themselues all together, not hauing any meanes at all to fynde victuailes eyther for themselues or for their beastes, they encamped the day following in certaine barren champaines, where there was neyther corne nor cattell, neyther could they learne that in those quarters there were any villages at all. By meanes whereof the hunger of their beasts encreasing greatly, (a thing affirmed by dyuers faithfull & credible souldiers that were present in those calamities) they were constrained to geue to their horses and mules the leaues and stalkes of verie drie and withered reedes, & such other like thinges of no sustenaunce at all. And the men themselues were faine to satisfy their hunger with those vttermost

Night was the occasion that more then half the hoast went not ouer.

8000. Turkes drowned in wading ouer the riuer of Canac.

A meruelous kind of Foord.

The calamities of the Turkish hoast,

reliques, that they went vp and downe piking & gathering out of those poore victuailles, which now by corruption were abhominable to mans nature. There was not a man in the whole army, but perceaued that it was high tyme to rid himselfe of these inconueniences: howbeit to returne backward was odious to them all, in respect of the present famine, and to go on forward was more terrible vnto them, in respect of the great feare that they had, to continue some longer tyme in these commenced miseries. Notwithstanding needes must they follow the fortune of their captaines: among whom Mustaffa the next morning, before all the rest, set himselfe forward on his determined iourney. Hee had not long marched onward, but there was discouered good store of sundry plantes, & neere vnto them a very large plaine all greene and flourishing, & garnished with many trees: by the onely sight whereof euery man was refreshed for the hope of good harbour, and hastened their paces somwhat more then ordinary, vntill they were entred into those champaines, being abundantly fertile in all kind of corne and fruites, that could be desyred of hungry man and horse. In this place did euery man satisfy his appetite with meat and his body with rest, and forgat in parte the calamities and damages that were ouerpassed: and the next morning with willing mindes they were all ready to follow Mustaffa, who remouing his campe, and leading it still through the fruitfull and pleasant fieldes, abounding in all thinges necessary for mans sustentation, arriued at the citty of Eres, beeing (as we haue before declared) the chiefe cittie in that coast of Siruan, as you trauaile from Georgia.

 This cittie of Eres was forsaken by a great number of her inhabitantes, as soone as it was noysed that the Turkes were come to Canac, and they all followed the Standards of Samir Ghan, Gouernour of the said cittie, beeing allured there vnto by the example of Ares-Chan, (whome also a good while before the Persian king had trusted with the gouernement of the cittie of Sumachia, and assoone as he likewise heard that Mustaffa was come to Canac, abandoned his owne cittie, and withdrew himselfe into the mountaine, as a sure and safe place,) There did Samir Chan remaine with him, and other the Gouernours of Sechi, and other places of the said Prouince, all of them, ioyntly together, attending the end of these great nouelties. So that the entrie of the Turkes into Eres, was not by the enimies sword in any sort disturbed, nor yet with any spoyles, that were found therein, any thing enriched, for that the people had carried away with them all the best thinges they had, and euery man endeuored in the common losse of his countrey, to keepe and preserue his priuate goods at the least, and his owne proper life. Two & twenty dayes did Mustaffa remayne vnder Eres: in all which time, although somewhat long, there was not one man that felt any inconuenience

The Turkes refreshed with victuaile, & other commodities.

The Turkes at Eres in Siruan.

Eres abandoned by the Persians.

hee Samir-Chan: & Ares Chan Persian Gouernours withdraw themselues into the mountaines.

The entry of the Turkes into Eres not disturbed by the enemy, nor enriched by spoile and victory.

Mustaffa remaineth in Eres 22. daies.

in any matter of sort, but during those dayes employed himselfe to the erecting of a Fortresse within the said citty: vpon whose walles were placed two hundred peeces of shot, and for the custodie thereof was appointed Caitas Bassa, one of the voluntary Captaines, with fiue thousand souldiers.

Eres fortifyed & fenced by Mustaffa.

In this meane time, for that the cittie of Sumachia, now called Sumachi, stood not farre distant from thence, it being the Metropoliticall cittie of that Prouince, and of great accompt, because it standeth vpon the way that leadeth to the cittie of Derbent, now called Demircapi, but in tymes past Alexandria,) Mustaffa commanded Osman Bassa, one also of the voluntarie Captaines, as before we haue noted, to possesse that cittie with ten thousand men, vnder the tytle of Visier, & Gouernour Generall of Siruan: Giuing him further in charge, that in any case hee should cleere the passage to Derbent abouesaid, and so giue present aduertisement to the Tarrarians of his arriuall, who without all doubt hauing passed through Colchis, could not choose but by this time be arriued in those quarters, at the least: for so had they promised to Amurath, with al faith and fidelitie. Osmen departed to Sumachia accordingly, and had frendly entertainement of those that remayned there, and were determined to commit their liues to the fury of the conquerers: so that he did presently surprise the cittie, entreating all the inhabitantes in frendly maner, without doing or suffring any outrage to be done vpon them. Which vsage being vnderstood by the Alessandrians, (a people that by naturall inclination, in ceremonies, in worship, and in obseruation of that their religion, liued not as Persians in deede, but subiect to the Persians, & principally to Mustaffa Sultan, the gouernor of that cittie, & yet for all that being of the Turkish beliefe:) they sent presently to offer themselues to Osman, beseeching him to receiue them into his protection, and in all occasions to defend them from the Persians.

Mustaffa appointeth Osman bassa to keepe Sumachia & Derbent.

Osman Bassa frendly entertayned at Sumachia.

The Alexandrians yeeld themselues to the Turkes.

Of all these matters Mustaffa had aduertisement before he departed from Eres: from which place, (after hee had finished his Fortresse, his Garrisons, and all his Rampiers, beeing infourmed of these good aduenturds, follioited there vnto by the Giannizzars and the people of Grecia, and somwhat enforced so to do by the season of the yeare which was vnfit for so long a voyage as was yet behind, & perswading himselfe that he should leaue his affairs there in good and reasonable state) with great confidence hee departed, and turned his course towardes the country of Leuentogli, otherwise called Alexander the Great, as he had entreated him to do in his late passage to Siruan: and hauing traueiled a long iourney, he lodged at the foote of a certaine mountaine, where hee wanted no kind of good victuailes: And from

Mustaffa departeth from Eres.

thence sent Engines and Pioners to make a bridge ouer Canac, that his Armie might passe-ouer without any daunger. On the hether side of the riuer they tooke vp their lodginges: and from that place Mustaffa sent to giue notice of his arriuall to Sahamal, the inhabitant and Lord of the mountaine of Brus, (whereof we haue heretofore made often mention:) who presently came to yeeld himselfe as vassall to the Turkes, and being entertained with his accustomed pompe, and rewarded with apparrell, sword, battell-Axe & Target all guilt, he tooke his leaue and returned to his old withdrawing places of the mountaine.

After that Sahamal was gone, Mustaffa departed also, and trauelled forward by night, because hee would not loose the opportunity of faire wether: but so it happened through ill guiding, that hee lost his way, and knew not whither he went, being conducted through rough waies, and vneasy and difficult passages, whereby he was enforced to set vp his tentes, & wait for daylight: which rising very cleere did manifest vnto them, that they were nowe entred into the countries of Leuentogli. And therefore he caused proclamation to be made fourthwith ouer all his army, that vpon paine of death no man should be so hardy; as to molest or disquiet anie of the subiectes of Alessandro, but to haue good respect vnto them, and to entreat them with all curtesy. The day following he still continued his iourney in the saide country of Schender, where he wanted no victuailles, and the rather for that the same day there arriued from Zaghen certaine embassadors of Alessandro, with great aboundance of cattell, of corne, of fruits, & of other relief, which was sent by him for a presēt to the Generall, with a solemne excuse that he came not himselfe, because the infirmitie of his body would not suffer him. Wherewithall Mustaffa rested satisfyed, and leauing the cittye of Zaghen on the right hand, he caused the messengers of Alessandro to guide him, and so tooke his way toward Teflis: and by them was so directly conducted, that within the space of three daies, without eyther hunger or thirst, or any other inconuenience of his army, they brought him to Teflis, from whence they returned homewards, being wel contented for their paines by Mustaffa.

But those that he had left at Teflis before for the custody thereof, he found so miserably plagued with famyne, that they were constrained to eat Cattes and Dogges, and Sheepe skinnes, & such like vnwonted & strange thinges. Many of them also he found sicke, and some dead, by reason that they could not obtaine lycence of Mahamet Bassa their captaine to go out of the castle to prouide victuaile, for feare of the enemyes. By whose prouidence such care was taken for their corne, fruit, and cattell, that, although those of Teflis had issued outfor that purpose, yet was it all preserued in very safe and secure places without any daunger. Which thing was credibly certifyed to me not

A bridge built vpon Canac to passe ouer.

Sahamal yeeldeth himselfe to Mustaffa.

Mustaffa by night looseth his way.

Mustaffa in the countrey of Leuent.

The embassadors of Leuentogli with reliefe & presentes receaued by Generall Mustaffa.

Mustaffa at Teflis.

The famine of the souldiers left in the Castle of Teflis.

by one alone, but by many of the Georgians, with whom I was familiarly acquainted both in respect of my trafficke with them, and also of my practise in phisicke. But Mustaffa refreshed and relieued them all with words, with money and with meat, and gaue them plenty of all thinges, And after he had remayned there two daies, he raised his army, and put himselfe in the way towardes the champaines that were subiect to the said citty, to put all to sworde and fyre, as indeede he did. Onely the sepulchers (wherein rested the bones and ashes of Simons progenitors, and neere whereunto he tooke vp his first lodging) were leaft vnhurt and vntouched, by the Turkish fury. The day following they trauelled ouer rough and ragged mountaines full of a thousand difficulties, which were the more encreased by wonderful great snowes that were fallen, by meanes whereof, together with diuers other annoyances, many souldiers, horses, cammelles and mules did perish. In this distresse they continued two whole daies, during which tyme all the people were fallen into such a disorder, that forgetting the feare of their enemies country, without any regard or respect, euerye man tooke vp his seuerall lodging aparte, and one on this syde, and another on that syde shrowded himselfe, where he might fynde either some thicke bushe, or some small cottage, or some quyet valley to shelter him from the winde, from the snow, and from the stormes.

Mustaffa releeueth them with meate, money and wordes.

Great snowes breed many annoiances to the Turks.

The Turkes dispersed by cold weather.

But certaine Georgian captaines (and peraduenture euen the same, that had before so euill entreated the people of Soria,) hauing sent out scouts to watch the Turkish army from time to time, & being throughly certifyed of the disorder wherein it was, did ioine thēselues together, & in the right approched neer vnto it, secreatly, quietly & boldly searching out some opportunity, how they might coole the burning desyres of their enemies bloud. In the end hauing obserued Hossain Bey, my good frend and acquaintance, among many others the sonne of fruitfull Giambulat, (I terme him fruitfull, for that in one night there were borne vnto him 7. children by diuers women, & he himselfe saw at on time aliue fourescore & six heires of his owne body begotten,) that hee had withdrawen himselfe alone vnder certain mountaines to defend himselfe from the storme & the wind: they were perswaded that this was a sit occasion to gaine them some spoyles: and hauing assaulted him, they slew all his slaues, and all his squadrons of souldiers, tooke a great booty of many loades of mony and apparell, led away with them all his horses, and whatsoeuer els they could fynde, and scarce gaue him any leasure to saue himselfe, by flying into the Tentes of Beiran Bassa. And it may be that he had also remained for a pray to the Georgians, had it not beene for Hala Bey, captaine of the Zaini and Spahini of Aleppo, an old man as any among the Turkes, of an extraordinarie bounty, of a sincere mind, of free speech, and

The Georgians ly in wait for the Turks.

Hossain Bey the authours frend.

Fruitfull Giambulat that saw 86. children aliue at once that were his heires.

Hossain Bey assaulted by the Georgians, & greatly discomfited.

Hala Bey the authours frend.

well exercysed in feates of Armes, from whome I liberallie receaued many particularities of these thinges that I haue written. This man being wakened by the noise, & raising the people of Beyran Bassa, ran out himselfe to meet Hossain Bey, and shewed him the way to escape as afore. And vpon this rising of the Turks, the Georgiani retired themselues with their gotten pray, and so the rest had leasure to withdraw themselues together into more sure & safe places.

Hossain Bey escapeth to the tentes of Beyran Bassa.

The next morning the Campe remoued, and in the euening came to a castell called Ghiurchala, where it stayed a whole day to make prouision of victuaile, which was attempted by sending many of their slaues abroade into the fieldes, conducted by the men of the said castell. In the meane while, there arriued certain embassadors from one that was then called the nephew of Simon, signifying to Mustaffa, that (if it would stand with his good pleasure) their lord would come to salute him, & to offer himselfe vnto him as his vassaile. whereof Mustaffa was very glad, and declaring vnto them that his comming should be very acceptable vnto him, he sent them backe againe with presentes and curteous wordes. But although hee was expected all that day, yet made he not his apparance, & indeed all those that were sent out into the fieldes for reliefe, were miserably hacked in peeces, to the great griefe of Mustaffa, thinking himselfe too much abused by those fained embassadors, who in truth proued to bee cunning and craftie spyes, rather then embassadors.

The nephewe of Simon veeldeth himselfe faynedly to Mustaffa.

From this place the army departed with great hunger, ouer diuers vneasy hilles and rough places of the Georgianj, where they were faine oftentimes to rest themselues, & at last came to the confynes of the widdowes territory, vpō the feast day of the Turkes Ramadan. In the entrance whereof they must needes passe through a narrow strait betweene certain mountaines, where the riuer crankleth it selfe with a thousand tourninges and windinges about the low valley: A very difficult place and indeed so narrowe, that no more then one man alone could passe through it. Betweene this straite, and a very thicke and hilly wood, they lodged vpon the banks of the said riuer, and from thence the next morning they remoued, and trauelledouer very steep mountaines, and wooddy Forrestes, ouer ice and snow more harde then marble-pauemente, and ouer other hanging rockes, in such miserable sorte that many camelles, mules and horses, aswell for cariage as for saddle, fell downe headlong into the whirlepittes of the riuer to their vtter spoyle. Through this ruinous cragges, and dyuers other miseryes they iournyed all the next day, and after that, another day also as miserable and dammageable to the Army as the former: but at last being shrewdly spoiled and ill handled by hunger, foyled and slaughtered by their enemies, & afflicted with the harde season and

Hunger among the Turkes.

The straite of the mountaines of Georgia, watred by Araxis.

Misery of the Turkes.

Their misery continued.

situation of the place, they arriued within the territories that lay vnder Altunchala, the widdowes Pallace, where they had all manner of desyred reliefe, for all the miseries that they had endured since their departure from Chiurchala vntill this place, being the space of sixe daies, which ordinarily, if it had beene a common trauelled way, would haue beene performed in one onely daies iourney.

The Turkes releeued at Altunchala.

The Widdow with her elder sonne Alessandro, came downe from the Castel, and went to the pauillion of Mustaffa, offering him dyuers presentes, and promising vnto him all faithfull obedience. Mustaffa receaued her curteously, and declared vnto her the good entertaynement, that he gaue to her yonger sonne Manucchiar, that went with him to Siruan, who being there present shewed euident token thereof to his mother. Mustaffa, (dissembling for the present tyme his priuie displeasure, that hee bare the widdows son Alessandro) embraced him courteously, and praied her that she would bee pleased to leaue him also there with him, for that it should turne to both their contentmentes, signifying furder vnto her, that he would send both her sonnes to Constantinople to Amurath, with letters of credence for their yeelded obedience, for their fauour shewed to his army in giuing them so secure passage, and so many helpes, & lastly for their good deserts, the rather that by the said Sultan they might be honourably entertained, and enriched with honours & dignities.

The widdow and her sonne Alessandro come to Mustaffa.

The Widdow, although her mynd was herewithall sore troubled & perplexed, yet outwardly in her countenance shewed her selfe to be pleased, and seemed curteously to yeeld, what she was of necessity constrained to grant: aswell because Mustaffa had one of her sonnes already in possession, as also for that her selfe & her whole state were now in his power, & as it were at his deuotion: & therefore leauing both her sonnes behind her, she returned to her Castell.

The Widdow leaueth both her sonnes in Mustaffaes handes.

Mustaffa, after hee had stayed in that place with his army two whole dayes without feeling the want of any thing departed thence towarde Chars, and so did all the rest, who hauing now no feare of the enemie, as being in a sure and frendly countrey, deuided themselues into seuerall companyes, by fiues, by twenties, by fiftyes in a troupe, as euery man thought it best and conuenyent. The first day they lodged at Clisca in the widdowes countrey, where they wanted no manner of necessaries, but had most plentifull aboundance of all thinges. From thence they tooke their next lodging vnder certain rough mountaines by which they trauelled two whole dayes through many difficulties, where some of them also dyed for cold. Then they came to Messeardachan sometimes belonging to the Georgianj, but now to the Turkes: & so to Biucardacan, belonging also to the Turkes, where they kept the feast of Ramadan, which till now they could not celebrate. And from thence to

The Turkes at Clisca

Some dye for cold.

Olti a Castell also of the Turkes, where the Sangiacco, that gouerneth those quarters is resident, a countrey very fertile in all thinges, well situated, and very conuenient for these and greater passages. From Olti by the way of Neneruan in two daies they arryued at Hassanchalasi, a Castell likewyse of the Turks, called also Passin, and from thence afterward they came to Erzirum, with the great reioicing of the whole army, which was there presently discharged by Mustaffa, without any numbring or mustring at all, and so they returned all home into their owne countries.

But Mustaffa setled himselfe in Erzirum, dispatching Poastes with letters of plentifull aduertysementes to the king touching all thinges that had passed, but yet in such sort that he magnifyed his owne exploites without measure: and among diuers other newes, that were scarce true, which he wrote, one was, That Teflis, which hee had taken, was in greatnes & beauty equal vnto Damasco, besydes the situation that was exceeding strong. He certifyed him also of the battelles that he had with the Persians: the obedience that he receaued of the Georgiani, & the Siruanians: the stirres and insurrections of the people of Constantinople & of Greece: the Fortresse built at Eres: the garrisons of souldiers left in that Citty with Caitas Bassa, and in Sumachia with Osman Bassa: the offers of the Alexandrians: and in briefe whatsoeuer els had passed, & whatsoeuer he had taken from the enemy. Neither did he faile to propound to Amurath his opinion, what hee thought conuenient to be attempted the next yeare, for the strengthning of those places that he had already conquered, and for preparing the way to newe enterpryses. And principally he put him in mind of a fortifycation to be made at Chars, a place very fit for any passage to Georgia or Armenia, by situation fruitefull and commodious both for men and cattell. And withall he sente vnto the said king, the widdowes two sonnes Manucchiar & Alessandro, signifying that they would bee alwaies ready to performe whatsoeuer it should please him to command them, and that he had receaued in their country all good entertainemente and frendly welcome not omitting for all that, to declare his opinion, that Manucchiar was a meeter manne for the gouernement then Alessandro for that Manucchiar had shewed greater valour, & was more willing and ready to serue him then his brother: and the rather because it was a generall opinion, that Alessandro had his hand in those treasons and mischeefes which happened to the victuailers and to the Sorians in Georgia. Greatly did the king commend the diligence and vertue of Mustaffa, and pleased himselfe highly with this conceit, that of these pretty beginnings there might growe mighty conquestes and singular successes to the enlargement of his Empyre, and hoped that by this meanes hee should bee able

The Turkes at Olti.

The Turkes at Hassanchalasi.

The Turkes in their returne at Erzirum. The army discharged by Mustaffa to winter themselues.

Mustaffa magnifyeth his owne exploites to Amurath.

A fortification to be at Chars.

The widdows sonne sent to K. Amurath.

to surpasse the glory of his predecessors, and the more his thoughtes were occupied about these warres, the lesse did he trouble himselfe with thinking how to annoy Europe with his forces.

But now it is high time to return to the narration of the accidentes that happened in Siruan, where (we told you) Caitas Bassa was leaft at Eres, and Osman Bassa at Sumachia, with expresse order, that Osman should call the Tartarians to his aide: the Tartarians, (I say,) that hauing leaft the Fennes of Meotis, and the vnmountable shores of the Blacke Sea, passed ouer the rockes vpon Colchis, & surueighed the frosen cragges of Caucasus, were now arriued in the confynes of Siruan, and there staied, attending the commandemente of the Turkes, to inuyte them to spoile and victory. Among the Tartarian Precopenses, there was one Abdilcherai, a Capitaine of great valour and fame, a yong man of comely countenaunce and well sett of person, who, according to the faithfull promise of Tatar-Chan (surnamed Mahamet) geuen to Amurath, brought with him about thirty thousand souldiers, his subiectes, with a full resolution to attempt whatsoeuer any Turkish captaine should command him in the name of Amurath. And therefore Osman called him, and inuited him to succour the forces of his king, and to furder these beginnings of his glory, & these his conquestes, or rather these magnificall and famous termes of victory. Hee aduised him withall, that assoone as he had arriued in the countrey of Siruan, before he passed any furder, he should send aduertisementes of his arriuall there, by two or three seuerall letters dispatched by two or three seuerall messengers for the more security, to the end that he might be againe enformed what course he should take, to make his coming more profitable and more glorious. All which was not onely throughly vnderstood, but also most diligently put in execution by Abdilcherai, and therefore hauing entred the Iron gates, where Derbent standeth, (which by the Turkes at this day is called Demircapi, and signifyeth, The Gates of Iron,) and from thence passing on into the country of Siruan, there he staied, and gaue aduertisement thereof to Osman, as he was appointed.

Now in the meane time, that Mustaffa hauing subdued Sumachia and Eres, was departed out of the confynes of Siruan, Ares-Chan (who after was gouernour of Sumachia,) and other Gouernours of that region, of whom we made mention before, hearing the newes of the departure of the Turkish Generall, were determined to returne to their forsaken country, & to find some meanes, whereby they might in parte (at the least) reuenge the great iniuries, wherewith Ares-Chan was most greeuously offended and damnifyed, and so with victorie eyther of spoile or of slaughter vpon Osman Bassa, to gaine honour & commendation with the Persian king, by the publike shame and confusion of his enemyes. For in deed great was his anger and wrath, when hee beheld his owne Citty remaine for a pray to the enemy, and was not hable by any outwarde acte, to shew any signe of his greefe. And so hauing passed vnder Sumaohia, (not far from which place he had put to the sworde som fewe victuailers of Osmans, that more boldly then wisely had issued out of the citty,) and being with all his people encamped in certaine freshe fieldes, a little on this syde of the said Sumachia: I knowe not how, but he was so well fauoured by good fortune, that he surprysed certaine spies or messengers, sent from Abdilcherai, who first went to carry the news to Osman, of the arriuall of the Tartarian Captaine, and according to the order taken betweene them, to knowe his pleasure, what should be put in execution. These Tartarians were brought before Ares-Chan, who after much torture disclosed the letters that they carried: which the Persian captaine read, and considering the great number of the Tartarians that were come, (for the letters made mention of thirtie thousand) he was vtterly resolued not to stay any longer in those quarters, but presently raysed his Campe, & retired towards Canac, meaning from thence to certify the Persian king of all these nouelties, and vpon the bankes of the saide riuer to encampe himselfe, attending an answere from his said king.

But Abdilcherai, who had now sent out his second, & his third spies, caused Osman Bassa by som other means to vnderstand of his arriuall, who then very wel perceaued that the suddaine and vnlooked-for departure of Ares-Chan could not be vpō any other occasiō, but vpon knowledge of the coming of so great an hoast: but when he saw that the first spies neuer came, which Abdilcherai accused in his second letters, he was more then assured thereof. Howbeit the Tartarian captaine was called to Sumachia, where sitting in consultation with Osman, they fell to agreement that Abdilcherai should passe Canac, and so onwardeeuen vnto Genge the countrey of Emanguli-Chan, to destroy and wast his fields, his townes and his Citties, bringing away with him, men, cattell and corne, and enriching his arriuall by all the most terrible & strange meanes he could. The Barbarian captaine longed to see the time that he might staine his dartes and sworde in the blood of his enemies entrailes, and to charge himselfe with the expected pray: and therefore presently departed, and with poasting iourneyes passed ouer Canac, where Ares-Chan was as yet encamped, and assaulting him in furious manner, (without allowing him any time of defence,) lyke a rauening and deuouring flame, discomfited all his hoast, and taking him aliue, sent him to Sumachia to the garrisons of Osman, who forthwith caused him to bee hanged by the necke out of a lodging in the same Diuano or Councell house, where he had heretofore sitten as Gouernour.

The spyes or messengers of the Tartarians taken by the encamped Persians.

The Tartariā spyes disclose their letters to Ares-Chan.

Ares-Chan retireth to Canac fearing the comming of the Tartarians.

The Tartarians at Sumachia, in consultation with Osman.

All the Persian army of Ares-Chan discomfited by the Tartarians & Ares-Chan himselfe hanged.

From thence, wading ouer the riuer, and coursing a little aboue Genge, he found Emanguli-Chan, among certaine vallies, with his wife, all his familie and a great parte of the nobilitie of Genge, hunting the wild-boare, & suddenly put him to flight, tooke from him his wife, all the Ladies, and many slaues, and slew many of the rest, that vnawares were brought thither to see such disport. And after roade on to Genge, and yeelded it wholy to the furie, licentiousnesse, lust, and wickednesse of his souldiers, who left no maner of inhumanitie or crueltie vnattempted, but satisfied all their most immoderate and barbarous affections, that naturall fiercenesse, or present occasion could minister vnto them. And so beeing loaden with spoyles, satiated with bloud, and weary with the slaughter of their enimies, they returned merrily towardes Siruan, and passing againe ouer Canac, they came on the hether side of Eres into certaine low champaines, enuironed about with hilles, and there hauing pitched their tentes, without any feare they setled themselues to sleepe, and with rest to repaire their fore-wearied fences.

Genge sacked

The Tartarians encamped in certaine fieldes on the hether side of Canac, fall to sleepe.

In this meane-while, and long before these actions, were the newes come into Persia of the battailes that happened in the plaines of Chielder, and in the Demi-Islande betweene Canac and Araxis: Whereupon the Persian king, who neither would nor could goe himselfe in person, hauing gathered new forces, had dispatched Emirhamze Mirize his eldest sonne with twelue thousand souldiers to passe into Siruan, to see what hurtes the enimie had done, to attempt the reuenge of the forepassed iniuries, but especially and aboue all to punish the villanie of those of Sechi, and other Cities of Siruan, that voluntarily, and not induced thereunto by any necessity, had yeelded themselues to follow the Religion of the Turkes. The Persian Prince had now remoued from Casbin, accompanied with his mother Begum, who would needes follow her beloued sonne, and had taken his iourney towardes Siruan, vnder the guiding and gouernement of Mirize Salmas, chiefe of the Sultanes, and had already left behind him the countrey of Ardouil and Caracach: when hee was certified of the aduertisements come from Ares-Chan, touching the arriuall of Abdilcherai with his populous hoaste of Tartarians, and thereby was stricken in a greate quandarie, & almost without comfort. But yet his feare was not so great, as it could stay his ambitious and burning desyres of reuenge and glory, but rather enflamed with a fresh anger for the great boldnes of the Tartarians, and set on fire with an vnquencheable thirst of reuenge, hee was encouraged more then euer he was, to prosecute his intended enterpryse: and so came to Siruan, still leading people with him from such places as he trauelled through, & hastening his iourney came to Eres, long before the king his father did thinke hee would. Very fit

Emirhamze the Persian Kinges eldest sonne, at Siruan.

Begum the Persian Princes mother followeth him in his Army to Siruan.

& conuenient was this his notable celerity: for that Caitas Bassa had boldly issued out of the Fortresse, & went spoyling all the country about, carrying away with him what pray soeuer he mett withall, and committing such other insolences, as hungry souldiers beyond all honesty, vse to doo in strange and fruitefull countries. But when hee was in the middest of his spoyles, and leaste feared his enemyes forces, he was suddenly encountred and assaulted by the said Prince, without hauing any meanes to his furie: so that in this extremity and necessity, which brought Caitas to a sudden death, ther followed a bloudy battell, wherein although the small nomber of the Turks shewed many effectes of valour, yet in the fight they were all destroied with their captaine, who together with his lyfe abandoned the world, the Fortresse, and the spoiles, & left the country free, that was committed to his custody. Which the Persian Duke hauing once againe gotten into his possession, he tooke away the two hundred peeces of shot, that were left in the Forte by Mustaffa, and presently sent them to Casbin to his father.

Mightely did courage encrease, and hardines quicken in the Persian Prince by this good successe, and therefore leauing his mother in Eres, he followed on his iourney towardes Sumachia: but in passing by the way where the Tartarians were encamped, and in descending the hilles, that enuironed the plaine, he discouered their tentes that were there pitched: whereupon he stood in great doubt what to attempt, whether by venturing vppon so populous an hoast to proue the perrill of battaile, or yeelding to so great a danger to returne back into Persia. Too great a shame he thought it to returne, & rather then he would with ignominie refuse so good an occasion offred him, he did choose with honour to endaunger himselfe to the most manifest perrill of his lyfe: and therefore descending the hill, and drawing nigh to the pauilions of the enemy, he perceaued that all the army was laid downe, enioying their quiet rest and sleep, and their horses, some couched & some standing, but all of them void of saddles or horsemen. Whereupon without any stay, setting spurres to his horse he pricked forward with all his hoast, and in all hast and terrible manner ran to assault the Tartarians, who were now both buried in their spoiles & sleep: & hauing slaine their first watch, and their second, although with some losse, among the tumultuary souldiers hee made an vniuersall confusion, & common slaughter, putting some to flight, killing others, and taking diuers of them Captiues. Among whome was their Captaine Abdilcherai, who was taken aliue and sent to the king in Casbin, vnder good and sure custodie.

After these victories, the Persian Prince scoured to Sumachia, and compassed the Cittie round-about, wherein the new Turkish Captaine Osman sate as Gouernour, to the great reproach of Persia: and there

The Persian Prince suddenly arriued at Eres.

escape Caitas Bassa assaulted by the Persian Prince. A bloody battell. Caitas Bassa & all his people slaine.

Eres recouered by the Persians.

Begum left at Eres.

The Persian prince disconereth the encamped Tartarians.

The Tartarians destroyed & Abdilcherai taken aliue by the Persian Prince.

The Persian Prince vnder Sumachia threateneth Osman.

encamping himselfe, sent word to Osman, that if he would yeeld himselfe, he would let him goe with his life and goods: but otherwise if he would stand-out obstinate, and not yeeld vp the cittie, which vniustly he possessed, he should be compelled to surrender it by force, and his life withall. Osman, that knew nothing of the Tartarians ouerthrow, but hoped, that entertaining his enimies with faire wordes and goodly promises, the Tartarians might in the meane space returne, and hew them all to peeces, gaue the sayd Prince a most courteous aunsweare, saying that hee was very ready to yeeld vp the Cittie, but withall entreated him that he would make stay but for three onely dayes, & graunt him time to put all his thinges in readinesse, that so he might freely depart, as it pleased the prince in courtesy to offer him. The Persian Prince was very glad to receiue such an aunsweare, & well knowing the ouerthrow which he gaue to the enimy, did verily perswade himselfe that Osman frankly, and with a true & constant mind had made this promise: & therefore expected that what the Turke had offred should be performed. But Osman not meaning to commit himselfe to the faith of his enemy, though hee was vtterly resolued to withdraw himselfe into some stronger place, yet was he very curious to find meanes to escape into those safer refuges, and not to come within the fingers of the prince. And therefore somwhat before the assigned terme of the three daies appointed, seeing that the Tartarians whom he looked for, did not appeare, he resolued to saue himselfe by secreat flight: because he was sure, that if hee should remaine in Sumachia, hee had good reason to feare the inhabitantes themselues would betray him, and that if he should yeeld himselfe to the Prince, he might be by him also easily deceaued.

And thereupon determined with himselfe, by the help of the darke night, and a difficult way, (though very couert by reason of the high cragges and bushie places of the mountains neere to Sumachia) to take his flight, and withdraw himselfe to Demircapi, as hee had already promised to the Alessandrians. And so he iourneyed ouer the said mountaines with great secrecie and silence, leading away with him whatsoeuer either in the tyme of peace or of war he had laid vp in store, and without any daunger or threate of the enemy he escaped safely to the said City of Derbent. On the morning the inhabitants of Sumachia, without any stay opened the gates of the city to the Persian Duke, who seeing their infidelity, that they were not onely ready to giue entertainement to Osman, but also to help him to escape without giuing to the prince any inckling of his departure, did put in execution the effectes of his wrath and indignation which euen in Casbin he had conceaued in his minde against them: and with great cruelty did punish the miserable and infortunate Commons of the Citty, making their houses euen with the ground, destroying both the old and new walls therof, and bringing the whole lande to nought, that sometime was so desired a receit of the Turkes. But when he should depart from thence, he was in a great deliberation with himselfe whether he should passe on to Derbent, or returne into Persia. The citty well fenced, the cold time of winter, and the long voiage that hee should haue had homeward, persuaded the Prince to lay aside the enterprise of Demircapi, and so he made choise to returne to Casbin. But first for all that, he determined to make his retyre by the people of Eres and of Sechi, and vpon them as vpon rebelles to inflict deserued punnishment. For the effecting of which his purpose, he made his present repaire thither, and spared neither sexe, norage, nor any condition, but though the persons were vnequall, yet was the punishment equall to all. And after the execution of this his reuenge and indignation, he with his foresaide mother Begum, and with his armie, though somewhat diminished and endamaged, yet victorious and triumphant turned home to Casbin.

Young Abdilcherai the Tartarian, was kept within the kinges Serraglio in good & safe lodgings, neither did he in this his captiuitie find want of any thing, but agreeably to his calling he was appointed a very tolerable and easie imprisonment: which day by day was in such sort enlarged, that he seemed to liue not as a prisoner or captiue, but rather as a companion of those of the court, and as it were in apparant liberty: by which occasion, hauing insinuated himselfe into the loue of Begum the kings wife, he spent his time in courting of her, and she again in courting of him in all secreat and couert manner. These mutuall affections proceeded in such sorte, and these interchaungeable fauours discouered themselues so openly, that in the Serraglio and ouer all the City, there was a rife report, how shameles Begum had participated her bed & herselfe with the Tartarian prisoner. Howbeit neither the king nor the prince knew any thing of it: but the king perceauing that the yong gentleman was generally commended to be valiant and curteous, began to thinke of a matter, which might easily fall out to bee a very great commodity and help to himselfe. For the king fauouring these good qualities, being conioined with proportion of body and nobility of birth, (because he noysed himselfe to be the brother of Tatar-Chan) persuaded himselfe verily, that it could not but proue a meruellous benefite to him, if in steed of a captiue he should make him his kinsman, and giue him his daughter to wife. Whereby (hee was in good hope) there might grow such an amity and vnion between the Tartarian Precopenses, & himselfe, as they would not onely refuse from thenceforth to fauour Amurath in these warres, but also that they would bee enemyes vnto him, and in the fauour of Persia turne their armes & affections against him. Very considerate assuredly

Prince deliberateth whether he should returne home or go forward to Derbent.

The people of Sechi & Eres punnished.

Abdilcherai prisoner in Casbin well entertained.

Abdilcherai the prisoner enamored, & beloued of Queene Begum.

The report of the loose life of Begum the Persian kings wife.

The deep consideration of Mahamet the Persian King.

was this cogitation of the king: but yet did it greatly displease the Sultans of Casbin: who either because some of them was a suiter to the said daughter, or because they did naturally hate the Tartarian Nation, or els because they had a mischeeuous conceit of the loues of Begum, did all their endeauours to turne the king from so strange a purpose, and vsed all the arte that possible they could deuise, to cancell out of his mind that detestable opinion, as they thought. Howbeit they could nothing preuaile either with their eloquence or other their cunning deuises: but the king was now vpon the point to make a conclusion of the marriage, when as the Sultans entring into the Serraglio with a company of their people, and finding there the vnfortunate Tartarian, ran him through the body, cutting of first his priuie members, and flapping them vpon his mouth after a most barbarous and filthy maner. It is reported that Queene Begum likewise was then also murdered by them, but (how soeuer it came to passe) it is a cleere case, that the death of the Tartarian Duke was procured in the maner aboue mentioned, and that the poore lady neuer after that day, saw the light of the sonne. Which whether it was put in execution by the appointment of her husband, who had beene aduertised of all thinges that had happened, or that the Sultanes wrought it for the publike interest: they know best, that haue had the meanes to insinuate themselues into the innermost places of the Realme: For vnto our knowledge neuer came there any other report touching the particulars thereof.

The Kinges purpose doth not please the Sultans of Casbin.

Abdilcherai slaine in the Serraglio of Casbin, by the Sultans.

Vpon the death of this Tartarian there sprung-vp many ciuill dissentions in Persia, and so thereupon followed also the banishment of some, the flight of others, and sondry miseries, that lighted vppon many. And the great hopes whereby the king was mooued to desire the marriage, were chaunged into most turbulent and troublesome passions, and daungerous calamities, that threatned the vtter confusion of the Persian affaires, to the singular benefit & commodity of Amurath. And yet for all these strange accidents, the king ceassed not to prepare new forces for the next yeare, and as much as in him lay to quiet all tumultuous disorders, brideling his owne priuate affections, and the motions of his sonne Emirhamze Mirize, and procuring at last a perfect vnitie, which hee thought most necessary to continue the defence of his kingdome. And these were the stirs that happened in the Persian and Tartarian affaires the first yeare, being the yeare of our saluation, 1578.

Vpon these murders there arose many calamities in Persia.

But Osman Bassa being in Demir-Capi, after the returne of the Persian Prince to Casbin, continually employed himselfe in laying platfourmes for the enlarging of the conquestes already begon, and for the assuring of those places vnder the gouernement of Amurath. Among other occasions, that he tooke for the better establishing of his owne matters, one was the friendship that he entred with Sahamal, Lord of the mountaine of Brus, of whome I haue more then once made mention before. With this man did Osman practise many tokens of good will, and he againe interchangeably towards Osman, wherevpon there arose a faithfull frendship betwene them, if not thoroughly and inwardly, yet at the least in outward apparance: wherevnto in short time there was added a straight knot of alliance, for that Osman tooke to wife a daughter of the sayd Sahamal, and hauing celebrated the marriage, hee thought he was sure of all sides, & could not desire greater signes of the sinceritie of his loue. But soone after, grounding himselfe vpon reasonable coniectures, he toke a suspicion that Sahamal, for all his inward and outward practises of frendship towards him, might notwithstanding receiue some secrete order from the Persian king to betray him, and to deliuer the Cittie from the Turkish oppression, and so reduce all the Prouince, as before it was, to his aunctient deuotion. Among other occasions, whereby Osman was moued and induced to suspect it, (al being of great force and importance,) the speeches of his wife (being Sahamals daughter) gaue him greatest cause. For she being rauished with the valour, riches, and magnanimitie of her husband, would not conceale any thing from him, that she knew was deuised against his life, but freely vttered by word of mouth vnto him, that her father hauing reconciled himselfe to the Persian king, did continue his confederacy and frendship with him, and that letters went betwene them of great matters, and particularly of the affaires of Siruan. By this discouery Osman Bassa grew into a great suspicion, that Sahamal should deceitfully practise his death, and perswaded himselfe verily, that the frendship, the mutuall offices of loue betwene them, and the marriage that was made, were wholy direrected to that end. This aduertisement Osman kept secreat to himselfe, and made shew to his wife that hee kept no such reckoning of it, as in deede he did, & ought to doo, being a matter of so great importance: But yet in his hart resolued to keep it in store to his benefite: in such sorte, that not onely the deuise which Sahamal had imagined against him was quite frustrated and auoyded, but also Sahamal himselfe was punnished with deserued death. And therefore Osman caused Sahamal to come to him, & thereby feasting him, courting him, & entertaining him, as it became him to vse his beloued father in lawe, and by many other apparant and confident behauiours, he made Sahamal strongly presume, that he might take oportunity to put in execution those designementes, for effecting whereof he had thus procured the frendship and alliance of Osman. But Osman preuented the intent of Sahamal. For hauing inuited him (according to the custome) to come and celebrate with him certain of their solemne feastes, he made the most valorous and trustie

Osman practiseth frendship with Sahamal the Georgian.

Osman marrieth a daughter of Sahamals.

of his esquadrons acquainted with his determination, and enioyned them, that assoone as Sahamal was entred into his court, euen in the very dismounting from his horse, they should all fall vpon him, cut of his head, and put all his retinue to the edge of the sword. Old Sahamal failed not to come accordingly, being inuited by his son in-law and daughter to the solemne feastes, & in his lighting from his horse all was performed that Osman had commanded: & forthwith there were dispatched two thousand horsemen to spoile & sacke all the lands, & country of the said Georgian Lord, to the great maruell & astonishment both of farre & neere. The newes thereof came to Casbin, euen to the kinges eares, who tooke the matter very greeuously, and beganne to foresee, that the conquering of that countrey would proue very difficult, and so feared greatly that the Prouince of Siruan would remaine still in the Turkes handes. And this was the end of the stirres in Siruan the first yeare: & so the winter comming-on very sharpely euery man ceased from battell and forraging, forsaking the forrestes and the fieldes, and attended wholly to the conseruation of such things, as they had already conquered.

And now by this time all these aduertisementes were arriued at Constantinople, & Amurath had receaued all the particular intelligences of all thinges that had happened. Also Ali-Vcchiali, who in the port of Trebizonda had discharged his appointed carriage, was now returned to Constantinople, & made relation of his sayling into Colchis, declaring how hee had built a Castell in the Territorie of Tatiano, in the confines of Iurello, and that he had strengthened and enlarged those borders in Georgia on that side also: insomuch as these beginnings seemed to Amurath, to bee of great importance: the successe whereof in the continuance of the history, we will describe vnto you in the bookes that follow.

The end of the third booke.

Sahamal beheaded by the appointment of Osman at Demir-Capi. The country of Sahamal wasted by Osmans people. The Persian king bewayleth the deaths of old Sahamal.

Ali-Vcchiali buildeth a Castell in Colchis.

The Fourth Booke

The Argument.

The deliberations of Amurath, what enterprise he should take in hand.

He resolueth thereon, and sendeth out new Commissions.

He causeth Manucchiar to be circumcized, and deliuereth his brother Alessandro into his custody.

In Persia, Emanguli-Chan maketh new offers to the king.

Simon maketh request to the Persian king.

The causes, why Simon chaungeth his Religion.

Simon is dispatched by the Persian to annoy the Turkes in Georgia.

The new assembly of the Turkish Armie.

The Insurrection of the Souldiers.

Chars fortified by Mustaffa.

Mustaffa falleth into new cogitations for the succours of Teflis.

Hassan is sent by him into Georgia, where there happeneth a battell full of losse to the Turkes.

The Georgians do assaile the Turkes a fresh.

Alyculi Chan is taken prisoner.

Victorious Hassan succoureth Teflis, and returneth.

The Stratagemes of Simon.

Hassan deceiueth Alyculi Chan,

Simon being also deceiued, and all in a rage, vtterly destroyeth the Turkes.

Hassan arriueth at Chars.

Alyculi emprisoned at Erzirum.

Abas Mirize accused of rebellion by Salmas, who had made the eldest Persian Prince his Sonne in law.

Mustaffa discharged of his Generall ship.

A comparison betweene Sinan and Mustaffa.

Sinan accuseth Mustaffa.

Two Deftardari or Treasurers of Mustaffa emprisoned.
The death of Mahamet the chiefe Visier, and the maner of his death.
Sinan elected the chiefe Visier.
Mustaffa and his two Treasurers released.
Sinan elected Generall.
The Persian king sendeth Embassadours to Constantinople.
The conditions of Peace.
The arriuall of the Embassadour Maxut Chan at Constantinople.
His speech to Amurath.
The Persian king at Tauris.
The leauie of Souldiers in Persia.
The consultations of the Persians.
The Turcomannes follow the Persians.
Tocomac chosen to goe with an Armie in to Georgia.
The treaty of Peace with Amurath at Constantinople.
Maxut Chan made Treasurer or Chamberleine of Tauris.
Maxut-Chan accused by Emir-Chan.
Maxut Chan flyeth out of Persia, and runneth to the Turkes.
Maxut-Chan at Constantinople.

THE FOVRTH BOOKE

As soone as Amurath was certifyed by the letters of Mustaffa, of all that which had happened since his departure, vntill his returne to Erzirum, and vnderstoode the battelles that followed, the obedience that was yeelded by the Georgianj, the conquering of citties, the building of new Fortes, and to bee short so good a beginning of so desired an enterprise. Of these prosperouse successes, which by Mustaffa were described to bee far greater then in'deed they were, (hauing geuen order, that Alessandro & Manucchiar, who were sent vnto him by Mustaffa, should bee safely kept with all good entertainment,) he began to cast many deuises in his head touching such matters, as were to bee attempted the next yeare. And especially there arose at one instant many & sundry considerations in his mind, which told him that the manner of sending his army to a newe resting place might be altered diuers waies, & so amiddest so many doubts he remayned in a mammering what to doo. On the one side hee was of opinion, that it must needes be necessary to passe againe into Siruan, and to recouer those Cities that were first conquered by Mustaffa, and after subdued againe by the Persians. For by that meanes it would come to passe, that the countrey of Siruan should remaine quietly vnder the gouernement of Amurath, and so the great trauells, the troublesome voyages, the

The considerations of Amurath.

harde conquestes, the bloud already spilled, the dangerous perrilles, & the losses of the next yeare should not altogether be frustrate. But this opinion of his, hee himselfe (euen of himselfe) chaunged, as it is reported, for the great hope that he had in the aide that was promised him by Tatar-Chan, who did faithfully assure both him and Osman, that he would ouerrunne that region anew, and set forwarde those notable designementes that he had intended, and gaue his word to doo great matters in his seruice. In respect of this hope (which notwithstanding fell-out to be but vaine, through the default of Tatar-Chan, as in place it shalbe shewed) hee laide Siruan asyde, and committed the defence thereof to the false promises of the Tartarian, & to the valour of Osman: consulting with himselfe, whether it were not expedient to send his army in a straite course to Tauris, & to find meanes that there might be erected in that Citty a Fortresse, which being well fenced with artillary and arcubuse, and strengthned with the vertue of valourous souldiers, should neuer be subdued by the power of Persia. And so bringing this his purpose to effecte, without the other difficulties, (which if the warre should fall out to bee long, hee must needes endure) there might remaine in his possession all the cuntrey that lyeth betweene Tauris and Erzirum. The easinesse and speed, wherewith this his purpose might be brought to effect, did fauour his conceit in this pointe wonderfully: for there was no man but thought that the Forte might be built in very few daies, & euery man perswaded him that it was an easy matter for so great an hoast not onely to pierce into Tauris, but also to passe whether soeuer hee would desire. This his designement was of great weight & importance, neither did there want some that priuily and familiarly did aduise him, that it was to be preferred before the rest, and comforted the king to goe forward withall, by promising prosperous successe therein.

But albeit that Amurath had his minde enkindled with ambitious desires and lustes, burning after glorie, and being pricked on with sharpe spurres of Auarice, longed to carrie away the victorie ouer his enemies landes: Notwithstanding, laying aside all his foresaid consultations, as being too eager and importunate, and weighing his affaires in a more vpright ballance, he deemed it better to preferre the safetie of his Armie, the honor of this warre, and the certaintie of victorie, before the doubtfull speed in attempting the enterprise: and in the end he did resolutely conclude with himself, that he had rather (though but slowly) ouercome & triumph ouer his enemies, then (too soone with shame) to forsake and abandon his designements begun: and therefore did fully determine first to assure and strengthen his owne borders, to lay open the wayes that were shut against him with woods & bushes, to confirme his conquests that were as yet but doubtfull, to discouer all secret and treacherous ambushments, and to make the voiage plaine and open: rather then to runne headlong with vncertain conceits into another mans coūtrie, and to conquer places, that were farre of, fenced and defended not onely by mightie enemies, but also by Nature it selfe. In this his resolution he was confirmed by the state of the Georgiani, whom he perceaued as yet not to be reduced to such assured obedience, as he durst altogether trust them: and in particular he feared the treacherie of Daut, and more then that, the comming of Simon. For by these occasions it might fall out, that his Armie going to Tauris, might be assailed on the one side by the Georgiani, and on the other side by the Persians, and so brought into verie great miseries. And this misfortune might happen vnto him, as often as he should haue occasion to send new supplies to the Fortresse.

By these deliberations, and with this resolution Amurath being moued, he did absolutely signifie to Mustaffa by writing, that it was his pleasure, that against the next spring he should prepare all such prouision, as he thought necessarie for the buylding of certayn Fortes in the waies that lead from Erzirum into Georgia, to the end, that hauing made all those wayes safe and secure, and brought that people into due obedience, the next yeare he might employ his courage to more noble and haughtie enterprises. Hereupon Mustaffa presently directed out his precepts to the Cities of Aleppo, of Damasco, of Caraemit, and to all the other places of Soria and Mesopotamia, that they should take-vp cunning workmasters, Pioners, and other such persons, to the number of twentie thousand: And likewise wrote to all the Countries specified in the first Booke, that all their Souldiers, (yea, and in greater number then they were the last yeare) should be in a readinesse the next Spring, to returne to the warre: Whereof he caused the rumour to be spread euen as farre as Egypt. He commaunded likewise, that they should make collection of the Taxes and Tenthes, and that in greater quantitie, then it was the yeare before: and made such prouision of Money from the Chambres of Aleppo, and other places, as he thought necessarie for these purposes.

Mustaffa sendeth out commaundement for a new Armie.

In this meane while at Constantinople, the two Brethren, the Widdowes sonnes, who (as we told you before) were sent by Mustaffa to Amurath, expected the end why they were come to the Court. As touching Alessandro, he perswaded himselfe that no wrong should euer be done vnto him, to whom by the course of his age the gouernment of his kingdom belonged, or rather who alreadie was put in possession thereof by his Mother: and besides that, was in a great hope, that some means should be deuised how he myght be established & confirmed therin after a more sure and safe maner, and that Manucchiar, his brother, should be honoured with some

Georgian Alessandro & Manucchiar at Constantinople.

other Office worthy the magnificence of Amurath. Wherein although he had some litle kind of doubt that troubled him: yet did he euer carie a constant resolution, that he would not in any case chaunge his Religion, nor staine hys conscience wyth so fowle and infamous a blot. On the other side, Manucchiar the yonger Brother, who the last yeare had followed the Campe of Mustaffa, and had shewed some good tokens of manhood, with an expresse kind of Militarie vertue, that he might the rather enter into the gouernment of his Mothers State, induced therunto by the flattering desire of Rule, was vtterly resolued with himselfe to do any thing, so that he might not liue as a priuate souldier, but rather to take from his brother his birthright and enheritance, and with the vtter losse of his countrie-Religion wherein he was borne, to purchase a vyle and base kingdome, yea, and rather then he would liue inferiour in dignitie to his brother, he would make himselfe the slaue of Amurath, and the Deuill. Neither is their opinion false peraduenture, that thinke this agreement and conspiracie to haue beene secretelie contriued betweene him and Mustaffa, vtterlie to disgrace and ouerthrow his Brother. Hereupon they were both examined, which of them would be content to submit hymselfe to the Religion of Mahamet: whereunto Manucchiar aunswered, that hee would so doo, and beeing become the vassall of so great an Emperour, would desire no other thing, but to manage his owne State in his seruice, and vnder his protection. Whereas on the other side Alessandro, although he should be depriued of his State, which alreadie hee had begun to gouerne, yet would he not consent to the vyle and infamous chaunge of his Religion, but remayning constant in his former fayth, he onely desired, that as a priuate souldier, and bereaued of that inheritance, whereof Nature and God had caused him to bee borne the lawfull successour, he might not be denyed at the least to goe and lyue in his owne natiue Countrie, and so to be buried neere vnto the Ashes of his predecessors: promising withall, at all times; all obedience to Amurath, and loue to his brother. The Turkish king willed Manucchiar therein to do as he himselfe thought good. For that for his owne part, he did greatlie feare, least Alessandro by some treacherie myght depriue him of his lyfe; and so succeeding in his former place, might make that State more rebellious then euer it was before. Howbeit, for somuch as Manucchiar consented vnto it, he was also to content himselfe withall, and to commit the custodie of that State to such care, as Manucchiar should take for the preseruation of himselfe. Heereupon Manucchiar was circumcised, and had the name of Mustaffa gyuen him, wyth the title of Bassa and Gouernour of Altunchala, and of all his Mothers and Brothers Countries: (for the which there were great signes of ioy ouer all the Serraglio,) and hee beeing thus created a Turke, had his

Manucchiar consenteth to chaunge his Religion.

Alessandro remayneth constant in Christian Religion.

Manucchiar circumcised, and named Mustaffa.

Brother Alessandro committed vnto him, and they both returned into their owne Region.

But in Persia, in the pallace of Casbin, many consultations were had in this meane time. For Emanguli Chan, gouernour of Genge, perceiuing himselfe to be in great daunger of loosing his beloued and honorable gouernment, by means of the late sacke and spoyle of his Cittie made by the Tartarian, and taking occasion of those plottes that were dayly in contriuing to sende people into the confines of Siruan: to the ende that Osman Fassa shoulde not intend his new works, and withal (if it were possible) shuld be hunted out of Demir Capi, and out of all that prouince, he purposed with himselfe to make an offer to King Mahamet, that he should bind himselfe vpon paine of his head, to defend Siruan, and not suffer Osman to attempt any newe buildings or further conquestes in that Region: and therein wrought so much with the King, that his request was not denyed him. Whereuppon the charge of the gouernment of Genge, & guarding the Prouince of Siruan from the forces of Osman, was frankly committed vnto him. Neither were his offers extended any further: For the Persian King knew wel ynough, that if the Tartarians or the Generall Mustaffa should come thither, hee should stand in need of greater prouision and stronger defences. And therefore he gaue order to Emir-Chan, gouernour of Tauris, to Tocomac Gouernour of Reiuan, to Serap-Chan gouernor of Nassiuan, and to diuers other Captaines that were neerest, that at euery instance and request of Emanguli-Chan, they should be ready (if need so required) with their power to resist eyther the Tartarians or the Turkes, when they should enter into the countrey of Siruan. Neither did Emanguli forget to solicit the sonne of Sahamal, who succeeded in the Lordship of Brus, that he would ioyne himselfe with him, and they two together woulde take occasion to reuenge the grieuous losses that they had receiued of the Turkish army, and especially to chastise Osman Bassa, as hee deserued for the death of Sahamal his father. Howbeit the saide sonne would not by any meanes endaunger himselfe, neither durst in any wise shewe himselfe an open enemie and persecutor of the Turkes, but was content to beare the losse of his father in such sort, as he thought most behoouefull for the preseruation of his owne estate,

And this was the prouision that was made for the securitie of that Prouince, concerning which, euerie man almost was of opinion, that Mustaffa should not returne thither againe, but they knew well that hee shoulde chieflie be employed about the strengthening and assuring of the conquestes of Georgia: and therefore there was no further prouision made there. But the King turned all his counsels and cogitations to send people towards Teflis, for he knew of a certentie, that either all the Turkish Armie or els some great bande of it shoulde

The offer of Emanguli-Chan.

Emanguli inuiteth the son of Sahamal the Georgian to ioine with him.

The Persian king mindeth to send men towards Teflis in Georgia.

come to bring succours thither, or els it must needes come to passe, that the Fort should fall againe into the hands of the Georgiani. About this matter was the King verie busie and intentiue, when as Simon the Georgian, who was sometimes imprisoned at Cahaca (of whome we made mention before) and being throughlie enformed of all thinges that had happened, thought with himselfe that hereby he might take opportunitie to obtaine at the Kinges hand such helpe as hee had long desired, and purchase those honours that he had long expected, For hee deemed it a verie likelie and reasonable matter, for the King to desire and wish with all his heart, that hee (carrying the name of a famous Captaine, & throughly acquainted with al the aduantages, that might be taken in Georgia, to the great losse and anoyance of the Turks) would offer himself to go into that prouince and there gathering his souldiers together with a soueraigne authoritie ouer all that people, to defend those cities that were yet vntouched, far better than his brother Dant could doe, and in another maner a sort (than he also could) to trouble and offend the Turks, which must needes come that way to succour Teflis. Neither did hee protract the time long, after he was entred into this cogitation, but with conuenient speed dispatched his supplication to the King, wherin he declared his request, & reproouing his brother for his cowardise & flight, promised to perfourme greate matters himselfe. *Simon the Georgian.*

Simon maketh a request to the Persian King.

This Simon in the time that he remained prisoner at Cahaca, entred strait familiarity with Ismahel (late son to King Tamas deceased) who, as we told you before, was sent thither by his father to be safelie kept: & in this mutual familiarity there passed such enterchangeble offices of loue betweene them, that as Ismahel shewed himselfe louing and affectionate to the conditions of Simon, so much did Simon for his part shew himself dutiful & deuoted to the vertues & magnanimity of Ismahel: wherby there arose an extraordinary loue of the one towards the other: which cōtinued in such sort, that Simon (I know not by what sophistry deluded or by what flattery enticed) was perswaded by the Persian prince to forsake his religion, and to follow that barbarous superstition. What might be the reasons that were able to change the mind of Simon, being before so constant, and so wel instructed in the Greek-Christian faith (for the maintaining wherof he had chosen to liue depriued of his libertie and estate.) it can not bee so precisely declared: but it seemeth, there were three principall and powerfull respectes, that wrought this vnexpected noueltie in him Namely, the perpetuall imprisonment, which he knew hee could not auoyd, as long as he continued of that mind: the friendship of Ismahel (friendship I say, that oftentimes changeth mens natures, much more their opinions:) and thirdly the great honours that Prince Ismahel did *The familiarity between Ismahel and Simon.*

Simon induced to change his religion, and the reasons why.

dayly promise him, whensoeuer it should happen that hee were named King. While they were thus mutually affected one towards another, it happened that King Tamas died, and Ismahel being accompanied from Cahaca to Casbin, was with meruellous pompe saluted King of all his father dominions. Among all the rest, whome the King full dearely beloued, hee could not forget, but preserue in memorie the vertue and fame of Simon, who was already according to the Kings pleasure circumcised, and made a Mahometan, yea, and in such sort did he remember him, that hee was most desirous to bestowe greater honours and rewardes vpon him than he himselfe could request. But sudden and vnexpected death lighting vpon, before he was aware of it was the occasion why Simon remained without any aduancement, and yet so greatlie contented, as his recouered libertie could breed contentment in him. Notwithstanding among the many varieties of his thoughts did Simon long time wander, being after the death of Ismahel shreudlie destracted in his mind, coursing and discoursing with himself whether it were better for him, either to remaine still in Casbin and to stay the comming of the new King, or els to resolue vpon departure, and so to returne to his forsaken faith, and wasted Citties. But in the end, after many consultations, hee concluded that it should bee more safe and commendable, considering the state of his affaires, to stay for the new King, and vnder his protection and fauour to find some means, that he might berestored to the dignity and rule that was vsurped vpon him, rather than to flie away alone, and (hauing no stay to leane vppon) to seeke for quarrels and contentions with his brother, yea and peraduenture to purchase himselfe a bitter death. And therefore he did willingly maintaine himselfe in Casbin, looking and hoping, that the chaunge of his schisme (for so it is rather to be accounted than a religion) his imprisonment endured, his libertie recouered, his fame of great valour, his present necessitie, his deuotion and obedience to the king manifestlie declared, should deserue at the new kings hands some honour and reward, or at least, if it would please him to commit any charge of the warre in Georgia to his care, a constant and assured protection of him. And therefore when Mahamet was now established in his kingdome, and was certified of the losse of Teflis, Simon besought him of lawfull leaue, to returne vnder his protection into his own ill-defended countrey, offering himselfe withall to venture vpon any perill or trauell whatsoeuer, and promising that he would neuer either feare any great enterprise, or auoyd any base exployt, so that he might know he might do good seruice to Mahamet. With great satisfaction did the King consent to the requests of Simon, and named him the Chan of all that kingdome, which hee possessed before by the name of a Christian: and with all diligence was he sent with Aliculi-Chan into

The power of friendship.

The diuers cogitations of Simon.

Simon named (by the Persian king) the Chan of all his kingdome.

THE FOURTH BOOKE 89

Georgia, for the endammaging of the Turkish Armie, and defence of his neighbour Citties. And to them both were deliuered certaine peeces of Artillerie, that were taken at the rocke or Castle of Eres, when Caitas Bassa was slaine, (as in the booke next going before we haue told you) and besides the Artillerie, there were assigned vnto them fiue thousande Horsmen, that were leauied out of the Citties, bordering vpon the one and the other Media. Simon afterwardes comming to Georgia, where hee was greatlie welcommed and honoured, pressed about three thousande Souldiers out of all those countries, both of his owne and of his neighbours, signifying vnto them all, (though with a false and impious excuse,) that he was now become a Persian, not because he preferred the faith and lawe of Mahamet before Christian Religion, but onely because he might bee deliuered of his imprisonment, and imploy his forces in the seruice of our Sauiour and onely Prophete Christ Iesus, and so by that meanes also maintaine his owne estate. And in this order were the affayres of Georgia assured and strengthened, after the best maner that might be.

Artillarie appointed for Simon & Aliculi Chan.

Simon presseth souldiers in Georgia.

Simons excuse, why he changed his faith.

But now was the new season of the spring in beginning, and euery man prepared himselfe to the discontinued trauels of the warres begun. And nowe were there met together in Erzirum, out of all the woonted prouinces, all the souldiers: & withal were gathered together all the Engines, all the Moneys, al the prouision of corne, Barley, and Rise, and all other things necessarie for the sustenaunce of Cattel & Souldiers. Aegypt also had sent thither her squadronst whereof notwithstanding little more than the one halfe arriued at Erzirum, partlie by reason of the sandie wilder nesse, through which they must needs passe, as they came towards Soria from Memphis, where now Cair standeth: and partlie by reason of the pestiferous maladies, which they found in the Cittie of Aleppo, and places heere thereunto, where besides Carbuncles, Iaundisses, and blacke botches, there raigned also a venomous and contagious Feuer, that replenished the Cittie with great terrour, lamentation, and death. So that this Armie at Erzirum, was equall with the first: and thereupon Mustaffa taking due suruey thereof, determined to remooue, and to iourney towards Chars. And so holding on his way to Hassen-Chalasi, hee came in twelue daies to Chars, not perceiuing so much as one small word awry in any of his Souldiers. And forasmuch as here they must rest, & put themselues in defence, by fortifying with walles, & compassing with ditches the ruinated City of Chars, which must be done in the best maner that might be, and with as great speed as was possible, ther was no reremedie, but besides the Pioners and Engyners (that were brought for that purpose) there must be set to worke many Spaoglani, many slaues, and some Ianizzaries also. But it was not presently put in execution, as the necessity required. For all

The meeting together of a new armie at Erzirum.

Aegypt sendeth souldiers, whereof scarse the one half came to Erzirum.

Pestilent sicknesses in Soria.

This Army equal with the first.

Mustaffa at Chars.

	these kind of people suddenly made an insurrection, and in a tumult
The soudiers in a tumult against the General.	began with bitter protestations to let the Generall vnderstand, that their stipends, wherewith it pleased the Sultan to fauour them, were not bestowed vpon them, 'to employ their forces and vertues in workes so vise and so far from the Arte of warre but only with their swords and other weapons to exercise that force and hardinesse, for which they were esteemed worthy of that honour.' The General gaue them their answer againe in verie haughty tearms, and although he knew wel ynough, that the smallest summe of mony that he should haue bestowed among them, would soone haue quieted them, yet would he not yeeld one iot to their inciuility, but vsing al means of authority & terrour, he brought them to work as much as he desired. And so within the space of 23. daies, the towers and wals were erected, the ditches digged, the
In the space of 23. dayes Chars fensed.	bathes builded, the artillery disposed in order vpō the wals & the water brought round about it, either frō som branch of Eufrates, or frō som other riuer (not much lesse famous than Eufrates) that springeth out of the mountain Periardo. Many inconueniences happened in the Armie, while they were busie about this worke, and namelie vpon the xxv. day of August, when they had almost euen finished the whole building, the souldiers endured a most sudden colde, by reason of much snowe
Snowes at Chars in August.	that then fell in greate aboundance. But so vehement it was not, that it coulde not bee borne, but euery man was the rather forwarde to execute anie commandement, that according to the pleasure of Amurah should bee enioyned them by Mustaffa, all of them being generallie of opinion, that the only repairing and building of Chars was but a small matter, in regard of so greate an Armie gathered together with so greate diligence, no doubt for some greater and further purpose.

For the accomplishing of this fortification nowe there remained nothing to doe, it being fullie finished, and therfore nowe it was time to attempt some newe enterprises: Whereupon the Generall resolued to sende succours into Georgia to the fort of Teflis, without which it was most certaine that the Fortresse would be yeelded to the Georgians. For this purpose he must needs take one of these courses, either to choose some valiant Captaine that should go thither, or els to go himselfe in person, with all his Armie, about so great an enterprise as that was. In which cogitation he remayned very doubtfull, casting in his mind on the one side a certaine feare, that if he went not with all his armie, some mishappe might light vpon the Captaine that should goe in his steed, and on the other side bethinking himselfe, that if he shoulde goe thither with all his people, he should hardlie satisfie Amurah, whom he had already made to beleeue, that he had sudued all the Georgians and reduced all that prouince to his obedience and deuotion. Notwithstanding in this his ambiguity, the desire that he had

The consultations of generall Mustaffa touching Teflis.

THE FOURTH BOOKE

to preserue his credit with Amurath, preuailed, and hee thought that it would be as sufficient to sende succours thither by a Captaine accompanied with twentie thousand chosen souldiers, as to go himself with all his campe: being of opinion, that in the straites of Tomanis and other places, so huge a multitude might giue occasion to their enemies rather of praye than of feare, and might breed to their own forces rather lettes and impedimentes, than any fauour or help. Wherein hee was highly commended of all men, though therby with the King in particular he lost his credit, to whom he had heretofore made so goodly promises, that he wel hoped, without sending any such preparation thither, to haue receiued of that people much greater obedience.

Now forasmuch as it was verie needful to fortifie and strengthen that place, he made choise of Hassan the Bassa of Damasco, son to that Mahamet that was the principal Visior of the Court, as famous as any that euer had any gouernement in the Ottoman Empire, a man no lesse faire in face & countenance, than valourous and venturous in sudden and important cases, and to him he deliuered between eighteen and twenty thousand souldiers, some of Greece, some of Damasco, and some of Caraemit: ioyning in company with him one Resuan-Bassa, Captaine of certaine Aduenturers (comprehended in the forsaid number) that voluntarily offered themselues to follow the forces of Hassan: and assigned vnto him likewise fourty thousand Duckets, and many loades of Meale, Rise, and Barley, with other thinges necessarie both for diet, and for warre: and so set him forward for Teflis.

Hassan Bassa of Damasco, chosen Generall for the succouring of Teflis, with 20000. souldiers.

Resuan Bassa Captain of certain Aduenturers.

40000. Duckats caried to Teflis.

This Hassan caried a haughtie mind, with high thoughts agreeable to his magnanimity, and did determine with him selfe to loose all that he had, yea, and his veric life withall, rather thā he shuld not bring these succors within the wals of Teflis. But when he was now come to the famous strait of Tomanis, & passed the ruins of other treacherous places, he arriued at a dangerous passage (without perceiuing any footing of an enemy) wher the woods on the one side, deep valleyes & craggy rocks on the other side, wold make any man astonied that shuld come thither: and, behold, euen on a sudden, the Persiaus, togither with the Georgians, vnder the conduct of Aliculi-Chan & of Simon, at vnawares set vpon the armie of Hassan, & ioyned battel with them. For Aliculi-Chan and Simon-Bech (as we told you before) being sent into Georgia, & hauing therabouts gathered souldiers togither to the number of 8000. did still remaine for the most part in the borders of Teflis & Tomanis, wayting for some opportunity to annoy, either those of the Fort of Teflis, if happily they shoulde at any time issue foorth, or els the other that shoulde come to succour them. Howbeit the famine, wherewith they were afflicted at that time, could not woorke so much vpon them, as induce them to issue out of the fortresse, & so

Allculi-chan and Simon.

Anoysome famin in Teflis.

the Persians could find no opportunity to do them any harm as they desired: but hauing continual aduertisement, that Mustaffa had sent succours to thē being thus besieged, they stayed there, & watched, to hear on what side any newes wold appear frō them. At the last they vnderstood by certain spies, that they kept the way of Tomanis & that Hassan Bassa with twenty thousand men was comming to this aid. This news caused them foorthi with to seatter themselues among the woods, all along the length of the said straite, hoping from thence to assaile the Turkes, and ouerthrowing them headlong into the deep valley, to bereaue them both of their goods and life.

But Hassan, who had not so much care of any thing, as he had to auoid that grieuous daunger, chose rather to make his iourny through the woods, & eschuothe ambushes & trecheries that his enemies might lay for him, & so minister means to his people to escape the perill of that headlong ouerthrow. And therfore in steed of leauing the wood on his left-hand, he entred within it, to discouer all the wiles that might be plotted against him, and so did al his souldiers with him, & therupō began the battel. Wherin they fought with a thousand windings & turnings in and out, through a thousand crooked pathes, and doubtful cranks, in a most confused Medley, till there ensued therupon a great slaughter of the Turkes: who being not accustomed to this kind of fight, nor acquainted with the situation of the place, were in the skirmish driuen so far, that downe they fell, and not being able to recouer themselues, were presently slain. In this confusion, among others that were ill handled, was Mustaffa Bey of Caisar, a place in Caramania, who lost his banner, being taken away from him by the Georgians, hauing also his Standerd bearer thrust through, and all his horses surprised, which he had caused to be lead out on the right hand, and done many mischiefs with them. And in this maner did they passe the straites of Tomamis.

Now although they were not very far from Teflis, yet wold they needs make stay nere to the said straits, & faining that they wold fauour and rest their men and their cattell, (and peraduēture meaning to nourish a foolish opinion of fear in the minds oftheir enemies) they waited to see whether they wold come againe to trouble them a fresh or no. Hassan Bassa burned, til he might perform som famous and notable act, thinking with himselfe that hee had receiued a great ignominy, in suffring his enemies being in number so far inferiour vnto him, to escape frō him & remembring that in such places sleights and stratagems are more auailable than open forces, he took aduice, that a band of the souldiers of Greece with a certaine troupe of the Aduenturiers, vnder the conduct of Resuan-Bassa, should lay themselues in ambushment within the thickest shades of the strait, and so being hidden, should

The warinesse of Hassan.

The battell, wherin there was a great slaughter of the Turks.

The Turkish stratageme

diligentlie watch euery stirre of the enemy. Two dayes together did the Turkes remaine there thus diuided asunder, and were now resolued the third day to remooue from thence, and not to stay any longer from conducting their succours to Teflis: when as Aliculi-Chan and Simon Bech (vainely imagining that this stay of the Turks was for feare they had of the Persians) with all their people freshly, but boldly, and foolishly returned and gaue a newe onset vpon the flancke of Hassans Squadrons, who foorth with raising all his souldiers, and giuing a signe to Resuan and the rest that lay in ambush, with all speed compassed-in his enemies, and straightning their wings on both sides, tooke some of them aliue, hacked some in peeces, and put all the rest to flight. Among others that were taken aliue, Aliculi-Chan (the Persian Captaine) who ouer-rashlie ran euen vpon the face of Hassan, with al his band, that continually followed him, was taken prisoner, and so fell into the hands of Hassan. Who victoriously and ioyfully arriued at Teflis, the next day following, being the verie 11 day after his departure frō Chars: where hauing passed ouer the riuer, and entred the fortresse he found among the poore besieged soules many miseries, by occasion whereof some had died, and some were yet sick. For they were so plagued with famine, that they had not only deuoured their horses of small price, but they had also eaten the verie skinnes of the same horses, of Muttons, and of dogs, and had passed away the time in most miserable wants. But Hassan did comfort them all with the newes of victory, and more with the relief that he brought thē, distributing to euery one of them gifts and good words, and exhorting them all to perseuere in the seruice of the King, whose honour was neuer more then now to be respected: For that it is no lesse commendation for a man to preserue and keep a conquered country in the midst of the enemie and the enemies forces, then it is at first to conquer it. And for asmuch as al the souldiers of the Fort did with one voyce request Hassan, that he would appoint them a newe Captaine, because they did all mislike Mahamet-Bassa, who the last yeare was left by the Generall in that Forte: Hassan remoued the said Mahamet, and put in his place Amet Bassa Aggibeogli. And when he had filled vp the places of the dead souldiers with a newe supply, he tooke his leaue, and recommended the charge and custody of the Fort to their trust and vertue.

Hassan passed ouer the riuer with all his people, and put himselfe on the way backe again towards Tomanis, so that he came to the very strayt, without any trouble or impediment of his enemies. But being come to the mouth of the strait, he was aduertised by his Scoutes, that it was shut vp with verie strong trenches of Artillerie, and defended with a great nūber of souldiers. And these were they that remained aliue in the last skirmishes (that we told you of) when Hassan martched

The Georgians assault again the Turkish Armie.

Aliculi-Chan taken aliue.

Hassan victoriouslie arriued at Teflis.

A great famine in the sieged city of Teflis.

Hassan returneth from Teflis.

The entrie of the strait fenced with Artillarie.

towardes Teflis. For Simon thinking (as in deede it fell out) that Hassan shoulde returne backe by the same way of Tomanis could not find any better meanes to represse his boldnesse, to reuenge the losses of his owne people and to redeeme the prisoner Alieuli-Chan, but this, Namely, thus to shut vp the mouth of the Straite, hoping thereby, that the Turks being enforced to runne vpon the artillerie, so laid for defence of the said strait, shuld be all consumed and vtterly destroyed. But Hassan as soon as he vnderstood that the passage was […]th it sort shut vp by Simon, sought means to make his iourny some other way, and declyning that great danger to frustrate and delude the ambushes and stratagems of Simon. Whiles he remained thus doubtful in himself, discoursing many conceits in his mind: Alyculi-Chan, who would not haue bene squemish to haue committed any villany, so that he might thereby purchase his libertie out of prison, made offer to Hassan, that he wold shew him a safe and a short cut, wherby he should not onlie eschue the prepared mischiefe, but also auoyd all assaultes of his enemies: but yet vpon this condition that Hassan shuld promise him to set him at liberty. The Turkish Bassa did not stick in large maner to promise Alyculi his liberty, although indeed he did not perform his promise to him afterwards, which (to say the truth) did not a litle obscure the glory of his actions: And therfore bending his iourny towards the right hand, he was guided by Aliculi-Chan through strāge and vncoth waies out of those woods & dangers, not meeting with so much as the sword of one enemy. The Persian Duke put the Turk in mind of his promise for his liberty, but al in vain: For the Turk dissembling the wicked intention, wherby he was induced to giue him his word, pretended with great & deep sighs, that he was very sory he could not perform, asmuch as his intent was to doe for him: because it lay not in his power to set any man at liberty, that in battel was taken prisoner by the souldiers & vassals of A murath & yet for a noble & magnifical pledge he gaue him his faith, that so far as his intreaties & fauours with captaine Mustaffa could preuaile, he would not suffer him to receiue any wrong, but would vse all the most earnest meanes he could to procure him al liberty, & return to his own cuntry.

In this meane while, Simon perceiuing that the Turkes were remooued from those places that were neere vnto the straire, could not perswade himselfe that they were returned to Teflis, but imagined that they had taken this new way. And being afterward certified that it was so indeed, and informed of the trueth thereof by his faithfull spies, he ranne all headlong and as it were desperate to meete with that so happie Armie. And burning in anger and all inflamed with rage for this great fortune of the Turkes, cursing and blaspheming the heauens, hee arriued vpon the tayle of the Turkish hoast, which with vnmeasurable

---

Hassan seeketh to auoid the great danger of the strait.

Hassan promiseth to set Aliculi-Chan the Persian at libertie.

Hassan breaketh his promise.

Angry Simon destroyeth the taile of Hassans army

fury he did wholly destroy & discomfit, leading away with him al the people, all the horses, and all the treasure of Mahamet Bassa, which was brought from Teflis, & all the treasure of Hassan Bassa likewise: putting to death & taking prisoners the slaues & vessals of both the Captaines, and shedding the bloud of many other souldiers. Among whō although he sought greedily and diligently for Aliculi-Chan, of purpose to deliuer him, yet could he not finde him, for that he was committed to the charge and safe custody of a Turkish captaine in the front of the Army. After which medley, there fell againe great store of snowes, so that the cold thereof, biting and nipping the woundes of such as had, valiantly fought in the battel, the greatest part of them perished.

<small>Aboundant snowes.</small>

Hassan followed on his voyage, and being come to Chars in the space of eight dayes after his departure from Teflis, he presented Aliculi to Mustaffa, declaring vnto him the battels that hapned his succors performed at Teflis the dangers that he had passed, & the great losses that he recerued in his return: & the Turks say, that he did not fail most instantlie to deal for the libertie of Aliculi, which notwithstanding I leaue to the iudgement of those that can iudge more profoundly, than I with truth and credite can write, I my selfe being one of those, that do verily beleene, He can not keepe his faith with man, that denieth his faith to God. Sufficeth it, that poore vnhappy Aliculi by commaundement of Mustaffa was caried away to Erzirum, and ther committed to prison in the Castell. And this was the ende of the stirres of the yeare 1579.

<small>Hassan come to Chars,</small>

<small>Aliculi-Chan imprisoned at Erzirum.</small>

Mustaffa returned to the said Citie of Erzirum with al his Army, which was presently also by him discharged. And afterwards he sent aduertisementes of all these successes to the Court to Amurath, recounting vnto him the deserts of Hassan aswell for the succouring of Teflis, as also for the taking of Captaine Aliculi-Chan. And forasmuch as the last yeare the said General had perswaded Amurah, that the prouince of Georgia, and the people thereof were reduced vnder his obedience: to the end that he should not maruell at so many losses and so many battels, and thereby doubt of some lying and false information, hee declared vnto him, that all these difficulties were not raised by the natural and home-bred Georgians, who the last yeare had promised him al due obedience, but by two certain Captaines, Simon and Aliculi, sent out of Persia, who had mooued all these stirres, prepared all these dangers, and layd all these ambushes, although one of them now remayned with him in prison, a worthy punishment for his malapert temerity. The king sent by two of his Capigi (or Gentlemen Hushers) to Hassan, a battle-axe al gilt, and setful of iewels, a Target of gold and pearle, and a garment of cloth of gold, in rewarde of his

<small>Amurath honoreth Hassan.</small>

noble enterprises atchieued, commending him eat lie for his vertue and valour: and with great delight did he read-ouer all that Mustaffa had written vnto him, giuing order withall, that Aliculi should be kept, where hee was, in diligent and safe custodie.

The King of Persia lying at Casbin was aduertised of all these successes, which being added to his newe thoughts touching his sonat Heri, wherof Mirize Salmas had enformed him, did greatly molest him. For on the one side, the euident dangers, wherin all Georgia stood, did shrewdly trouble him, considering that the Stratageme so well deuised by Simon had no better successe, and the Turks had now made themselues throughly acquainted with all those passages, in the difficulty & roughnes whereof consisted al his hope of defence: and moreouer vnderstanding that the Widowes sons wer become vassals to the Turk, which course Leuentogli also propounded to himselfe, as one that was greatly inclined to be in confederacie with the Ottamans: and to bee brief, perceiuing that all the Georgian Captaines had setled themselues vnder the standardes of Amurath, hee could not but feare greatly, that his enemies would begin to pierce into the noble cities of Medili the greater, yea and peraduenture euen vnto Tauris before any of the rest. On the other side, he was as it were with a worm inwardly consumed, for the newes that were brought him by his Visier Mirize Salmas, of the euident suspition, which he told him, that his son Abas Mirize of Heri, shuld (like a rebel and an ambitious youth) goe about to proclame himselfe king of the Persian empire, to the great ignominy of his father, and of Emirhamze his eldest sonne, who only was worthy to bee named his successour in that crowne.

Abas Mirize suspected of rebellion against his father, by Mirize Salmas the chief Sultan of Casbin Mirize Salmas hauing made the Persiā prince his son in law aduanced his estate.

This Mirize Salmas, according to his longing desire, had maried a daughter of his to the saide Emirhamze with the consent of the king his father: but yet not content with that great honor, he ceased not continually with ambitious deuices to seek out meanes, how he might make the Persian estate free from all other Seignuries, & bring it to that passe as it might wholly remaine to his son, vndeuided & entire, from the participation of his brethren. And therfore little regarding the perilles that might happen from the Turks, and blinded with the desire of his own greatnesse, he went about to turn the King against Abas Mirize, either to take him & commit him to prison, or at least to leaue him void of all authority to command. And the better to perswade the king therunto (being a man very credulous & nothing considerate, but putting more confidence in him than in any other) he began to discourse, that Abas Mirize his sonne had not greatly respected him in diuers occasions, declaring vnto him, that sundry times hee had very rashly scorned his commandements, and because he would not shewe himself obedient & inferiour vnto him,

The Persian king verie credulous & inconsiderate

he wold not send so much as one souldier towards this war against the Turks; and in fine he had caused himselfe not onely to bee called king of Heri, but he had also giuen it out, that he meant to claime the succession in the kingdome. And that therefore it was necessarie to feele the mind of the young youth, and to establish the tranquility and quiet of the Empire: to the end that if these stirres against the Turks went forwards, Abas Mirize should not be so hardy, as in the greatest heat of war to raise sudden tumults, & to make himselfe Lord of that, which by right appertained to Emirhamze. Of these complaints he gaue the king diuers euident prooffs, which both in respect of the loue that he bare to Emirhamze, and also of the faith that he gaue to his Visier, caried a greate sway with him in his mind, especially they being accompanied with the crafty packing of the said Visier, who as hee was very cunning in such practises of himselfe, so did hee make them much more effectuall with the effeminate king by the means of diuers Ladies & other occasions that were familiar and vsual with him. But the most euident prooffe of all was this, that the saide Visier enformed the king, that whereas both by letters and commandements he had summoned the gouernours of Sasuar, Coran, & other places subiect to the iurisdiction of Heri, to come to Casbin, and so to passe with Emirhamze to Siruan, yet neuer a one of them wold stir a foot, answering, that they were enioyned so to do by Abas Mirize their lord. This euidence was the most principal occasion, why euery thing that Mirize Salmas alleaged, was beleeued by the King, & why he did continually bethink himself, how he might find opportunity to represse the boldnes of his disobedient son. And yet notwithstanding al these difficulties being otherwise perswaded by his most loyal and faithful Sultans, he did not fayl to temper these his internal motions, & to tame these vnruly affectiōs of his mind: & remaining resolute in his important cogitations against the Turks, to prepare such prouision, which should be sufficient to inhibit their passage to Tauris, if they had had any purpose so to do. Vpon which resolution arresting himself, he neuer ceased til he had furnished all those prouisions, whereof a litle hereafter we will make mention, for that it is verie conuenient first to prosecute the history of those things that were reported of Mustaffa.

He being returned (as we told you) to Erzirum, after so many external stirres & troubles, was surprised by certain more intrinsecal, & domestical quarrels at home: for manie grieuous complaints were there made of him to Amurath, whereupon the said king was induced to take frō him the charge of the Generalship, & to cal him to the court to giue account of his actions. Neither did this thing happen vnto him without iust cause, for that he had before raised a great discontentmēt

Obiections against Abas Mirize.

The Persian king effeminate.

Mustaffa discharged of his Generalship, and called home to Constantinople.

The occasion of the depriuation of Mustaffa from his Generalship.

in the mind of Amurath, by sending so much people to the succours of Teflis, whereby hee coniectured that the affaires of Georgia were not in such security, as Mustaffa had already informed him they were. Moreouer hee had also greatly displeased al the souldiers of his army, who thought themselues to be much deceiued by him, for that now this second year, with so much adoo, he had gathered together such a number of armed men, and made so greate prouision with such a charge and expences to their Lorde, and with such a trouble of al the whole empire, and yet had not any worthy or notable enterprise to performe, wherby either the glorie of Amurath might receiue increase among his enemies, or the souldiers themselues might be contented with some good bootie, or for any other action of importance. Whereupon they were all in an vprore, & accused him of improuidence and prodigality, in that he had no regard of the wealth and subiects of his king. With these accusations did they the more odiously taxe and reprooue Mustaffa, for that in the space of two years, wherein they had followed his wars, they neuer receuedfrō him any smal sign of curtesie, no not so much as the smallest reward: but alwaies like a tyrāt, he did reserue to his own vse althose presents and tokens of gratification, which by order from the king were due to all the souldiers, to encourage them that they might the more lustily cōtinuein this war. These and such other complaints that were made of Mustaffa, although they were of some moment, yet woulde the king neuer haue construed them so hardly against him, as for the same he wold haue bin induced to depriue him of his place: and without all doubt they had bene vtterly cancelled by reason of the great fauours which Amurath did beare vnto him, it the enuie which Sinan. Bassa did carie towards him, being now exasperated by ancient and inveterate hatred, had not ministred strength & force to all these accusations, & set (as it were) an edge vpon Amurath to do what he did.

A comparison of Sinan Bassa and Mustaffa, two ancient aduersaries.

This Sinan was a most ancient enemy to Mustaffa, and thought himself to be his match in al things. For if Mustaffa had broght the Iland of Cyprus into the power of the Turks within the space of so many moneths, Sinan had also in very few dayes subdued La Goletta in Africa. And if Mustaffa were a man of great courage, and reuerend for his yeares, Sinan would be his equall both in the one and the other: yea and Sinan would not sticke to think himselfe to be his better (which indeed was supposed to be the originall of these bitter indignations) for that in the enterprise of Giamen, where Arabia Felix is, Sinan himselfe did an exployt, which Mustaffa neither durst nor was able, nor yet knew how to put in execution, and Sinan alone caried away the glory and entire honour of that famous victorie and important conquest. And euer after wardes there was nourished between them a thousand dissentions, so that the one of them did alwayes shewe himselfe aemulous and aduersarie to the other both in act and speach, as occasions fell out. At the last happens this opportunitie for Sinan, to declare vnto the King how the matters of Mustaffa were but slenderlie grounded, and taking occasion of the complaint of so many against him, he caused a great number of the to frame their supplication to the king, which he for his part did in most m [...]lignant maner inforce, and exaggerate against Mustaffa, accusing him; that this second yeare he had manifestlie shewed himselfe to haue gone into the warre, not as a worthy Captaine, and one that was desirous of noble and honourable enterprises, but as a man greedy to make merchandise of bloud and of his souldiers payēs employing the most liberal prouision of corne and money, not as rewards for wel-deseruing men, nor to the foundation of such fabrikes as were needful, and might haue bene builded therewithall, but only to his owne proper gaine, and to enrich himselfe with his peoples losses, to the great shame of the king, and endommagement of the publike treasurie: adding hereunto, that if those things which haue bene executed by the said Mustaffa, were rightly serched, it would be found, that he had pretermitted manie good opportunities, that he had attempted many things in vaine, and generally that he had not done anie good either to the king, or to his souldiers, but onely to himself. Whom rather than they would follow againe as their Captaine, all his people being in an vprore, shewed themselues readie and willing to aduenture themselues in any other far greater labour, that by their Lord and king shuld be commanded them. These and other such like complaints, which the king heard of Mustaffa, of whō (as we told you before) he had already conceaued a hard opinion, because hee perceiued that the affaires of Georgia were not in any great security, were the occasion why Amurath was resolued to put him from his place. Wherunto he did the more easily condiscend, because he did alwaies think it very dangerous to suffer one and the self same General to be any long time the minister of so great an enterprise, and Captaine of so many Squadrons: and besides, that he alwayes deemed it to be a small honor to him, if he should stil imploy but only one man, and that it would be greater honour to him, to shew that he had variety of subiectes, that were worthy of so great a charge. And therfore being desirous to find out the truth of that, which was reported vnto him touching Mustaffa, he sent for him to the Court, causing also two of his Deftardari or Treasurers to be brought with him, that they migh shew the accounts of such moneys as he had receiued & laid out, and to be short, giue vp an account of whole office. Mustaffa came to Constantinople accordinglie, where the two Deftardari were committed to safe custody: and he in the mean while,

Sinan accuseth Mustaffa

Mustaffa his two Treasurers brought to the Court.

vsing the mighty and potent mediation of diuers Ladies, laboured by al possible means, that Amurath might be perswaded to admit him to his presence and to receiue his honourable and rich presents: wherwithall the wrath and indignation of all angry harts is woont to he appeased and extinguished, especially among the Barbarians, in whom Couetousnes subdueth humaine reason and iustice, and doth in such impious maner ouer-rule the Mahometical Empires, & principally the empire of the Turks, that there remaineth not so much as the shadow of such a vertue, but it is altogether gouerned onlie by meere Tyranny. Further than this, was there no proceeding against Mustaffa, but yet he was neuer admitted to those honours, which in recompence of such actions as he had perfourmed both in peace and in warre, for the seruice of the Ottomans, he perswaded himself were due vnto him.

<small>Ladies mighty mediators with Amurath.</small>

<small>A detestation of the Turkish gouernment.</small>

In the time that Mustaffa remayned General at Erzirum, there departed out of this life Mahamet the principall Visier, who by a fraudulent & treacherous mad foole, while he sate to giue audience in an open place, within his owne house, was suddainly, and to the common astonishment of all the companie, stroke through the bodie with a sharp Gangiara or (as we call it) a dagger. And after him dyed likewise of an infirmity Agmat Bassa, who succeeded in the place of Mahamet that was slaine, so that the said soueraigne dignity by rightfull succession was due to Mūstaffa. But yet he was not thought woorthy of it by him that might and ought to haue gratified him therewithall, as wee shall declare vnto you a little hereafter, because I take it to be verie conuenient, in this place to insert the death of the said Mahamet the Visier: as a matter verie notable and famous in those daies, & for an example of such, as administer iustice in such great offices, worthy to be registred not in one onely, but in a thousand and a thousand histories.

<small>The death of Mahamet, the principall Vice-Roy.</small>

This foresaid Mahamet, in his greatest managing of the vniuersall gouernment of that empire, for certaine causes and respects, that seemed to him reasonable (whether they were so or no, the curious searchers of al particulars can tel) had depriued a certaine souldier of Constantinople of his yearly stipend, which with many labours and dangers hee had gotten to maintain himselfe withall, which stipend he had bestowed vpon another, whō the said Mahamet either for friendship, or for bribe, or for desert had made capable of it: and so, that other poore soul remained in miserie, and in deed altogether depriued of all meanes to sustain his life. To which miserable estate seeing himself now brought, & not guilty to himself of any fault that hee had committed, worthy of so great punishmēt, he determined with himselfe to reuenge the iniury with the bloud of Mahamet the Bassa, & to bereaue him of his life, that had bereued him of his ho non &

<small>The occasions and maner of the strange death of Vic-Reoy Mahamet.</small>

liuing. And because he could not haue any fit means to put this his designment in execution, vnles hee might compasse some familiarity with Mahamet, by haunting his house, and conuersing domestically with him (for otherwise he could not be permitted to come neere him, that inioyeth that barbarous estate, by reason of the guarde of slaues, that keep the person of the Visier) he resolued to apparell himself like an Eremit, which the Turks cal Dreuis, and to present himself euery morning before Mahamet to aske him his almes. And so he did, counterfeiting withal a certaine kinde of folly and lightnes of minde, to the end he might make the people beleeue, that the same had hapned vnto him through the grief which he had conceaued for his money and his honour taken from him by the Visier. For in deed principallie and aboue al other things, those that take vpō them the life of a Dreuis, do count erfet a certain kind of worldly foolishnes and a contempt of all earthly things, whereby the variable and ignorant people is brought into a beleefe, that they are enamored and inspired only with heauenly cogitations. Mahamet, not only the first time, but also at all other times that the counter-feit Eremite did present himself before him, caused him to be comforted with his good almes, and as it wer with a kind of priuat stipend enioyned him, that euery morning he shuld come vnto him into the Diuano, and there together with othous (appointed for the same purpose) hee should say his deuout prayers, and singing prayses to their wicked prophet, entreat God for his saluation For it is the oustome of all the Noble men, that at the ordinary houres of saluting (or rather blaspheming) God, all their impious and prophane priestes assemble themselues in the Diuani, which are made ready for them, and there all together the Infidell wretches do mumble vp with their vnclean monthes those their wicked blasphemies, whereby they do irritate and prouoke the bounty and Maiestie of God. By this meanes did the Eremite insimate himselfe into very great familiarity, and this his practise endured so long; that the counterfeit foole went in and out of the Diuano at his pleasure, without that euer any man gain sayd either his going in, or his comming out and dayly he sate in the presence of the Visier, and so hauing saide his prayers and taken his almes in quiet and welcome manner, with all reuerence departed. At the last, when the crafty Begger thought that his time was come, wherein he might very fitly execute his purpose, without any feare of death, or of torment (which sometimes is more grieuous and terrible than death itself) hauing vtterlie resolued with himselfe most willingly to die, so that he might satisfie the desire of reuenge, which priuily he had fostered in his hart: hauing put a verie sharpe Gangiara secretly in one of his sleeues, he went according to his custom to require his alms, with an assured resolution (when he had said his praiers, &

A custome of the Barbarians.

reached out his hand to receaue his wonted alms) speedily to charge vpon the Visier, and with his sharpe weapon once or twise to strike him to the heart. According to the accustomed maner, was the counterfet Priest (for who would euer haue feared so long a designment and so traiterous & fraudulent a mischiefe at his handes:) brought into the Diuano, where Mahamet the Visier sate within his house for publike audience & after the vsuallmaner, before any of the suters, that attēded for answers & dispatch of their busines, did suspect any such deceit, he was admitted here vnto Mahamet, & sitting right against him, according to his old woont poured out those maledictions which those barbarians doe vse to mūble vp in their vain praiers: which being finished, whiles the Visier of simplicity reached vnto him his wonted almes, the traiterous foole in steed of receiuing it, drewe out his dagger with great speed, and thrust it once or twise into his breast, whereby there gushed out both his blood & his life. And therupon al the stāders by, astonished with the strāgenes of the fact, ran in vnto him, & saw this strange spectacle the olde hoary Visier al soyled in his own blood, & deadlie pale, breathing forth his last gasp, & yeelding vp his miserable ghost. Presently did they bind the mischieuous Dreuis with strong cords & by and by did the rumor therof flie to the kings eares, who suspecting that some of the chiefe Gouernors, that they might mount into that high dignity, had prouoked the traitor to doe this detestable act, would needs vnderstand of the traiterous Murderer, what occasion had mooded him thus to betray his Visier. Who answered him againe, that he did it to deliuer the Citie of Constantinople from the tyranny of him, by whom he was vndeseruedly depriued of the stipende that hee had demerited, and of the honour that he had atchieued. But when the King coulde receiue no other answer from him, the Rebel was deliuered into the hands of the slaues belonging to the deade Visier, and so put to death with vnspeakeable torments.

And thus died Mahamet, and a litle while after, Agmat also died of sicknes (as is aforesaid) so that it was Mustaffa his course to succeed in that chiefe roome: for hee was the third in the order of the Bassas. But, although he did vse al the possible meanes hee could, that the saide charge (being due vnto him) might be bestowed vpon him, yet wold not the King grace him so much as to grant it him vnder seale, although in effect he made him sit as a Visier, and all matters of state were brought vnto him as the chiefe Visier: but in his steed the seale was sent to Sinan-Bassa, who was now made Generall, & was on his way towards Teflis, as in due place it shall be shewed Greatly was Mustaffa discontented here withall, and much grieued at this iniustice of Amurath, neither was he altogether void of feare, least some other strange accident should light vpon him. Howbeit notwithstanding all

Mustaffa not thought worthy of the roome of the chief Visier.

Sinan chosen the chief Visier.

these malecontentments, he did not faile to purge himselfe throughly of the accusations laid against him, and caused also his two Defterdari to be enlarged, after their innocencio was made known, which whether it wer so known to be indeed, or whether it was made to seem so by the means of his presents & of gold which amōgst the barbarous & corrupt people is wont to make vile matters to appear noble, & to couer & cōceal al soul & dishonest practises, I wil not define. Mustaffa and his two Treasurers quit.

After the depriuing of Mustaffa from the charge of the Generalship. Amurath was enforced to elect a new General aswel for the preseruation of Chars and Teflis, as also to reduce the enemie to some good cōditions of peace, for which purpose finding Sinan to be a fit man, as one that euer shewed himselfe an enuious imitator of Mustaffa, and one that peraduenture would be glad to receiue such a dignity, yea, and perhaps one that by some secret seruice had induced the King to make choyce of him, he nominated the said Sinan to be General for this expedition, and to him he gaue the soueraine authoritie to command, and to set in order all those preparations, which hee thought necessarie for such enterprises, as he shuld think good to attempt in this his first year. But Sinan although by reason of this great fauour he grewe haughtie and glorious, yet did he not fore slowe to discourse thoroughly with himselfe vpon all his designmentes, and namely besides the succouring of Teflis, hee determined to build a Fortat Tomanis, to assure the wayes that lead thither from Chars, and withall to attempt all the means he could to induce the Persiā king to send Embassadors for peace, with such conditions as should be acceptable to Amurath. With these and such like discourses did he busie himselfe, whiles he was making preparation to passe towards Erzirum.

Sinan chosen General.

The purposes of Generall Sinan.

Of all these changes and alterations the Persian king was aduertised, who employed himselfe, (as we told you before) in preparing for the disturbance of his enemies, and to minister also matter himselfe of some attempts that he likewise entended. And being certified (whether by the meanes of Sinan or of any other, the certenty is not yet come vnto vs) that this new Turkish General was a man greatly giuen to cogitations, how this war might be quieted, & these wrathful broiles reduced to a good peace whiles he was setting al things in order & areadines to send me into Georgia, & to gather an army for the defēce of his cities, he be thought himself that it was very conuenient to put this matter in execution, being exhorted thereunto by Leuentogli, who although hee had bene iniured by the Persians, yet he could not but think it a dangerous thing to haue these warres so neere him: and being likewise hartened in it by his Visier Mirize Salmas, who was more intentiue towards the vniust suppressing of Abas Mirize of Heri, then he was for any sufficient reparations or due prouisions for this warre,

The Persian king resolueth to send Embassadors to Constantinople. Maxut-Chan dispatched as Embassador.

Maxut-chan to Sinan.

Conditions of peace offered by the Persian king.

The speach of the Embassador to Sinan

he resolued to sende Ambassadors to Constantinople to demand peace of Amurath. And deeming Maxut-Chan to be a man very fit for that purpose he made choyce of him to performe that businesse, adioyning vnto him for an Assistant an old Priest belonging to the said Leuentogli, as one that was a common friend to both parties, and very desirous of this quietnes. And so hee dispatched Maxut-Chan, with charge that hee should goe to Sinan, and of him receiue guides, to conduct him to Constantinople with letters vnto the king: and that he should, as much as lay in him, labour for the pacifying of all these troubles, and in any case conclude vpon it, so that Amurath would be contented with Chars and Teflis. And thus being departed from Casbin, keeping the way of Sultania, Zanga, Miana, Turcoman and Tauris, leauing on his right hand Chiulfal, Nassiuan, Reiuan and by Coy & Van, wher the Bassa appointed him one to guide him, he arriued at Chars. It is generally known, and I haue in particular vnderstood, how great the ioy was, which the Turks conceaued of the comming of this Ambassadour, and how Cicala-Bassa did with all diligence dispatch certain postes to the court with these good newes. From Chars the saide Embassadour was sent by the way of Hassan-Chalasi to Erzirum, & from thence with new guides he went towards Amazia. But when he came to Siuas, there he found Generall Sinan encamped, gathering together his Armie from the cities aboue named, to lead them with him to the execution of his designements.

The Persian Embassadour entourmed Sinan of all that, whereof hee had to treat with the Turkish king on the behalfe of his king Mahamet: and laboured earnestly to perswade him of the honesty of the request, and the equitie of the cause, declaring vnto him, that as vnder the lawe of Mahomet their common Prophet, both the nations are conioyned together, so that they ought with one vnitie and speciall concord defend and encrease their Names, by subduing the Christian people, who professing to worship the true God and the true Prophet, do possesse the most noble Cities of Europe: so was it a matter very inconuenient to contend among themselues, and seeke to ouerthrow, yea and vtterly to destroy one another: it being a thing quite contrarye to that vnion, which should be among people of one & the selfe same religion: it being also rather the property of brute & sauage beasts thā of men, to driue & expulse out of their natiue nest, those that are the followers and worshippers of one & the self same Prophet. And although among so much people, and in such bredth & largenes of cuntries ther be found peraduenture some signe of contrariety, & some small shew of difference, yet for all that the matter is not so great, as that it shuld deserue such troublesom stirs, and kindle such ardent indignations, wherby he that is of greatest power shuld be moued to enter into another mans cuntries, & endommage his neighbours. And that therfore he did hope to obtaine at the hands of Amurath this desited peace, if hee had no other cause wherwith he did find himselfe agreeued, as in trouth there was not, no nor euer was there any such thought towards him. Wherefore he besought him, that he woulde conueigh him with trustie guides to Amurath, to the end, that, if it were possible, they might not suffer these bloudy warres to goe forwards, at the report whereof, the most remote Nations of the East, yea and of all the whole worlde did reioyce, and stood wayting attentiuely to see what would be the issue of them.

Sinan entertained the Embassadour after the best maner, that the rudenesse of his nature woulde permit him: and thinking with himselfe, that not onelie the losses and disaduantage of the Persian king, but also the very fame of his valour in matters of warre, had wrought in the mindes of his enemies this resolution, to come and demaund peace (which he procured afterwards) he determined to pleasure the Embassador in the request which hee made vnto him for the conueighing of him to the Court: and accompanying him with a sure conuoy to send him to Constantinople: And wrote to Amurath in his letters all that which (hee thought) was fit to be demanded, representing vnto him what great and important matters (he hoped) might now be obtained, and raising in him woonderfull expectation of all happie successe, rather than motioning vnto him any feare or suspition of any vaine treatie. But before he dismissed the saide Embassador, he thought it good to aduise him, not to go to Amurath without resolution to offer him some great good conditions, and to yeeld vnto him all those landes and all that countrey, which he with the valour of his Subiectes and with Armes had conquered, by ouercomming the forces of his enemies, by passing through the most hard and difficult waies, by climing the rough and craggierockes, by vvading ouer the moste violent riuers, that are in all Media and Iberia: For hee knewe the minde of Amurath verie vvell, that hee vvas resolued in himselfe, not to yeeld so much as one hande breadth of that grounde which his subiects had valiantlie and worthyly won with the sword.

This demaund did greatly trouble Maxut-Chan, so that he began to fancie within himself, that he should not be able to conclude any thing, and (if the said Embassadors son did not tell vs a lie, who diuers times did moste familiarly discourse with vs vpon euery particularitie, whiles we visited him in Aleppo) he was in a peraduenture to returne into Persia againe, and not to passe ouer to Constantinople. Notwithstanding considering better with himselfe what belonged to his dutie, and doubting that this protestation might bee but an ambitious demand of Sinan himselfe, and hoping to r eceaue more reasonable

Sinan receiueth the Embassador.

Admonitiõs of Sinan to Maxut-chan the Embassador.

Maxut-chan feareth that he shal not conclude any thing.

conditions of peace from the mouth of the Turkish king and also to the end his own king might be the better certified, that he had not fayled fully to perfourme his duty in so waighty a businesse, he gaue large words to Sinan, and made him beleeue that he had order and authority from Mahamat (his Lord) to conclude, what hee thought best and most conuenient, for the matter of peace. And so the Embassador departed, with a safe companie from Sinas, and keeping on the way of Caisar, leauing both Conia and Angori, he arriued at Isnic (in old time called Nicea) a city situate neere vnto the Moore, anciently called Ascania, and from thence came to Scutar, passing ouer that litle gulfe which ioyneth those two seas together, and so was conducted to Constantinople.

Maxut-chan the Embassador come to Constantinople.

In the meane time the Persian King withdrew himselfe out of Casbin, and vpon the rumour of the Turkish nouelries meant also himselfe to giue out a noyse of some important matters which he likewise intended. Whereupon by his Royall commandement he called all the Chans, Gouernouts of his Subiect Cities, together with all their military forces to Tauris, and he himself with the Prince Emirhamze passed into Sultania, and hauing there visited certaine of his Ancestors sepulchers, hee went to Zanga, from thence to Miana, and then leauing Giurgi Chalassi on his left hand, and Ardoutl on his right hand, he came to the place called Turcoman, from whence afterwards in foure dayes space hee arriued at Tauris. There he assembled together all his people, which came running in most obediently at his commandement, and there also had many consultations what he were best to do, For as yet he did not assuredly know, what Sinan meant to attempt, and therefore beganne to cast in his head diuers doubts, but all vncertaine, and as it were in the dark: but yet in the end, among a thousand ambiguities, hee resolued with himselfe to send souldiers into Georgia towards the coaste of Teflis, where it was of necessitie that succours should be sent to those of the Fort: and withall determined also himselfe to goe foorth with all his Armie from Tauris to Caracach, a place very commodious and neere to guarde both Tauris and Siruan, being situate euen in the middest betweene the one and the other, and there to expect theremouing of Sinan: whose ambitious nature the king knowing, did think it would fall out, that to surmount Mustaffa in glorie, he would haue enterprised to run euen vpon Tauris, and to attempt some strange matter in those quarters. And so resting in this determination hee caused sufficient prouision to be made of corne, and of al other things needfull for the nourishment of cattell and men.

The Persian king stirreth and maketh famous preparations.

The Persian King at Tauris. The assembly of the Persian souldiers. The consultations of the Persian king.

Prouision of necessaries.

The Turcomā Nation followeth the Armie of the Persian King.

Among all the rest, that followed the kings Armie, a good company of the Turcoman Nation came vnto him also this yeare: so that the Persian hoast was verie great and sufficient, and able to attempt any famous enterprise. But when it came to the poynt, that he shuld send some of his Captaines into Georgia, he meant not to make choyce of any other for that purpose, but only of those, which by reason of their experience in those cuntries, and neare neighbourhood to the Georgiani, both could and by dutie were bound the rather to aide their neighbours, and endommage their enemies. And yet he made choice of Tocomac, and the rest, that hetherto in this warre had fought those battels, which before wee haue described, and comaunded them, that gathering their people together, they should depart into Georgia, and there ioyning themselues with Simon they shoulde worke the greatest annoyance to the Turkish armie that possible they could not fayling continually to aduertise him of their successes, and of the Turkes purposes: of whom if they shoulde learne either by the report of spies, or by any other means, that they would passe to Tauris, they shuld not sayle to pursue them, to the end they might ioyne together with him, and so encounter their enemies Armie. All these Captaines were most resolute men and most perfect in all militarie exercises, and being warned by the captiuity of Alyculi-Chan, they walked much more circumspectly & with the greater aduisement, but yet ful of a thousand desires to attēpt some great matter. They led with them about ten thousand persons, which being, ioyned with the people of Georgia, amouunted to the number of thirteene thousand: who presently assoone as they vnderstood of Sinans arriuall at Erzirum, put themselues on their way towards Teflis. And to the end the Turkes should not heare any newes of them, they kept that way, which as yet was not discouered by the enemies, sauing only by the Tartarian spoylers and robbers, and that was the way of Genge, which is situate in a certaine Champayne, wherein there are neither Cities nor townes, but such as were either their friendes, or their subiectes, or their confederates, neither are ther either any trecherous or rebellious people between it and Tauris. And thus the Persians being arriued at Genge, sent word thereof to Simon, giuing him withal to vnderstande, that as soon as he perceaueth the Turkes to be remooued from Chars, he must sende them a watch word, for that they were ready to performe great matters in his behalfe, & keeping on the way of Grin, they wold come and ioyn thēselues with him, and so being vnited together, they wold cause the Turks to feel the disturbances and annoyances which were prepared for them.

But nowe was the Persian Embassador incountred and receaued in Constantinople with al due kind of honour, and after certain dayes brought into do his embassage: wherin (as I vnderstood by many credible persons whiles I was in Constantinople, & afterward it was confirmed in Aleppo by the said Embassadors son, when rebelling against his king, and entertained by the Turke, he was placed in the gouernment of the said City of Aleppo) among other things,

Tocomac selected to go with an army into Georgia.

13000. Persiand Georgians

The situation of the citie of Genge.

The Persians at Genge aduertise Simon what he should do.

The Persian Embassador brought before King Amurath.

The speech of the Embassador.

whereupon he did most eloquently discourse with the king, hee framed his speech in such sort, that it was sufficient to disswade and withdraw him from this war, deliuering vnto him all those reasons, that might haue relation thereunto, and telling him, that his King Mahamet, who had but lately succeeded with great glorie in the happie kingdome of Persia, was alwayes greatlie grieued at these troubles of the wars, which if he thought hee coulde pacifie with the shedding of his blood and the spending of his life, he would not haue spared either the one or the other, and would also most willinglie haue tryed all the remedies for it, that possibly he could. For he did at the first consider with himselfe howe contrarie it was to the mercifull nature of their common Prophete Mahamet to nourish contention & much more to cause the publike spilling of the blood of his nations. Secondly he did manifestly perceiue, how inconuenient a thing it was, that warre should succeed so suddenly vpon a peace, which was so royally and with so many sworre Capitulations concluded betweene Tamas and Soliman: after which peace Armes should neuer haue bene raised, but vpon some great quarrell and offence that should be offered. For certain it was, that the soule of him, who in his lyfe time was so readie and willing to sweare to peace and amity, was nowe for the violating and breach thereof much grieued and offended in that happy life (he might better haue saide in Hell) and was now also accused for the same before God by the elect soules of Persia. And yet at his first comming to the kingdome his Maiestie might well perceaue, how greatly Persia reioyced at his happinesse, hauing made publike declaration thereof, by sending vnto him an Embassage to that purpose by Sultan Tocomac, whereby hee might manifestly perceiue the good mind, and the maintenance of good faith and peace, on the behalfe of the Persian kings. And although in the shorte time of the raigne of ambitious Ismahell there was some rumour raised, that he meant to go into Babylonia, and some such like newes: yet it was but a youthly part, and an effect of that heat, which is commonly proper to such persons, as being kept a long while in strait prison, cannot vse their liberty with moderate termes, and as they ought, and therefore he had receiued due punishment for it by his sudden and vnexpected death. But the king that now is, aboue all other embraced amitie with his Maiesty, and did earnestly desire not only, that he might not make war against him, but also that he might find fauour to bee linked in friendship and loue with him, and so they two together might prosecute the noble and worthy enterprises against the Christian Nations: which warre could not be but iust and honest, for that it tended to the inlargement of their natiue religion, and to the suppression of the enemies & rebels to their own Prophet Mahamet. And that therefore his Maiesty would be pleased to temper and quench his anger conceaued, which had incensed him to take Armes against a king that was so friendly to him: and not to disturbe the peace of so many cities, that were nere vnto him not only in situation but also in religion, and more kind vnto him, then all the rest of the Nations in the world.

The King dismissed the Embassador without any other resolution at al: but only gaue order; that whatsoeuer he had to discourse touching this peace, he shoulde communicate it with his Visier. Many were the courses and discourses that happened in this businesse: for that the Turke required all those Cities and Countries, which till that time hee had conquered with the sword: and the Embassadour on the otherside had no warrant from his king to yeeld any more than was contained within Georgia, on this side the riuer Araxis, which hath beene so often mentioned heeretofore. Whereupon the said Ambassador coulde not but remaine in great feare, least he should be suspected for a spie, and so be ill entreated: where withall he did finde himselfe too manifestlie charged by the speech that the Visier vsed towardes him. But hauing no further warrant, than is abouesaid, hee knewe not wherupon to resolue himselfe, or how he might remedie the euident danger of imprisonment or of some other smister accident, and so finde meanes to be licensed to returne. In the end, when he perceiued himselfe straitned to the grant of these demands, receiuing also some threatnings withall, hee determined with himselfe to enlarge his speaches with the Visier in diuers & sundry particularities, and to giue him good hope, that he should be able to perswade with his king Mahamet, the yelding vp of so much as Amurath had & did demand. And the rather to make the Turks beleeue that he should obtain the same, they say, that he discoursed with Mustaffa and the other Visiers vpon the late stirs, by occasiō wherof the Persiā king was called to Heri, about the foresaid suspition, raised against Abas Mirize his son: and withall declared vnto the Turks, with what facilitie, vpon his return into Persia, he would acquaint the king with this demand, and so induce him to be contented with it: But whatsoeuer was then concluded betwixte them, (for in this point Maxut-Chan himself did alwayes forbeare to tell the trueth either to me, or to any other, with whom he was familiar. And it is a very dangerous matter for an Historiographer to write diffusedly and at random of matters so secrete, for that in such extrauagations he may easily slip into a lie: the greatest monster & absurdity, that can be in one that writeth an historie) certaine it is, that Maxut-Chan was friendly and without any outrage sent from Con stantinople to Chars, where Sinan was then with his army, & commission was giuen to Sinan, that without delay, and with all fidelity he should cause the Persian to be accompanied to Van, and from thence into Persia, wheresoeuer

The order, which Amurath gaue touching the Persian Embassador.

The demands of the Turkish King, for the conclusion of a peace.

The resolution of Maxut-Chan with himselfe.

Maxut sent without any outrage to Chars.

the said Embassadour did especially desire: all which was vndoubtedly performed, as shall be set down in due place.

And now it is time to returne to Sinan, who from Siuai had sent the said Embassador to the Court, & being departed from thence, arriued at the last in Erzirum, wher he took a suruey of al his souldiers, of al his corne, of al his munition, and to be briefe, of all that which was necessarie for this expedition: & when the fit season was come, wherein all those preparations were brought to their ripenesse, he withdrew himselfe from Erzirum with al his Army, and keeping on the way to Hassan-Chalasi, hee went towardes Chars, from whence he had dispatched the Persian Embassador into Persia, as we haue told you, being verie sory and greatly discontented that no other conclusion could be wrought.

Sinan in Erzirum surueigheth all his people, & prouisions for warre.

At the last Maxut-Chan arriued in Persia before the King, to whom he reported al that which hapned in this his Embassage: the sum whereof was, that the Turkish king would not otherwise condiscend to any condition of peace, vnlesse there might be yeelded vnto him al the whole cuntry of Siruan, euen as far as Demir-Capi inclusiuely, presuming that all that country belonged vnto him, which he had already gotten and conquered by his famous battels. Neither did olde Maxut forbeare to tell him, that being growne into greate suspition with the Turkish King, that he was come thither rather to spie how matters went, than to treat vppon any agreement of peace, and not knowing by what other means to auoid the manifest danger of imprisonment or death, but only by large offers & promises, he was faine to giue Amurath to vnderstand, that he was able to obtain of his Lord & master asmuch as Amurath demanded; but yet for all that, it now lay in his Maiesties power, either to cause the said conclusiō to be performed or not. The king for the present time remained very well satisfied with that which Maxut had done, & willed it shuld be signified vnto him, that he shuld require some reward of his trauell and trouble, for he was minded to requite him for it. Maxut requested nothing in particular, but referred all to the liberality and bounty of his king, who presentlie and without any delay bestowed vpon him the gouernement of a certaine small place nere vnto Reuan, which notwithstanding, with the Kings fauour hee refused, desiring some greater rewarde, that might make him recompence for his greate expences Wherein it pleased the King to fauour him, and gaue vnto him the charge of the chamber of Tauris, naming him the Chamberlaine, or as the Turkes call it, the Defterdar of that rich and large Citie.

Maxut-Chan telleth the K. what he had done.

The Persian king seemeth contented with the trauel of Maxut, and meaneth to reward him.

Maxut-chan made Chamberlaine of Tauris by the kings grant

But because one Emir-Chan, an ancient enemy and persecutor of Maxut-Chan, sate in Tauris as chiefe Gouernour, (whom the Persians call Chan, and the Turkes Bassa) he was not wel pleased with this new office, though verie honourable and of good importance, and yet without the displeasure and anger of his king he could not refuse it: wherof not withstanding he perceaued he could haue but small ioy, in respect that he could not endure the neighbourhead of Emir-Chan, from whom hee greatly feared some pernicious treacherie. And therefore he resolued with himselfe to forsake Tauris, and to leaue a Vicegerent, there in his steed, and to withdraw himselfe to certaine lands of his own, about two small dayes iourney distant from Salmas towardes Tauris, (the village or country, tearme it whether ye will, is called Cassangich, a pleasant and delightful place, and the ancient inheritance of Maxut-Chan) and there he meant to passe away the time, till it came into the Kings mind to dispose otherwise of him, as he should thinke good. But Emir-Chan, who still nourished the antike poyson of his anger and hatred against him, being not able to omit this occasion, which he thought to be most fit to bring him into disgrace with the king, caused the king to vnderstand, that Maxut was not contented most impudently to refuse the first office bestowed vpon him, but nowe also in contempt of his guifts & rewards, he had abandoned Tauris, & substituted in his place a most vile person, to represent the kinges Maiesty, and to manage his treasure: and that he himself remained absent, far from that citie & the Court there; hauing withdrawne himself into the confines of Turky, no doubt for some mischieuous intent, either to yeeld himselfe vnto them, or els to haue intelligence with them touching this war, & peradventure he was guilty to himself, that he could not commit a greater error, thē he had alredy cōmitted, by offring Siruan to the Turkish king, & making promise of so large conditions. For the Emperor Ottoman might well make as importune & vnreasonable demands as he thoght good, & might alwaies well hope to obtaine al good conditions of peace, but Maxut-Chan hauing done al this to rid himself out of the Turks hands; and hauing had such a safe and sure conuoy to guide him, it could be no otherwise but that he had discouered himselfe to be very familiar & partial on the Turks side, & a rebel to his own king. And that therfore it wer good to make trial of his inclination, & so peraduenture auoyd som great change, tending to the losse and dommage of Persia.

Maxut-Chan forsaketh Tauris, and withdraweth himselfe to Cassangich.

Emir-Chan accuseth Maxut-chan

Very grieuously did the king take this refusal, that Maxut had made of these his rewards, & this his retire to Cassangich did put in his head a shadowe of that suspicion which Emir-Chan had motioned vnto him, & withal weighing in himself the foresaid reasons & considerations of Emir-Chan, he was the more confirmed in his hard conceit against Maxut, and in the end was perswaded to cal him before himself, & (if he could not by any other means, then) by torments and torture to vnderstand the trueth of matters how they went. And therfore he

King Mahamet displeased with Maxut-chan.

The king appointed Emir-Chan to bring Maxut-chan to him.

commanded Emir-Chan, that secretly he should send for him, & bring him before him Exceeding great was the ioy of Emir-Chan, when he sawe that the king did not only go about vpon his request to punish his enemy, but also that it was to be done by his own hands: & therupon he thought long til he had brought this shame vpon Maxut-Chan, who hauing already heard some inklings and priuie whisperings of that which Emir-Chan intended, had vtterly resolued with himself to do any thing, rather than he wold suffer himselfe to be deliuered into the kings hands. And therfore when there came vnto him frō Emir-Chan, xv. sellowes for that purpose, who in the kings name summoned him to the court, without making any shewe that he tooke the matter otherwise then wel, he entertained thē curteously, & made them great cheare, bestowing vpon them both words and meates most bountefully.

The seruants of Emir-chan let down into a wel by Maxut-chan, and there couered.

But they being ouercome with sleepe, which crept vpon them by reason of the good chear, which they took more liberally then they shuld haue done, were straitly bound, & with long cords hanged & let down into a deep wel, & there shut vp & secretly couered. And he himself, presently gathering together the most precious things that he had in his house, his gold, his siluer, his iewels, and his richest apparel, and setting his wiues, his daughters, his sons, his brethren & his Neuewes on horsback, & to be short, remoouing with him al his family, in the euening (for the day was not yet shut in) he put himself on the way towards Salmas, where the next day he arriued in very good time, and was there friendly entertained by the Turkish Bassa, & from him conueighed to Van, where he was also curteously welcommed by Bassa Cicala, and afterwards with an honorable cōpany of men, & large fauors of letters he was set on his way towards Erzirum to Generall Sinan: who being very glad of his comming; wrote by him to Amurath, and so sent him vnto him with al diligence. And this was in effect the end of this first enterparlance of peace.

Maxut-chan flieth out of Persia, and goeth to the Turks. Maxut-chan at Salmas. Maxut-chan at Van.

What after wards became of Maxut-Chan, vpon his arriual at Constantinople, it shal be declared in due time and place, for that it is now requisit to return, where we left, to speak of Sinan, who (as we told you before) by the way of Hassan-Chalasi was come to Chars, and had dispatched away Maxut-Chan, who was sent vnto him from the king into Persia.

Maxut at Constantinople.

The end of the fourth Booke.

The Fifth Booke

The Argument.

Sinan stayeth eight daies at Chars, and departeth for Teflis.

Talogli and Homar are assaulted by Simon, by whom they are discomfited and Homar is slaine.

Sinan succoureth Teflis.

The Georgians and the Persians expect the Turkes to assault them.

They assault be Turks and discomfit them.

Sinan with all his Campe goeth against the Persians, who doe vtrerly refuse to […]oine battel with him.

Sinan goeth to Chielder, and mustreth his Armie.

He is mocked of his souldiers.

Sinan returneth to Chars where he stayeth a moneth, and then returneth to Erzirum: and so is called to Constantinople.

Ebrain-chan the new Embassador of Persia commeth to Sinan.

The Ambassador at Constatinople with Sinan.

Solenine feasts for the circumcision of the Ottoman Prince.

Ebrain-Chan is sent prisoner to Erzirum.

Amurath committeth the succors for Teflis to Mahamet the Bassa, who with twenty fiue thousand persons departeth in the latter ende of August from Erzirum.

Mustaffa the Georgian ioyneth with Mahamet at Archelech.

The Georgians and the Persians send to defie the Turkes, and to bid them to battell

Mahamet the Bassa refuseth the Battell.

The Turkes passe ouer the riuer, and are assaulted by their enemies, and shamefullie discomsited.

The Turkes being so discomfited, retire themselues to Teflis.

Mahamet the Bassa maketh a publike oration to his souldiers at Teflis.

Mahamet leauieth a taske among his souldiers and so departeth.

A disorder in the departure among the Curdi.

At Altunchala a counterfeit Counsel-house called to betray Mustaffa, who woundeth the Lieutenant of Mahamet, the Bassa of Caraemit, and Mamet himselfe.

Amurah being angry at these misfortunes; reproueth the Bassas of his court for their improuidence and follie and particularlie findeth himselfe grieued with Sinan, who maketh a proud and an arrogant answer to the king: Whereupon he is banished from the Court, and Sciaus the Bassa, sonne in law to the King is chosen chiefe Visier in the roome of Sinan.

Sinan at Chars 8. daies.

Sinan remayned at Chars eight dayes, during which time, hee surueighed againe all his souldiers, & al his corn, & thē set himself on his way towards Tomanis, with resolution there to build a Fort, as I told you before. He passed by Archelech, and left behind him Peruana Giol & Triala, and in the end arriued at Tomanis; where, a litle before he came thither, was arriued also the Capigilarchechaiasi from the Court, bringing with him the seal and the writ, wherby the king had named him to be chiefe Visier. For which good newes all the Bassas in the army shewed great signes of reioycing.

Sinan receiueth newes that he is chosen chiefe Visier by the King.

Great raine at Tomanis.

At Tomanis he consulted with al his chief Bassas, touching his designment for the Fort that was to be made, and euery one of them deliuered diuers Models of it: but none of them all could be put in execution, by reason of the raine, which fel so largely, so aboundantly, and so continually, that the souldiers had neither leasure nor meanes to employ themselues in that work, and especially because Sinan did greatly fear, that the enemy taking the oportunity of this rain, of the strait, and of the building, might peraduenture assault the armie, and finding it out of order & in ill plight, might greatlie endommage it. This raine continued falling for the space of eight daies, in all which time neither did beame of the Sun break out, nor the skie cleare: Howbeit waxing at the last somewhat lightsome, Sinan determined to remooue from thence, and to cary onwards his succours to Teflis.

Talogli and Homar goe out to fetch in corne and cattell,

Assoone as the Army was raised, and presently after they had passed the strait of Tomanis, Talogli the Aga or Captaine of the Ianizzaries of Damasco, and Homar the Sangiacco or Lord of Saffetto, who had alwaies hetherto kept company together in the Army, because they were neighbors, whiles they dwelt at Saffetto and Damasco, had now also determined to go togither to seeke their fortune. For they had receiued priuie intelligence, that hard by a little out of the way there was good store of corne and cattel, and thereupon they resolued to fetch in that booty. And so gathering together a company of souldiers, to the nūber of two thousand, who were all very desirous of some refreshing, because they were insome necessity for corne, they went out for this pray. But Simon-Chan, who hauing aduertised the Persians of the departure of Sinan from Chars, and ioyned himself vnto them, had withdrawne himselfe to follow the Army a far off, and had diuided his souldiers into such places, where there was either corne, or water, or any such like thing, that might allure the Turkes to scatter themselues from the Campe: Assoon as he was aware of them, that they had carelesly run out to lay hold on this desired booty, being accompanied with his owne people, & a fewe other Persians, he fel vpon thē, & hewed thē al to peeces, scarle leauing the Aga of the Ianizzaries any leasure to fly, who being ayded by the swiftnes of his horse (or whether hee were in the front marching before al the rest, I know not) put himselfe to flight, and so scaped with his life. In so much as the Sangiacco aboue named and all the rest were there slaine, and in brief there escaped nor one, but only the foresaid Aga.

Sinan pursued on his iourney, & in the space of two daies came to Teflis, where presently he gathered together all the chief of his Army, & calling also into the Diuano the Capilarchevaiasi, he began to take order, that euery man vpon his oath should depose the truth, touching the greatnes of that cuntry. And all this was, but onely to make it euidently appeare, that the information which Mustaffa had giuen to the king, that Teflis was a citie lik to Damasco, was vtterly vntrue, for that Teflis was but a small peece of ground, containing but a few houses, and few inhabitants in them, and not only vnequal to Damasco, but also vnworthy in any sort to be compared vnto it, for that it did far surpasse Teflis in all things, aswel for riches and bignes, as for multitude of people. At the same time also he distributed his treasure, and the succors which he brought, among the souldiers of the sort, comforting them with good speeches, & with lustie & liuely promises of great matters. And foramuch as all the souldiers there made great complaints against the Bassa, that was their Captain in the fortresse, Sinan caused an information, or (as the Turks cal it) a Teflis to be framed against him, & hauing found him guilty that he had conuerted the souldiers pay to his own vse, he condemned him in restitution thereof, and discharging him immediatly frō his office, he did substitute in his place Giusuf Bey, one of the Georgian Lordes, who for the ancient enmity between him and Simon had yeelded him self to the Turks, & was by them so welcommed, that Sinan trusted him with the oustody of that fort, which with so many dangers had bene maintained and defended till that day.

When this was done, Sinan departed frō thence with al his army, & while he was vpon his departure ther arriued Embassadors from

The preparation of Sinan

Simon assaulteth Talogli and Homar.

Homar the Sangiacco slaine, and all his people discomfited.

Sinan enquireth of the greatnes of Teflis, to the reproch of Mustaffa.

Sinan succoureth the Fort at Teflis.

Guisuf Bey, the Runegat put in trust with the keeping of Teflis fort.

Leuentogli lord of Zaghen (of whom we haue oftentimes made mentiō before) who wer very wel welcom to Sinan, especially for that aswel by their relation, as also by the testimony of the souldiers of Teflis thēselues, he had bin certified how much good Leuentogli had done vnto thē, by sending to the fort vittails, money, & whatsoeuer els he had that might be commodious for them in that their continual necessity, Which in trueth was so great, that it was an occasion of spreaidng abroad a general fame, whereby it was reported, that the said Fort was yeelded by the Turks to the Georgiani, yea and the rumor of it passed euen into Italy. But it was all false: For notwithstanding so great penurie of all things, and so great a siege, yet was the Fort still maintained and held in the possession of those fortunate people: Which was afterwardes the matter and occasion of continuing those motions and mutations, which after fell out so commodious to the state of Christendom. The Embassadors excused their Lord, for not comming himselfe in person, to do reuerence to Sinan, for that his sicknesse and certen other priuat respects did hinder him from doing that, which hee both desired, and also ought to haue done. All which was most acceptable to Sinan, who in sign therof caused the Embassadors of Leuentogli, to be apparelled in cloth of gold, and sent vnto himself a battel-axe and sword all gilt and set with iewels, promising vnto him great matters, and with gallant words declaring vnto him his exceeding affection of loue & confederacie with him. Yea and some say, that Sinan sent letters to Alesiandro himself, wherein he made a motion vnto him for some treaty of peace, telling him, that hee being a friend both to the Turks and to the Persians, ought to trie al the means he could to pacifie these troubles, and to reconcile the minds of the two kings. But in truth what was done in so secrete a matter, I could neuer yet learne any certenty to write: and therfore without any further speach of it, wee wil prosecute the progresse of Sinans armie.

 The day following, Sinan & his army passed the strait of Tomanis, & then came before him Mutafsade Bassa, borne in Aleppo, & now gouernor of the same city (whō I had often-times in cure) declaring vnto him, that not far frō them ther was great store of corne & cattell, and no body to keepe the same, but only a few Georgiās, & therfore it wold be wel if he would send for the saide praie, whereof (yea though it had beene much greater,) his Armie stood in such need. Sinan did carrie a good affection to Mutafsade, and therefore was easely induced to send for the bootie: but because he was in some feare, that if he shoulde not send out a good Company of Souldiers for it, there might haue happened to his vittailers some accustomed mishap, & being principally mooued with the fresh remembrance of the sinister accident that lighted vpon Talogli and Homar, he gaue order, that to fetch in

Ambassadors from Leuentogli to Sinā

The rumour prooued false that Teflis was yeelded.

Sinan honoreth the Embassadors.

Mutafsade to General Sinā.

Sinan appointeth 10000. souldiers to goe with Mutafsade.

this Corne and Cattel there should goe out ten thousand horsemen and their seruants: among whom was also the said Mutafsade, as Captaine of them all.

Now Tocomac, Simon, and other Persian Captaines had gathered themselues together, & stood waiting & watching, when any band of the Turkish Souldiers should come down for these reliefes of Corne, & hiding themselues in certaine treacherous valleis neere vnto them, expected occasion, wherein they might make some notable discouery of themselues. Whereupon the foresaide Souldiers beeing come, according to the appointment of Sinan, to fetch away these vitailes, and beeing arriued at the place where they were, they beganne to load their beastes withall: and whiles they were most delighted with the sweetnes of their pray, and had nowe charged almost all their Mules and horses with that which it most pleased euerie man to choose, the hidden Persians, all on a sodaine, issued out of their treacherous valley and entred among them. But Mutafsade, as soone as he discouered the Persians in so great number, & in so good time to come vpon thē, foreseeing the vniuersall slaughter of all his people, was the first man that fled, and with an vnhappie signe of ill lucke, he left the rest, that either woulde not, or coulde not saue themselues by flight, to the furie of their enemies: who pursuing their desired victorye, hewed in peeces seauen thousand of them, and some they carried away aliue, leading with them their Mules and horses laden with their stolen bootie, Mutafsade was the first that broughtto Sinan the vnhappie newes of the Persians treacherie, and after him the slaughter that followed, was also reported vnto him by the fugitiues that escaped by flight. And thereupon Sinan dispatched away the Bassa of Caramania, and a great band of Souldiers with him, with commandement that in what place soeuer, and in what sorte soeuer he found them, hee shoulde ioyne battel with them. And these squadrons of fore-runners being gone afore, he him selfe presently, raising all his campe, withal speed followed the said Bassa of Caramania. But neither the one nor the other ariued in time, for the Persians immediately after the foresaide victory, without any staying, hauing recouered their pray, had withdrawen themselues betweene the Mountaines into certaine secure places, which were knowen onely to such, as by daily experience had perfectlie learned the diverse & difficult passages of Georgia. The army of Sinan marched on for the space of some miles, till they ascended a certaine hill from whence they discouered the Persians, who hauing disposed of their pray in the places before named: were now returned to pursue the army & to watch some fresh occasioni of new battell. As soone as the Persians deserued the whole army, they were afraid to meere with them, yea and feared also leaste Sinan would descende from the hill, and so assault

The Georgiās & the Persians watch for the Turkes, to set vpon them.

The Persians set vpon the Turkes.

Mutafsade flieth first of al.

7000. Turkes hewen in peeces. Mutafsade bringeth newes to Sinā of the discomfiture.

Sinan with all his Campe remoueth to set vpon the Persians.

The Persians refuse to ioine battel, & retire to their safe places.

them to their exceeding great losse. For they did well remember, what dangers and losses Mustaffa had prociued vnto them whē they too boldly & carelessely had suffered themselues to be induced to carry for him, with so great a multitude & so many fires, in the Champaines of Chieldern: & therefore they tooke a better course for their owne security, and so resolued to returne backe into their strong places within the mountaine. And yet they could not be so quick in this their retire, dont that the Turkes who following Sinan were now descended to pursue them, ouertooke some fewe of them, & destroyed about fifty or threescore of thē whose heads in signe of triumph they carried a good part of their way vpon the point of their speares: and aliue they tooke not in all aboue threescore and ten.

trecheries Sinan beeing at Triala with al his army, vnderstādeth that the King of Persia with a very great army is comming against him.

At the last Sinan with all his hoast passed these of his enemies, & came to Triala, where he vnderstood by diuers inhabitants of those villages, that of sundry Persians & Georgiās also which had trauelled that way, they had secretly learned, how the king of Persia, in his owne person, with an exceeding great army being departed out of Tauris, was comming to meete the Turkish hoast, & to bidde it battel: & that his purpose was, that the 4 captaines which were cōbined together with Simon, keeping on their way towards Georgia, should set vpō the hinder part of the Turkish army, & at the very same instant, hee himselfe with his forces would set vpō the forefront. At this news he made pre-

Sinan proclameth, that all his army should make ready to go to Tauris.

sent proclamatiō through al his army, that al the heauy cariages, & such as were vnprofitable for battel should be sent before towards Ardachan, & that euery mā should put himselfe in order & readines with armor & munition for the viage to Tauris, whither he himselfe meant to go & to meete with the king his enemy. In the meane while

A general coniecture.

(as it is reported by many aswel Persiās as Turks.) he dispatched certen Volachi or posts to the Persian king being at Caracach to intreat him, that he wuld send ouer some Ambassador, for a peac, thinking with himself (as some doe conicture) by these meanes he should remoue out of the Kings mind, his resolution to come & assaile him, if any such meaning hee had. The proclamation was put in execution according

Sinan with his army in the plaines of Chielder.

to his appointment, and hauing sent away the saide cariages & heauy burdens towards Ardachan, he himselfe with certaine loads of corne & vittels, (so many onely as were sufficient for the voiage) descended into the open & large plaines of Chielder, where presently he mustred al his people that caried weapons, and gaue notice, that before he would settle himself towards Tauris, he meant to make triall of the readines & nimblenes of al his army, & to set forth such a shew, as though they

The order of the Army.

ioyned battel with their enemies: which presently the next morning without any further delay he put in execution accordingly. For first he set forward fiue hundred peeces of final artilery, placing thē in

THE FIFTH BOOKE 119

good order after the manner of a large trench, & after this shot, three rows of Ianizzaries, & behind them he tooke vp his own place. Then followed al the army which he parted into two great & wide wings, which after the fashion of a moone cōpassed about a great deale of ground entermingling also heere and there some footemen, with his horsemen, & some harcubuses among his darts & lances. Behind al the armie were placed al the cariages which were requisit for the vrgent necessity of vittaile, and behind the cariages went the Arrie rewarde conducted by two Bassaes with viii. thousandmen. The army being thus ordered and disposed, hee sent out some fewe Turkes, to shewe themselues vpon the top of certaine hilles, and as though they had bin enemies, that came to seize vpon his army, he presently caused al his artillery to be discharged, and commaunded euery man to skirmish, & to bestir himselfe, after the same manner and altogether with the same kinde of behauiour, as if their enemie were present before them. And so the tempest of the Harguebuzes being ouer passed, the launces or Indian canes discharged, & the exceeding thicke storme of arrowes ceased, there did shine round about on all sides, such a brightnes of swords, helmets, and brest-plates, yeelding forth great lightnings & as it were fierie beames, that it enkindled the mindes of them all to battel: and then againe the drums & trumpets made such a noise, the Ensignes, creasts, liueries, and deuises were so turned and tossed & the aire so replenished with seuerall colours of blewe and yellowe, & to be briefe there was such a medly of al things, as though it had been the turmoile of a very battel indeed. After a while he caused the retrait to bee sounded, and then setting all his army in order againe, there was such another like shewe commaunded the second time, and after that the third also: which indeede was performed rather with the scorne and derision of all his souldiers, who thought it to be as it were but children play, then that any commendation did indeed arise thereby to ambitious Sinan.

Sinan maketh three shewes with his army & exerciseth it with fighting & skirmishing

Sinan derided by his Souldiers.

When these counterfeit shewes of war were finished, yet did he not got forwards towards Tauris, as he had apointed, but remained eight daies in those plains of Chielder, at which time there ariued out of Persia Aider the Aga, as Ambassador from the King, who was entertained by the general with great ioy. Diuerse and sundry things did this Embassador propounde, which were likewise propounded by Maxut-Chan: but the conclusion of alwas, that the king of Persia would voluntarily relinquish Chars and Teflis, and remaine (as hee did before) in amitie with Amurath: and therefore hee desired Sinan that he would not faile to conclude of a peace because he himselfe had commandemēt to returne back into Persia, Sinan promised to deale with Amurath for this peace, if king Mahamet would send a new

The King of Persia offereth Chars vpon conditiō of peace.

Sinan promiseth to intreat a peace: & rerequireth a new embassador.	embassador to Constantinople. Vpon which cōclusion the said Aider returned into Persia, & being accompanied with sure guids ariued at Tauris before this king to whō he declared what things he had seene, & what promises he had receiued of Sinan, and withal exhorted the king to send a new embassador to the Turkish Court, causing him first to enter couenants with Sinan (as he had promised,) for so it would bee an easie matter to procure a good and speedie resolution. After this, when the publike rumor was found to be false, that was spread abroad of the comming of the Persian king, Sinan in steed of going to Tauris, resolued to goe to Chars & so to returne into his confederate Countries. At Chars he remained a whole month, in very meere and absolute idlenes, with the generall maruaile & murmur of his souldiers, who indeed were astonished, when they perceiued they were come out, not to fight, not to passe into their enemies Countrie, not to make any conquest by war, but to be Idle and to play, to the great dammage & expenses of their Kings Reuenues, and the disturbance of his whole kingdome.
Sinan returneth to Chars & there remaineth in Idlenesse a whole moneth. Sinan reproued by his souldiers.	
Sinan departeth from Chars to returne to Erzirum.	At the last he departed from Chars, for that it was now winter, & the frosts and snows round about thē wrought his souldiers vnaccustomed miseries. In Hassa-Chalassi they celebrated their most solemne feasts, and afterwarde with all his Army hee withdrew himselfe to Erzirum from whence he did presently [...]misse euery man to goe and winter in his own Country and he himselfe remained still in the said Citie.
Sinan sendeth aduertisement to the court, of al that had happened.	From this place he sent diligent information, aswel at the departure of the Capigilarohecaiasi, as also by certaine Volacchi dispatched away by post, of the succours that he left at Teflis, of the losses that he receiued by his enemies, of all that wherein he had found Mustaffa an arrant her, of the cōming of the Persian embassador, of the promise made vnto him touching a newe embassador, and to be short of al his whole actions. And besides all these Narrations, he aduertised the king that the enterprize of Persia was a very hard, long, and difficult matter, & such a one, as there needed another kind of preparation, then as yet was appointed for it, & that if Amunath did desire to subdue & ouercome Persia, it was then very necessary, that he should speake with him at large, & discourse vpon many particularities, which neither might he commit to paper, neither coulde they bee declared by pen, without exceeding great tediousnes: & in this point he did write very much, & shewed himselfe to be very petemptorie. And again, besids these first Velacahi, he dispatched also new messēgers, to be very instāt & importunate with Amurath for his returne to Constantinople, continually telling him, that it was not possible for him to signifie by writing, what he purposed to report vnto him by word of mouth, for the easie accomplishmēt of his cōmenced en terprize. Nothing in the
Sinan reporteth the enterprize of Persia to be very hard.	
Sinan maketh ernest request to goe to Cōstantinople.	

world did Sinā hate more thē this war: & for the appeasing thereof he did not omit to attēpt al possible meanes, hauing his mind altogether bēt against the affairs of the christians in Europe, & for yᵉ diuerting of these wars from the east into some other quarters, he vsed & practised continually a thousand deuises. At the last he wrought so much, be intreated so much, he writ so many letters, & solicited the matter so ernestly, that the king was persuaded to sēd for him to Constantinople assoon as euer he was certified of the ariual of the new embassador frō Persia, of whom Sinan had before aduertised him. For among the difficulties, which Sinan had propounded to Amurath, he was resolued vppon this conclusion that it woulde bee conuenient either to receiue the new embassador of Persia, if he came with honorable conditions, and so to grow to a peace, or if the embassador came not, or if after his cō ming they coulde not agree vppon the peace, then to put in execution those his conceits and designements, wherof he must needes in particular talke with him by word of mouth. The promised embassador, called Ebrain-Chan, a man of great eloquence, and in Persia esteemed to bee of great valour came to Sinan accordingly: whereof Sinan presently gaue intelligence to Amurath, beseeching him againe, that he would permit him to come to Constantinople.

Sinan obtained his desire, and hauing secretly sent forth of his Statiōs certaine succours to Teflis, which came vnto thē in very fit time, he went himself to the court where he attended the vniuersall gouernment of the whole empire. But at his first comming to the presence of the king, (wherein he neuer discoursed with him vpō any thing but onely of the comming of the Persian embassador) the conditions were established, which they had to require, for the reducing of the Capitulations of this peace to a good end. After which agreement the embassador being nowe come, & most magnificently receauet in Constantinople was brought in who with magnifical & glorious speeches endeuored to persuade Amurath, that his king had a most ardent desire to be reconciled and to ioine his forces with him, & that for this purpose hee was now specially come thither & withal, that if he also would answere him with the like mind, there would ensue thereof the greatest vnitie & friendship, that euer was betweene the Mahometans, since the time that their great Propher had deliuered to the world that wicked law of theirs. Amurath caused answere to be giuen him, that hee should talke with his Visier, and with him treat of al the matter touching the peace: & so he was by the king entertained & dismissed, both at one time.

In the meane time, the Turke had resolued to cal to Constantinople, his eldest sonne Mahamet, who was to succede him in the Empire, and to circumcise him according to the custome of the Barbarians, following

Sinan abhorreth the wars in Persia, and desireth that they were turned against the Christians.

Sinan called to Constantinople.

Ebrain-Chan the new Embassador of Persia commeth to Sinā.

Sinan goeth to Constantinople and sitteth in his place of vicier

Ebrain-Chan speaketh with the king & exhorteth him to peace.

The answere of Amurath to the embassador Ebrain-Chan.

Embassadors of diuers princes come to Constantinople. The Venetians send Giacomo-Soranzo to Constantinople.

therein the inueterate Lawe of the Hebrewes. And for this purpose from al the prouinces of Christendome, by messengers dispatched in poste, were the catholike Princes solemnely inuited to the feastes, that vpon this occasion were prepared. According to this their inuiting there came thither embassadors out of many countries of Europe with great giftes and presentes in token of peace and confederacie. And among the rest the Venetians sent thither one Giacomo Soranzo, who by the great satisfaction, which he made to the king & all those of his court, reuiued the amity and friendship, which flourished betweene the king and that Senate.

Feastes at the circumcision of Prince Ottoman.

In the great market place of Constantinople, which the Turkes call At Maidan, there were rounde about in all places erected certen high Scaffoldes: where the multitude should sit to behold the pleasant fight, of firewoorkes, of bankets, of musikes, of wrastlings, and of whatsoeuer else, was there to be shewed for the declaration of so greate a ioy. The king himselfe was present at the said triumphs in a certen Palace, (situate in the most open place of all that large and broade streete,) where within a great lowpe or windowe alost, all closed about and couered aboue with plancks and boords, through the transparent holes & lattises therof, not being seene of any body, in the company of his wife, he discouered and beheld al thinges that were there performed. All the embassadors had their scaffolds prepared and furnished, & the Persian embassador had his so affold also seuer all to himselfe, but yet with a farre different intent & respect then the rest is for that the other embassadors were honored & regarded, as it was conuenient and agreeable to their degrees and estates, and receiued such entertainement as might he shewed at such a kind of Barbarons spectacles but the Persian, by reason of the scornes and iniuries done vnto him, did not onely not reioice at the saide feastes and triumphes, but also ministred himselfe great matter of laughter and sporte to the beholders. For among sundrie other wrongs and outrages, that by the commandement of. Amurath were done to the Persian nation by hauging vp certaine counterfect pictures of Persians made of lathes and stickes, and then burning them, and in many scornefull sortes abusing them: the king, for the great disdaine that he had taken against Ebrain-Chan, as one that not condescending to the conditions of peace which he expected, not yeelding any more then Maxut-Chan and Aidere Age had done before, seemed to haue come as a spie to marke the Turkish affaires, or to mocke King Amurath, rather then to put in execution any good matter, that he had to spacific the mindes of the two mightie princes commaunded that the said embassador, vnder sure and trustie

Ebrain-Chan sent prisoner to Erzirum.

custodie in should bee ledde prisoner to Erzirum, vntill further order were taken with him.

How be it Sinan for all this remained still in his office of Chief Visier, and attended the publike gouernement of the kingdome, without any intermission, vntill suche time, as those matters fell out, which in place conuenient shall be declared vnto you: for that now it is time to returne to Teflis and Chars where wee left, which two places without further succours must needes fall into the enemies hands. For Sinan being nowe gone to Constantinople, and the souldiers beeing besieged in Teflis, and hauing receiued none other reliefe, but onely that little, which in the beginning of the spring Sinan had secretly caused to be conueied vnto them; and which would scarce be sufficient for all that yeere, so that (it is to be thought) they were in verie great necessitie, there was no remedie, this other yeere, whiles Sinan remained at the court, but to send some new succors vnto thē, & the rather for that it was not possible to meet with so good an occasion to send them any help, as he found before his departure from Erzirum. In this greate necessitie therefore he did boldlie & freely counsel the king, to send a new garrison of souldiers to Van, to the end that no Persians shoulde passe on this side Van to endamage those countries: and next, that vnder the conduct of some fit Captaine he would send some succours to Teflis. Vpon which point the king asked Sinan his opinion, & willed him to be thinke himselfe of one, to whom this expedition might bee committed. Sinan propounded diuers and sundrie persons vnto him: but none of them pleased Amurath who was minded to bestowe this charge vppon Mahamet the Bassa, Nephew to Mustaffa Bassa, and in that respect enuied and hated by Sinan, whom, albeit hee told the king that he was not a fitte man for suche a seruice, yet woulde hee needes emploie him in this supplie, as it were in despite, and derision of the aduice, which Sinan gaue him. And therefore hee sente this Mahamet to Erzirum, with the title of the Bassa of that Prouince, displacing from thence Kesuan Bassa the Gouernor of that Region, and withal added thereunto the honor & dignitie of the Captaineship ouer the army for Teflis. Presently vpon this resolution commaundement was giuen to the Bassa of Caraemit, called Hassa the Eunuke, to Mustaffa sometime called by the name of Manucchiar the Georgian, who (as wee tolde you before) exchanged his Natiue religion with the Turkish superstition, to all the Sangiacchi, the Curdi, & al the souldiers of Erzirum, that reducing themselues vnder the Standerd of Mahamet Bassa, they shoulde followe him to Teflis, and obey him in all thinges that hee should command them. Whereupon there assembled together out of all the saide places about fiue and twentie thousand persons, and treasure sufficient was appointed for the reliefe of the Souldiers in the besieged fort, together with Corne and all other necessarie prouisions for them, so that euery thing was put in readines for this enterprize, in

Sinan aduiseth Amurath to send a garrison to Van: & succour to Teflis, vnder some good Captaine.

Amurath cōmitteth the succours of Teflis to Mahamet Bassa.

25000. men follow Mahamet Bassa to Teflis for succour thereof.

such large and liberall manner, that it might abundantly haue suffised. Commandement likewise was giuen to the Bassa of Aleppo, & to the Bassa of Maras, that with al their souldiers, which they had in pay, they should repaire to Van, and there abide till winter. These two Bassaes performed the Kings commandement, and were not disturbed nor molested in any sort by the enemy. Mahamet the Bassa also performed it likewise, together with all his Souldiers aboue named, but yet with a farre different and contrarie fortune for that there happened vnto him diuers grieuous & pernicious accidents, which made this enterprize vnfortunate and miserable, whereof it is now fit time to discourse in prosecuting the due course of our historie.

Mahamet Bassa the Generall departeth frō Erzirum.

In the end of August Mahamet the Bassa departed from Erzirum, with the Bassa of Caraemit, all the Sangiacchi, the Curdi, & all the souldiers subiect to his gouernement, carrying also with him money, corne, & all other necessarye munition. At the end of eight daies he arriued at Chars, & from thence passed to Archelech, being in the meane time neither assailed nor disturbed by any enemie. At Archelech he found Mustaffa Bassa, the Widowes Sonne, and al his souldiers belonging vnto him, who excusing himselfe with liuely reasons for that he came not to meete with him at Erzirum according to his duty, was most ioyfully entertained, & honored by Mahamet with Cloath of Golde, and Sworde and Target all guilte, and withall admonished to continue obedient and subiect to Amurath, not failing to conduct him with his garrison appointed for Teflis, and to choose that way, which he thought to be the shortest, the safest, and the most commodious for them: for that some were of opinion that it would be lesse danger to trauel by the way of Tomanis, & some other by the way of his country. Wherein after many discourses Mustaffa did readily resolue him, that the easiest and shortest way lay through his owne countrey, as being also the safest in his opinion. The counsell of Mustaffa pleased Mahamet greatly, who made choice of him to be the guide of his army, reposing himselfe wholly vpon his good aduise, and so they departed together from thence towards Teflis, passing through Altunchala & Carachala, both belonging now to the said Georgian, but in times past to the Widow his mother: abounding with all thinges necessary for the sustenance of man: neither were they euer disturbed by the enemies forces. From these quarters they went forward to a Castell called Gori, sometimes appertaining to the Georgiani, & gouerned by a brother of that Giusuf who had yeelded himselfe to the Turkes, but now by reason of that brothers death it is fallen into the hands of the Turks: from which place they discouered in certaine fieldes a great army of Georgians, mingled with Persians, but yet apparrelled after the manner of Georgia.

Mustaffa the Georgian commeth to Archelech to meet with Mahamet Bassa going for Teflis.

By the aduise of Mustaffa Generall Mahamet resolueth to goe to Teflis through the Widowes country.

THE FIFTH BOOKE

These were those Captains of Persia with Simon-Chan, so often mentioned heertofore: who were sent from the Persiā king, (as in diuerse yeers before they also were) to succor & aid the Georgian forces. For the king thought, that they were sufficient enough to performe that busines, vnderstanding, that the Turkes had sent no greater armie thither: and so by their good helpe there might peraduenture ensue a quiet end and pacification of al these troubles. And therfore staying himselfe in Tauris, hee had sent the aforenamed Captains into Georgia, who keeping on the way of Genge and of Grin had secretly conioyned themselues with Simon, and dissembled & counterfeited their apparel only because the meanes of peace should not bee disturbed, and their king accompted a falsifier of his faith, who vnder the vaile of a treaty vpon truce & amity, whiles Amurath attended nothing else but to succour and defend his conquered Countries, without any annoyance or disturbāce to any other places, went about to procure the slaughter and ouerthrow of the Turks. These then, assoon as they saw the Turkish army, & perceiued that they thēselues wer also descried by them, sent swift haraulds vnto thē to bid them battel, & with haughtie and iniurious words to defie them to fight. *The Persians counterfeit their apparrel, to the end the meanes of a peace should not be disturbed.*

Mahamet Bassa, who had no other desire, but onely to bring his succors safe to Teflis, receiued this defiance with great griefe of minde, and hauing dismissed the hearaulds, hee went about (in the best manner he could), to delay the execution of this their prouocatiō to battel. That euening hee was fauored in his purpose by very great & continuall raine, which couertly excused his delay & feare, euery man thinking that it proceeded rather vpon some reasonable & iust impediment then vpon his cowardise. But the next morning, when the sun shined bright vpon the face of the earth without any cloud at all, the Georgians & the Persians, hauing vnited themselues, & waxen more resolute then euer they were, drew neer to the Turkish armie, & followed it while it marched. And so both the armies kept in sight one of another, without any act at al or motion of war, vntil about fowre howrs & a halfe before night, at what time the Turks ariued neer to a riuer, that separated the one army frō the other. Mahamet and Mustaffa fell into consultation betweene themselues, whether they should passe ouer the riuer, before night, or else without any further trauel to stay on this side of the water vntill the next morning. Mustaffa the Georgian aduised him to stay and not to go ouer fearing lest they coulde not possibly bee so readie, & haue all their cōpanie together on the other side, so soone, but that their enemies would be first vpon them, & finding the camp in disarray & confusiō would greatly annoy them. Notwithstāding Mahamet disliked this aduise of Mustaffa, hauing taken a strong conceit, euen vpon the very first discouery of the enemy that there was

The Georgians and Persians defie the Turks to the fight.

Mahamet Bassa refuseth battell.

Mustaffa aduiseth not to passe the riuer

Mustaffa misliketh the Georgians aduise.

some intelligence & agreement between Mustaffa & the Persians, & that malitiously to that end he had perswaded him to come that way, & not by the way of Tomanis: & therfore Mahamet thinking if there were any deceit intended & plotted between Mustaffa & his enemies, to set it in some confusion and disturbance, would not in any case follow the counsell of the Georgian, to stay that night on this side of the riuer but commaunded that with all the greatest speede that might be all his souldiers with their Casenda and their Nosul, that is with their treasure and Corne should passe ouer, to the ende that before night they might lande on the other side of the water in some good place, to the scorne and derision of their enemies. The Checaia or the Lieutenant of Mahamet Bassa, a bolde young-man and a hardie, was the first that went ouer, and after him the carriages of money, and of corne, & then al the whole Armie with verie great speed; although some of the confused multitude were drowned in the waters, being rather ouer troden with the horses & camels, then brought to their deathes either by the swiftnes of the waters course, or by the depth of the Channel. For indeede neither the one nor the other could possiblie be the cause or occasion of this mischaunce.

Mahamet commandeth to passe the riuer presently.

Some drowned in the riuer.

Assone as the Georgiani perceiued, that the Turkes had passed the Riuer, without any staying til they might settle themselues in any good order, in great haste & furie they ran to encounter them, & presently assailed them, whiles they were all in a confusion and out of array, by meanes whereof the Turkes durst not almost sustaine their furious assault. And yet was there not in them such basenesse of courage, but that they turned their faces, and ioyned battel with thē, wherein within a verie short time you might see the bankes of the Riuer in manie places be sprinkled with the Turkish bloud, and many carcases of the Turkes here and there scattered, without any apparance at all of any losse among the Georgians and the Persians, that could be perceiued. Among those that fell in this slaughter, there were a number of Sangiacchi, Curdi, and certaine Mesopotamians: whereby it was manifestly discouered, that if the Turkish Squadrons had not vsed the greater valour, out of all question they had bene all miserablie destroied: with the rest of the Sangiacchi, Curdi, & Mesopotamians fearing and coniecturing by the ouerthrowe of their owne the losse also of the others, they turned their backes, and put themselues to flight: the like did the remnant also of Caraemit, and after them at the last all the whole Armie. And because the Georgians, foreseeing this their flight, had made a great wing, and turning themselues vpon their enemies on the lands side, had left them no passage to flie, but sought by al meanes to driue them backe againe into the Riuer, the fugitiue cowards could not choose, but euē in their flight receiue verye

Georgians & Persians set vpon Mahamet Bassa.

The Turkes discomfited by the Persiās & Georgians.

The Turkes flie from the battell.

great hurt intermingled with shame. Which notwithstanding some of thē desiring to auoyd, thought it lesse harme to cast themselues into the riuer, and so escape (though hardly) with their liues, or else with desperation to bee drowned in the waters. Great was their shame, great was their confusion, but greatest was their losse, for that in the heat of the battell, the Kings money and the Corne was taken in pray by the Georgians and Persians, euery man sauing (onely) somuch for himself, as he could secretely hide vpon his owne bodie, or conuey by the meanes of some trustie slaue, which by the helpe of their swift horses, was preserued rather by fortune then by valor. *The Turkes in their flight greatly damnified.*

In this maner were the Turks handled who being thus discomfited, and wounded, full of shame and dishonour, & spoyled of all their reliefe, the next morning gathered themselues together again, one with another cursing the heauens, their king, & their aduerse fortune, some of thē also threatning that Georgian rinegate, as though all this mischiefe had happened through his treachery & secrete intelligence with the enemie. Notwithstanding, when they founde that they had still remaning so much money, and other easements, as might suffice to comfort the afflicted mindes of the souldiers besieged in the forte, they re solued to goe onwardes to Teflis, & the day following they made so good speed in their iourney, that for all the difficulties of the waies, which trauellers do commonly find in those quarters, they ariued there in the euening. Greatly were all the souldiers of the fort astonied whē they saw the Turks, whom they had so long expected, ariued in such bad order & so il furnished, & were wonderfully grieued at this common losse: by reason where of they were all in a greate confusion and protested to Mahamet, that they would abandon the defence of that countrie, if they had not necessary prouision made for thē: yea their protestations were so vehemēt, & their mutinie so tumultuous, that therby was confirmed a certaine generall rumour which was alreadie raised vpon this vnfortunate battel, that Teflis was recouered by the Georgians, the reporte whereof came also into Italy, as a thing most certaine and true, and yet proued to be but a lie. Besides which losse of the foresaide souldiers and prouision, certaine other mischiefes were also like to ensue, which euery reasonable man woulde expecte vppon so happie and fortunate a successe but that they were met withal. For Mahamet after he had with large promises pacified & mitigated their first furies & insolences, presentlie in the morning he caused a Diuano to bee called within the castel, where hauing the multitude of the Sangiacchi, the Bassaes, the Zaini, the Spahini, & the Giannizzaries gathered together, he spake vnto them in this manner.

'Forasmuch as it hath pleased GOD, that so great and so important an occasion of victorie, which was offered vnto vs for the exaltation

The treasure and corne taken from the Turkes.

Mahamet Bassa being discomfited gathereth together his scattered souldiers.

The besieged souldiers in Teslis protest to Mahamet Bassa, that they will abādon the fort.

The oration of Mahamet Bassa in the Castel of Teflis.

and glorie of euerie one of us, is nowe fallen out so infortunately that 'it hath not onely not ministred vnto vs anye matter of triumphing ouer our enemies, as wee shoulde haue done, but rather it hath made them (I knowe not howe) to carrie away from vs both the triumph, and also our Armor, our Horses, our slaues, and our spoiles: yea and the remembrance wheof doth most grieuously trouble & afflict me,) our Sultans money, and our publike munition and sorces, solemnely deliuered to our conducte, is nowe become a bootye and pray vnto them: that the honour which might haue made euerie one of vs to bee famous among Noble and valourous Souldiers, is nowe fallen from our foreheades, and to our great detriment doth adorne the heades of Straungers, or rather of our enemies: And that notwithstanding all this, wee are nowe come to these couragious Souldiers, which with their great labour and valour haue defended this forte euen in the middest of their enemies weapons and treacheries, & to whom wee should yeeld that aide and reliefe, which the vertue of euery one of their minds doth deserue, & which king Amurath had put in our handes to bring hither vnto thē: there is now no remedie but to resolue vpon some good means that we fall not wholly into the vtter disgrace of our Lord & King, & that is to maintaine these souldiers in the custody & defence of this forte, & though it bee with all our own wants & al our own dishonors, to comfort these that haue so long time looked for vs, & so wel deserued all mā ner of reliefe. We cannot excuse our selues, that our enemies were better then we, either in number or instrumēts of warre: (for both in the one and the other we were farre beyond thē) neitheryet can, we say, that they set vpō vs by night, or at vnawares:) for when we saw their nūber, their weapons, their horses, and finally their approch, and their manner of assault, yet we would needes passe ouer the Riuer, and ioyne battell with them: which we nowe knowe hath fallen out verie lamentable to vs, because wee were more readie to take our flight then to endure the fight, & to vse our feete then to occupie our handes.) And therefore it is very requisite, aswel to satisfy the rigor of Iustice, as to performe the duetie of Souldiers, that we suffer not our Lorde and Kinge to loose his Money which hee trusted into our handes, and which is gone from vs, not by greater strength nor by any treacherous stratagem of our enemies, but through our owne too-too importunate feare, and too base a regarde of our liues, before which it was the duetie of euerie one of vs to haue preferred the care of our honour. For if by fighting and couragiouslie sustayning the assaults of our enemies, though they had bene stronger and better armed then we, this misfortune had happened vnto vs, & that we could in any sort haue represented to the King and the world an honourable & bloudie battell, wee should not now haue had anie neede to seeke meanes, howe to repaire this losse, and to restore the thing that violently was taken from vs by such as were more mightie then our selues, and these honorable souldiers also should more easilie haue digested with vs this lamētable calamitie. But we haue lost that money, & in verie deed, hauing (as it were) willingly bestowed it vpon the Georgians & Persians to redeeme our liues and to saue vs from their furie, wee are bound to repay it, or else for euer hereafter to be challenged as lawful debters to the King for it. And therefore, my good friends & companions, if you will take a good course, let euery one of vs without any further consultation put his hand to his priuate purse (if he haue not foolishly cast that also into the handes of his rauenous enemie) and with our owne monie let vs succour the necessitie of these men, and haue regard to the honor of our King. So shall wee make our flight lesse blame-worthie, wee shall iustifie our actions the more honestly, and (that which is of greatest importance) we shall the better pacific the wrath of King Amurath, which most iustly he might conceiue against vs. I my self, before you al, am most ready to disburse fower thousand Duckats towards it: if it please you al to followe mee accordingly; wee shall deliuer these Souldiers from their great necessitie, and acquite our selues from the intricate bonds of most troublesome displeasures.'

A man might there haue seene a thousand countenances chaunged a thousand maner of wayes: for one softly whispered many a cursse and shame vpon the King, vpon Mahamet, vpō God: another denied to disburse any thing, another determined priuilie to steale away, and some practised one thing & some another, but in the end euery man was induced to follow the purpose and example of Mahamet: and there vpon hauing made a purse according to euery mans habilitie, there was collected thirtie thousand Duckats among them. Presently after this, word was sent to Leuentogli at Zaghen, that he should send thē grain, Muttons and other necessarie prouisions, that they might the better continue the defense of the Fort. *The Turkes make a purse among themselues in Teflis of 30000. dukats.*

Two onely dayes did they remaine in Teflis, and then hauing chaunged such souldiers as desired to bee dismissed, and hauing also appointed for that gouernement Homar Bassa in the rowme of Giusuf, that was in it before, Mahamet departed. But before his departure, consultation was had whether they shoulde keepe the way of Tomanis, or the other through the Countrey of the Georgian Mustaffa: and in the ende they resolued, that it was better to keepe the way of Tomanis, and thereupon order was taken that they shoulde all passe ouer the riuer, for that they were determined to goe that way. The Sangiacchi Curdi were the first that went ouer, and had alreadie pitched their tents vpon the further side of the water, (when Mahamet beganne to reuoke his former order, and sente thē word that they should return, *Mahamet departeth from Teflis.*

Mahamet giueth order to passe the riuer to returne by the way of Tomanis.

Mahamet reuoketh his order: but is not obeied by the Curdi.

because he was now determined to leaue the way of Tomanis, & to go back by the same way that he came, by Carachala & Altunchala. Al the Sā giacchi were in a great rage at this message, being alreadie exceedinglie greeued aswell for the losse of their friends as also for disbursing their Money, and in plaine and expresse tearmes, sente him answere that they were accustomed to warre, and to great exploites fitte for men and not for boyes: and that these mutabilities seemed to them to bee rather childrens plaie then manly resolutions: and as for themselues, that they were not minded to chaunge their iourney, but as they had alreadie separated themselues, so would they goe forwardes, and followe on their voiage. Verie hotely and earnestlie did Mahamet entreate them to returne backe, but no meanes could hee find to reuoke them from their obstinate purpose, but forwards they went the

The Curdi come to Chars long before Mahamet Bassa.

same way and arriued at Chars, long before Mahamet, who was much greeued at thē & greatly reprooued their disobedience. But when he perceiued he could not otherwise do, he with the Bassa of Caraemit and the Bassa of Altunchala put themselues on their Iourney, euen in the same waies, wherein they had receiued their shamefull and ignominious discomfiture.

Mahamet at Altunchala.

At the last Mahamet arriued at Altun-Chala. And for asmuch as partly by his own earnest desire, partly through the secrete prouocation of the other chiefe Bassaes, he was vrged to seeke some meanes, how hee might reuenge the treasons and losses, which the Georgians had wrought and brought vpon them, yea euen with the death of Mustaffa, who was nowe suspected of all men. Mahamet and the rest thinking (as wee tolde you before) that Mustaffa had had some priuie intelligence with them, and that they together had plotted this treacherie: Or at the least (for that was thought to bee the principall intent of Mahamet) forasmuch as hee was minded by this meanes to make Amurath beleeue, that in trueth all the mischiefes that lighted vpon them, did not happen through their cowardise, but through the treacherous treasons, and malitious aduises of the Georgian, and so make their receiued losses seeme more worrhie of excuse, and their flight more pardonable hee deuised with himselfe how to finde out such an artificiall plot, as without any stirre hee might bring to effect what hee had entended.

Mahamet deuiseth howe to betray Mustaffa the Georgian in Altunchala.

And that which he had in his minde was this: To call a Diuano vnder his owne Pauilion, faining that hee had receiued some commaundement from the Courte, and then hauing caused Mustaffa to come into that rowme, whiles the said commaundement shoulde bed in reading, to cause his Checaia or Lieuetenant with those chiefe of his bande that stoode about him, to fall vpon him and presently cutte off his heade. So

Mahamet calleth a fained counsel.

Mahamet called the said Diuano, wherein there sat with him the Bassa Eunuke of Caraemit, certaine Sangiacchi subiect to the Iurisdiction of Erzirum the Capigi Bassi (that is, the chiefe Gentleman vsher) and the Checaia of the saide Mahamet: with all whome vpon the Lawe of a solemne oath hee had communicated his intended deceyte. The Georgian Mustaffa was called accordingly, who, both because he was beloued of moe then one, and also because hee vsed all diligence and forecast, and specially because euen in the army he had perceiued some priuie whisperings of such a matter, knew full wel, that all this was deuised against him, and imagined that the conspiracie had beene farre greater then indeede it was: whereupon he also prepared for his owne defence. And touching his going to the Diuano, he thought he might not deny so to doe, least by his absence he should be condemned for contumacy, & so he himselfe shoulde make himselfe guilty and culpable of the fault, that (peraduēture not without reason) was imputed vnto him, and thereby leaue his cities for a pray to their enemies. But seeing that he must needes goe, hee deuised a very safe and sure meanes, how he might escape the hands of the Turkes, and peraduenture to the great dommage of Mahamet and example of the beholders, giue a taste of his owne vertue and valor. And therefore hauing chosen out fiftie of his most faithfull Souldiers, he gaue them to vnderstande, that there was no remedie but they must needes follow him to the Diuano, that was appointed with in the Pauilion of Mahamet, and being come thither they must there stay ready and attentiue, to the end that at his first & one onely call, they should all sodainely & forceably rush into the pauilion with their weapons, and rather then any wrong should be done vnto him, they should exercise their strength against the Turkes without exception of any person. They being by nature verie great enemies to the Turkish bloude, and vnderstanding full well what he had said vnto them, setled themselues to put it in execution, and hauing gathered vnto them other of their owne faithfull and trustie friendes also, they set Mustaffa before them and so followed him euen to the Pauilion of Mahamet. Mustaffa entred into the Diuano, and standing vppon his feete required Mahamet to tell him what hee had to say to him: who presently caused the coū terfaite commaundement to be read, whereunto hee gaue an attentiue eare. But when the other Sangiacchi and Bassaes beganne to sit down (for it is the manner of the Turkes whensoeuer anie of the Kinges commandementes are in reading, alwaies to stande vp, and not to sit downe vntill it bee fully read,) the Georgian tooke his leaue, promising that hee woulde euer bee readie, not onely to performe that order of the Kinge, but whatsoeuer else hee shoulde commaund, how hard and difficult so euer it were. While he was retiring out of the Pauilion, the Capigi Bassi (or gentleman Vsher) of Mahamet Bassa, came vnto him, and plucking him by the sleeue of his garment, (adding deeds also to his wordes,) willed him to sit downe.

Mustaffa the Georgian prepareth his gard to defēd himselfe from Mahamet.

Mustaffa the Georgian at the tent of the Diuano.

The custome of the Turkes, whē the Kings commandements are in reading, to stand vp.

Mustaffa cryeth out and woundeth Mahamets Lieuetenant.

When Mustaffa felt himself plucked by the sleeue, he cried out aloud, and drewe his sworde: wherewith hee stroke Mahamets Checaia that was right against him, and with his left hande hauing raught his roll from his pate, with his right hand, sodenly, to the great astonishment of all that were present, at one onely blowe, he parted his heade, his necke and his brest in twaine, euen to his verie stomacke, so that hee died (a strange spectacle to beholde) being thus cut in sunder, with his two shoulders hanging downe vpon their seuerall sides. After this first hee redoubled his seconde stroke, and aymed at the heade of the Eunuk Bassa, but it beeing defended by the writhen Rolles of his Turbant, it slipped downe by his eare, and besides a peece of his saide Turbant caried his eare quite away, with a little also of his flesh of his checke. Then being all enraged, & eagerlie enflamed with desire of reuenge he did set vpō Mahamet Bassa (who being now alin a confusiō was risen at this tumult) & wounded him with fiue mortall wounds: two whereof notwithstanding, being the deepest and the sorest, although they brought him euen to the extreeme poynt of death, yet by cunning hand were healed. At the cry of this Rinegate Georgian all his people had runne in together: vpon whose confused tumult and the feare that Mustaffa through his furie had put into them, the Campe was raysed and euery man with all speede departing from thence, set himselfe on his way towardes Chars, whither also were brought the two wounded Bassaes, and the rest, that were ill handled and greatlie scarred with these sudden and vncouth stirres.

Mustaffa sent present information to the King, of all that was practised and wrought against him, finding himselfe greatly greened at the false suspition that Mahamet had conceyued of him, to his great dishonour: wherein he did so cunningly write, and so much dissemble, by shadowing the trueth with lying and cogging, that hee perswaded the King to shewe him a manifest token of his good liking and contentment, by sending vnto him both cloth of gold, and a battell Axe all guilt. Mahamet also, entermingling here and there; with all the arte that possiblie hee coulde deuise, all hatefull and injurious tearmes, sent large aduertisements of all the misfortunes that had happened, and aggrauated to the King both the treacheries of Mustaffa, and also the slender securitie of those wayes and countries.

Assoone as King Amurath vnderstoode the calamitie of his souldiers, the losse of his money, the great dishonour of his people, and the apparent danger, wherein the Fort of Teflis stoode, when it was like to bee abandoned: beeing all inflamed with rage and anger, hee called vnto him the Bassaes of his Court, among whom sate as chiefe the proud and haughtie Sinan, and rated them all diuerse and sundrie wayes, reproouing their leawde counsell, and recounting the losses that

Mahamets lieuetenant dieth, being cut in sunder downe to the stomacke.

Mustaffa cutteth of the eare of the Bassa of Caraemit.

Mustaffa woūdeth Mahamet with fiue mortal woūds

Mahamet being wounded retired to Chars with his people.

Mustaffa aduertiseth king Amurath of al that had happened.

Mahamet also informeth the King howe matters had fallen out.

Amurath being angrie reprooueth the Bassaes of the Court.

he had receyued, as though they had happened through their defaultes, and especially Sinan, the principall occasion of all these mischiefes, who like an improuident foole woulde needs relinguish the charge of his Armie, and like a King sitte idle at Constantinople, standing (as it were) at some publike triumph, to beholde and heare the miseries and misfortunes of others. Sinan coulde doe no lesse, but make aunswere to the wrathfull King, yet not with such mildenesse and modestie, as in so sinister an occasion he shoulde peraduenture haue doone, but rather in all proude and arrogant manner, without any reuerence or regard, hee tolde him plainely, That as the last yeare, (beeing the fifth yeare of this warre) whiles hee was ready and prepared to returne to Constantinople, the succors were brought into Teflis with so great quiet and ease, that euen his owne subiects (much lesse his enemies) scarce knewe of it, the Persians and the Georgians in the meane time occupying their mindes about anie other thing rather then about this, (wherof we haue not in deed made any mention at all in his due place, for that there fel out nothing worthie to be written, sauing that the sayd supplie of money & corne (vndoubtedly to the iust commendation of Sinā) was so safely & warely cōducted to Teflis, that neither the Turks made any preparatiō of souldiers for the conuoy of it, nor yet the enemies had any suspitiō of such a matter, neither was there any shew of battel or cōtention about it.)

Sinan answereth the king proudly and arrogantly.

Succours brought to Teflis, without any thing else worth the writing.

Euen so it would haue fallen out this yeare also, if the King had put his aduise in execution, asmuch as hee despised & contemned it: For he did then giue him to vnderstand that Mahamet Bassa could not be a fit man for the leading of those succours, especially to such a station or place, and that it was very necessary to haue chosē in his rowm, some other person of valor, of worth, and of wisdome: but seing he would needs make choice of the same Mahamet, hee was not now to blame any other for this errour, but onely himselfe. And touching his comming to Constantinople, it was a thing long before thought to bee very needfull, not onely for his aduise howe the matter of peace might bee brought to some good passe, but also because (if that treatie came not to the desired issue,) then hee had to talke with him, howe hee might easily compasse the ouerthrow of his enemie: which matter as yet he had no fitte time to declare vnto him, but was now most readie to reueale it, if it would so please him. Wonderfully was Amurath greeued with this his answere, when hee considered that a slaue of his owne, should thus reproch him with a matter that was so odious, and so manifestly touched his follie and improuidence: notwithstanding he dissembled his discontentment conceiued against him, and was verie desirous to know of him, what that secrete and important matter was, which he had to reueale vnto him, for the easie compassing of

Amurath greeuously offended with Sinan.

this commenced enterprise: and therefore after he had framed him a glosing replie, he cōmanded Sinan to display all his conceites, and to disclose those his deuises, which he had to vtter. All the rest of the Bassaes helde their peace, & euery one of them, omitting the ouersights of Sinā, were cōtent also to omit the occasiō of answering the king, al of thē being wholy bent against him & ioined with the king (as it were) in disdain & scorne of his arrogancie, who for a briefe of al his aduises propounded these two thinges. First, his counsaile was, that they should not proceede in this warre as they had hithereto done, that is to say, by seeking with fortes and fortresses to hold and keepe their enemies countries. For (as in the verie beginning of this war, whiles consultation was had in what manner and sorte it should be made, hee had expresly protested) he did manifestly foresee, that their Casende or treasuries were not able to yeeld such store of money, as was sufficient for the maintenance of necessarie garrisons, and so the error of Mustaffa (that nowe is dead) was euidently conuinced, who so obstinatelie had persuaded such a dangerous and difficult manner of warfare. His secōd aduise was, that the true meanes to bring these stirs to a wishid ende consisted especiallie in the resolution of the king himselfe, whom if it would please but to remoue a little frō Constātinople, for three or foure daies iourneys onely, and to passe either into Caraemit, or into Aleppo, or at least into Amasia, hee might assuredly promise to himselfe all speedie & honourable victory, for at the onelie name of his remoue, either the Persians would not stande too obstinately vpon conditions of peace, but would easely come to any agreement, or els he might continue his wars, & so obtaine great cōquests. These were the reasons that Sinan propounded whereof it seemeth no other thing followed but onelie an enuious affectiō of the king against him, quite contrarie to the conceit which before hee had of him, & (which was a matter of greater importāce) a further suspition (fostered by these mightie Ladies,) that Sinan had thus counselled the king himselfe to goe in person from Constantinople, not for any good that coulde arise by his departur, but onely that so hee might finde meanes for the Prince his Sonne to make himselfe King & driue out his father. This suspiciō was in such sort nourished in the minde of Amurath, especially being assured of the great affection which the prince carried towards Sinan, that he was enforced to ridd him out of his sight, and to depriue him of al charge, driuing him presentlie out of the court and out of Constantinople, and banishing him into Damotica, a place neere to Andrinopolis: from whence afterterwarde, through speciall fauour which by humble supplication hee obtained, he was sent into Marmara a little beyond Siliurea, where he yet liueth. And into his place of Visiership was assumed Sciaus Bassa, the Kings

Sonne in lawe, by contrey an Hungarian, a man verie gracious of countenance, and of honourable iudgemente, but aboue all the men in the worlde, a seller of Iustice and benefites, and yet a great friend to the peace with Christian Princes which Sinan did so wickedlie maligne.

Sciaus the chiefe Visier, and his manners.

In the meane time the Persian captaines had withdrawen themselues to their places of Residence, and by verie speedie Postes had imparted to their King their obtained victories, and so euery man for this season had made an end of those great stirs that were raised in the years. 1580. 1581. and a good parte of 1582. wherein also followed the election of a newe generall, who notwithstanding went not forward in his troublesome busines, vntil the beginning of the yeare, 1583. as in the next booke we wil declare vnto you.

The Persians at their places of residence

The 5. 6. and 7. yeere of this warre

The ende of the fift Booke.

The Sixt Booke

The Argument.

The Persian King resolueth to ride to Heri, against his sonne Abas.
Emir-Chan promiseth the King to defend his Territories from the Turks
The Gouernour of Sasuar beheaded.
The King attempteth to get his Sonne Abas into his handes.
Abas writeth to his Father, and the Tenor of his Letters.
The two Persian Princes reconcile themselues one to the other.
Salmas accused and beheaded.
The Persian King, and the Prince his Sonne returne to Casbin.
Ferat chosen Generall of the Turkish Armie.
Ferat repaireth Aggia Chalasi, and Reiuan.
Tocomac seeketh meanes to bee reuenged of the iniuries of the Turkes.
Ferat returneth to Chars, and causeth a Sangiacco of the Curdi to be beheaded
Manucchiar the Georgian beheadeth the Messengers and Gentlemen-vshers of Amurath and deuideth the Treasure betweene himselfe, and his cosin Simon.
Hassan goeth to succour Teflis.
Ferat is at Erzirum, and dismisseth his Armie.
The Persian King is affraide of newe stirres, and commeth to Tauris with a great Armie.
Generall Ferat gathereth a newe Armie at Chars▪ he goeth to Lory: he passeth to the streites of Tomanis and cutteth down the woods.
Daut Chan yeeldeth himselfe to the Turkes.
Simon goeth to assault Resuan the Bassa: he hath his horse slaine vnder him and is strangelie deliuered from extreame daunger.
Tomanis defended by Hassan.
A great dearth in the army of Ferat.

Ferat is threatened by his Souldiers.

Ferat goeth to Clisca, and meaneth to fortifie it.

Resuan is hardly entreated by the Souldiers, who also threaten their Generall againe.

The Generalls life is saued by Amurath the Bassa of Caramania.

A most confused tumult in the Armie, and Ferat the Generall is enforced shamefully to yeeld to his Souldiers, and returneth to Erzirum.

The Originall occasion and manner of the escape of Alyculi-Chan.

The Persian king dismisseth all his Souldiers, that he had gathered together.

Emir-Chan is imprisoned, and hauing his eies put out, by the kings appoinment, he dieth miserablie in prison.

New displeasures arise among the Turcomannes for the death of Emir-Chan.

Amurath conceiueth great hope of the valour of Osman the Bassa.

Sciaus writeth to the Tartarian of the comming of Osman to Constantinople.

Osman with foure thousand souldiers putteth himselfe in the way to Constantinople.

Osman is assaulted by the Tartarians, but Osman ouer commeth them.

Osman putteth the Tartarian king to death, and appointeth his brother to be his successor.

Osman departeth from Caffa by Gallies, and arriueth at Constantinople.

Osman is chosen chiefe Visier in the rowme of Sciaus, and Generall in the rowme of Ferat.

Osman departeth from Constantinople, and goeth to Erzirum.

Osman gathereth a greater armie, then all those that haue beene hitherto gathered in these warres, besides the Souldiers of Egypt and Damasco, who did not goe with Osman.

THE SIXT BOOKE

The Persians reioyce & are full of good hopes.

After that these victorious Warriers, loaden with spoiles and diuerse of their Enemies ensignes, were with great ioy receiued at home in Persia, at the last to the greater comfort of the Persians, the discord also that fell out between Mahamet Bassa, & Mustaffa the Georgian was declared vnto thē, whereat they did no lesse reioyce, then they did before fortheir obtayned victories. And euerie man thought with himselfe that this newes might greatly further the matter of peace, or at least if that came not to the wished ende, yet it might hinder the Turkes from passing to anie place that was neere vnto them, & might also keepe them occupied, is Teflis had hitherto done, in such places as are farre distant from their Royall Cities. Which coniecture of theirs might verie well be grounded vpon a reasonable foundation, aswell because the iniurie was verie great, that Mustaffa had done to Mahamet the Generall of the Turkish Campe, as also for that the Territories of the saide Mustaffa were no lesse replenished with places most fit for treacheries and ambushes, then the Territories of Sinion. In these and such like good hopes remayned the Persians; when by the way of Georgia there came tydinges to them that Sinan was displaced from his Office of Generalshippe, and therefore the Turkes must of necessitie send foorth some newe Captaine, if they were minded still to continue this warre. With great griefe of minde did the Persians receiue this aduertisement, knowingful well howe much Sinan was inclined to peace, & how deadly he hated the continuance of these long and troublesome contentions. But much more greiuous was it vnto them, when they vnderstoode withall, how their treaties of peace were all in vayne, and howe besides those indignities that so dishonestlie were offered to the Persian Nation at Constantinople, their Embassador was also at the last sent prisoner to Erzirum. And yet notwithstanding all these sorie newes the Persians chaunged not their former hopes, but verilie perswaded themselues that these discords, & the outrages committed vpon the Turkes by Manucchiar, might happelie hinder their enterprise, which this yeare they minded to attempt to the great preiudise of Nassiuan, and Tauris: For they imagined, that seeing their newe Generall must needes be sent as farre as from Constantinople, the new yere could not serue their turne to any other purpoce, but onely to succour Teflis, and to reuenge the shame receyued by the outragious furie of Manucchiar. In which poynt they discoursed also with themselues, that euen in that respect Manucchiar and Simon would make a league together, aswell because they were neighbors in Territorie, and were likely both of them to run one and the selfe same course of fortune, as also (yea & so much the rather) because Manucchiar hauing taken to wife a sister of Simons, they could dono lesse in these innouations but ioyne themselues together, & one of them be a protector and defender of the other, and so vniting their forces together they shuld be able to annoy al such, as should be sent to conueigh new succors to Teflis.

The Persians are sorie for displacing of Sinan.

The Persians greeued at the indignitie done to their Embassador.

The Persians are still in good hope.

Vpon these occasions the Persian King, perceyuing that he could not haue a fitter oportunitie to employe himselfe against Abas Mirize his some, determined with himselfe to leaue the matters of this side of his kingdome in their present state, and to march towards Heri, whereunto hee was earnestly solicited by his elder son Emirhamze

Mahamet the Persian King resolueth to ride to Heri against his sonne Abas Mirize.

Mirize, but principally by Mirize Salmas his Visier, whom his said son in lawe did likewise dayly animate to this resolution, and could not well brooke that anie other thing shoulde bee in speech, but onely this, And therefore seeing there was no other remedie, but that the king must needs satisfie the request of these mightte entercessers, and also establish all thinges in as good securitie as possibly hee might (besides the great confidence and trust which he reposed as we told you, in his cosins the Georgiās) he called vnto him Emir-Chan being at that time the Gouernour of Tauris, and opened vnto him the resolution which he had to ride into Heri, 'declaring vnto him withall, that he meant not to take this viage vpon him, and quite to leaue at randon all these his Cities that were so neere and commodious for the fury of the Turkes, but he would set a trustie garde to keepe them, and make choice of such a person to attende them, as shoulde be able to yeelde him a good account of them, whensoeuer the Turks should aduenture to endammage those coū tries. And forsomuch as Emanguli-Chan had taken vpon him the charge to defend Siruan, & not to suffer that Osman Bassa should proceed anie further in his conquestes there, but to keepe him straite and to restraine him within the narrow boūds & holds of Demir-Capi, he had foūd out also another person that had promised him, whensoeuer occasiō required to gather an armie together, and to vse all other good meanes to resist the Turkes, if they should at any time seeke to annoy these borders of Tauris, Nassiuan, Reiuan, & such lik. And further signified vnto him, That he was minded to discharge him of the Office that hee had, namely the Gouernourshippe of Tauris, and would substitute in his place the mā that had so readily offred himself to this seruice, bestowing vpon him the name and title of the Gouernour ouer Reiuan and Nassiuan, and ouer all the other places and Captaines in those quarters. But if Emir-Chan himselfe woulde promise the like, and besides other helpes, would vse also the seruice of the mightie Turcoman Nation when neede should so require, he would not onely suffer him stil to inioic his charge, but also, not harkening to the promises of the other man, he would honour him further, with the dignitie of Captaine Generall against the Turkish Armie.'

The speech of the Persian king to Emir-Chan.

A long time did Emir-Chan remaine in suspence hereat, not knowing wherupon to resolue himself. For on the one side, he knew that he had many aduersaries & cōpetitors, who no doubt would very boldly haue made the like offer to the king, of purpose to oppresse him, and to hoist him out of his possessed dignitie: & on the other side he saw the promise was verie difficult, for he vnderstood ful wel what great power the Turkish Armie had, against which he coulde not promise to make any resistance, no nor to looke them in the face, with so slender and weake prouisions as he had. Neuerthelesse, he being deceiued as wel as

Emir-Chan wondereth at the speech of his King.

the rest with those common hopes, that whiles the King himselfe might be busied about the winning of Heri, the Turkes neither could nor would attende any other thing, but onely to reuenge the iniuries of the Georgians, to chastise those troublesome and treacherous people, and to succor Teflis: couragiouslie at last promised the King that he woulde not suffer the Turkes, no not so much as to approch, either to Reiuan or Nassiuan, but would maintaine and keepe him and his landes safe and vntouched from any of their forces. And if it shoulde fall out that through some extra-vagant or extraordinary resolution of the Turkish Captaines, the enemies should come into those borders, hee woulde then gather together the Turcomans and all their confederates, and so imploy his whole power and forces against them, to the ende, that such iniuries should not bee attempted, at the least without reuenge.

Emir-Cham promiseth the king to garde his Frontirs from the Turkes furie.

This resolution beeing concluded, King Mahamet sette himselfe forwardes towards Casbin, with an Armie of twentie thousande persons, and leauing on his left hande Gheilan and the Caspian sea, and on his right hande Siras and Cassan, and beyond all that, euen vppon the coast of the saide Sea Massandran, Saru, Pangiazar, and Culbat, by the way of Terrachan, Imamadulasis, Cur, Sembran, Bestan, & Dagman, he arriued at the Citie of Sasuar, being on that sid the chiefe of all the Cities that are subiect to the iurisdiction of Heri. Nowe the gouernour of this Citie had fortified himselfe, by keeping the gates locked, and maintaining a vigilant guarde about it, hoping that delaying the King and so auoiding his first assaulte, hee might also peraduenture persuade him, that this his comming was not necessarie, and purge himselfe before him of any accusation or fault, wherewith all he might be charged. But this his designement, though indeed both iust and reasonable could not fall out according to his desire. For Mirize Salmas, who in the delay of this their besieging, had continuallie among other surmises, entermingled also some feare and suspition of Nouelties, did still sollicite and hasten the enterprise, and himselfe encouraging the Souldiers thereunto, with ladders, with ropes, with timber, and with other engines did so much, that in a shorte time the Guarde of the Citie was taken, and the Gates opened to the King, who swarming in with all his Armie, lefte no leasure for Chan the Gouernor to escape, but presently caused him to bee beheaded, although he alledged a thousand excuses for himselfe, and obiected a thousand accusations against the seditious Visier. The King after this departed from Sasuar, and ioyning vnto him all the strength of the cities of Nisaur, Massiat, Tursis, Turbat, Giem, Malan, and Coran, hauing also put to death certaine captaines and Sultans, that were accused by the Visier to be Confederates in the rebellion of his Sonne, hee arriued atlast at the desired Citie of Heri. Very strong is this Citie by situation, compassed about with a good wal,

King Mahamet with an armie of 20000 persons rideth towardes Heri.

Mahamet at Sasuar.

The Gouernor of Sasuar beheaded by the kings commandement.

The gouernour of Sasuar beheaded by the Kings commandement.

and watered with deepe channells of running springes, conueighed into it by Tamerlane their Founder or Restorer: so that the winning thereof coulde not but prooue very long and difficult: especiallye because there were in it many valiaunt Captaines, all enuious enemies to Mirize-Salmas, and readye to attempt any notable enterprise, for the defence of themselues and of their Lord. Assoone as the King had discouered the saide Citie, hee felte a rising in his minde the diuerse affections of griefe, and of pietie: and indeede greater was the griefe which hee conceiued, in respect of the businesse that hee wente about, then his pietie was. For hee greeued woonderfullye at his owne vnhappinesse and miserye, that hee shoulde cause such a one to bee borne into the lighte of the worlde, as in steede of maintaining his Fathers honour, and ioyning his forces with the forces of his Father to the destruction of his Enemies, shoulde rather bee a meanes for his arrant enemies to enter into his confederate Countreyes, and hee himselfe prooue the verye ouerthrowe of him, from whom he receiued his beeing, and present dignitye. It greeued him likewise and that with affectionate passions, to remember the bloud of his subiectes, that had heeretofore beene spilt vppon so straunge an occasion: yea and scarcelye durste hee enter into cogitation with himselfe, thence forwarde to shedde any more of the bloude of his peoples. Neuerthelesse, with all these his conceites and vnhappye fortune, beeing more and more sollicited by the Visier, hee attempted to vnderstande (if hee coulde) the minde of his Sonne, and (if it might bee possible) to gette him into his handes.

But the Citie of Heri was well fenced, (as we haue said) and therefore it must needes require the spending of many daies, before it could be obtained: which Abas-Mirize knowing full well, thought it good in the meane time to write diuers letters to his Father and his Brother, wherein hee besought them, that they would make knowen vnto him the occasions of this their stirre. For if desire of rule had mooued them to desire the depriuation of him beeing their Sonne and Brother, from the honour which hee lawfully possessed, and which his Father himselfe had procured for him, they ought to abandon that imagination, and not to seeke the disturbance of their peace, for that hee was alwaies to spende his wealth, and his bloude together with his estate, in their seruice, and acknowledged his Father to bee his good Father and King, who rather then hee: shoulde pursue this resolution, shoulde bee encouraged to encrease his Dominion ouer his neighbours the Indians and Bactriaus, which woulde bee more honourable and profitable for that Empire, and much more commodious for all Persia: And if they were not induced heereunto for this cause, but by a desire to reuenge some trespasse that hee had committed in preiudice either of the Crowne of Persia, or his Fathers honour, 'hee was most readie

King Mahamet at Heri. The Situation of Heri.

The winning of Heri difficult.

King Mahamet soroweth his vnhappy and euill fortune.

Mahamet seeketh to get his Sonne Abas into his handes. Abas writeth to the king his father. The tenor of the letters of Abas Mirize.

THE SIXT BOOKE 143

to submit himselfe to any amendes, and with all reason to yelde vnto them the kingdome, yea the worlde, and euen his owne life also, the rather to satisfie their mindes with a more full contentation.'

With twise and thrise reading ouer, were these affectionate and reuerent letters considered and digested, and at last both the Brother and the father, perceyuing in thē such liberalitie of wordes, and beeing ouer come with pittie, or (if not with pittie yet) with great admiration and contentment, they determined to put the matter in practise, and moderating their wicked desires of bloud, ruine and death, to attempt the reducing of the young mans minde to some good passe. 'Wherevpon they wrote backe vnto him, That no greedie desire to vsurpe his gouernement (An affection that was onely raysed in the gluttenous minde of prophane Salmas) had induced them to make so great a voyage, to trouble so much the people, and to shed such aboundaunce of bloud. For rather then they would depriue him of that gouernement, they would bee readie to bestowe vpon him newe benefites and honours of greater esteeme. But onely his disobedience and impudencie, in that hee caused himselfe to bee called the King of all Persia, and woulde not sende somuch as one Captayne to ayde them against the Turkes, these were the causes, why they proceeded to these great inconueniences: because they thought it their duetie to roote vp such wicked and obstinate desires out of their kingdome, and in Persia to preserue an vniuersall obedience and common tranquilitie among their subiectes.'

King Mahamet the father & Emirhamze the Prince writ backe to Abas.

The accusations against Abas Mirize.

The youngman, when hee vnderstood the accusations that were laied against him, was greatly comforted, & hoped to make it manifest before al men, how the king & his brother were misinformed in these particularities & therfore incontinently did write back againe vnto them, That if they would inuiolably promise, not to put to death, nor doe any outrage: 'to any his embassadors, he would sendvn to thē such euident matter, & so cleere informatiō touching those his accusations, as they should not onely plainly perceiue there was neuer any such kind of thought in him, but also that he had alwaies desired & laboured the cōtrarie: & peraduenture he should open vnto thē such a matter, as in respect of other men and not of himselfe, would cause their comming to proue profitable and commodious to all the kingdome of Persia.' Whereupon they both promised all good entertainment, and were now become very desirous to vnderstand, what those straunge nouelties should be: 'and so when they had yeelded their consent, and with solemne oath had offered to receiue the said embassadours with all friendly curtesie and regarde: Abas sent vnto them two of his chiefe counsellours, men of good accompt and reuerence both for their yeares and wisedome, with commaundement, That they should declare, how

Abas hopeth wel, and writeth backe to his father and his brother.

The promises that passed friendly betweene the Princes.

all these stirres did arise from none other man, but onelie from the Visier Mirize-Salmas: who as he had alreadie laboured this daungerous plot against Abas-Mirize the kings own son, so (if this his designment should bee brought to passe) he would not sticke to doe the like against the King himselfe, to satisfie the greedy and ambitious desire which hee had to place his Sonne in lawe Emir-hamze in the soueraigne seate, and himselfe to bee the man, that (as Lieutenant to the King) shoulde commaunde the whole Empire. Which notwithstanding they were to reueale without any blame or accusation of Emir-Hamze, and to make it knowen to his old father, that neuer any such conceits or affections were kindled in the Prince, but that he was also vnwares induced thereunto by the crafte and suttlety of malignant Salmas.'

The excuses of the embassadors in the behalfe of Abas Mirize.

The two Embassadours came accordingly, and after many speeches, in the ende, swearing (according to their custome) by the Creator that spread out the Aire, that founded the earth vppon the deepes, that adorned the heauen with starres, that powred abroade the water, that made the fire, and briefely of nothing brought foorth all thinges: swearing by the heade of their vaine Master Aly, and by the false religion of their impious Prophet Mahamet: swearing by their children, by their wiues, by their own souls, That such peruers thoughts neuer entred into the head of Abas-Mirize: 'They alledged many testimonies and euident proofes, that most loyally and faithfully, in all due time, aswell when hee was aduanced to the soueraigne degree of a king, as also in his battels against the Turkes, his Sonne had alwaies caused deuout prayers and supplications to bee made to God for his prosperitye, neither euer desired to heare any other but happie and fortunate successe of him. They brought with them a thousande and a thousand Precepts and Royall Letters, which the younge man had caused to be written, as occasions required, to the Gouernours that were his Subiectes for the gouernement of the state, wherein hee neuer named himselfe the King of Persia, but onelye your King and Gouernour of Heri.' They prayed the King also that hee woulde cause a diligent processe (which the Turkes call a Teftis) to be framed against his Sonne, and if there shoulde bee founde in him any signe or shadowe of so wicked a suspicion, that then hee woulde take from him his estate and libertie. For they woulde remaine as hostages for him. 'But when all this shoulde be done, and Abas-Mirize shoulde bee founde altogether free from these vniust and impious calumniations, then (falling euen to the earth and kissing it,) they besought him and coniured him, that hee woulde not leaue the matter thus imperfect, to the preiudice of his bloude: but returning to his counsellor, he would likewise take information, vppon what minde or consideration it was well knowen that he had aduised the King to take vpon him this vnorderly and

The Embassadors of the King and the Prince are receiued.

The Embassadors accusations against Mirize Salmas.

THE SIXT BOOKE 145

daungerous viage. For without doubt hee shoulde finde nothing in him but malignant, ambitious, and wicked affections, and such as euen deserued, that with his bloud there should be reuenged all the bloud of those, which till that houre had beene brought to their vnworthie and vndeserued death. And forasmuch as there remained one onely difficulty to be cancelled & cleared, wherof the Visier had informed the king, touching a commaundement that was giuen by Abas-Mirize to the gouernors that were vnder him, as namely to the gouernour of Sasuar and of other places, that they should not goe to the warre against the Turkes: they confessed in trueth, that such an order was taken indeede, but not to that vniust and slanderous end, as it was related to the king by the Visier, but onely in respect of the warres, that were reported to be begun in those quarters by the Tartarian Iesselbas, who by diuers into ades hauing robbed the Cities, the Townes, and the Fieldes of Heri, had put such a feare in younge Abas-Mirize and all his Counsellours, that they durste not emptye their Cities of their guardes and forces, and thereupon (as they should finde it true, if they woulde enquire thereof) the saide Gouernours were commanded that they should not goe to the war against the Turks, but that they should expect further direction, whereof they shoulde haue notice, if they should be called for.' And that all this was signified by writing to the Visier himselfe, but that hee of a malignant minde had concealed the same: onely to try, if in these common troubles hee coulde bring it to passe, that Abas-Mirize and the king might bee bereaued of their liues, and Emir-hamze succeed in their place, and so hee himselfe remaine the Super-intendent of his sonne in law, and Moderator of rather the Tyrant of that happie and famous kingdome. Which (they saide) they made knowen vnto him, not because they thought Emir-hamze to bee acquainted with so treacheious a traine, (for they knewe very well, how greatly in imitation of his Fathers pietie, hee hated dissension among kinsefolkes, & shedding of bloude) but onely because it was throughlye discouered to bee the most vnlawful and vnreasonable desire of the wicked traitor Mirize-Salmas.

Verie graue and strange cogitations did these auncient Orators raise in the mindes of the two Princes: and Mahamet the Father, beeing by nature credulous and inconstant beyond measure, began to make great construction of their speeches, and deepely to consider of their so earnest and important requestes, whose offers also seemed vnto him so vpright and equall, that he could not choose but accept thereof. And therefore calling vnto him the Gouernours, the Captaines, the Iudges and Treasurers of all the Cities that were subiecte to Heri, hee demaunded of them, how and in what sorte they esteemed of Abas-Mirize, and how & in what degree of honour he desired to be esteemed

The offers of the Embassadors accepted by the King and the Prince.

of them. And of them all he receiued an vniforme aunswere, that they helde him for their Lord, as the Lieutenant to the king of Cas-bin, and that he himselfe did alwais desire so to be taken & thoughtof. And euerie of them brought in diuers Letters, Precepts, and Orders, wherein hee neuer caused himselfe to bee honoured with any other title, but onely, your king of Heri. Hee demaunded further, whether those tumults of warres were indeede attempted by the Tartarian Iesselbas or no: whereof hee receiued also a large and solemne information, that so it was, to the greate detriment of all those territories. And thus the king was throughly persuaded of the innocencie of his son, who before was noted vnto him by his Visier to bee an obstinate rebell. Vpon which occasion onely, although hee might iustly haue put his Visier to death, as one that had beene the cause of the slaughters that happened, and of the bloud of so many valorous Captaines that was shed so iniuriouslie: yet because he would be better informed of the trueth of the accusations laid againste him by the Embassadours of Heri, the rather to ridd himselfe from so important and so iust a feare: and because he doubted also peraduenture, least there had beene some conspiracie plotted against him betwene the Visier and Emir-hamze: hee resolued to make a curious and diligent inquisition thereof. And therefore first of all, in great secrecie, calling vnto him Emir-hamze, and demaunding of him by all faire meanes, howe and wherefore hee had aduised and procured this iourney against Abas-Mirize, Son to himselfe & Brother to him, whereas indeede he had founde him innocent of al those crimes that were layde to his charge: he receaued aunswere from the Prince that hee had no other certeyntie of the pretended ill behauiour of his brother, but onely that which proceeded from the greate credite that hee always bare towardes his Father in Lawe Mirize Salmas, to whome, as to a Visier, and as to his Father in Lawe, and as to a Protectour of the Kingdome, and finally as to a person that had beene tryed in a thousande matters to bee true and trustie, hee had always yeelded assured credence, in all such matters, as daylye were in speech betweene them. Insomuch that hee discharged the whole Tempest of all these mischiefes vppon the Visier, Touching whome the King made diligent inquisition aswell among those of the Courte as of the Armie, and thereby founde verye straunge and vnexpected Nouelties. For there was not a man almost, that did not accuse him, for a seditious man, for a Cruell man, for an vniust man, and for a Tyrant, and to bee briefe that did not make him guiltie of very haynous crimes, and in particular for the accusation layd against him by the Embassadours of Heri, they all declared, that in trueth hee was always made acquaynted with the true occasions, which did restrayne the Gouernours subiecte to Abas Mirize (from

King Mahamet persuaded of the innocencie of his Sonne.

King Mahamet trieth the Princes mind.

All the mischiefes light vpon Salmas the Visier.

Mirize Salmas accused by all.

going to the Warre against the Turkes,) but that hee most malioiously had concealed the same, of purpose onely to hatch such a straunge and dangerous stirre; in hope to aduance his owne estate by the destruction of others. And so at last Mirize Salmas was detected for guiltie, & rewarded with that punishment, which he desired vniustly to conuert vpō others.

For the King, who had nowe founde such impietie in him, as besides that hee had caused manie Sultans of accompt to bee vniustly and vnworthely put to death, he also went about to procure, that the Father shoulde defyle himselfe with the bloude of his owne Sonne, (a thing so odious both to the King himselfe and all his kingdome, as euer anie cruell Action coulde possiblie bee,) the King (I saye) coulde not suffer this impietie, but acknowledging a fresh the innocencie of the one, and the guylte of the other, the one hee deliuered and embraced as his Sonne, the other he auaunted out of his presence, and punishing him as an impious person, hee caused his heade to bee cutte from his Carcase. In this manner, the ambitious Visier, as though hee had voluntarily gone to his owne death, tourned all these angers and tumultes against himselfe, and with his owne destruction pacified the dissentions and hatredes that were fostered in the two Princes mindes. And Emirhamze, when hee had nowe discouered the wickednesse of his Father in Lawe, tooke it also in verie good parte that hee was depriued both of his state and life. And so the two brethren beeing reconcyled together, and the Sonne to the Father, after that Abas Mirize had agayne promised his wished obedience (which hee afterwarde willinglie performed,) Kinge Mahamet returned with the Prince towardes Casbin, where by reason of sodayne and vnexpected newes hee had nowe along time beene looked for and desired.

Mirize Salmas beheaded by the Kings order.

K. Mahamet with the Prince returneth to Casbin.

Amurath, through the roughe speeches, and vnluckie prognostications of Sinan, was more and more settled in his purpose to continue this Warre, hopinge that hee woulde cause all the threatteninge of Sinan to bee but vaine, and to reape so much the more glorie by his happie successe in such an enterprise, as it should fall out contrarie to the common opinion of all men. And thereupon began to bethinke himselfe whome he might choose for his Generall, and to him not onelie to commit such a charge, but also to communicate all his deuises. Till that time, Osman Bassa was appoynted bee the man, but Amurath thinking that Osman might prooue more seruiceable in Siruan, and thereby the better assure and establish the conquest of that Region, durste not so soone remoue him from thence. Among the Bassaes of the Court there was one Ferat, a man of ripe yeares, but yet fierce of courage, tough in opinion, in counsell as hardie as might beseeeme his age, ready for all sodeine and strange aduentures, but aboue all a vassall most deuoted to the King, and happely he had performed some good office, why he was the rather now called forth by Amurath to this seruice. Of this man at the last hee was resolued to make choyce to bee the Captaine of his Armie. And therefore hee called him to him, and communicated with him all his priuie dessignements and secrete deuises necessarie for this warre, encouraging him to take paynes, to fight battels, to obtayne victories, and to doe all things else agreeable to so worthie an enterprise. Verie willingly did Ferat accept of this newe Office, and thought himselfe to bee highly fauoured by the King, and so disposed himselfe to performe the same, so farre as he coulde employ his strength, his wit and his diligence therein, and thereupon made him a large promise, that hee woulde put in execution, whatsoeuer shoulde be offered vnto him either by occasion, or by his Royall commaundement. Which although the King should not haue vrged any further, but onely to assure the passage to Teflis, and all Georgia, and principally to destroye the countrie of Mustaffa the Georgian, who had so audaciouslie iniured the Lieutenant of Amurath and set his whole Armie in confusion, yet beeing certified by Maxut-Chan the Rebell of Persia, and being aduertised by his subiecte Bassaes that remained neere to Tauris, howe King Mahamet was departed, or atleast was vpon the poynt of departing to Heri, to trie his Sonnes minde, hee chaunged his purpose, and deliberating the matter with himselfe, hee commaunded Ferat to employ all his Force and diligence to erect a Fabrike at Reiuan, a place belonging to Tocomac, and to assure the passage that leadeth from Chars to Raiuan. For so they shoulde be reuenged of manie treacheries and dammages which they had receyued by Tocomac, and the way to the Citie of Tauris shoulde bee made open, to the great glory of Amurath. Hee aduised Ferat also, that although hee knew verie well, it were his duetie to chastize Mustaffa the Georgian for his rash attempt against Mahamet Bassa, being then his Generall: yet he thought it better, that hee should dissemble and conceale his ill opinion of him, and (if it might bee possible) to worke so, as hee might conueigh the treasure and succours to Teflis. For by this meanes, the passage beeing made safe and secure, without anye moe Fortresses or Fabrikes, all Georgia woulde bee subdued, and the next yeare they might attempt the enterprise of Tauris.

Verie highlie did Ferat commende the deuises of Amurath, and shewed himselfe readie for anie attempt. And nowe was the time come, wherein it behooued them to set on foote these their important dessignements: and therefore in the beginning of the yeare 1583. commaundedements were sent out of all the Cities of the Empire, which were wont to make their appearance at these wars, that vpon fresh summons they should be readie to returne against the Persians, and to

Ferat a Bassa of the Court.

Ferat Bassa elected generall of the Armie in Sinans place.

Amurath deliberateth what should be done towards this expedition of Ferat.

Commandement sent out for the expedition of Generall Ferat.

put in execution, that which should be enioyned thē by their new captain: the Fame whereof flew as far as to Tripoli in Soria, to Damasco, to Aleppo, to all Iurie, to Palestina, to Mesopotamia, to Babylonia, to Balsara, to Siuas, to Maras, to all Bithynia, to Cappadocia, to Cilicia, to Armenia, and to all the Sangiacchi and Curdi of them, yea and beyond Constantinople, to the borders of Hungarie, and of Greece, and to bee briefe to all their subiecte Regions, that were wont to come to this Warre. All which sent their Captaynes and Souldiers accordingly, all readie and willing to performe the pleasure of their Lorde. And so at the last, Generall Ferat departing from Constantinople, and passing to Chalcedon by the way of Amasia, and of Siuas, hee came to Erzirum, where hee tooke a veiw of all his Souldiers, all his Pioners, his Buylders, his Treasure, his prouision of Corne, his Munitions of Warre, and leading with him the ordinarie Number of Artillarie, hee gathered altogether vnder his Standerd. Afterwardes in due time hee remooued from Erzirum, and in the space of eight dayes arryued at Chars: (in which his iourney hee vsed the seruice of the rebell Maxut-Chan, as his Guide, who in the Turkish language is called a Calaus:) and from Chars hee sette himselfe on his waye towardes Reiuan. Three dayes before hee came to Reiuan, of certayne ruines of an olde and sleepe Castle, which the Turkes called Aggia-Chalasi, hee erected a newe Fortresse, and left in it a Garrison of fower hundred Souldiers, together with a Sangiaccho and certaine peeces of Ordinance, and then went to Reiuan.

This Countrey lyeth neere to a Mountaine, whose toppe reaching aboue the clouldes, seemeth to touch the heauens, and is continually charged with snowe and yce. At the foote of this heigh and starke mountayne there lie fayre fieldes abounding with Corne and Cattell, and watered with diuers brookes, that falling downe from a lofte discharged themselues into Araxis. It is distant from Tauris, eight or nine dayes iourney: betweene which two places are situate Nassiuan, Chiulfall, Marant, and Soffian, all enriched with goodly Gardens and pleasaunt Greenes: but in the way many craggie mountaynes to bee clymed, and sundrie harde passages either for Armie or Traueller. It hath vppon the coast towardes the North, Teflis, vppon the South the playnes of Caldaran: and a little higher towardes the Tropike of Capricorne, Van and the Marciana Marish.

Heere then did Ferat Bassa encampe himselfe with all his Armie, and taking the aduise of his chiefe Captaynes, where hee shoulde builde the Forte, they all with one consent aduised him to seaze vppon the houses and Gardens of Tocomac, and to enuiron them with Ditches, with Walles, and with Ordinaunce for defense, and in the middest as it were in a Center within the Walles to erecte a highe Castle, which on

The Prouinces sent their souldiers and prouision this yeere.

Ferat departeth from Constantinople, and by Calcedon & Ciuas cōmeth to Erzirum.

Ferat being guided by the rebell Maxut-Chā arriueth at Chars.

Ferat repayreth Aggia-Chala.

Ferat at Reiuan, and the description of the situation thereof.

A Consultation touching the principall place where the Fort should bee erected.

euerie side rounde about might discouer both the hilles and the playnes, and beeing well fensed with store of good Ordenance might threaten destruction and ruine to all those that durst attempt to endammage them. And so they enclosed the gardens with walles accordingly, and hauing digged ditches rounde about them, they conueyed water into them from a certayne riuer, that came downe from the hilles and ranne into Araxis, and in this manner within the space of fifteene dayes they finished the Fort.

The forte of Reiuan 750. yardes about. Within the space of 15. dayes the works at Reiuan, the diches and all were finished.

It was a great affliction to Tocomac thus to loose his own Countrie, yea and so much the more greeuous it was vnto him, because it happened so sodenly and as it were vnlooked for: he himselfe, presently assoone as he vnderstood that the Turkish Armie was comming towardes that coast, hauing withdrawne himselfe and his men of war out of the Citie, and leauing the impotent to the mercie of the Conquerors, seeking by all meanes to bee reuenged, if not altogether, yet at the least in some part of this great iniurie. And therefore hee wrote to the King in Corazan, he wrote to Emir-Chan in Tauris, hee wrote to Simon in Georgia, hee gathered souldiers out of the villages, and vsed all his possible indeuour to make himselfe meete and able to annoy the enemies Armie. But neither from Georgia coulde hee receaue anie helpe, because they were too-much troubled with hindering any succours to bee brought for the reliefe of the beseeged in Teflis, (as in due place it shall be declared:) Neither from Tauris was hee releeued with so much as one Souldier: either because Emir-Chan woulde not, or coulde not stirre, or else because hee had some secrete intelligence with Generall Ferat, not to disturbe him in this his Fabrike. And so Tocomac could not haue the lucke to be fauoured with any poore ayde, that might at the least haue mittigated the bitternesse of his griefe. And therefore being not able to doe anie thing, but onely with those few Souldiers which he had, to lay some priuie ambushes for the Turkes, hee neuer ceased to sley sometimes a hundred of them, sometimes a hundreth and fiftie, and sometimes moe, and in that manner to coole the heat of his heart, which swelled with the burning desires of reuenge. And the better to ease his stomacke, which was infected with the poyson of hatred against Emir-Chan, who sitting still as it were to beholde his miseries, woulde not so much as shake a sworde to annoye these spoyling Turkes, and thereby performe his promise made to the Kinge, hee spared not to dispatch certayne horse men to the saide King in Corazan, and by eloquent letters to amplifie the vilenesse and cowardize of Emir-Chan, discouering vnto him some shadowe of suspicion, and intermingling with all some causes of iealousie to be conceiued in his minde, that Emir-Chan had some secrete intelligence with the Turkish Generall. And to be short he omitted no occasion,

Tocomac seeketh meanes to reuenge the losse of his owne citie by annoying of Ferat.

Tocomac neuer ceaseth to annoy the Turkes.

Tocomac hateth Emir-Chan.

Tocomac accuseth Emir-Chan to the King.

THE SIXT BOOKE 151

whereby hee might anie way qualifie the griefe that he had taken for the losse of his Citie.

The Turkish Captaine at last departed from his newe Forte, and returned to Chars, and for the custodie of the said Fortresse he appointed there as Captaine Sinan Bassa, sonne to that Cicala, who by misfortune was lately taken prisoner, whiles with great fame hee scowred and wasted the Tyrrhene Sea. And therefore this his Sonne (who was afterwarde cured and healed by mee of a certaine disease that hee had at Aleppo) partly for the goodlinesse of his person, and partly for the hope that hee raysed of his valour, was so greatly fauoured by Selim the late Tyraunt of Constantinople, and the arrant Enemie of the Italian name, that hauing scarce passed the flowre of his youth, in which age he was deerely beloued of him, hee, was created the Aga or Captayne of the Giamizaries, and after this his first degree of honour sent to bee gouernour of certayne Cities, and in the ende hauing beene imployed in diuers tumults, and perible of warress, hee was nowe appointed Captaine and Keeper of this Forte, together with Ossan Bey, Sonne to the late famous Giambulat, afore mentioned. With these two Captaines; but yet vnder the sole gouernement of Bassa Elicabi onely, and with the companye of eight thousand Souldiers; partlye Stipendiaries and partlye, Naturall Subjects, and with the Munition aboue rehearsed this Forte was strengthened and this Garrison of Souldiers, without expecting any yeerely succours to bee brought them by an Armye euen of themselues, in seuerall troupes of three hundred together in a companie, were alwaies woont at certaine appointed times to go & fetch their pay at the Citie of Enzirum and afterwardes at Aloppo, and other Cities of Soria, which they also continue to doe euen to this daye. And so with these saide Souldiers, and with good store of Artillarie artificially distributed vpon the new wall, Ferat left the Forte, and as we haue saide withdrewe himselfe to Chars, passing by the waye of Aggia-Chalasi, and performing his iourney in ten daies space.

Ferat departeth from Reiuan.
Cicala Bassa left for the custodie of Reiuan.

Cicala Bassa cured by the author at Aleppo.

Famous Giambulat, 8000. Souldiers at Reiuan.

Where when he was arriued, there arose very great and straunge newes. For there was sodainely brought before the said Generall, a Sangiacco Curdo, with his hands bounde behinde him all pale and astonished with feare whose heade without any more a doo hee caused to bee cutte from him carcase publishing to the rest that hee was a spie and a rebell. Which whether it were so or no, or whether this sodaine and vnexpected death lighted vpon him in respecte of some other displeasure, they knowe best, (if it bee lawfull at the least to know it) that are the curious searchers of such particularities.

Ferat by the way of Aggia Chalasi in ten daies returneth to Chars. A Sangiacco Curdo beheaded as a Rebell by Ferat.

At the execution wherof there was a rumour raised of a far greater importance. For by many reporters there was brought to the eares of the General a great faine of a wonderfull noueltie, namely, that

A woonderful strange noueltie brought to the eares of Ferat.	Mustaffa the Georgian, to whom Amurath had sent thirty thousand Duckates from Constantinople by two of his Capigi and two Chiaus or Nuntioes, to the end that with a Troupe of his Subiectes he shoulde carrie them to Teflis for the reliefe of those in the Forte, was fledde, and beeing nowe become a rebell to the Turkish King, had lefte the Fortresse in manifeste daunger to yeelde, if by some other meanes it were not relieued. Great was the maruel, the griefe, and the anger, that Ferat conceiued vpon these newes, and minding to haue a full certaintye thereof, hee called vnto him all suche as
Mustaffa seeketh meanes to be enformed cleerelie of the misfortune.	were the Messengers of this misfortune, and of them receiued a cleere and an expresse information of euery particular: so that in briefe hee was generallye certified that Mustaffa, the two Capigi and the Chiaus hauing put themselues on their iourneye towardes Teflis with the treasure, assisted with the company of fiue hundred of his Souldiers, in the midway had met with his Cosin Simon, by whom, after hee had setled himselfe to make some long discourse with him, he was sharpely reproued, that so prophanely hee had abandoned the sacred name of Christ that he was not onely content to liue in Turkish
Simon the Georgian exhorteth his Cosin Manucchiar to returne to his former faith.	impiety but also that he durst impugne the champions & defendor of the Christian faith, and that hee woulde become a slaue to another for a filthie superstition and impietie, raised and sowen with venerous and pestilent doctrine by a Prophane and heathen Prophet, that is dead, 'abandoning and forsaking the religion of that God, which is the onelie true and one God, in Trinitye.' And that with these and such like speeches, which very eloquently and with great zeale flowed from the mouth of Simon, he was persuaded to relinquish that infamous and wicked slauerie, and in any fitte occasion that God, (who is most mercifull towardes sinners and offendors) should minister vnto him, to reuenge the oppression, that Amurath had vsed towards him, and openlie to declare to the whole world, that he scorned and renounced the Diabolicall pompes and infernall riches of the Tyrant, thereby disclosing himselfe to bee indeede of greate courage and a true Christian. 'His cosin not ceasing in the meane time to repeate often vnto him, That God would not faile in peculiar and familiar manner to take
The Capigi and the Chiaus beheaded by Manucchiar. Manuchiar & Simon deuide the treasure betweene them & confederat themselues together.	knowledge of his Actions, and to fauour them, yea and at all times to sende vnto him all happie and wished successe: whereas on the contrarie side, if he would not resolue with himselfe so to doe, hee might well bee assured, that after manye labours and trauels, which hee should indure for the seruice of Amurath, he should obtaine none other recompence, but a harde and infamous captiuitle and in the endesome fraudulent and treacherous death.' Vpon which woordes Mustaffa beeing throughly moued, he caused the two Capigi and the Chiaus to be apprehended, and presentlie beheaded and so Simon

and hee, besides the bande of their kindred hauing solemnely vowed a perpetuall confederacie & strict frindship to bee inuiolablie kept betweene them, deuided the treasure, and withdrowe themselues to their wonted passages, there to annoy and endomage, whosoeuer shoulde be sent for the soccouring of Teflis.

These and such other particularities when Ferat vnderstoode, being all in a furye, and inflamed with rage, he did sweare that he would not returne to Erzirum, vntill all the Country of Mustaffa were put to fire and sworde: but yet in the meane time he bechought himselfe that vrgent necessity did shrewdly vrge him to send conuenient strength to the place that was in daunger: and for that purpose made choyse of Hassan Bassa, who alreadie in the last yeere of the Generall-shippe of Mustaffa had very couragiously conueighed the sayde succours and taken Alyculi-Chan prisoner. To him therefore did the Generall assigne fourtye thousande Duckates, with other prouision necessarye for that enterprise, and for suretie appointed him fifteene thousand persons of the best choyce and valour in all the Armye. In tenne daies space Hassan Bassa wente and came from Teflis: In whose iourneye too and fro, the Georgians made manye skirmishes with them, wherein there were slaine of the Turkes sometimes tenne, and sometimes twenty, and sometimes their mules and sometimes their horses were taken from them, but no matter at all of any great moment.

After this, the Generall elected one Resuan Bassa to bee Captaine of six thousand Souldiers to goe to Altu […]hala, Carachala, and other places and villages of Mustaffa the late rinegato, nowe become a rebel to the Turkes, and relapsed to the obstinate religion of the Greekes. Which Resuan, withot any long stay, ouerranne all his Territorye, burnt his townes and his lands, and committed vncouth outrages, euen vpon the poore insensible trees. Resuan brought home with him manye Captiue soules, with much Corne and Cattell, and to bee breefe wheresoeuer hee went, hee wasted and destroyed like a Tempest, whatsoeuer was before him: and if in any place he seemed to be any thing fauourable, and his fury pacified, it was because there was no resistance made by any vpon whom he might exercise his forces. The Generall was nowe also retyred to Ardachan, and thither came Resuan to meete him with his foresaide booty. But because there remained nothing else to bee done in those quarters, and the winter persuaded their returne, they remoued from Ardachan, and by the way of Olti retyred to Erzirum: from whence all the souldiers were licensed to departe to their seuerall places of aboade: and an Arz or Memoriall sente to the King of all the Actions that had beene performed, & principally of the good enterprise of Hassan Bassa, who for the same was nowe also once againe honoured by the King with cloath of gold, and

Ferat sweareth that hee will destroy al the country of Manucchiar. Hassan Bassa chosen to carry the succours to Teflis. 15000. Souldiers assigned to Hassan. with the reliefe.

In 10. daies Hassan goeth & commeth with the succours. The Georgians annoy the people of Hassan Bassa. Resuan Bassa chosen Captaine to endommage the country of Manucchiar: The harmes done by Resuan.

Ferat at Arda-Chan.

Ferat by the way of Olti returneth to Erzirum, and dismisseth his Armie. Hassan Bassa rewarded by the king.

a battell axe and Target al guilt. And this end had the troubles of the yeere 1583. of mans saluation, beeing the seauenth yeere of this warre.

All the rest of the yeere 1583. the Generall wintered at Erzirum, and afterward sent out his ordenary commandementes ouer all his accustomed Cities, to summon the souldiers against the next spring of the yeere 1584. appointing the taxes and tenthes to bee somewhat greater then they were woont to bee, and gathering together a greater number of pioners & enginers thē euer had been gathered heeretofore, and withall published a rumor abroade that they shoulde goe to Nassiuan, and there doe great matters. At the reporte whereof the Persians were much mooued, and began to cast many things in their heades about in. Glad they were for the vnion and amitye lately concluded beteween the two Cosins Simon and Manucchiar: (for nowe being againe reclaimed and become a Champion of his former faith, we may cal him no longer Mustaffa, the name that he had giuen him by Amurath at his Circumcision, but Manucchiar, whereby hee was Christened by the Priestes at his Baptisme.) And they wel hoped, that by the diligence of them both, the way of Tomanis would be sufficiently kept & guarded, or at the leaste that which they were not able to doe, the rest of the Persian Captaines woulde performe for their partes.

But aboue all others the king who was nowe arriued at Casbin, and had vnderstoode the confirmation of the vnhappy successe at Reiuan, and the newe preparations of the Turkes, beganne to thinke vpon further matters, and entred into many discourses with himselfe, all entermingled with a very great feare of some strange alterations. The fabrik erected the last yeere at Reiuan aforesaid, & the repaire of the castle called Aggia-Chalasi, had perswaded him, that the Turkes this yeere would passe to Tauris, or at least as the reporte was to Nassiuan, and build new fortresses in those borders. Which thing the king neither would nor could endure by any meanes, for that it might prooue a shrewd introduction to the ruine of Persia, and to the bringinge downe of so mightye an Empire. And therefore hee retayned still those Forces which hee brought home with him, and out of all the Cities that were Subiecte vnto him hee caused as manye moe to come as hee coulde, commaunding withall, that all the Chans vppon paine of Death shoulde followe him to Tauris, and so not longe after the arriuall of Ferat Bassa at Erzirum, hee also arriued at Tauris, being with all obedience accompanied by all his said Army.

This vnexpected comming of the Persian to Tauris, as it engendred expectation of verye good successe in the . mindes of all men, insomuch as the voice went ouer all Italye, that the Persian ment to haue meruailous conflicts with the Turke, whereat Christendome did not

---

Marginalia:

Ferat spreadeth a rumor that he would goe to Nassiuan.

The estate & expectations of the Persians, vpon occasions that fell out.

King Mahamet feareth some newe matter.

Mahamet the Persian king gathereth a great army. The Persian king at Tauris.

The comming of the Persiā king to Tauris breedeth great conceits

THE SIXT BOOKE 155

a little reioyce for the good hope that it bred of some happy euent in preiudice of the Turkes: so Ferat Bassa beeing certified thereof, before he proceeded any further, beeing thereunto aduised by Maxut-Chan his Guide, (as afterwarde hee confessed at Aleppo) he thought good to aduertise Amurath of the matter declaring vnto him, That his desire was to goe to Nassiuan, and there to build a fortresse according to his commaundement, (a woorke in his opinion verye necessarie, to make the passage for Tauris safe and secure.) But forsomuch as he had receiued intelligence by trustye Souldiers, that the Persian king was remooued to Tauris with a verye huge Army, and was vtterly resolued to come and encounter him, he thought it his duetye not to put in execution his foresaide determination, without the Kings expresse commandement, Amurath presentlie wrote backe vnto him, that if it were so as he had written, he should imploy himselfe about nothing els, but to quiet the passage of Tomanis and Lori, to the ende that the next yeere following there shoulde bee no neede to send any newe Army, to conuey the succors, but some small bande mighte bee sufficient, as trauelling through a country, that were at amity and confederatye with them. Which order Amurath did the more willingly set down, for that he saw the rebellion of Manucchair; and knewe fullwell, that the Fort of Teflis by reason of his Treacheries shoulde haue more neede nowe, then euer it had, to bee sustained and releeued. Yet not withstanding Ferat woulde not publish this newe commaundement, but caused the rumour to bee confirmed (more then hee did before) that hee woulde goe to Nassiuan, of purpose to feede the opinion, that the Persians had formerly conceaued in their mindes of his going thether, & so eluding them hee might without any disturbance of the enimie attend the building of the Forts, which he had intended for the quieting of the most dangerous passages of Lori and Tomanis.

Ferat hauing concluded vpon this resolution, and gathered together his people with all things necessarie for his purpose, remooued at last with his Armie from Erzirum towards Chars, where he arriued by the way of Hassan-Chalassi, not meeting with any annoiance or hinder and at al, & there he staied the space of tend ayes, to the end that all his companies of Souldiers and heape of prouision might beenewlie suruey ghed. And then departing from Chars, hee iournied low and Lori, and presently dispatched Hassan Bassa with fiue thousande valiaunt light horsemen to scoure the Countrie, and passing euen to Tomanis to retourne him newes, of all that hee shoulde see or heare in those quarters, and to bring home his Captiues with him, that hee might the better make diligent enquirie of the affaires of Georgiās. This commandement of the Generall Hassan performed duetifully, and making haste on his iourney passed to Lori, and from Lori to Tomanis,

Ferat writeth to Amurath.

Amurath writeth againe to Ferat, not to goe to Nassiuan but to Lori & Tomanis in Georgia.

A stratageme wrought by the Turkes vpon a false rumor.

General Ferat at Chars, where he staieth for his Armie ten daies.

Ferat departeth from Chars, sendeth out Hassan Bassa as a forerunner before him.

& speedily scoured ouer all the woodes, opening and disclosing all the passages rounde about without any occasion ministred vnto him to giue assay of his valour at the last hauing mete with certayne Cassuchi, (which wee may terme Robbers by the high way) he slewe them al, and setting their heads on the toppes of their Launces, he made his returne towards Lori. Where hauing staied one whole day, they discouered from thence aid he whole Turkish Armie, with a great and fearefull shew comming and approching towardes them. Whereupon Hassan went to meet the Generall, & to reporte vnto him the excursiō that he had made, declaring withal, that he had not encountered any other but onely certaine Cassachi, whose heades he might beholde vppon their Launces, for that hee thought it not necessarie to bring them aliue, because they were altogether ignoraunt of the Georgian and Persian affaires, and therefore were not able to deliuer any information thereof at all. And so they arriued altogether at Lori aforesaide, and there encamped themselues. This place did sometime belong to Simon, well strengthened with a high Castell, compassed about with verye deepe ditches, and a thicke wall almost a mile in circuit, but at this present somewhat weeakened and wasted by time. It is distant from Teflis two dayes iourney of a Cariers pace. Generall Ferat selzed vppon it, and hauing restored the walles in such places as they had most neede of reparations, and strengthened all the breachies, he planted therein seauen or eight thousand persons, of the Sangiacchi, the Giannizari, the Spahini and the Zaini, and for the guid or Captaine ouer them hee appointed Aly Bassa of Greece, and vpon the Castell and the Walles hee distributed two hundred peeces of small ordenance. All these prouisions beeing made hee wente to Tomanis, leauing order with the said Aly Bassa, that when hee thought hee might take fitte opportunitie, hee shoulde not faile to fortyfie Saitan-Chalasi, about tenne miles distant from Lori, & to place therein a conuenient garrison of Souldiers and Artillarie.

Fower daies long were they going to Fomanis for the Generall would needs make it fower daies iourney, being ordinarily but one daies woorke from the one place to the other, to the ende that those fieldes being very riche of Corne, of fruite, and of Cattell should euery where be wasted and burned by his spoiling Armye, and that the Countrey Inhabitants besides their other losses shoulde also endure the losse of their Rents. Now Tomanis in times past was also a Castell, whither Simon used often times to make his repayre: and when the heate of these Warres beganne, the Georgians themselues were in a consultation to raze it, to the ende that it shoulde not be surprized by the Turkes, and thereby that benefitte shoulde redounde to them, which it could not yeelde vnto the Georgians, for their want of Ordenance. And heere

Marginalia:
- Certaine thieues slane by Hassan.
- Generall Ferat at Lori. The Situation of Lori.
- The walles of Lori repaired. 7000 souldiers in Lori. Aly Bassa of Greece captaine of Lori.
- 200. peeces of ordinance in Lori. Ferat goeth to Tomanis. Order to fortifie Saitan-Chalasi neer adioining
- The state of Tomanis.
- Consultations about the erecting of a fort at Tomanis.

THE SIXT BOOKE 157

was greate aduise taken, howe and where the Forte shoulde be erected for the defence of the countrey, But after many discourses at laste it was concluded, that a Castell shoulde bee builte not in that place but a little furthers and that for this reason, because Tomanis standing a good long waye on this side the Straite, if they shoulde builde the Forte there, then coulde they not make that passage safe and secure and therefore it was needefull for them to proceede further euen to the very much of it and there to plant the Fortiesse And so the Armye marched forwarde a certaine fewe Miles, vntill beeing arriued at the very issue of the narrowe passage, they found the Ruines of another castell, and neere there vnto they stayed themselues. This stoepe head long Castel was compassed round about with a very thick wood of beeches pineaples & other trees, which hindred all discouerie of anything a farre off, so that it was not couenient to founde such a Castle there from whence their Ordinaunce coulde neither auayle them to whom the defense thereof should be committed, nor endommage those that shoulde come to offende it. And therefore the Generall commaunded, that euery man with vncouth outrage shoulde fell the trees, and with sharpe instrumentes hewe downe the Pyneapples, the Fyrres, the Beeches and the Elmes, and making way through thicke and thinne, should laye it out for a broade streete and an open Champayne, that before was the receptacle for a thousande dangerous treacheries. In verie short space were the trees layd along on the ground, the place made lightsome and open, and a very commodious situation prepared for the foundation of a Castle. The plot of the olde ruyned Castle was compassed about with a wall of a thousande and seauen hundred yards, and in the middle thereof was erected a Towre or rather a strong keepe, sundrie lodginges and chambers builded, and two hundred peeces of Ordinance distributed vpon the newe Walles.

 In this meane time there were diuers men of all sortes sent out to fetch in vittels and other booties who although they had beene abroad many days since their departure, were not as yet returned which ministred matter of great maruell and feare to euery man. Nowe the Generall seeing that they did not as yet shewe themselves, Determined to send Hassan Bassa with eight thousand horsemen, to scowre the Countrie round about, and to make the way fro the saide Vitellers to returne in safetie. The experienced Warriors went out accordingly, and meete them returning hime, loaden with Corne and well prouided of Cattell, and other ritch and plentifull booties, which was a great reliefe to all the Souldiers. Afterwardes the Generall sent Resuan, beeing nowe the Bassa of Natolia, and the Bassa of Caraemit to conueigh the succours to Teflis, with tweentie thousande persons in their companie, the most choosen and best armed in all the hoast, who marching all

A Castell among the woods.

The thicke woods cut downe and made open

The compasse of the walles of Tomanis.

Certaine vittellers sent abroad but not heard of againe.

Hassan Bassa goeth out to assure the way for returne of the vittelers.

Resuan Bassa goeth to Teflis with succours with twentie thousand persons.

closely together in the directe way, within one dayes space arryued at the sayde Fort, wherein they placed their Garrison, and chaunging the Gouernour thereof, substituted in his rowme one Bagli, beeing then, vppon this occasion onely, called a Bassa.

<small>Bagli Bassa left for gouernour at Teflis.</small>

Whiles Resuan lay thus encamped vnder Teflis, Daut-Chan the brother of Simon, who (as wee tolde you in the beginning of this warre) at the comming of Mustaffa into Georgia, had fledde out of Teflis and abandoned the Castle, came nowe with all his Familie to offer himselfe for a subiecte and a deuoted vassall to Amurath, promissing that hee would followe the Turkish Armie, and employ all his forces and all his wits in the seruice thereof: and therefore besought him, that he would vouchsafe to cause him to bee receyued with all good entertainment, being nowe come with a trustie and assured hope to finde peace and safetie among their weapons, and vnder their lawe and religion to enioy a quiet and peaceable life. Resuan entertayned them all with great promises, and large assurances of all good successe, according to their desires and necessities.

<small>Daut-Chan. yeeldeth him selfe to the Turkes.</small>

In the meane while newes were brought to Simon, that Generall Ferat, staying at the straytes of Tomanis withall his Armie, had sent Resuan Bassa to succour Teflis, and withall it was tolde him by certayne false and lying Spies that Resuan was gone, not with twentie thousande persons, but with a far lesse number of people, then indeede hee was. At which good newes hee tooke courage to encounter Resuan, and setting vppon him to ioyne a bloudye and mortall battell with him. Which his resolution hee caused presentlye to bee put in practise: for without any further delaye, beeing accompanied with fower thousand Georgians, partly Subiectes of his owne, and partly of Manucchiar, with all speede possible hee wente against Resuan. But whiles Simon was going thitherwardes, Generall Ferat (either because he was falsely informed that there were a greater number of Georgian Souldiers, or else because without any other aduertisement, he was of himselfe affraide that the Enemies Army was bigger then it was) had alreadie by chaunce dispatched away the two Bassaes of Caramania and of Maras with tenne thousande persons, to the end that ioyning themselues with the Souldiers of Resuan, they shoulde bee somuch the safer and stronger at all aduentures. Nowe Simon came vpon Resuan, being encamped with six thousand Souldiers onely at the roote of a certaine Hill, on the backeside whereof were all the rest of his people, neere to a certaine water, and presentlie made an assault vppon him. The Souldiers, behinde the Hill, beeing aware of Simons approch, were readie all at once with their weapons to annoy Simon, who nowe was exceeding sory for his error in beleeuing the false newes, and repenting himselfe, that hee had assaulted his Enemies, hee perceiued that hee

<small>Simon aduertised of the going of Resuan to Teflis.</small>

<small>Simon deluded by the liing spies meaneth to assaile Resuan.</small>

<small>Simon with 4000. Souldiers goeth to encounter Resuan Bassa.</small>

<small>The Bassaes of Caramania & Maras dispatched for aide.</small>

was vndoone. But when hee sawe, that by flight hee coulde not but encrease his griefe, and make the issue more lamentable and miserable, with those fewe Souldiers which hee had, hee endured the fury of the populous Armye of Resuan, and on both sides there was ioyned a moste cruell Battell: Wherein on the one side you mighte haue seene a straunge and vn-vsuall valour, and on the other a tumultuous superfluitie of a multitude, that in the encounter were rather sore wounded, then able to carrie away the Victorie: Howbeit in the end the huge number of the Turkish swordes and Speares did ouercome the small number of the Georgians, and the Barbarian fires and Artillarie did bring the Christian forces to an vnhappye estate. But Simon himselfe, whose Horse in the Medley was quite thrust thorough, fell downe headlong to the grounde, and his guilt Torbant with his Golden Horne from his Heade, and in his fall was verie neere to haue been taken prisoner. Which misfortune, as it happened to his Lieutenaunt and to his Generall, and to many other his followers, so must it needes also haue lighted vppon him, if hee had not beene relieued by an vnexpected and (as it were a meruailous fauor. For whiles the battel was euen at the greatest heat betweene them, Resuan discouered the two Bassaes of Caramania and Maras, who (as wee told you) were newly sent by General Ferat to succor him, but both by the said Resuan, and also by the rest of the Turkish armie were indeed thought to be Persians. Wherupon they were incontinently surprized with a sodaine feare insomuch that all of them waxing fainte and hanging in suspence, the victory, which before was sure their owne, became nowe very doubtfull, and the Turkes themselues feared, that they should bee the loosers. In this suspence & doubtfulnes of minde, the battel also was intermitted, & by those very frinds, which were sent thither to further this enterprise, it was vnawares disturbed whereby the Georgians and specially Simon, whose estate was almost desperate) tooke the opportunitie & benefite to escape & saue themselues, and to leaue behinde them many infallible signes of their valour among the Turks: of whō manie remained there slaine, many wounded, and manie replenished with verie great maruell and vnexpected feare. Thus escaped Simon, and thus remayned Resuan, who after that hee had discouered his welwilling Bassaes approaching neerer towardes him, and knewe them particularly to bee his Confederates and Furderers, coulde not bee quiet with himselfe for the escape of Simon, who without all doubt had beene vtterly ouerthrowne and all his people, if as hee feared great harme, by the comming of the two Bassaes, so hee had expected that helpe which hee shoulde haue expected. For without anye further trouble or difficultie, all the Forces of the Georgians had either beene taken prisoners, or miserablie destroyed. But poore Simon saued himself in

Simon repenteth that hee went to set vpon Resuan.

A cruel battel betweene the Turkes and the Georgiās.

Simons horse thrust though

An vnexpected chaunce deliuereth Simon from present destruction.

Simon escapeth out of the Turkes handes.

the places neere therabouts, which hee knewe by their situation to bee verie safe and secure, and there beganne a freshe to bee greeued at the false information that hee had receaued by the lying spies touching his Armies, bewayling the deathes and captiuitie of his subiectes, and yeelding thankes to God for the preseruation of his life and libertie.

Simon thanketh God for preseruation of his life.

The Turkes in this meane time were come to Tomanis, withall iollitie and triumph, drawing the standardes of Simon all along the ground, and bearing manie heades of the Georgians vppon their Launces to the great ioy of Generall Ferat, to whome also there were deliuered all the prisoners taken in the battell, and impious Daut-Chan, likewise presented, who hauing in times past abandoned his first faith was become a Persian, and now againe despising the vaine and wicked woorshippe of the Persians, had yeelded himselfe for a pray to the impure filthinesse of the Turkes, and made himselfe a voluntarie slaue to Amurath

Resuan at Tomanis againe.

The season of the yeere was nowe so farre spente, that euery man beganne to feare the winter approching, and therefore the Generall determined to remoue from those partes, and to withdrawe himselfe into some safer places: and so hauing set in Order all the Garrisons of the newe Forte, in such sorte as we tolde you before, hee appointed Hassan to bee the Bassa of Tomanis, and lefte with him eight thousand souldiers, which he had chosen out of the rest, for that enterprise.

Feare of winter approching.

Hassan left as Bassa at Tomanis with 8000.

Very deepely in his minde had Ferat layed-vp the oultrage committed by Mustaffa the Georgian, (beeing nowe returned to his old name of Manucchiar,) in taking away the Kings treasure, and killing the two Capigi and the Chiaus: neither could hee finde any rest, nor time to ease his stomacke beeing all inflamed and boiling with anger for the same. And therefore hee resolued with himselfe not to returne to Chars or Erzirum, vnlesse he had first passed into the countries of the said Georgian, and by annoying the same in the cruelest manner he coulde, reuenged the intollerable iniuries that were receiued. In three daies he arriued at Triala, where all the Turkish Army encamped themselues, and where they endured a very strange and vnwonted dearth and scarsitie of all thinges, and principally the want of ordinary, vittailes grew so excessiue, that after the rate of the Venetian Staio or Bushell, they paied fiue hundred Duckates for euerye fiue Bushels and a halfe (which amounteth to the measure of a Sorian Macuco to the vniuersall calamitye of the whole Army, Barley also was happilie solde at a higher price, as Hala Bey (of whom I made mention before) did for a trueth giue mee to vnderstand, and confirmed it by the testimonie of diuers others.

Ferat arriueth at Triala. A dearth such as was neuer hearde of among the Army.

From this place the Generall was minded to goe on forwardes, towardes the countrie of Manucchiar: but whiles hee was vpon the raising of his tentes, one Ueis, beeing then the Bassa of Aleppo, came against him, and aduertised him, that it was not good now to spend the time in wandring about those coūtries, for that there were three verie great enemies, which were confederate together, to make this enterprise very difficult, and almost impossible & desperate. 'One was the season of the yeer, beeing now ful of snows, frosts, and tempests, which in those Regions are continually noysome to trauellers. Another was the want & scarsity of all things necessarie for vittaile, without which no doubt the Armie would make an insurrection, and abandon all the enterprises that should bee attempted, & so in the greatest heat of their labors, their designements being put in practise, should be hindred and interrupted. And the third was the people of Georgia, who peraduenture might find opportunity to procure the ioynt helpe of the Persians in their fauour, and by a common vniting of themselues together, to worke some notable mischiefe against their armie. But Ferat did most sharply rebuke the Bassa, & reproued him with bitter termes, telling him flatly, that hee wel perceiued he was broughtvp among mountains & villages, & of a villein (as hee was) aduanced to the honor of a Bassa, vpō some od conceit & foolish importunity: and that therfore he should not haue presumed so much as to thinke it lawful for him, so impudently & shamelesly to come & giue him such aduertisments: but rather it had beene his duety to haue held his peace, and to harken to the commandements of his betters, & superiors, yeelding himselfe obedient & deuoted to performe the same with all his power. With this rebuke the General passed on to Archelech:' in al which passage he destroied & in a manner burnt vp al the plat countrie, though indeed it were in amitie & confederacie with the Turkes. But the inhabitants of Archelech had withdrawen themselues into the mountaine, abandoning the Citie, the Castels, and Villages, and leauing them open to the furie of the armie, to the great astonishment & maruell of al men, who thought that they beeing subiectes, rather then they should flie into the mountains, should haue run with al ioy & gladnes to salute the victorious Captaine, & to admire the armies, the deuises, the forces & the ensigns of their good friend the Generall.

 In Archelech Ferat encamped & staied the space of fower daies, among the rockie crags, & in a barren soyle, where neither cattel nor men had any store of necessarie sustenance, but rather euery man en dured vnspeakable miseries. Howbeit forfower whole daies the souldiers were content to beare this great calamity. But in the end therof, the fal of a huge snow being added to these extremities did so gret ly encrease their griefes, that all the Giannizzaries & Spaoglini of Constantinople arose in a tumult, and comming before Ferat, in

> Bassa Veis commeth before General Ferat, and speaketh to him.

> Ferat reprooueth Veis the Bassa.

> Ferat at Archelech.

> The miseries of the Turkish Armie.

despiteful & contemptuous manner, with very haughtie and resolute termes they said vnto him. And how long shall we endure this thy tedious and insolent gouernment? where is the due commiseration that thou oughtest to beare towardes the vassels of our soueraigne Lord, thou rustical & vnreasonable captaine? 'Doest thou think happelie, that we keep with our harlots, as thou doest, vnder thy sumptuous pauilions, all fat & in good plight with delicate viandes, whiles others liue in miserie? Doest thou beleeue, that we haue, as thou hast, our daintie Sugers, spices, and conserues, wherby to restore vs in the common calamities of others? And that we haue at commaund our neate & pretious wines, which thou minglest with thy cleere & plesant waters, partly prouided for thee by the Arte of the cunning Doctors, & partly brought vnto thee from farre places? From this daie foreward, it wil bee no longer endured, that so much people should continue in this famine & cold lying vpon the hard ground, and afflicted with nakednes and many other inconueniences: and therfore get thy selfe vp, and returne towards Erzirum: or else we shal be enforced to doo that, which wil breed more displeasure to thee, then to any man else.'

The souldiers being in a tumult speake despitefully to the general.

The general, being in a great agony & confusiō within himself, presētly caused a Dixano to be assēbled, wherin it was cōcluded, that they should all send their strong sumpter horses towards Ardachan, & all folow him into yᵉ widows coūtrey, whither he had appointed to go, only to make an Inrode to giue thē occasiō of spoile & bootie, & to refresh the minds of thē al, that were afflicted with the miseries both past & present. At the cōmandement of the general they al readely obeyd, aswell because he promised them a speedy vioage as also for that euerie man desired the sacke of Altun-Chala, & other the territories of Manucchiar: & therefore they al verie willingly followed the Standerdes of Ferat, who holding on his iourneye through certaine lowe valleyes, betweene the high and difficult mountaines (which could be none other but the Rockes of Periardo) and beeing continually accompanied with a verie great dearth and scarsitie, brought his Army to Clisca, a place belonging to the sayd Manucchiar, but now quite abandoned & forsaken by all the inhabitants, who at the onely voice of the Generalles comming, hauing gotten together all the best stuffe that they had, together with their wiues, their children, & al their deerest iewels, were departed from thence, & remooued into remote and safe places, till the furye of the victor should be ouerpassed. In the fields neere vnto this place there was good store of Rie, Barley, & other corne wherewith they might quench the hunger of the Cattell, yea and the souldiers themselues through the aboundāce of fruite and flesh were greatly comforted and refreshed. So that the Generall being encouraged by these commodities, and hoping that the whole Armie

Ferat promiseth the spoile of Manucchiar his countries.

General Ferat at Clisca.

The armie refreshed with plenty of vittailes.

woulde take it well to stay a while in such good ease, determined with himselfe to erect a newe Forte in the place, and to strengthen it with Armour and Souldiers: and with this resolution gaue commandement to Resuan Bassa, that he should goe vp to the towre, and in the top thereof plant a banner, with a proclamation and publike reporte, that he woulde fence that Fortresse, and in the name of Amurath Fortifie it, as other Fortes were woont to bee. Resuan being accompanied with the Bassa of Caramania, who was al so called Amurath, executed the commandement of the Generall, in the toppe of the Towre planted one or two Banners accordingly, whereat assoone as the Souldiers espied them, the forenamed Giannizzaries and the Spaoglani, sodainelye tooke great indignation, because they thought themselues to be too much abused by their captaine, and thereupon arising againe all in an vprore, replenished with furie and confused in tumult, with great despite and rage, they ranne vp to take downe the Banners that were planted vpon the Fort, and taking them in their handes, they strooke the saide Resuan Bassa once or twise about the pate withall, discharging a thousand iniurious and reprochful wordes vpon him, and sharpely rebuking him. And then returning to the Generall, who was nowe also come thither himselfe to countenance the Action of Resuan, and from that high place the better to behold the situation thereof, with gestures full of contempt and disdaine, reuiling him with many shamefull and scornefull termes, they protested vnto him, 'That they were not come to the Warres to exercise the occupation of Masons and Dawbers, and to bee employed in such vile and dishonourable offices, but onely to Manage their weapons, and thereby to demerite their ordinary wages, and to purchase to themselues glorie and renowme at their Kings handes. And therefore, if hee loued his heade, and woulde not shortly see those Armes turned againste him, which hitherto had beene the Reuengers of the enemies iniuries, hee shoulde resolue with himselfe to leaue these newe Buildinges, and these vnseasonable designementes, and giuing place to the contrary season of the yeere, hee shoulde haue due care of their common desires and necessities.' And whiles they were thus talking vnto him, there was one more bolde then the rest and beyond his dutie, that did not sticke to assault the Generall, and to threaten him, that he would wreake his fury vpon him, and chastife him with impious hands & cruell blows withall. But the forenamed Bassa of Caramania was readie to lende the Generall his owne Horse, and so rescuing him from the rage and tumulte of the Souldiers to conduct him to his Pauilion. Howbeit Ferat was pursued by the tumultuous Souldiers, and sharpely accused againe for the stay that hee hadde made there, and for not resoluing presently to remooue from thence: yea and after they had often repeated their contumelious speeches, and reprochful

The Generall commandeth that Clisca should bee fortified.

Resuan Bassa ill handled by the souldiers.

The souldiers reuile Generall Ferat.

The souldiers in a tumult threaten the General. Amurath the Bassa of Caramania saueth the Generalls life.

villanies against him, they vttered also at the last their manifest & expresse protestations, that if the next morning he did not remooue from those Quarters, without all faile, hee shoulde loose his life for it. Ferat, who could not abide to yeeld to them, that shoulde of duetie haue beene ready and obedient at euery becke that hee should make, seeking by all meanes (notwithstanding all this stirre) to staye there for so long time, as woulde bee sufficiente to builde a Forte, that woulde bee so noysome and iniurious to Manucchiar, coulde doe no lesse but aunswere these Protestations, telling them, 'that he made no accompte of their threatening him with his life, which hee had alwaies offered as readie for any seruice of Amurath his King: But if they had no care to serue their Soueraigne in this newe Building, they might goe their waies: for as for himselfe, he was vtterlye minded to obey his Lorde, in whatsoeuer hee had commaunded him, for the honour of whome euerye man ought to thinke his life very well bestowed.' Vpon this aunswere there followed diuerse railinges, and curses against the king, against the General, against them all: and in a most confused tumulte, that was raised, euerie man betooke himselfe to his weapons, and in euerie corner there were heard grommellings, & whisperinges, full of wrath and fiercenesse, so that there was great feare of some dangerous conflict, but greater was the suspicion of the Generalls life. For nowe euery man had withdrawen himselfe to the guarding of suche things as he esteemed most deerely, when as sodainelye and in a trice they sawe the pauilions of the Captaines and of all the Bassaes fall downe to the grounde, al the cordes thereof beeing cut by the wrathfull souldiers, and as it were in a Moment all the Muttons and other Cattell, which the Generall and Bassaes led with them for their ordinary vse, were seized vppon, and guarded with all diligence possible. And so farre off was it, that any man durste challenge or reuenge this their rashnesse, that they themselues returning a freshe vppon their Captaine, beeing nowe all in a maze and frightfull feare, they repeated the thirde time the protestations which they had twyse alreadye made vnto him, that if hee woulde not remooue from those Countries, and turne his Iourneye towardes Erzirum, without all faile those Valleyes and Fieldes shoulde become the Sepulchers of the Bassaes, and those Hilles shoulde retayne an eternall memorie of so famous a day.

The Generall might haue done with this people whatsoeuer hee had listed, if with a little liberallitye hee had bestowed but a small Quantitye of Money amonge them: but beeing loath to shewe, euen the leaste token of a gratefull minde towards them, he was enforced to performe their proud and arrogant demaundes, and to his great shame to obey them, whome hee might haue made obedient to him, rather with mildnesse then with rigor. And therefore the Captaine

THE SIXT BOOKE 165

was constrained to yeelde and obey his Soulders, and to auoide theire despitefull and sharpe threates, to his exceeding great reproach, euen as they had commaunded, to remooue from those quarters. The first day hee arriued at Ardachan, with the verie great annoyance and trouble of all the souldiers: for whereas the iourney was wont to bee two daies worke ordinarilie, aswell in respecte of the long waie, as also of the passage ouer a verie rough and difficult mountaine, the Generall woulde needes haue it dispatched in one onely daie, the rather thereby to afflicte and grieue the Souldiers. But for this his reuenge hee receiued euen the selfe same daie his due rewarde, for that the Chariots, wherein his wemen rode were conueyed away, together with their Eunuches that were their keepers: some saie, by the Georgians, that in those woodes and cragges of the mountaine lay in ambushe, waiting for some such occasion: and others say, by the Giannizzaries, who altogether to dishonour the Captaine, wrought him this iniurie. Great was the reproach which Ferat receiued, not onely in the Armie, but also, yea & farre greater at Constantinople, when these newes were knowen there: so that hee was continually replenished and inflamed with shame: and yet notwithstanding all this his wrath and ardent indignation, hee was compelled to endure the losse of his deerest Iewels, and in case as he was to iourney towards Erzirum.

In Ardachan hee tooke a surueigh of his Armie, and before hee commaunded any remooue, hee gaue them all leaue to departe, himselfe afterward arriuing at Erzirum, hated of all his Souldiers, enuyed by Veis Bassa and others the Captaines of the hoast, defamed for the losse of his wemen, and fallen into the disgrace of euery man. But no lesse then the rest, was the Turkish king discontented with him, for two verie mightie and weightie considerations. First, for that he was notable to make anie vaunt of any action that hee had doone in reuenge of the exceeding great iniurie of the Georgian: neither was it possible for him to learne the way how to behaue himselfe towards the souldiers, that they might become obedient & friendly vnto him. Secondly for that without any care, he had suffered Alyculi-Chan to escape away: about whose flight he could not choose but haue some intelligence and conference, as beeing the onely man, that in all the strange haps which happened in the former yeers of this warre had continually celebrated & renewed the fresh memory of his seruiceable actions. For Ferar, who (as we told you before) by the new order, which he receiued from the Court, was to diuert his iourney from Nassiuan, to the straites and narrowe passages of Georgia, beeing desirous to bee throughly enformed in all those waies, that with most ease might leade him into those places, and withall to bee acquainted with al those difficult & perilous corners, where the Georgians were wont to hide themselues in ambushes, and

Ferat at Ardachan.

Generall Ferat his wemen stolen away from him.

The shame of General Ferat

A muster at Ardachan.

Ferat at Erzirum.

King Amurath discontented with Ferat.

prepare their treacheries, resolued with himselfe (in the second yeare when hee remoued from Erzirum) to take Alyculi-Chan out of prison, who was apprehended by Hassan Bassa, and caused to bee imprisoned by General Mustaffa, (as it is aboue written in the fourth book.) This Alycul Chan did Ferat purpose to vse as his guid & counseller in this voiage, & to take his aduise in such difficult resolutiōs, as might happen vnto him in those narrow straites, and thereby to auoid the perils, that are ordinarily found in euery cornet of those Regions. And therefore he caried him with him, vnder a certain guard (whatsoeuer it was afterwards) of his most faithfull vassels, & caused him to be wel intreated, by yelding vnto him the benefit & enioying of whatsoeuer he needed. At the last they arriued in Georgia, at the streits of Tomanis, where we told you the forenamed Castell was erected, and from thence hee escaped secretly into Parsia. The manner of his escape is diuersly reported. For some say, that Ferat vpon this condition brought him from Erzirum, to set him at libertie whensoeuer hee should yeeld him any good aduise in this voyage: and that when he had so doone, for the discharge of his promise (which notwithstanding is a hard matter to beleeue in a Turkish Infidel:) hee gratified him with his libertie. Others say, that Ferat for the exceeding great bribes, which hee had taken of Alyouli, granted him opportunitie to escape. But what bribs or rewards could a poore prisoner giue, that was spoiled of al his substance in the battel, and left scareable to sustaine himselfe. And to bee briefe, others some say, that this escape was made neither for reward of money, nor discharge of promise, but by the onely vigilance of Alyouli himselfe, and the sleepines of his keepers, and that watching the opportunitie of the night, which is a friende to all scapes, hee started away. But whether this or that were the manner of his escape, in fine hee was then deliuered from the Turkish captiuitie, and returned into Persia, to the performing of those enterprises, which shall bee told you, when wee shall come to their fit times in this our Historie, for that nowe it is not amisse to declare a certaine particularitie, that happened before some of these actions that wee haue alreadie described, and that indeed may not be passed ouer in silence, and that is, the execution of the commaundementes that Ferat gaue to Aly Bassa, before hee departed from Georgia.

This Aly, who (as wee tolde you) remained in the Fort at Lory, founde his opportunitie to issue out of the Fortresse, and descending downe a certaine hill, at the foote whereof there was a Castell called Saitan-Chalasi, (which in our language may bee interpreted the Castell of the Diuel:) with great diligence hee fortified the same: Hee left therein fiftie peeces of Artillerie, and a thousand men, vnder the charge of a Sangiacco, and so quieted the passages from forte to forte in such

The Original, of the escape of Alyculi-Chan, late prisoner in Erzirum.

The manner of the escape of Alyculi-Chan the Persian.

Alyculi Chan flieth againe into Persia.

The Castel of Satan fortified.

sorte, as all the waies from Reiuan to Chars, and from Chars to Teflis were made easie and safe, and so all the enemies treacheries were discouered, and all their meanes taken away, whereby they might be able to plot any newe.

In this meane time, the King of Persia, who (as wee told you before) was arriued at Tauris with althose his forces, perceiuing that the Turkes had changed their purpose from Nassiuan to Georgia, so that there was no further need to employ his Armie against them in defense of Tauris or Nassiuā, at the last resolued with himself to licence his soul diers to depart, which he had brought thither with him for the repressing of those publike stirs: and to apply himselfe to more priuate reuenges. For calling Emir-Chan vnto him, whom he had lately left for gouernour of Tauris, & General ouer al the Cities & Captains aboue named he enquired of him the occasion, why he performed not the great promises which he had made vnto him before his departur to Heri, & did not his endeuor to hinder the Turkish fabrik at Reiuā, or atleast why he went not out with other souldiers appointed for that purpose, and namely with the Turcomannes (as hee had promised) to reuenge so great an iniurie, and in the best manner hee coulde to endomage the Turkish forces. For if there had beene none other promise to binde him, yet that had beene the duetie of euerie Persian Captain, much more had it beene his parte, who had tyed himselfe thereunto by a solemne promise. Sundrie excuses did Emir-Chan alledge for his manifest defaulte, and principallye the speedie departure of the Turkish Armie for that in so short a time, as the enemies Armie staied vnder Reiuan, hee had not leasure enough to call together either the Turcomannes, or the other Souldiers for that seruice: but for himselfe, hee was alwaies most readie to employ all his power and his life therein. These and other like excuses Emir-Chan alleadged to discharge himselfe from the burthen of the Crime, which the King and the Sultans had layed vpon him. But the king perceiuing too manifestlie, that there was no excuse sufficient to acquite Emir-Chan from so grieuous a faulte, and adding also peraduenture to these indignities, some auncient hatred, which hee had taken of old, and retained against Emir-Chan, euer since the death of Ismahel, determined with himself to bereaue him of his sight, & so cōmaunded, that with a hot burning Iron, applied to the eies of the wicked Chan, all the humor that maintained his sight should be dried vp, and afterwardes being thus blinded and despoiled of all his goods hee shoulde be shut vp in close prison: which accordinglye without any further delay was put in execution, and was the occasion, that within the space of a fewe moneths hee died miserably in prisone.

Thus was Persia depriued of a famous and courageous man, and amonge other her losses shee felte this also to be of that moment,

The waies of Reiuan, Tomanis, Lory and Teflis made secure.

King Mahamet licenseth all his souldiers of Tauris to depart home.

King Mahamet quarrelleth with Emir-Chan the Gouernour of Tauris.

Excuses alledged by EmirChan.

King Mahamet commandeth that EmirChan should haue his eyes put out. EmirChan being blinded dieth miserably in prison.

as although it were of it selfe of some importance, yet in respecte of the circumstances it was exceeding great. For the Turcoman Nation, who among other Captaines, (from whence Persia receiued her protection and dignities) made great accompt of Emir-Chan, and by him *The Turcomā Nation greatly offended for the death of EmirChan their captaine.* was greatly honoured, at this death of his became highly offended, and were notably discontended, yea, & their indignatiō encreased so at the last that being become rebellious and an vtter enemie to that Crowne, they did absolutely denie their forces to the publike defence thereof. This their wrath and anger was also much more aggrauated, when they hearde that the King had bestowed the rowme of Emir-Chan, vpon *Newe discontentments of of the Turcomannes.* Alyculi the fugitiue, who was escaped out of prison from Ferat, as is aboue shewed. Which Alyculi, although in respect of the great perilles, wherein he had beene, deserued all preferment, yet for that he was an auncient Enemie to certaine Turcoman Captaines, they coulde not in any wise endure that hee should be exalted to so great an honour. And therefore they waxed more disdainefull & ill affected towardes the *The Persian forces weakened.* king, and thereby the Persians forces became the more weakened and deuided. And these were the euents of this season of the yeare. 1584. An end whereof wee made, at the returne of Ferat Bassa the Generall to Erzirum, whose successes also doe nowe call vppon vs, after we haue thus briefely described the nouelties of Persia.

From Erziram hee sente a large aduertisement to Amurath of all things that had happened, and besoughte him to commaund what shoulde bee attempted at the nexte Springe. But besides the infor- *Ferat informeth the king of that which had happened this yeere.* mation of Ferat, there wanted not many other that did the like also, although in another manner. For the King was aduertised, and that in an odious sorte, of all the whole proceedings of Ferat, the escape of Alyculi-Chan, the shamefull losse of his wemen, his quarrels with the Giannizzaries, the disorders that fell out, through his want of wisedome, *Others informe the king more Particularly of the ouersightes of Ferat.* amonge all the Bassaes of the whole Campe, especially his enimity with Veis Bassa, who by the king himselfe was thought to be a man of valour and prudence, and to bee shorte all the particulars of the actions, that had not altogether so honorably beene performed in that yeere: which in truth of themselues onely were causes sufficiente to induce the king to remooue the saide Ferat from the Office that he exercised. To these occasions there were also added sundry other priuate respectes. *Osman Bassa thought by Amurath to be a worthy Captaine.* For euer sithens the departure of Ferat out of Erzirum to builde the Fortresses at Lory and Tomanis, Amurath had it still in his heade the next yeer following to attempt the enterprise of Tauris, and therein to make triall of the most famous Captaines that hee had: thinking with himselfe, that the estate of Reiuan and Chars being so safely setled, there was no reason any longer to delaye or slacke the passage to Tauris and thereby to stirre vppe through all the worlde a famous reporte of greate exploytes, and a glorie correspondent to so daungerous an attempte. Nowe among the Captaines, whom Amurath esteemed to be worthy men, to whom he might with trust commit this enterprise, he bethought himselfe of Osman Bassa who (wee tolde you) was lefte at Sumachia in Siruan by Generall Mustaffa, the first yeere of this warre, and whose iourney to Demir-Capi we described afterwards, together with suche other matters as hee performed againste Ares-Chan and Sahamal, in assuring the Conquest of that Citie. The good opinion, that Amurath had thus conceiued of Osman, did springe & arise in his head, not only for the exploits done by him, which wee haue sufficiently aboue declared, but also, yea and much the rather, for that hee maintained so greate an Armie, in a Countrey so farre distant, without any expences at al to the king, hauing nowe a good while leauied the Souldiers Stipendes vppon the landes and territories of that Region, and still exercised a kinde of gouernement and soueraigntie ouer those places. Of all which his good proceedings, Osman caused intelligence to be sent to the Court sundrie times in the yeare, discoursing vppon the State of all thinges, and howe without any helpe of the Tartarians, who since the death of Adilcherai neuer came to assist him, hee had assured and confirmed the Conquest for euer. By these meanes, and by other fauours which Osman had about the king, there was fostered in the minde of Amurath a wonderfull good opinion of him, but although (as wee haue sayed) euer since the departure of Ferat out of Erzirum the second yeere, hee was throughly perswaded of the vertue of Osman, yet was he not resolued (as then) to call vpon him, for that hee was hindered by the Nouelties that arose in Georgia, and stayed by a kinde of hope, that hee had conceiued of some better establishmente in the affaiers of Siruan. And nowe hauing settled all those borders, in such sorte as wee haue described, and opened the passage in manner aforesaide, he thought it good to stay no longer, but resolued with himselfe to cut of al further delay, & to cause him to come to him, to Constantinople: & for that purpose, before, that Ferat was ariued at Erzirū, the king had disparched certen Capigi & Chiaus to call this famous warriour vnto him: and thereupon, in the next spring, they began to make prouision of new attempts and new Captaines.

Amurath hath great hope of the valour of Osman Bassa.

But there wanted not some, that went about to hinder both his comming & also these dissignements that were of great importance. At that time by reason of the death of the three Visiers before named, and the banishment of Sinan aboue also declared, there had succeeded in the place of the chiefe Visier, Sciaus Bassa, son in law to Amurath, next vnto whom it was Osmans course to sit in the order of those Bassaes, that were aduanced to that honor. But Sciaus, who rather for the comelinesse of his person, and alliance with the king, then for anie

Certaine messengers and gentlemen vshers dispatched to call Osman to Constantinople.

other thing was mounted to those highe rowmes, did greatly feare, least partely for his experience in matters of warre, and particularly for the good affection and trust which the king did beare to Osman, at this his cōming to Constantinople he might perswade the king to what hee listed: and so peraduenture it might fall out, that he would take from him the chiefest office, and get the vniuersal gouernment of the whole Empyre, wher by so great wealth was to bee gained and purchased. And therefore hee had euerie date new stinges arising in his mind, and sundrie cogitations how hee might ridde himselfe of these feares, and finde meanes to auoide his comming to the Court. And because it was a verie dangerous matter openly to attempt the same, and might peraduenture be an easie meanes to make him forgoe his life, hee thought it better to make triall of a more commodious & trustie meane. This Sciaus, in consideration of many gifts and rewards, which the Cuman Tartarian had often bestowed vpon him, had continually endeuored to cleere him before the king of diuers accusations, which Osman by his letters was wont to lay to his charge, & for all his ouersights to alledge such reasons in his behalf, as if they did not perswade Amurath to bee altogether kinde and courteous towards him, yet at the least not to carrie a malitious & enuious conceit against him. And so farre had hee proceeded in countenancing and fauouring the Tartarian, that there was established and confirmed an enterchaungeable amitie and mutuall confederacie betweene them: but besids this their reciprocall friendship, there quickened in the heart of Sciaus a certaine assured imagination, that the said Tartarian king would vse al the waies and meanes possible, to hinder the comming of Osman to Constantinople, yf hee were but made acquainted with his comming. And therefore Sciaus, assoone as hee vnderstoode the certaine resolution of Amurath, to call Osman to the Court, before he saw the Chiaus and the Capigi dispatched, which went with the Kinges commaundement to fetch him, secretly wrote to the Cuman Tartar, who lay encamped neere to the hauen of Caffa vpon the Moore of Moeotis, certifying him that Osman was to come to the Courte: and that therefore hee woulde call to minde how great an enemie hee had beene to him, and how much hee had endeuored by letters to Amurath, to turne all his hatred and displeasure against him: 'and withall, that if hee was able to doo so much by letters, as if Sciaus had not defended him with verie reasonable excuses, the king had executed his wrathfall minde vpon him to his greate losse and detrimente, hee shoulde then imagine with himselfe, what Osman woulde bee able to doe, when hee shoulde come in person to the presence of Amurath, and without anie mediatour determine betweene themselues of all matters, whatsoeuer they shoulde thinke to bee conuenient for the common quiet.' These

---

Sciaus endeauoreth to hinder the comming of Osman Bassa to the Court in his place.

Freindship betweene Sciaus the Visier, & the Cuman Tartarian.

Sciaus writeth to the Tartar of Osmans comming to the Court.

& peraduentur worse were the letters, which Sciaus wrote to the Tartar, which ministred matter enough vnto him, to encourage him to his barbarous and cruell designement: and hauing fully resolued with himselfe, not to suffer so pernicious an enemie of his owne to arriue at Constantinople, and also to rid his mind of so great a feare, and especially perceiuing that Sciaus, in whose breast he reposed all his hope and all his protection, did so greatly feare his comming, he commaunded, that twelue thousand souldiers, chaungnig their weapons and apparrell, should goe and lie in await for Osman, in the borders betweene Colchis and Iberia, towards the Tartarian Nomades, and so making an assault vpon him, to bereeue him of his life, hoping that such an outrage either could not or would not bee imputed to his procurement, but rather either to the Tartar Nomades, or to the Mengrellians, or to the Georgians, or to the Moscouites, or to the Theeues by the high way: and to bee short, rather to any bodie else then to him. The commaundementes of the Tartar king were put in practise by them accordingly, and without any further stay they ioyned themselues all together, and so rode towards the place appointed. *The order, which the Tartarian taketh to prohibite Osmās comming to Constantinople.*

The, Volacchi, and the Capigi, which were sent from the king, were now come to Osman, who readily had put himselfe on his way towardes Constantinople, hauing left behind him at Derbent, and at Sumachia two Bassaes, which he thought to bee the most sufficient men and the best of all those that were in Siruania: hauing also appointed verie good orders in the same, and an assured establishment of all those Countries and places, which Mustaffa first had subdued, and hee himselfe afterward had mainteined and kept vnder the obedience of Amurath. Hee had also made good prouision for the naughtie and dangerous passages, through which hee was to iourney, by chosing out fower thousand souldiers, which hee had tried in diuers battels, and brought vp (as a man may say) vnder his owne custody and militarie discipline: by meanes of whose valour hee was in good hope he might passe safely through the treacheries of the Albanians, and the populous Squadrons aswell of the Tartarians as of the Mengrellians: so that hee perswaded himselfe to bee safe and sure from all daunger and feare. And to bee short, hee was not troubled with any other care (as those which were neerest of counsel with him, had told me a thousand times) but onely the exceding desire, wherein hee liued, that he might be able to reuenge the wrong, which the Cuman Tartar had doone to Amurath and to him, by failing in his promises that he had made vnto them, and omitting to sende any more souldiers into Media for these appointed enterprises. *The Tartarian Souldiers ride to the enterprise against Osman*

Osman departeth from Derbent, and leaueth two Bassaes in it and at Sumachia.

Osman setteth forwarde with 4000. souldiers.

Osman desireth to bee reuenged on the Cuman Tartarian.

Thus departed he from Derbent or Demircapi, as we may call it, and coasting along the rockes of Caucasus, (Caucasus I say, that in all seasons of the yeare is all white and hoarie with continuall snowes,) Leauing on his left hand Media, Iberia, and Colchis, and on his right hand the two famous riuers of Tanais, and Volga, euen as his entrance into the first shores of the Euxine sea, hee was by the abouenamed twelue thousand Tartarians, being apparrelled like the Cassachi or Theeues that kept by the high waies, sodenly assailed and fought withall. But, like a huge rocke lying open to tempestes and waues, standing fast & vnmooueable in it selfe, resisteth the thundrings and rushings of the vaste and fearefull billowes, so stoode Osman sounde and firme and couragiouslie sustained this treacherous assaulte, neither was there anie in all his bande, that to auoide this vnexpected onset, resolued to fly vpon it: but al of them, turning their bold countenances against the rebellious multitude of those Traiterous Squadrons, endured the shock of the Assailants, who (as indeede it is their custome in the beginning to vse great force, but afterwardes lightly to languish and withdrawe themselues) finding so stoute a resistaunce in those fewe, which they thought with their onely lookes and shoutinges to haue put to flight, became verie sorrowfull and fowlye discontented. Howbeit forsomuch as they were the Assailants themselues, they could not resolue to flie, and shamefully to abandon their dueties, in pursuing so vnequal a battaile: Whereunto the Souldiers of Osman were alreadye in such sort inflamed, and he himselfe also so enkindled, that with a verie small losse of his owne, and in a verye shorte space of time, hee sawe the great discomfiture of them. Whereby taking fresh force as it were at this conflicte, and sweetned in the taste of victorie and bloud, they were also encouraged and reuiued, that the battaile was not abandoned by them, vntill partely by taking a number of the Tartarians as prisoners, partly hewing others in peeces, and partly driuing a many of them to shamefull flight, they had obtained a most happy victory, and found themselues not onely free from this deepe danger, but also Conquerors and Reuengers of an iniurie so fraudulently contriued against them. By the Prisoners that were taken in sundry sortes, and by meanes of diuers tormentes which he put them too, he was informed that for the feare which their king had cōceiued, least when he came to constantinople he would procure his destruction from Amurath, he was come downe with this Army to seeke his death. Assoone as Osman had receiued certaine intelligence of this treason of the Tartar, hauing caused a perfect processe to bee made of it, together with the dispositions of the saide Tartariaen prisoners, he sent the same by the shortest, safest, and easiest wayes that hee coulde deuise to Amurath at Constantinople. Which processe accompanied also with his Letters, wherein he gaue aduertisement of the treacheries most vniustly contriued against him, and of the battaile that ensued thereupon, prouoking and inflaming

---

The iourney of Osman Bassa.

Osman assaulted & fought withall by the 12000. Tartarians apparrelled like Cassachi.

The Tartariãs at first shewe great valour, but afterward withdrawe themselues.

The Tartariãs discontented.

Great losse of the Tartarians.

The Tartarians destroyed and put to flight.

The prisoners reueale the treacherie plotted against Osman.

Osman aduertiseth Amurath of euerie particular.

THE SIXT BOOKE

him to reuenge so grieuous an iniurie, and so wicked a rebellion. Amurath hauing receiued these reportes, according as the necessitie of the matter required, secretely and resolutly tooke order, that certaine Galleyes should bee sente to the hauen of Caffa, to fetch Osman Bassa, and with all that there shoulde bee conueighed thither a brother of the saide Tartar, commaunding Osman by Letters that he should put to death the Cuman Traitor, and substitute this his Brother in his place, to the ende hee might serue for an example to all men, that such wicked and mischieuous offences doe neuer passe without due punishment.

Amurath taketh order that gallies should be sent to Caffa. Amurath writeth to Osman to flay the Tartarian King and to substitute his Brother in his rowme.

But that wee may the better vnderstand, why this Cuman Brother was at this time so readye for this businesse, it shal be wel in briefe to set down some of the particulars that may open the light of this truth. Among other potēt Princes, that cowardly & basely yeelding to the Ottoman power doe lead a very vile & troublesome life vnder them, the Kings of the Cuman Tartarians called Precopensi did also submit themselues, and gouerned those peoples that were subiecte vnto them, according to the wicked and damnable pleasures of the Ottomans whom they serued. Amonge the rest of these Cuman Kings this present King, who beeing wholly deuoted vnto them, was placed in this kingdome, besides the slaughter of his parents had himselfe also indured diuers & sundry afflictiōs, so that he greatly feared to be remoued from that gouernement and committed to prison. And therfore this his brother, who as we told you was now so ready for this action, as one that for the constitution of his bodie, and for the guiftes of his minde, beeing adorned with the knowledge of Astrologye and Philosophie, was better esteemed by the Subiects, then his brother nowe raining was, (for that by reason of his excessiue tributes, and besides his tributs, of his Ordinarie bribes that he often bestowed at the Court, he was become most odious to his Subiects, from whome he sucked those Reuenues and presents) this his brother (I say) beeing rauished with the conceite of himselfe, and perswaded by the comfortable woordes of his best friendes, resolued to passe to Constantinople: and although hee were younger in yeares, and naked and bare of money and wealth, whereby he might haue obtained that, which hee hoped for, ouer his Brother: yet trusting vpon the common voice and reporte of the people, from whome hee had carried with him verie earnest supplications and intercessions to the Ottoman king, and also relying greatly vpon his owne eloquence, and other vertues whereby he thought he was able to purchase the fauour of the king, hee imagined it to be a reasonable suit and easie to bee graunted, to require that thing of Amurath which age and riches had denyed him: that is to say, that hee woulde driue his Brother out of the kingdome, and to substitute him in his place. And thus wente the good young man to the courte, where hauing bestowed a fewe small

The purpose of the Tartars brother, to bereaue him of his state.

presentes, he did not sticke to shew himselfe to bee a suiter for the rowme of his Brother: who hauing had intelligence before, of his going to Constantinople, had presentlye written to his Embassadours there, that they should not regarde any expences, they should not omit any duety or intreatie, they should not forget any Art or diligence, to retain him stil established in his possessed dig nitye, & to procure his foolish & audatious Brother to be clapt vp in some place, where he might not disturb him in his kingdom. And so whiles the one labored with the power of his toung, and by meanes thereof conioyned with the other ornamentes of his mind hoped to haue become his Brothers superiour, the Agentes of the other did not cease to imploy also the force of their guiftes and Stratagems: and in the end it fell out, that neither learning nor beauty of person, nor good reporte, coulde preuaile somuch for the one as rich presentes and crafty deceites legitimated by gold, could doe for the other, notwithstanding a number of filthy vices that were in him. (And what is it, that money cannot doe amonge couetous people at this day, if it bee bestowed in measure and in time, and distributed in fitte occasions? The young man was committed prisoner, & sent by safe watch to Gogna, sometimes called Iconium a City of Licaonia, and his Brother stil confirmed in his possessed kingdome. With great patience did the vnhappy young man remaine at Gogna, apparelled like an Eremit, and in that his captiuity liued a life altogether conformable to his miserye, and (as al men iustified it vnto me, at my passage through that Cytye, when I went to Constantinople) by his continuall and treacherous execrations, and a kinde of externall innocencye, hee made shewe that hee was voide of all hope or ambitious desire to be brought to a kingdome, but rather sought nothing else nor expected anything else, but onely like a forelorne and vnhappie wretch, with vaine affliction & impious deuotion, to prepare himselfe to a laudable and honorable death. And loe, whiles hee thus liued separated and sequestered from all worthy cogitations, vpon the discouerie of the king his brothers rebellion, with an vnexpected noueltie he was called againe to the dignitie, that hee had sometimes so greatly desired, and of late altogether abandoned. For assoone as Amurath had receiued the aduertisements from Osman, hee sent certaine Volacchi to fetch the young man, & with vnspeakable speed hauing put him in the Gallies, he sent him to Caffa, with letters to Osman of the tenour aforesaid. Osman had no sooner receiued these letters, but aswell for the desire hee had to serue his Lorde, as also to be reuenged vpon him, that so manifestly by not sending his promised aides into Siruan had hindred the enterprises, which hee had so desired, & the Ottoman king commanded, but especially and aboue all for the deadly treacheries that he had contriued against his life, hee himselfe put the Tartarian

The remedie that the Tartar king vsed against his brother.

Mony among corupt people can doe all thinges.

The authour in Gogna had intelligence of the Tartarian youngmā

to death, whom, foreseeing (as it were) and assuring himselfe that he should receiue such order from Amurath, he had alredie by cunning means got into his hands and presently thereupon caused the young man to be saluted King, & acknowledged to be their Captaine and their Lord, and Lieutenant of Amurath.

From the foresaid shores of the Euxyne Sea, Osman Bassa departed afterwards, and having imbarked himselfe in the forenamed Gallies at the Porte of Caffa, passed ouer the great Sea, and entered into the Thracian Bosphorous, arriued at Constantinople in the yeare of mans saluation 1584 where he was receiued with greate pompe and singular significations of good loue. But with most euident and expresse kindes of ioy was hee saluted by the king himselfe, when by his owne speech and presence hee had occasion to declare vnto him euery particularitie of the matters that happened in his long and important voiage, and of the state of Siruan. For hauing deliuered his rich presents to his soueraigne, and being admitted to haue speech with the king himselfe, hee concealed nothing, that might represent the perils and trauels that hee had passed, and the conquestes that hee had made in Siruan. After all which discourses Amurath, who carried a most ardent desire to see the Persian King somewhat bridled, and the Citie of Tauris brought vnder his subiection, beganne to enter conference with Osman about that enterprise, and in the end would needs knowe throughly of him, what issue he could promise him of this his desire, and in what sort, by his aduise and counsel the forces should be employed, and the Armies disposed, for the subduing of that Citie, which ouer all the Nations of the world was so famous, and of so greate honour to the Persian kingdome. To all these demaunds his answere and resolution was, that for so much as now by the late building of the fortresses the matters of Georgia were fully settled and all the borders of Reiuan euen to Erzirum made safe and well guarded with the new fortes erected there, and the Prouince of Siruan also reduced to a kinde of laudable obedience, and to bee short, for somuch as they had now throughlie discouered, what treacherie or deceit soeuer the enemie was able to contriue in all those quarters: and seeing there was no feare left of anie sodaine assault to bee made by anie traitorous assailants to the detriment of those that shoulde passe to Tauris, hee thought, the matter was nowe no longer to bee foreslowed but that it was verie expediente to attempt the famous enterprize of Tauris, and by erecting a Forte in that Citie to raise a terrour ouer al Persia, and a glorirous renowme of their mightie conquestes, amonge the Nations of Europe. For it was alreadie well knowen what the Georgians were able to doo, the people wherof had already partly of their owne voluntary motion, and partly enforced by necessity & feare, yeelded their dutiful obediēce: & although Mustaffa

Osman slaieth the Tartarian king, and substituteth his brother in his place.

Osman departeth by Gallie from the territories of the Tartarians towards Constantinople.

Osman receiued at Constantinople ioyfully.

Osman in speech with Amurath.

Osmans resolution.

Osman aduiseth the enter prise of Tauris, and sheweth the manner how.

had rebelled & returned to his former libertie & natiue Religion, yet he might peraduenture by this time repent himselfe thereof: neither was there any cause at all to feare the treacheries of one, that beeing without any traine to followe him, and of himselfe verie poore: woulde rather seeke to saue himselfe in his obscure and base villages, and to keep his pittifull holdes within the mountaines: neither could bee able to endure the sounde of their victors, much lesse bee so hardie as to assault the victoreis. So that all thinges now were open, neither was there any feare of any noueltie arising, but that the iourney to Tauris might resolutely bee performed: for the accomplishment wherof hee thought that either the same Armie, or at the most a verie little greater would suffize, so that it were of the choisest souldiers.

A letter of Sciaus that was found is the cause why hee was dismissed from his chiefe Visiership.

By reason of one of the letters, which Sciaus Bassa had written to the Cuman Tartar, and was founde I know not howe, Amurath had depriued the saide Sciaus from the office of the chiefe Visier, and banished him from the Courte, so that hee liued afterwardes about Calcedone, vpon the borders of Asia towardes Constantinople, in a certaine Serraglio or close Palace, that yee had there builte for his owne pleasure and recreation. And in the rowme of this his son in law, he had appointed Osman to bee chiefe Visier in the ranke of the Bassaes of the Court: and not contented to haue committed so great a trust vnto him, hee nominated him also the Generall and Soueraigne Captaine in the enterprise of Tauris.

Osman Bassa chiefe Visier.

Such power and force hath vertue, that euen from the verie skomme of the rascall sorte, and out of the rustical route of Mountaine Peasauntes (which notwithstanding cannot bee truely iustified of this Osman) it doth oftentimes in this variable worlde drawe diuerse men into Princes Courtes, and aduaunce them to the highest dignities. This Osmans father was a Circassian borne, who in the common losse and conquest of his countrey, was one of those, that to escape the slaughtering sworde of Selim, submitted themselues to the Turkish yoke, and afterwardes fighting in defense thereof, hee ouercame the Aethtopians, and thereby obtained immortall renowme. Of these his vertues hee lefte the saide Osman his heire, who beeing broughte vppe in aboundance of all thinges, and trayned vp in the Arte of warrefare, became verie couragious and skilfull therein: and at last, from a priuate Souldier was called to the highest dignities of so greate an Empyre, and from thence to the chiefest place of authoritie in the Armie of the Easte, and to bee shorte, was at one instante created a Counseller and Generall of Ottoman. Greate was the ioye that Osman conceiued hereat, and greate was the desire that hee had to make himselfe woorthie of so honourable fauours: and the greater confidence that hee perceiued Amarath had reposed in him, the more eagerly was he

The offspring of Osman Bassa.

Osman chosen General of the Armie to goe to Tauris.

spurred on to doe any thing possible whereby hee might shewe himselfe to haue deserued the same. And therefore aduising with himselfe, that forasmuch as there must bee a greater Armie nowe Leuied, then there was in the former years, & so sent into very far Countreyes, it was also necessarie for him the sooner to send out his aduertisementes into all his subiect Prouinces, and he himselfe by his owne example to prouoke the other Captaines and Souldiers therunto, he determined euen in winter (thought it were as yet somewhat troublesome,) to passe to Chalcedon, and from thence to Angori, to Amasia, to Siuas, and in those territories to driue out the time, vntill hee might vnderstand, that all his souldiers, which were summoned were gathered together. But because vpon this his great speed, it might fal out peraduenture, that his enemies also woulde beginne to prepare a greater number of Souldiers, if they should vnderstande for certaine, that Osman had appointed all these preparations for Tauris: he thought it a better pollicie (for so it pleased Amurath also: to spreade a rumour abroade, that they must goe for Nassiuan, whither Ferat Bassa had giuen out speech that he should haue gone the last yeere before: to the end that the Persians, beeing so beguiled, shoulde not regard the gathering of so mighty an Armye, as they woulde haue done, if they should haue heard of their passage to Tauris.

The diligence of Osman Bassa.

A fained rumour of going to Nassiuan.

And so this Generall cosening Rumour touching Nassiuan, was published abroad, not onely through all the Cities subiect to the Turk, but the fame therof flew also euen into the Countries of the Persians, who notwithstanding beeing very iealous of the Citie of Tauris, and fearing that the matter would fall out, as indeed afterwardes it did, ceased not to make curious & diligent enquiry about it. And although the indignitie and disgrace, that was offered to his Embassadour, dissuaded him from sending any other for treaty of peace, yet to spie out the secretes of the Turkes, and to vnderstande certainely whether their intent were to passe to Nassiuan or to Tauris, hee coulde doe no lesse but dispatch diuers Chiaus or Messengers to Osman, and by making a shewe that he ment in very deed to feele his minde touching conditions of peace, to try whether he could learne and discouer the trueth or no. But by all the meanes, and by all the cunning that he could possibly vse, he could neuer find out any certaine knowledge thereof: so that there still remained in him many doubtfull and confused cogitations, which were engendered and fostered by some carelesse and simple reporters, that Osman had giuen out speeche for the enterprize of Nassiuan.

The Persian iealous of Tauris.

The Persian cannot come to any certen knowledge of the designement of Osman Bassa.

And nowe according to the commandement gone out through all the Cities of the Empire, the Souldiers of all sortes beganne to flocke together: and all those that either were desirous to be established in their former charges and gouernementes of Cities, or sought ambitiously

Osman gathereth together a huge treasure by presents.

to bee honoured with some Office and dignitie, made repaire vnto him as vnto a king and Soueraigne moderator of the Ottoman Empire, presenting him with very large & liberal guiftes. Wherby his estate was so greatly enriched, that through these meanes he had gathered together a huge heape of infinite treasure. And so entertaining them with all affable curtesie, and also with promising both rewardes and honours to all that woulde followe him in his purposed voiage, he leauied a wonderful great number of Men and Moneyes. But nowe was the time come, that called him away to goe towardes Erzirum, where hee was greatlye expected by his huge armie there assembled together, & notwithstanding the great of all things belonging to vittel, that commonly raigneth in those quarters, yet he was enforced to make his iourny to that citie, where he arriued about the latter end of the Moneth of Iuly, and there, with all possible speed taking a viewe of his whole Army, and of all the prouision necessary for so important and famous an enterprize, he dailye laboured to hasten his departure. In the saide citie of Erzirum were mette together all the souldiers of the Prouinces that were woont to send helpe, but yet in a greater number, then euer was gathered by any Generall before, for that euerie man forsooke and abandoned his own priuate busines, & vpon assured hopes of new rewards & vnwonted honors, they were al induced to follow the fame of, their newe Visier. Onelie the people of Aegypt and Damasco were busied with other more priuate Quarels, wher of because they are both of great importance, and also fel out at this verie instant, it wil not be amisse to make some briefe rehearsal, for a manifest, and euident example heerafter, how great harme and mischiefe the diuersitie of opinions, and dissension of neighbours doth breed among all sortes of men.

dearth Great dearth in Erzirum. The greatest Army that euer was gathered was this. The souldiers of Aegypt & Damasco went not with Osman.

The ende of the Sixt Booke.

The Seauenth Booke

The Argument.
HAssan the Bassa of Cairo in Egypt is called to the Court.
Ebrain the Bassa, chosen to be the Kings son in Lawe, is sent to Caireo in the rowme of Hassan.
Hassan in the companie of the Master of the Kings horse goeth to Constantinople.
Hee is committed to prison, and spoiled of all his wealth.
At the instant suite of the Queene, Hassan is set at libertie.
Ebrain is called to Constantinople to finish the mariage.
Ebrain commeth with an Armie of twelue thousand horse.
The Ofspringe, religion, customes, Territories, and weapons of the Drusians.
Three of the chiefe Lordes of the Drusians come to meete Ebrain.
Serafadin also commeth to Ebrain.
Serafadin being accused by his three enemies, speaketh in his owne defence.
Serafadin is committed to prison.
Manogli standeth obstinate and refuseth to come to Ebrain, but writeth his letters vnto him.
Ebrain resolueth to burne the countrie of Manogli.
Veis the Bassa with his sonne the Sangiacco of Ierusalem discomfited by the Drusians.
Gomeda is sent to Manogli, but returneth without speeding in his Message.
Aly the Bassa goeth to Manogli and speedeth.
Manogli sendeth his Mother to Ebrain.
Gomeda goeth againe to Manogli, and returneth with a verie rich present.
Gomeda goeth once againe to Manogli, and returneth with newe presents.

Andera belonging to Manogli is sacked, and nineteene other townes burnt.

Three hundred and fiftie persons belonging to Manogli, hewen in peeces.

The Matademo or chiefe Agent of Manogli, is slayed quicke.

The Souldiers of Serafadin slaine.

The Souldiers of the Turkish Gallies sacke all the Sea coast of Serafodin and Manogli.

Aly Carsusogli buieth the Title of a Bassa with a hundred thousand Duckats.

Mansurogli laied in chaines, and sent to the Gallies.

The territorie of Mansurogli is sacked.

Ebrain is ioyfully receiued into Constantinople.

Ebrain giueth great presents to the Sultan.

Quarrels betweene the Arabians, and the Sangiacco of Ierusalent.

The Subassi of Bethlehem is slayed quicke, by appointment of the Sangiacco.

Osman the Bassa is in a readinesse to departe from Erzirum, with speeche giuen out, that hee woulde not goe to Tauris, but to Nassiuan.

THE SEAUENTH BOOKE

Hassan-Bassa the Quenes Eunuch, sent to Cair, to be Bassa there.

AMurath had heertofore taken Hassan the Eunuch out of the Serraglio, from the charge that hee had there, to serue in the Quenes Court, and had sent him as Bassa to Cair in Aegypt: in whose fauoure, for recompence of his continual seruice employed in het behalfe, the Queene had obtained this great Office, which besides the honour belonging vnto it, was also verie beneficiall and profitable vnto him, as in deede it is to any other person, whose good happe it is to bee aduaunced thereunto: the riches and multitude of people inhabiting therein being so great, that it seemeth not to be one Citie, but rather that it containeth within the large Circuite of it, a number of Cities. This man beeing

Cair seemeth to bee many Cities rather then one.

coueteous of money, and desirous to handle the matter in such sorte, as this place of gouernment might yeelde him so great benefit, that hee shoulde little neede to seeke for any more suche grauntes at the kinges handes, by all manner of meanes, aswel indirectly as directly, sought to oppresse al the whol Nation, and spared neither any state nor age, nor sexe, but by all importunities and vndue courses, hee would wring and extorte rewardes and bribes from euerie man. By which his sinister and corrupt dealing, hee had now made himselfe so odious and intollerable vnto them, that there was not a man, but would choose to doo anie thing possible, rather then to remaine vnder these his continual tyrannies. And in the end, when it was plainely perceiued, that neither Religion, nor Loue, nor Iustice, nor Reason, could remooue his coueteous minde from his vsuall cruelties and rapine, a great number of such (as were moste vexed and molested by this newe Tyrant,) beganne daily, in close and quiet manner to goe to Constantinople, & make humble petitions to the king, that hee would bee pleased to displace so cruell and vniust a wretch, as thought it lawfull for him to drinke vp the bloude of their poore families, without any cause or offence at all. Neither were these complaintes made once or twice by one or two alone, but oftentimes and by manie seuerall persons: soe that generally in the Courte, there was no talke of anie thing else, but onely of the villanies and mischiefes, that were reported of the Eunuch. At the last, Amurath seeing that these publike exclamations wente dailie so farre, that it was nowe a shame for him to let them goe any further withoute due punishment, hee resolued with himselfe to call him to the Courte, and hauing sent vnto him certaine Capigi and Chiaus, hee admonished him sondrie times to returne home. But the Eunuch, whome it highlie grieued to forsake so fitte an occasion of enriching himselfe, did still delaye his returne, and beganne to alledge newe-coyned excuses for his longer stay. Which when Amurath vnderstoode, thinking rather that he was mocked thereby, & peraduenture also entering into some suspition of some publike alteration in those quarters, with a newe deuise hee determined to prouide for so greate a disorder, and by punishing the mischieuous nature of the coueteous Eunuch, in some parte at the leaste to satisfie the people that were in a mutinie, and to pacifie their pittifull exclamations and complaintes.

There satte at that time amonge the chiefe Bassaes of the Courte, one Ebrain, by Nation a Sclauonian, and of a place called Chianichie, a shorte daies iourney distante from Ragusa, a yoonge man of the age of two and thirtie yeares or thereaboutes, of verie faire conditions, and of reasonable iudgement, vpon whome Amurath him self had heretofore determined to bestow his own daughter for his wife and to make him his sonne in law. Whereof before this time there had beene diuers treaties and speeches. And therefore nowe beeing minded to remooue the Eunuch from his Office, and to satisfie the Citie, and hauing no other person, to whom he thought hee might better committe that truste, and beeing also willing withall, to minister occasion to his saide sonne in lawe to make monie and enriche himselfe, hee was resolued to send him as General Syndic and soueraigne Iudge into Aegypt, giuing him in particular charge, that hee shoulde remember howe wickedlie his predecessor had dealt before him, so that all the whole Territories of that huge and large Citie, were come vp euen vnto the Court, to

The Tyrannie of the Eunuch

The Eunuch Bassa of Cair, called home to the Court by Amurath.

Amurath desireth to pacifie the complaints of the Aegyptians.

Ebrain, a Bassa of the Court.

Amurath purposeth to bestow his daughter vpō Ebrain, for his wife.

Amurath findeth meanes for Ebrain to enrich himselfe, by sending him as Bassa and Syndic to Cair

exclaime againste his Tyrannie and coueteousnesse. And so this newe Bassa tooke his iourney towardes Aegypt, although there ranne before him a greate rumor of his comming, and of the greate authoritie, wherewith hee was sente. At which reporte as the Aegyptians rested contente and ioyfull: so the Eunuch waxed verie sad and sorrowfull: and did verilie perswade himselfe, that this alteration coulde not but engender some strange issue & effect against him. Which opiniō did so much the more deeply settle it self in his mind, for that he did not knowe one trustie person in all Aegypt, of whom hee might hope for any helpe and protection, in case that Ebrain Bassa shoulde driue him to any streighte. Whereupon aduising with himselfe to prouide better for his owne affaiers, and safety of his life, hee was resolued not to stay for the arriuall of the Visier, but departing out of Aegypt, with great care and circumspection, he trauelled towardes Constantinople, in hope to appease the kings wrath, or at leaste by the mediation of bribes and by the intercession of the Queene, to finde him of a more mild and placable disposition, then hee should finde Ebrain, who without doubt would not haue spared any extremitie or cruelty, to bereaue him both of his goods, & also of his life. Thus the craftie Eunuch departed from Aegypt, and put himselfe on his iourny towardes Constantinople, vsing greate diligence and care, that hee might not meete with Ebrain, who beeing alreadie certified by many Aegyptians of the escape of Hassan, gaue speedye aduertisement thereof to Amurath at Constantinople, to the ende hee mighte take suche order as was conuenient. Amurath hearing this, and hearing withall, that hee kept not the highway, that leadeth ordinarilye from Memphis into Thracia, feared leaste hee might flie to straunge Princes, and particularly suspected, that beeing arriued in Soria, he would passe into Persia to the Soffian king, and so worke him double and treble dommage, as one that had already gathered a huge treasure, and hauing liued in the Court, knew the most secret affaires therof & learned althe priuy deuises and fashions of the Serraglio. Wherupon with all diligence hee dispatched his Imbrahur Bassi (whome wee may call the Maister of his horse) with fortye of his Capigi, all Gentlemen vshers, and Officers of the most secret and neerest rowmes about him, with charge and commandement, that if hee met with him, he should bring him aliue to the Court, vsing all the assistaunce and aide of his people, that might bee requisit, and for that purpose deliuered vnto him very effectual & large letters, written after the best manner that is vsed in the Court. The kings Messenger with his appointed traine departed, and without any extraordinarie enquiry after the Eunuch, hee founde him in Soria, encamped in the plains of the Apameans, neere to the citie now called Aman, but in times past Apamea, the Principall Citie of that Countreye, where the Riuer

The Aegyptians ioyful, & the Eunuch sorrowful for the comming of Ebrain.

The Eunuch hopeth to pacifie the king by his going to the courte. The Eunuch departeth from Cair.

Amurath feareth that the Eunuch would flye to strange Princes.

Imbrahur Bassi dispatched by Amurath to meet with the Eunuch.

Orontes with his pleasaunt course watereth the greene and beautifull hilles, and from thence running along to the Walles of Antiochia, dischargeth it selfe afterwardes into the Siriac Sea, neere vnto Seleucia Pieria, which nowe they call Soldin. Assoone as the Eunuch vnderstood of the comming of the Imbrahur, he gaue order vnto his gard of slaues, which in great number with speares and Arcubuses did ordinarilie keepe his pauilion, that they should not grant entertainement into his Tent, to any other but onely to the Imbrahur himselfe, & in all rigorous manner to keepe the rest of the Capigi from comming in. This order was giuen in verie good time. For assoone as the Kings Officer had discouered the Tentes of the fugitiue Bassa, in all haste hee ranne towards the same, and seeking out the greatest among them, wente presently thither to enter into it with all his followers. But the slaues beeing in Armour opposed themselues against them, and permitting the Imbrahur to passe into the pauilion, entertained the rest of his traine without. The Imbrahur read vnto him the commaundement which hee had from the king to bring him to the Court, and instantly moued him that without any resistaunce hee woulde quietlye goe with him. But the cunning Eunuch, Behold (quoth he) howe without any calling of the king, or conducting by you I come of my selfe, and am assured that I shall finde not onely pardon and pitie, but also speciall fauour and grace in the sight of my Lord. For the wicked treacheries of my false accusers cannot abuse the vprighte and milde nature of the king, to the preiudice of mee, beeing an Innocent. And so they wente all together towardes Constantinople, keeping the high way of Antiochia, of Heraclea, of Gogna, and of Nicaea.

 The politike and crafty Eunuch had in this mean time dispatched diuers postes with letters to the Sultan Ladies, certifieng them of his comming, and principally beseeching the Queene, to protect him, and to purg the kings minde from all affection of anger and in dignation that he might haue conceiued against him: and so he arriued at Chalcedon. Assoone as the king vnderstood of his arriuall, hee caused all the treasure which he had gathered, to bee taken from him, withall the rest of his priuate substance, and the same to be carried into the great store house, and himselfe to bee shutte vppe in prison within the seauen Toweres: Where after hee hadde woorne out many daies, wherein hee still feared some deadlie blowe, hee receiued from the Queene an vnexpected aduertisement, that hee shoulde bee of good cheere, and quiet himselfe for that his wealth had alreadie excused his life, and that shee hoped in verie shorte time to gette him restored also to his libertie: which indeed she brought to passe. For she her selfe made earnest petition to her husband, that forasmuch as hee hadde bereaued her Eunuch of all his goods, hee woulde at the least deliuer

Imbrahur Bassa findeth the Eunuch in the champaines of Apamea.

The Eunuch and the Imbrahur go together to Constantinople.

The Eunuch at Chalcedon.

him out of prison, and restore him vnto her. This requeste of the Queene was graunted accordinglye: but all the treasure that hee hadde vniustlye scraped together out of the Families of Aegypt, remained still amonge the Golde and other iewels of the king.

But Ebrain Bassa, according to his newe commission was nowe arriued in Aegypt, and in shorte space, by farre more sinistre deuises, then the Eunuch before him had vsed, besides the annuall and Ordinarye Reuenue, of that Prouince, amounting yeerely to the summe of six hundred thousand Cecchini, he had got together an infinite heape of riches, that was able onely of it selfe to make him woorthie of his promised wife. And therefore he was called home to the Courte, to accomplish the intended Mariage. With this comman dement to returne to Constantinople, he receiued also in charg, that he shuld make his iourny through the people of Drusia, and such as hee shoulde find truely obedient vnto him, he should confirme them in their due obedience and make them pay their ancient duties: but such as were disobedient, he should quite root them out and destroy them: & from euery one of them, as wel friends as enemies in any case, to take away their Arcubuses, & al other kind of wepons whatsoeuer. Ebrain presently put this commandement in execution, & hauing leauied the foresaid treasure, put together all his owne priuate riches that hee had gathered in the time of his gouernment, and raised good store of Souldiers in that prouince, hee tooke with him especially thirteene Sangiacchi, that were ordinarilie accustomed to sit as assistauntes in the ruling of those populous Territories of Cair, vnder the gouernement of the Visier, the king or the Bassa of that Countrie, If ye list so to terme him: and so sette him selfe on his iourneye towardes Gasa, passing ouer those waste and huge wildernesses of Sande, that lie betweene Memphis and Gaza, and are a great parte of Arabia Deserta. From Gaza ioyning the Sangiaccho thereof with him, hee wente to Ierusalem, and from thence causing the Sangiaccho there also to followe his trayne, hee iournied by Saffetto, by Lezium, by Naplos, (called in times paste Samaria) still taking with him the Sangiacchi of all those places, and at the laste turned himselfe towardes Damasco, so that before hee ioyned with the bande of Damasco, hee had gotten together eighteene Sangiacchi, with all their Squadrons of Souldiers and Slaues. Besides these, hee had also his owne priuate Courte, which was woonderfull populouse, and two hundred Ianizzaries of Constantinople, whome the king woulde needes haue him to take with him at his departure from the Courte: so that in somme, hee had an Armie, almost of twelue thousand horsemen, From Damasco there were come to meete him, euen as farre as Ierusalem, all the Ianizzaries of that Citie, vnder the Conduct of their Aga, or Captaine, and all the Zaini and the Spahini, and the other souldiers

The Eunuch set at liberty.

Ebrain called to Constantinople to accomplish the intended mariage.

Order giuen to Ebrain to surucie, and subdue the Drusians.

Ebrain departeth from Cair with 13. Sangracchi.

Ebrain in the way of Damasco.

Ebrain with an armie of about 12000. horse.

that were vnder the gouernment of that Bassa, who at that time was one Veis, mentioned before in the troubles of Generall Ferat, in the laste booke: al which were no more in number there, but onely two thousande persons. There came from Aleppo Aly Bassa, being then out of Office (whome the Turkes call Mosul: that is to saie discharged or dismissed) and a Companie of two hundred Slaues with him. Ebrain also sente for Giaffer Bassa, beeing at that time the Eunuch or Captaine of Tripoli, a craftie man, and cruell of Nature: but hee beeing enflamed with the fame of Osman Bassa, who loued him verie well, woulde not in anie case obey the commaundemente of Ebrain. There came to him besides by the waie of Sidonia, which they nowe call Seida, the Aza of the Ianizzaries of Cyprus, with all the bande of that desolate and destroyed Isle: which Captaine was transported ouer in the Gallies, that by the kinges appointment were sente to fetche Ebrain: who beeing nowe made stronge with all these Souldiers, had purposed the vtter ruine of the disobediente Drusians, and the purchase of his owne glorie by triumphing ouer them. But because this my Historie shall not proceed vnder vnknowen names, wee are to declare, who these Drusians are, for whom there are nowe so greate preparations made by the newe Captaine, and of whome the king is so suspicious and doubtfull.

The Drusians are by Nation and Ofspring, French-men, the Reliques of those, that with deuoute mindes did in times past fight those memorable and Christian battels in Iurie, and recouered the holie Sepulchre of Christ: and beeing afterwardes subdued partly by the plague, and partlie by the furie of the Barbarians, mingled their seede with the Circumcised Nation, and so together with their authoritie and commaunding, lost also their first faith and religion: so that hauing extinguished their former sacred knowledge, they grew into a hatred of the Turkish superstition, and abhorred the Circumcision of the other, and betooke themselues to a newe Prophet, well knowine and beloued among them, called Isman. The true and right Drusians doo liue vncircumcised, neither doo they forbeare wine, which the Turkes are forbidden. They make it lawfull for themselues, without any conscience or respect, to take their own daughters to their wiues: So that (if it be true which Aristotle writeth, That amonge certaine brute beastes there is a kinde of respecte obserued in bloude) coupling themselues together by these prophane and filthie Mariages, they liue more beastlie, then the verie brute creatures. And as by their prophet and their factions they woulde needes bee separated from the Turkish sect, so in Dominion and gouernement they haue soughte by all meanes to bee different from them: for notwithstanding al the chaunges and troubles of the Turkish Tyrantes, yet haue they alwaies beene subiect

The Drusian people, what they are.

Isman the prophet of the Drusians.
The Drusians are not circumcised, they drinke wine liberally, and take their owne daughters to their wiues.

to their owne Naturall Princes, which by aunciente descent had the rule ouer them, and woulde neuer admitte any Captaine or Gouernour of the Ottomans to bee within the Countreyes, which they possessed. They are a people verie warrelike, stoute, obstinate, bolde, vndaunted, and religious obseruers of their lawe, although indeed some of their chiefe Rulers, to saue their liues, haue beene enforced to followe the pleasure of those that were mightier then themselues, by reason of their dissention with their neighbours. In battaile they vse especially the Arcubuse and the Scimitarre: and yet some of them at this daie doo serue with Launces and Dartes. They are apparrelled like the Easterne people, with a Turbante on their heade: and breeches they neuer weare, but in steede thereof they couer those partes with their Coate, which reacheth downe to their knees in length, by buttening it vppe before. They are also accustomed to grosse and Mountaine Meates. They inhabite all the Countrey that is inuironed within the confines of Ioppa aboue Caesarea in Palestina, and within the Riuers of Orontes and Iordane, stretching it selfe euen to the playne of Damasco, neere to the hilles that compasse it aboute, vpon the coast of Mounte Libanus.

marginalia: The Drusians would neuer admit any Turkish Gouernour.

marginalia: The weapons of the Drusians.

marginalia: The Countrie which the Drusians inhabit.

They were all in times paste good friendes, and confederate together in loue and concorde, so that they were in those daies greately esteemed: but nowe, beeing sette in a confusion throughe greedinesse, and couetuousnesse, they are deuided amonge them selues, and one of them contrarie and enemie to the other, but especially and principally at this daie, there are fiue chiefe Captaines or Heades of them, which they call Emir, One of them is named Ebneman, whome the Turkes call Manogli: Another Serafadin: the thirde Mahamet Ebnemansur, (the Turkes call him Mansurogli:) the forth Ebnefrec, by the Turks tearmed Feracogli, & by the Moors surnamed Acra, which we may interpret Scuruy or Scald,) and the fift, Ali Ebne-Carfus by the Turks called Ali-Carfusogly. Vnder these, who indeede carry the title and auctority of an Emir, that is to say King or Chiefe, there are diuers others, whome the Drusians themselues call Macademi, that are either Deputies to the Emirs, or els their Factors or Agentes, or both: amonge whome, in this alteration of matters, which wee intende to write of, Gomeda and Mendel were two verie famous persons, who kept their residence, the one in Baruti, and the other in Tripoli for Mansurogli, and called themselues Emirs, rather for flatterie then of any duetie, for that they were indeede no other but the Macademi of the saide Emir-Mahamet Ebnemansur.

marginalia: There are at this day fiue Captaines or chiefe rulers among the Drusians.

Ebneman, he inhabited the Mountains & fields, that are contained vnder the Iurisdictions of Caesarea, of Ptolemaida, of Tyrus, and of Sidonia: the inhabitants at this day call those places, Cheiserie, Acca, Sur, Seida, all of them, (as farre as I coulde see, when I trauelled in

marginalia: Ebneman or Manogli.

THE SEAUENTH BOOKE 187

Pilgrimage to the holye sepulchre of Christ) beeing desolate Countreyes and vtterlie destroyed, and hath his residence for the most parte vppon the hill, in Andera. Hee is verie mightye in men and Armour, and since the time that by treacherie and treason his Father was murthered by Mustaffa then Bassa of Damasco, he hath beene a deadly Enemy to the Turkish name.

Ebnemansur enioyeth al the Territorie contained with in Baruto and Anafe, and keepeth his residence vpon the hill in Gazir. Hee, beeing driuen thereunto through the controuersies that hee had with Ebnesuip, sometimes the Emino or Customer of the Kay at Tripoli, and with Ebneman aforenamed, yeelded himselfe as a pray to the Turkes, and was made the Sangiacco of Laodicea, called Lizza, hauing also the charge of the Custome house of Tripoli committed vnto him, where afterwardes Gomeda remained for him: But at the reasonable and honourable requestes of Giouanni Michaele, sent as Consul by the Senate of Venice into Soria, and by me in this Historie, oftentimes but not worthelie enough mentioned (for I was the meanes and practiser for the saide Consul, though vnworthie I were for such businesse) the said office was taken from him, whiles he was prisoner in Constantinople, in the yeere. 1586.

Ebnemansur or Māsurogli

Serafadin keepeth his state betweene Ebneman, & Ebnemansur: beeing in good league and confederate with the first, and at mortall enimitie with the second. Hee is the weakest of all the rest in forces and reuenues.

Seferadin.

Ebnefrec inhabiteth that parte of Libanus, that is towardes the East, and runneth downe euen to the foote of Libanus, ioyning vpon the plaines of Bacca. Of which plaines, together with the Citty (called by the inhabitantes there, Balbech, and by some thought to be Caesarea Philippi.) Emir Aly Ebnecarfus was euer the Lorde and owner, who also in this chaunge of Fortune, bought the Title of a Bassa; and would needes submitte himselfe wholly to the seruice of the Turkes. And heere along runneth the vale, that is so famous amonge the Phisitians, and Poetes, betweene Lib anus and Anti-Libanus, where also are to be seene the Lakes of Orontes and of Iordan, called Ior and Dan.

Ebnefrec or Feracogli.

EbneCarfus or Carfusogli.

The vale betweene Libanus and anti-Libanus famous among Phisitians. Ior and Dan, the two heads of Iordan.

Ebnefrec, Ebnecarfus and Ebnemansur, were alwaies great friends, but now especially at the comming of Ebrain Bassa, they shewed themselues, more straitly confederated together: Serafadin and Manogli were euer opposite against them: so that the one side procuring the ouerthrowe and mischiefe of the other; they haue vtterlye loste their strength, and haue no meanes left them to defend themselues from the Ottoman forces. Nowe assoone as the newes came among them, that Ebrain the Visier beeing departed from Cair woulde come into Soria, to subdue the Drusians, the three confederats aboue named, of purpose to turne all the mischiefe vpon Ebneman and Serafadin their enemies, resolued to goe and meet with the Bassa to shewe themselues subiect and deuoted to king Amurath, to carrie with them large and liberall bribes, and by accusing Serafadin and Ebneman of infidelitie, of disobedience, & of rebellion, to entreat their vtter destruction and ouerthrowe. And so hauing packed vp together greate store of money, cloth of silke, cloth of Woollen, and cloth of Gold, with many loades of other silkes and things of exceeding value, euery of the three beeing accompanied, one with some twoo thousand, and another with some three thousand, put themselues on their iourny towardes Ebrain, and met him at Ierusalem, where hee was already arriued. This their comming Ebrain Bassa tooke in woonderfull good parte, and verye courteously accepted those rich and great presentes which they brought him, and perceiuing such offers of their fidelitie and obedience: and such accusations of the two Drusian Captaines their enemies, hee began to bee in good hope of his intended enterprise. Neither did he forslow to vse moste sweet speeches vnto them, promising due rewardes to euery one of them and putting them in great expectation that he would encrease their honour, and enlarge their estates. By which liberall promises they beeing nowe become bold and venturous, beganne in more sharp, and bitter manner to accuse their two enemies. Which thing did the more highlye please Ehrain for that hee plainely perceiued, that nothing could more easely compasse their ouerthrow, then this their discorde. And therfore most readilie hee promised them, not onely that hee woulde procure the destruction of those their enemies, as rebells to the Turke, but also that hee woulde make themselues the Meanes and Ministers of their owne reuenge and chastisement. And thus beeing all accompanied and ioyned together, they came by the way of Damasco to the Champaigne of Bocca beforenamed, and in those plains incamped themselues. This was in the month of Iulie and in the yeere of mans redemption. 1585. And the whole Armie, that was with Ebrain, reconing also the Souldiers of the three Emirs, was about the number of twentie thousand horsemen strong.

In this place there came people out of all quarters, with presentes to honour the Visier, to whom he likewise yeelded such fauours & reliefes, as his coueteous nature could afford them. Among the rest, Giouanni Michaele, mentioned a little before, sente Christoforo de Buoni his Interpreter to salute the saide Bassa, who againe for his parte shewed diuerse signes and tokens of the Loue and Reuerence that hee carried towardes the Venetian estate. And for that the saide Christoforo de Buoni was of the same Nation and language that Ebrain was off, both of them beeing Sclauonians, and of Ragusi, hee esteemed of him so deerly, that hee woulde needes retaine him still, with him

The three Drusian Emirs goe to meete Ebrain as far as Ierusalem with a greate traine.

Ebrain expecteth good successe ouer the Drusians, by their discorde among themselues.

The Army of Ebrain in the plains of Bocca encreased to the nūber of 20000. hors

Giouanni Michaele the Venaetian Cōsul sendeth Chtistoforo de Buoni his interpreter to visite Ebrain the Visier with honourable presente.

as his familiar Companion, during all the time, that hee remained in Soria, about the subduing of the Drusians. By which meanes I attained to the precise and faithfull knowledge of all the proceedings in Drusia.

From these plaines also, Ebrain presently sente Letters to Serafadin, and to Ebneman, whereby hee inuited them to come vnto him, and declare themselues to bee Subiectes and obediente to the Sultan, to the ende hee mighte make intercession on their behaulfes for all suche honorable fauour as they desired: but if they woulde not come, then they must bee assured, that they shoulde bee depriued both of their estates and of these liues. Manogli would not come by any meanes: But Serafadin beeing poore both in wealth and in forces, and sarre more weake then Manogli, resolued to come, hoping that by his presents hee might rid himselfe of all trouble, for that he had hearde of the fortunate successe that had hitherto happened to the three Emirs, who (as all the worlde thought) had made the kings Champion their great friende and protector. And therefore hauing packed vp together diuerse loades of silkes, greate store of Money, and many cloathes of good value and beautye, hee carried them with him to honour the newe Duke, by whose Letters hee was so largely inuited. Hee caused also diuerse of his Subiectes to goe with him, and at last arriued at the Pauilion of Ebrain with his rich presentes, hauing first commaunded all those, that had accompanied him thether, to sequester themselues from him. The guiftes were readilye receiued, and the speech of Serafadin hearde with great attention, which in effect tended to no other ende, but onely to perswade the Visier, that he had alwaies beene deuoted and a vassall to Amurath, and that hee had carried a continuall desire to bee imployed in any seruice for him, and that nowe beeing led by the same affection, and assured by the friendly & courteous offers made him in his letters, hee was come to shewe himselfe vnto him to be the same man, & proffered him whatsoeuer lay in his slender power to performe. Ebrain made no answere to any of his speeches, but onely asked him the cause, why he liued continually in discord & bralles with the three Emirs (who also sate at that time in the same Pauilion.)

'Wherunto Serafadin answered, that neuer any Act proceeded from him, that might be the cause of any quarels or dissentiōs, but al sprong frō those three, who, because they were more mighty thē he, did continually woorke him great disquiet, & oppresse him intollerably: so that if he had at any time taken vp armes against them, he had done it al simply in his own defence, & onely to withstand their insolent molestations, & not because he was desirous of warres and dissentions, for that he did principally loue peace with al men, but specially & the rather with those that were his neighbours. Heerat the three conspirators arose, & by their grim looks bewraying their mindes

From Christofero de Buoni the Authour all the particulars of the Drusian people. Ebrain by letters inuiteth Seferadin and Manogli.

Serafadin in the presentes of Ebrain. The speech of Serafadin. The accusetiō of Serafadi. His defence.

full of hatred, they tolde him, that he was euer the occasion of al the bralles. For that by his continual disquieting of those quarters, those hils, those champeignes, & those hauens of the sea, he had procured a perpetual losse & hinderance to the customes of the Sultan, (whose officer Ebnemansur was.) Adding withal, that at this day his insolency was growen so great that from any other coasts or maritimal places, there durst not any strange vessel ariue at those Portes of Sidonia, of Tyrus & of Berito, nor any merchant or merchādize passe ouer the plains: But as thogh those countries were a pray & spoile to the theeus of Arabia, they were generally auoided of al trauelers both by land & sea. Serafadin would gladly haue replied in defēce of himself, by saying that neither Baruto, nor Seida nor Sur were vnder his iurisdictiō, but in troth partly vnder the authority of Manogli, & partly vnder the tyrannie of Ebnemansur.' But Ebrain preuented him, and surcharging him with manie iniurious words, commaunded the Captaine of the two hundred Ianizzaries of Constantinople, to take him into his custodie, and so beeing placed in a rotten Tente, that was appointed for him, hee was euerie night from thence forward put in the Stocks & in chains and guarded with a trustie gard of Ianizzaries.

In this meane time, came the aunswere of Manogli, who wrote backe to Ebrain Bassa, in this manner. To the Lord of Lordes, Soueraigne aboue the greate ones, the mightie, the Noble Captaine, Cosin to the Graund Lord, and the worthiest among the elect of the prophet Mahamet, the Noble and famous Lord, Ebrain Bassa. God giue good successe to his haughty enterprises, and prosperitie in all his honour. I doe wish (euen as thou doest louingly inuite and exhort mee) that I might come before thee, and follow thee, and serue thee alwaies, in any occasion, that it may happen thee to stand in neede of my helpe. For I knowe that thou wouldest rest assured of the reuernce that I beare towardes the Lorde, and of the most feruent desire, wherein I liue, to serue him, and to employ both my substance & my life in his seruice. Wherof I haue also giuen some testimonie, though but small, in the mannaging of the Customes, that I haue receiued. Wherein I haue alwaies so carried my selfe, that I am not his Debtor of one Aspro. A thing iwis, that Ebnemansur (who is nowe with thee) hath not done. For although by his comming to meete thee, euen as farre as Ierusalem, hee would make a shew of his sidelitie, yet doeth hee vsurpe more then two hundred thousand Duckates of the kinges, which hee doth most vniustly detain frō him of his customes. 'But my hard fortune will not grant mee the fauour, that I may come vnto thee. For there are at this present with thee three of mine enemies, who (I know well) beeing not contented to haue alwaies disquieted and troubled my estate, doo nowe seeke to bring mee into so great hatred with thy heart, that if thou haddest mee

Newe accusations of Serafadin.

Serafadin by the commandement of Ebrain imprisoned.

The letter of Manogli to Ebrain Bassa.

in thy handes, without any consideration thou wouldest bereaue mee of my life. And I am assured, that this sending for mee, doth import no other thing but onely a desire that thou hast to imprison mee, and so to kill mee. For I know, how much thou art giuen to greate enterprises. Besides this, my comming is also hindred by mine ancient oath, that I tooke, when beeing as yet but a child, I sawe mine owne father, so villanously betraied by the murdering sword of Mustaffa, beeing at that time the Bassa of Damasco: who vnder the colour of vnfeined freindship, got him into his handes, and traiterousslie stroke of his head. For in trueth I carie the image of my fathers reuerend head, al pale, & yet as it were brething, imprinted in my minde, which oftentimes presenteth it selfe to mee, aswell sleeping in the darknesse of the night, as also waking in the light of the day, and talking with mee, calleth to my remembrance the infidelitie of that murdering Tyrant, and exhorteth mee to keepe my selfe alooffe, from the handes of the mightie. And therefore I neither can, nor may obey thy requestes, and in that respect it grioueth mee, that I shall seeme disobedient vnto thee, beeing in any other action, and in all my cogitations, wholly addicted to doe anie seruice, not onely to thee, who art most worthie to bee reuerenced of farre greater persons then I am, but also to euerie the least Vassall of Amuraths.'

Thou wilt pardon me, I hope, and thou shalt well perceaue, that if there be any thing neere me, that may be acceptable to thee, all that I haue whatsoeuer, though in respect of thy selfe it may seeme vile and base, yet is it thyne, and is now reserued wholie for thee and not for me. Farewell, and command me, and hold mee excused, vpon these iust causes, which thou hearest, for my being so backward in comming to honour thee, as my duety requireth. The letter was subscribed in this manner. The Poore and the least amongst the sclaues of the Graund Lord: The Sonne of Man.

When Ebrain had read this letter, coniecturing thereby the constant opinion of Ebne-Man, that by no means he would willingly come within his power, hee resolued himselfe to go vpon him with all his Armye, and by burning his Townes, and threatning him in all terrible manner, either by force or by slight to get him into his hands, and in case he could not at last bring that to passe, then at least to try, whether he could draw from him as many arcubuses, and as great giftes and tributes, as possibly hee might. And therefore hee raised all his Campe, and turned himselfe towardes the countrey of Manogli, and leauing no place vnattempted, hee burned and destroyed foure and twenty Townes that were subiect vnto him, so mounting vp certaine rockes of Libanus, vpon the top of a large hill, (that standeth ouer Andara, and other places belonging to Manogli,) he encamped himselfe. But whiles

Ebrain resolueth to destroy the cuntry of Ebne-Man.

& 24. towns of Manoglies burned by Ebrain the Visier.

the armie of Ebrain was thus marching forwarde, Veis Bassa, with a great part of his people and his sonne the Sangiacco of Ierusalem, with his souldiers likewise, being in all to the nomber of a thousand & fiue hundred persons, were leaft behind in the champaines of Bocca, and (as it were a Rereward) had separated themselues from the rest of the army. But whiles they were busie in raising their Tentes, by a very great band of the Drusians of the faction of Manogli, that by vnusuall & vnknowen waies descending downe vpon them, found the said Bassa, and his son, with all the foresaid souldiers euen vpon the point of departing, they were furiously assaulted, and with the first tempest of arcubuses, & suddain blowes of their swords, they were so annoyed and terrified, that their enemies continuing their present victorie, became the Lordes of the pauilions, the wealth, and the armour of the Turkes, and leading away with them their horses & their carriages, in all terrible and stout manner they put to death about fiue hundred persons, and scarce gaue any leasure to scape, either to the Bassa the father, or to the Sangiacco the sonne, who fled straight to Ierusalem, and neuer returned againe to Ebrain: but Veis followed the army, and was thought worthie to be pittied of all men, and especially of Ebrain, who promised him great rewards and honours at the Kinges hands for his seruice.

Veis Bassa with the Sangiacco his son discomfi ted by the Drusians.

Vpon the hill aforesaid, the Visier continued foure & twentie daies together, with aboundance of all thinges necessary for victuaill: during all which tyme he attended nothing els, but to trye all deuises, how hee might draw money and presentes from Ebne-Man, or how hee might traine him into his handes. For the compassing whereof, he dispatched Gomeda the Agent or Factor of Ebnemansur, to the said Ebne-Man, being in Andera: and sent word by him, that for asmuch as he would not giue creadit to the promise that was made him, nor aduenture himselfe to come into the handes of his frend, he should send vnto him all the Arcubuses he had. For the Sultans pleasure was, that his people which went not to the wars in his seruice, should not be furnished with so great store of weapons, to the daunger of their neighbours, and of the subiectes themselues. With great griefe of mind did Ebne-Man behold the said Gomeda, as the man whom hee well knew to be the Factor of his deadly enemy, but yet durst not in any sort doo him anie iniury, nor giue him any reproach. But when he heard the demand for the Arcubuses, he aunswered him, that all his people and weapons were dispersed abroade ouer his Territorie, so that hee could not tell what Arcubuses to send him. And so Gomeda returned without any aunswere, that good was. Which when Aly the Bassa of Aleppo before named, vnderstood, he offred himselfe to the Visier, that hee would go vnto him, and that to good purpose. Many reasons did Aly Bassa

Gomeda goeth by commandement of Ebram to demand Arcubuses of Manogli.

Aly Bassa goeth to Manogli.

vse, to perswade the wary Drusian, that hee would come and yeeld his obedience to Ebrain, swearing that no manner of outrage should be doone vnto him, & promising him great and honorable fauours. But neuer could he remoue the sound and prouident mind of Ebne-Man, or winne him to yeeld himselfe into the handes of a man whom he thought to be so murderous: which when he had found to be more then certain, then did he labour to perswade him, at the least, that he would send Ebrain a good nomber of arcubuses, & withall som honorable presents in signe of the reuerence that he did beare towardes him, and of his obedience to Amurath: wherein although he found the mind of the Drusirn to bee as yet somewhat harde, as a man that would giue neither little nor much, knowing that all would be but cast away in the wind, yet at the last he brought him so about, that he was content so farre to pleasure him, as to send a present to Ebrain. And thereupon gaue him three hundred & twenty arcubuses, twentie packes of Andarine silkes, and fiftie thousande Duckates, to carrie to the Turkish Bassa for a gift, and to reconcile him vnto him. For the better effecting whereof, and that he might be rid of him, the next morning he sent his owne mother before him, who in the behalfe of her sonne, did performe a very worthie message, excusing him, aswell in respect of his enemies that sate there so neere vnto him, as also in regard of his oath, which he had solemnlie sworne, that he would neuer commit himselfe againe into the handes of a Turke. For the which she alleadged very good testimony of the deceitfull and lying promises of Mustaffa, being then the Bassa, or rather the Tirant of Damasco, by whose handes she herselfe saw her owne husband so barbarously murdred: and therefore she besought him, that hee would accept of the giftes which were sent him, and therewithall a mind and harte most ready to serue and obey the kinge in all occasions: and that hee would hold him excused, and allow his excuses to be lawfull, for that they were both iust and reasonable. The Turke replyed vpon her, that although she had found so foule a fault and offence in Mustaffa, who, vnder the assurance of his promise and fidelity, betrayed her husband, yet for all that, she ought not to feare any such wicked or infamous action, at his handes, who made profession of an honorable person, and a Souldier of his woord: and so by oath protesting all faithfull and constant friendship towards him, he cast a white vayle about her neck, and put another vpon himselfe, and a third he gaue the woman in her hands, willing her to report to her sonne the oathes he had made, and to carrie him that vayle, and bring him with her, for he should not be otherwise handled, but like a friend, and a brother. The peaceable old woman went her way accordingly, but she neyther could nor would go about to alter the purpose of her sonne, so that she returned to Ebrain

The present that Manogli sendeth to Ebrain, by the hand of Aly Bassa.

Manogli sendeth his mother to Ebrain in his steed.

Ebrain promiseth faith and peace to the Mother, to the end shee should fetch Manogli.

an aunswere not greatly pleasing him, and therefore hee licenced her to depart.

After which time, he sought more then euer he did before, to get the stubburne Emir into his hands, or at least to draw from him more presents and weapons, without regard of any shame, thinking euery thing lawfull that came into his mind, whatsoeuer. And therefore once againe he sent the craftie and malignant Gomeda, to exhort him, that vpon the faith and promise which he had geuen him, he would come vnto him. But for all the craftie and lying speeches, that the treacherous messenger could cunningly vse, he could obtaine nothing at his handes, but words onely. Which when he perceaued, and yet not minded to returne altogether in vaine, and without any profit, by the appointment of Ebrain himself, he told him, that forasmuch as he was not willing to go, yet he should be contented at least, in his presence to peruse the Accompts of those Monopolies, that he had managed for the King in times past, to the end that if they should be found to be paied and discharged, then he should rid the Turkish Captain from those mountaines, and so remayn in quiet. Manogli vnderstanding this fraudulent request, which in the end tended to no other purpose, but onely to get some money, & some presents, determined therein to satisfie Gomeda, with an expresse condition notwithstanding, that he should cause Ebrain to depart out of those quarters, and that he should not returne any more to request any thing of him. Which he verie largely and liberally promised, onely desiring him, that because he should not haue any occasion to send againe any others vnto him, hee would also giue him a good quantitie of Arcubuses, and thereby make the Visier fully contented and well appaied. And so he gaue him fiftie thousand Duckets more, and fower hundred and fower score Arcubuses, with a thousand Goates, a hundred and fiftie Camels, a hundred and fifty Buffes, a thousand Oxen, and two hundred Weathers. With this rich and honorable present came Gomeda to Ebrain, and declared vnto him, that this he had gotten from him, vpon promise that he should not molest the Drusian any more. For which the Visier did greatly reproue Gomeda, telling him that if he did not shew himselfe a more diligent and faithfull executor of his commaundements, he would not be well pleased with him, and that he would make euery man know, what a weightie matter it is for men to take vpon them so inordinate, and so dangerous a libertie. And for the greater despight both to the one and the other of them, Ebrain would needes haue Gomeda himselfe to returne againe to trouble the Drusian. Wherunto although he went in great feare, least some great mischiefe might happen to him by the hands of Manogli, yet was there no remedy, but needes he must follow the commaund of him, who was able to take from him both his honor,

Gomeda returneth to Manogli.

A new present of Ebne-Man to Ebrain.

Ebrain reproseth Gomeda

and his life. And therefore to auoid the greater danger, and to pleasure him, he made no great scruple to belie himself, and to become infamous in the sight of the Drusian. As soon as Manogli saw Gomeda, thinking with himselfe that he came to him again about his wonted requests, he was greatly troubled in his minde, and had almost prenented his arriuall with a dart, which the angry Drusian was minded, and euen at the verie point to throw at him, for the great desire he had to rid him out of his sight but that refraining his anger, least it might peraduenture haue bred more dangerous effectes, he quenched his choler with ignominious wordes and deadly threats: protesting at last, that the time would come, wherin he would recouer at his hands, whatsoeuer he had now taken from him by the meanes of so wrongfull and so wicked a treacherie. Notwithstanding Gomeda could do no lesse but accomplish the effect of his fraudulent requests, and so wrought with him in deed, that he drew from the Emir, fower burdens more of Arcubuses, tenne swordes, and tenne guylt Gangiares or daggers, certain siluer beltes, tenne packes of silk, and some few pence: Causing him withall to protest vnto him, that he would neuer suffer himselfe to be perswaded to come again vnto him: for if he did, he should be enforced to depriue him of his life, happen afterward what might happen of it.

Gomeda again goeth to Manogli.

The new present that Ebneman sendeth to Ebrain.

With extreame ioy and triumph did Ebrain the Visier see all this present, and thinking now with himself, that he had gotten a sufficient bootie of him, he determined to raise his Armie, & to sack all the rest of the Countrey that was subiect to Manogli, not leauing any part of it sound of vntouched. And therefore sending certain fore-runners before him to discouer the Countrey, & to prouide some commodious place to pytch his Tentes, (the Captain of whom was the Emir-Ebnefrec, otherwise called Acra the Scuruie) he raysed his Campe, and marched on the other side of the Mountain: and passing by Andera, which was the place of residence where Manogli remained, he commaunded that it should be sacked and burnt: which was put in execution accordingly, with vnspeakable effects of cruelty, committing all things to fier & sword. After this, the Turkes ouerran all the Countrey, and in two dayes space burnt & destroyed nineteen Townes besides, carying away with them whatsoeuer they could find worthie of spoyle.

Andera sacked.

19. Townes burnt.

After all this sacking and rasing, the Visier with all his Armie mounted vp to the large top of a Mountain, which was also neere to Andara, and from thence sent a thousand messēgers to Ebne-Man, to trie whether he would yet be perswaded to come vnto him. But neither all these siers, nor all their entreaties, nor their terrifying, nor their myldnesse could euer moue Manogli to commit himself into his hands, but still more stoutely and constantly resolued to auoyde most certain death. And therefore the Visier, not contented to haue burned and destroied the Countrey, to haue drawen so much treasure from the Drusian, and to haue plotted so many treacheries against him, bethought himselfe in the end to satisfie his inward affection to crueltie and reuenge, with the slaughter of his miserable people. And hauing vnderstood by a Spie, that the Captain of Andara, being one of the Factors of Manogli, with three hundred and fiftie persons was ascended vp to a certain hill into a safe and secure place, he sent Ebnefrec to entice him, & to tell him, that seeing his Emir Manogli would not come and yeeld himselfe, he should come vnto him, and assuredly, if he did so, in despite of Manogli he would make him a Sangiacco of some of those places, which hee most desired. The ambitious and vnheedy Macademo suffered himselfe to bee easely perswaded with this most malicious lie, and being accompanied with his three hundred and fiftie followers, went with the said Ebnefrec towardes the Visier. And beecause the voice was giuen out, that there were no moe Arcubuses in all the Countrey of Manogli, the Macademo commaunded all his men, that laying aside their Arcubuses, they should arme themselues onely with their swordes, and their bowes; And so going before them, walking still on the right side of the Emir Aora, thereby to giue him his due honor. (For it is the custome of the Mahometanes, and of all the East, and peraduenture it was so also among the Auncients, that the more honorable place is on the leaft side, as that which is (as it were) vpon the sword of his fellow whom he walketh withall, and the lesse honorable is the right side, as being subiect to the blow of the weapon, & readie to be stroken.) At the last he arriued at the Pauilion of Ebrain, hauing first caused his foresaid men to stay behind in a certain valley, two or three miles distant from the Tentes. Ebrain would not so much as see the Macademo, although both in respect of the nimhlenes of his person, and also the fiercenesse of his lookes, he was worthy to be seen, but commaunded that he should be safely kept in a seuerall place from Serafadin: and in the mean time hauing called to counsell the Emirs, and Aly the Bassa of Aleppo, to deuise some wyle, whereby they might put to death those three hundred and fiftie, wyth as little losse of their owne souldiers as possibly might be, it was concluded, that the foresaid Ebnefrec should leade them into a certain Vineyard, and afterwards at vnwares set vpon them, and hauing so brought them to a straite, hew them in peeces, and cut them off: for hauing no Arcubuses, they could work but small hurt to his souldiers. Acra went like a common butcher, and conducted the poore wretches into the appointed vineyard and while they waited for their Captaine, and expected some great reward, because they had so confidently beleeued their promises, they were sodeinly enuironed with the Armie of Ebrain, the Sangiacchi making a wing on the one side, and the Iannizzaries on the other: who beeing become greedie of

Ebnefrec or Feracogli goeth to inuite the Macademo of Manogli.

The custome of the Mahometans in their ceremonies and ciuilitie.

Acra like a common hangman.

the blood of those miserable soules, hauing brought them into a narrow compasse, fell vpon them with their Arcubuses and their speares, and suffering not one of them to escape, most cruelly slew them all. The vnhappie wretches defended themselues the best they could, with their arrowes, with their swordes, with their hands, and with their bodies, but all to no purpose, for they were all destroied in this common and miserable slaughter. Of the Turkes there were none slaine, but only three Iannizzaries, one of their Vlu Bassi, and some of the subiects of the two Emirs, Ebnefrec and Ebnecarfus, who were mistaken and thought to be their enemies, for that wearing the same kind of apparell, which the other souldiers of the Macademo did wear, they could not be distinguished in the medley the one from the other. Through which incircumspection no doubt there had been slaine a great number moe, but that they were aduised euery man to put a vyne leafe in his Turbant, that so being discerned from their enemies, they might be preserued, and as the slaughter light vpon the rest.

As soone as this massacre was finished, Ebrain would haue the death of the Macademo to follow, and causing him to bee brought before him, he commaunded that without any delay he should be stripped, & flayed quick. The Macademo stoutely vpbraided Ebrain with his promise, and his oath, and among diuers speeches, that sometimes smiling, and somtimes threatning he vttered whiles they stripped him: 'Cut me off (quoth he) my members, and first putting them into the priuities of that infamous Ebrains wife, put them afterwards into the mouth of himselfe. For so (I trow) he will be contented and satisfied with my flesh. And pursuing his threates, he spake thus to those, that were to be the executioners of his dolorous death. It is your great good fortune in deed (quoth he) that with such violence, and so needlesse deformitie yee are now resolued to drink vp my blood, and to take my life from me. For I do not think that any of you all, either had bin hable or durst, man to man, to draw one drop of my blood from me, no not to haue endured my countenance. But go to, proceed in your wicked and vnsatiable desire, and follow the impious commaundements of your Visier: for in the end there will light also vpon you, the worthy punishment of this villanous fact.' With these and diuers other speeches, which the Macademo thundred out of his inflamed brest, the miserable wretch (hauing been too credulous) was stripped, and three great slashes made on his back, where they began to flea him, he in the mean time not ceassing to blaspheme their Religion, and to cursse their King, and their false Prophet also. And then the barbarous souldiers, pursuing their cruell action, made certaine other gashes vpon his brest, and vpon his stomake, and so drawing his skinne downeward, they

The 350. souldiers of the Macademo, slaine.

The aduise of the Drusians.

Ebrain commandeth that the Macademo should be flaied quick.

The Macademo is in fleaing.

could not bring it to his Nauel, before he was dead, with most dolorous paines.

After this, the Visier caused Ebne Serafadin to be called into his pauilion, who (as we told you before) was by his commandement deliuered into the custodie of the Captain of the Iannizzaries of the Court, and gaue charge withall, that whiles Serafadin was in his Tent with him, all his men, that came with him, should be put to death. According to his appointment it was done, and when Serafadin was brought before the Visier, all his souldiers, which might be about a hundred & fiftie, were miserably hewen in peeces, and order giuen that Serafadin should be returned againe to his chaynes, and all his Countrey wasted and spoyled. This commaundement all the souldiers were readie enough to put in execution, and besides the booties that they took, they brought away also a hundred and fower score heades of the people that were subiect to the said Emir.

The countrie of Serafadin wasted.

Whiles this wasting by fier, & this slaughter by sword was in hand, the Visier dispatched Postes to Sidonia, where the forenamed Gallies were at road, by whom he sent commaundement, that disbarking iiij. thousand souldiers, they should sack all those Countries, euen as farre as Caesarea in Palaestine, sparing neither age, nor sexe, nor any condition of persons whatsoeuer. Which likewise was presently done, and three thousand soules brought captiues, great booties made of diuerse rich marchandizes, many Townes burnt, sundry Castels ruynated and made euen with the ground, and to be short, all the whole countrie of Serafadin and Manogli vtterly desolated. But Serafadin himself was afterward sent to Damasco, with all his wealth, money, and presents, vnder the gard and custodie of Bassa Veis, and Bassa Aly: who brought all things thither safe and sound, and so from thence to Tripoli, where on a certain plain betweene the land and the sea, they encamped themselues, and stayed there, waiting for the arriual of the Visier with his Gallies.

The souldiers of the Gallies sack the Sea coast of the Drusians.

Ebrain the Visier, was now in a readinesse to depart and to returne to Constantinople, where he was expected by the King, aswell for the greedinesse of his gold, as for the accomplishment of the Mariage. But bethinking himself, that whatsoeuer hither to he had don, would be accompted either little or nothing, vnlesse he prouided in some sort for the quiet of those peoples vnder the Turkish obediēce, he determined to nominate one of the three Emirs, that accompanied him to Ierusalem, to bee the Bassa of all those regions. Now the Emir Aly Ebnecarfus being the richest and the most obedient of them all, hee thought good to commit that charge vnto him, & honoured him with that dignity. Neither did he this without a bribe or rewarde, but for the price of a hundred thousand Cecchini, which the Emir Aly presently

The Emir Aly with 100000. peeces of gold buieth the title of the Bassa or Bocca, and Generall ouer the Drusians. Ebrain at Damasco.

paid vnto him, to make him seeme the more worthie of so great an honour. And therefore hee apparrelled him in cloth of gold, hee gaue him a mase and a sword all guilt, and deliuered vnto him the kinges commission, causing him withall to sweare faith and obedience to Amurath. And so hauing (at least to the shew) set in order the affayres of those mountaines, he determined to returne to Damasco.

There he continued for the space of twelue daies, where he ceased not to draw money & bribes from diuers persons, by most vnreasonable shiftes: and at last hauing no furder to doo in those partes, he turned himselfe towards Gazir and Baruto, two places vnder the gouernement of Ebne-Mansur, where hee arriued with all his army, and found that the Gallies, which had left the Port of Sidonia, were now in the hauen of Baruto, accordingly as hee had before commanded. Now vpon a certaine hill aboue Baruto, neere vnto the sea (called by the inhabitants San Botro) he placed himselfe, and pitched his owne Tent onely and none other, hauing caused his great pauilion, & all the rest of his best and goodly thinges, which he ment to carrie with him to Constantinople, to bee conueighed and laide vp in his Gallies, and shrowded himselfe onely in a very narrow and base tent. Thether he called Ebnemansur vnto him, and in pleasant manner signified vnto him, that now it was time for him to make paiment and satisfaction of the debt, which he ought the king his Lord, of a hundred and three score thousand duckattes for the custome of Tripoli and Baruto: for that he could not stay any longer in those quarters, but was constrained to returne to Constantinople: and thether he knew not how he might well go, vnlesse he carried with him the discharge of that debt. Ebne-Mansur made aunswere that it could not be long, before his Macademies would come with his monies, and then the next day after, certainely and without all delay he would disburse it. Ebrain who knew that all this was but a lye, determined to cause him to bee put in the Gallies, and because hee could not carry the money to his king, yet at the least to bring him his debtor. But in putting this his determination to effect and execution, he was affraide, of some insurrection among the people, aswell because he was within the territories of the said Ebne-Mansur, as also because he saw him greatly beloued and fauoured by Ebne-Frec and Ebne-Carfus. And therefore he thought it better policy, by concealing this his purpose, to shew him in his outward actions all good countenaunce, and by subtile deuises and treachery to take him prisoner. And thereupon told him, (like a deceitfull and lying companion) that for asmuch as hee was to stay there for his busines, that night and the next day, he was resolued to make a road into the countrey of Manogli, and praied him to doo him the fauour, that he would be contented to be his guide: and for that purpose when he should send

Ebrain at Gazir and Baruto.

Ebrain beguileth Mansurogli.

for him at midnight, that he wold come vnto him closely & quietly, because he was minded to depart without any stirre, onely with fiue hundred persons in his company. The Mahamet verily beleeued the matter, that so it was, and withall was in good hope by that meanes to finde some way to escape out of his hands. Whereupon, being called vp at midnight, he readily conueighed himselfe into the pauilion of Ebrain, who presently charging him most shamefully with many abhominable and foule termes, caused a chaine to be cast about his neck and his armes, and commanded him to be carried into the Gallies. The fiftie men which hee had appointed to be ready armed, hee sent forthwith to Baruto, to fetch Mendel aliue vnto him, who was by the common people intytled with the name of an Emir, but in deed was no other then a simple Macademo to Ebne-Mansur: willing them also, vpon a sudden to sack all the whole countrey of Ebne-Mansur. Whereby there was leauied so rich a pray, and so great a booty gathered, that it was a maruell to all men. For besides money & siluer, wherof there was a very huge somme, the store of clothes of silke and gold was such and so great, that it was worthy for a great Prince, and not fit for such a Mountainerusticall Lord as this was.

Mansurogli in chaines sent to the Gallies.

The country of Mansurogli destroied.

Hauing conueighed all this into his Gallies, hee sailed to Tripoli, where he found Serafadin in the custody of the two Bassaes aboue named: and hauing stayed there some few daies, wherein he committed sundry villanous and abhominable robberies, hee caused the said Serafadin to bee put into the Gallies, with all his silkes and his other wealth, and so departed for Constantinople. When he entred into the chanell of the citty, accompanied with foure and twenty Gallies, encountred and receaued by a wonderfull troupe of kinsfolkes and frendes, and saluted with an honorable peale of Artillary out of the Serraglio, I was also my selfe at Constantinople, where I had good meanes to see the bountifull and beautifull presentes, which the spoiling Bassa gaue the Turkish king. The somme whereof, (besides the yearely reuenue of Cair, amounting to sixe hundred thousand Cecchini,) was a Million of gold: threescore horses most richly garnished, of singular beauty, and particularly of the Arabian race: a liue Elephant, and a lyue Giraffle: (which is a beast like a Cammell and a Panther,) two very great Crocodiles dead: a chaire of gold and precious stones: a Casket also beset with precious stones and gold: many packes of most fine clothes, wollen, and silkes: certaine other clothes with fringe of gold and siluer, and the Barbarian cut-work: most fine linnen of Alexandria, and all the Arcubuses, taken from the Drusians.

Serafadin put into the Gallies.

Ebrain receiued into Constantinople.

The liberall presentes giuen by Ebrain to the Turkish king.

But now returning to the place from whence I was caried into these digressions, I say againe, that excepting the soulders of Egipt, and those of Damasco and Iurie, all the rest of the souldierie, that was bound to these enterprises, was raised with their newe Generall Osman Bassa, as wee told you before. And the multitude of them that came both to Siuas and to Erzirum was so great, that neuer was there seene a greatter in all the occasions that happened about these warres, as in the boke following shalbe shewed vnto you. For now hauing made mention of the Sangiacco of Ierusalem, it will not be amisse to declare the feates of Armes, that passed betweene him and the Arabians of Palestine before Ebrain the Visier came into those quarters.

In the confynes of Sodome, & in the places that lie not onely betweene the Lake Asphaltites and Damasco, but also in the plaines, and in the valleies of Iericho and of Samaria, and in other places about Bethlehem, Emaus, Bethany, Bethphage, Capharnaum, Nazaret, Leuir, Betsaid, Naplos, and other townes of name thereaboutes, there do haunt and liue sundry Arabian captaines, who spreading themselues euen as farre as Rama and Ioppa, ouer-runne all the countries there round about, and continually commit diuers outrages, aswell against the said Citties, as also vpon the goods and wealth not onely of the Inhabitants there, but also of Straungers: yea and their insolency oftentimes groweth so great, that they dare assault the fenced Cities, besides the spoyling of poore traueilers, that by reason of their businesse haue occasion to passe from one cittie to another. They handle a speare well, and are perpetuall shooters, but Armour of defence, they haue none at all. The horses, which they ride, are very swifte to runne, and spare of diet: they are very bold in pilling and theeuing. Neither could I my selfe escape their handes, when I traueiled to the holy Cittie, to worship the great Sepulcher of our Lord. These Arabians hauing had intelligence before hand, that the foresaid ambitious yongman, was appointed the Sangiaccho in Ierusalem, and that hee was in minde to raise all the Sangiacchoes thereaboutes, and ioyning himselfe with them, and his Father the Bassa of Damasco, to worke some great annoyance to their Libertie, & to put diuers of thē to death; resolued with thēselues, not to stay in any case, till he and his confederacy were ready, but rather by making sondry inuasions vpon him, euen to the very Cittie of Ierusalem, to prouoke him to come out into the field. And to induce him so to doe, they conspired with a certaine Subassi of Bethlehem, who was their frende, that he should encourage and embolden the Sangiaccho therevnto, by promising him great successe and fortunate euentes. The ambitious youth, being moued with the perswasions of the Subassi, of whome hee made good reckoning, and beeing shrewdly prouoked by their insolencies, resolued with himselfe to issue out of the cittie into the open field: and therevppon hauing armed a hundred of his Vassalles, and raysed all the horsemen that were vnder his gouernement to the number of sixe hundred, he made

The Arabians purpose to fight with the Sangiacco of Ierusalem.

The Arabians of Iurie, Samaria & Galilie, theeues & robbers.

a roade towardes Iericho, sending before to defy them to battell. The Arabians came accordingly, and against the Arcubuses of the Souldiers of the Sangiaccho, opposing their Indian Canes and their Arrowes, ouer-whelming hym withall as it were a floud, they wrought him great mischiefe. And in the very nicke, euen while the bartell was at the hoattest, the traiterous conspirator the Subassi fled towardes Bethlehem, and leaft the souldiers of Ierusalem in the handes of the Arabians, who put them all for the most part to the edge of the sword, & scarcely gaue any liberty to the Sangiacco to saue himself by flight. The Sangiacco was certainly enformed of this fraude of the dissembling Subassi, and to reuenge himselfe vpon him, hee began also to practise deceit with him, faining that he wold once more try his forces against the same Arabians, insomuch that hee caused the Subassi to arme himselfe and to come vnto him, without shew of any suspition, that he went about any mischeefe against him: But when he came to him, he tooke him aliue, and in most dolorous maner caused him presently to be fleaed quick. Such end had these youthly and sudden stirres of Iury, by occasion whereof, as being thereunto induced in a resonable respect, we were constrained with a due digression, to runne out a little from our first course of the affaires of Persia. And now staying vpon the same, we will returne to Osman Bassa, who being now come to Erzirum, and there hauing taken a muster of all his souldiers, was . in a readines to depart for Tauris, with a speech notwithstanding giuen out & published altogether for Nassiuan. Of whome, seeing wee are now to continue our History, without any intermission, we will reserue to make further narration in the next booke following: to the entent that the declaration of so famous & so important actions, be not in any wise interrupted by any other thing whatsoeuer.

The end of the seuenth booke.

Marginalia:

The Subassi of Bethlem flyeth. The Sāgiacco discomfited by the Arabians.

The Subassi of Bethlehem flayed quicke by the Sangiacco.

Osman in a readines to depart from Erzirū. with a speech to go to Nassiuan

The Eight Booke

The Argument.

Osman departeth from Erzirum with his Army, which is so great that is seemeth to be many mens powers vnited together.

Osman dismisseth forty thousand Souldiers out of his Army, as being superfluous and needelesse.

Osman taketh a review of his Army: departeth from the Caldaranes, and in steede of goyng to Nassiuan, turneth towardes Tauris: wherevpon the Souldiers of Greece and Constantinople are angry with him, but he appeaseth them mildely with fayre speeches and some small quantity of money.

Osman passeth on to Coy, to Marant, and to Soffian, and deseryeth Tauris.

The Vauward of Osman is assaulted and ouerthrowne by the Persian Prince.

The Army of the Persian Prince.

The Army of the Persian king.

Osman sendeth out a new Company against the Prince in reuenge of the discomfiture giuen to his Vauwarde: wherevpon followeth a bloudy battell, which was parted by reason of the night.

Alyculi assayleth the Turkish Army, and retyreth againe.

Alyculi assayleth it a fresh in the night time, and returneth not into the City Tauris, but withdraweth himselfe into the tentes of the Persian king.

The Persians that garde the gates of Tauris, fight with a rascall band of the Turkish Army.

The Persians retyre themselues into the City, and in the turninges of their streetes and places vnder the ground, they worke great mischiefe vpon the Turkes that followed them into the Citty.

A description of the situation of Tauris.

Osman maketh choyce of certaine gardens for a plot to build a Fort in.

The Fort is finished in the space of sixe and thirty dayes.

Certaine Turkes are found strangled in a bathe within Tauris, and Osman commaundeth that the Citty of Tauris should be sacked: wherevppon there doth ensue most miserable and horrible spectacles, and a mortall battell.

The Persian Herauldes returne to prouoke the Turkes to a fresh battell.

The ordering of both the Armies.

Most bloudy battels betweene them both.

The Bassa of Trebisonda, and the Bassa of Caraemit, with certeine Sangiacchi are slayne.

The Bassa of Garamania taken prisoner.

Osman is at the point of death, by reason of a greeuous disease.

Giaffer Eunucho the Bassa is chosen Generall, and gouernour of Tauris.

The Taurisians recouer the spoyle that was taken from them in Tauris.

Osman the Bassa, Visier and Generall dieth at Sancazan.

The ouerthrow of the Persians.

The muster of the Army at Van.

Teflis is succoured quietly without any trouble or hinderance.

Maxut-Chan is named the Bassa of Aleppo.

A Letter sent from the Campe to Aly the Bassa of Aleppo.

THE EIGHT BOOKE

Osman departeth from Erzirum.

Osman, the General of the Turkish campe, departed out of the Citie of Erzirum, about the eleuenth of August, in the yeare 1585. vsing the Rebell Maxut-Chan for the guide of his Armie: which although it was in deed at that time verie great, both for men and cattell, yet it appeared euery day to become more populous, and daily new Souldiers were discouered in it, though they were but vagarantes, and of small valour. The occasion whereof was, not onely the multitude of warrants sent abroad through all the subiect Cities, but also the affection that euery man did beare to the fame and renowme of Osman, vnto whom, aswell for his valour, whereof all men caried a good opinion, as also for his soueraigne aucthoritie, whereby he ruled as Chiefe Visier, but especially for the confidence, which (was well knowen) the King reposed in him, they all ran by heapes with most willing minds: And he wisely cherishing and fostering them in their good forwardnesse, entertayned

Osman entertaineth al that come.

them all with faire promises, and hope of rewardes. Insomuch, that the Generall had gathered together about a hundred and fiftie thousand horsemen, some seruing with bowes, some with battel-axe or sword, some with Arcubuse, some with launces, some stipendiaries, and other some voluntaries. And besides these, so great a multitude of seruile people, of craftes-men, of pioners, of cariers, of Iudges, of Treasurers, of Clerkes, of Collectors, and of all sorts of men: So great abundance of Camels, of Mules, and of Horses, and to be briefe, so huge an assemblie, that it would make a man beleeue, it was not the power of one King alone, but rather the forces of many Kings vnited and confederate together. Osman therefore perceauing that he had gathered too great a number of people, and too huge an Armie, and that it might fall out so great a multitude should want vittaile, perswading himself that his prouisions could not suffice the common necessitie, neither fearing his enemies forces so greatly, that he needed to lead so populous an host against them, he determined to discharge a great number of such as he thought to be most weak, and least apt to endure trauell, and to sell them their desired libertie at a good price. And the common fame is, that by this occasion out of that first number he drew out about fortie thousand persons, who with liberall and large brybes, accordingly as euery mans estate would beare it, redeeming the ordinarie perills of the warres, returned home to their owne dwellings. And so there remayned in the Armie of Osman, the number of a hundred and fower score thousand persons, or there aboutes.

The Generall, accompanied with this multitude, departed from Erzirum, & moued towards Tauris, still continuing (for all that) the speech for Nassiuan. But scarse were there two daies passed, when diuers souldiers of Grecia and Constantinople, presented themselues before him, and vpbrayded him with mvatter of great improuidence, telling him, that they began alreadie to feele the intollerable penurie of victuall, by wanting the same day their ordinarie allowance of Corne for their horses: so that if in the verie beginning, and (as it were) in the entrance of so long a iourney, they felt such a want, they could not tel with what iudgment or discretion he meant to lead so great a companie so farre as Nassiuan, nor by what cunning conceit he had presumed to sustain so great an Armie in the seruice of their Lord. Osman quietly heard their complaints, and presently prouided for them, by causing such store of Barley to be distributed among them all as they desired, and seuerely punishing the Officers, that had the charge for allowance of Corne, who most couetously began to make merchandise of the common prouision, by conuerting it to their owne priuate vses. And hauing thus quieted their troubled minds, he followed on his iourney, and by the way of Hassan-Chalassi, and of Chars, he arryued vpon

150000. horsmen.

The Armie of Osman seemeth to be the forces of manie kings vnited together.

40000. mē taken out of the Army, and returned home.

180000. persons in the army of Osman.

The souldiers of Greece and Constantinople complaine to Osman.

Osman myldly pacifieth the souldiers that were in a mutinie.

A reuiew of the Armie.

Osman departeth from the Caldaran plaines.

The souldiers of Greece and Constantinople, in pride & anger cōplain of Osman.

the Caldarane plaines, a famous place for the memorable battels, that were there fought betweene Selim and Ismahel, the father of Tamas, surnamed the Soffi. In these plaines he took a general reuiew of all his Armie, wherein there wanted a number, that by reason of sicknes, and diuers other infirmities, being not hable to continue the iourney, were enforced to stay behind, some in one place, & some in another. From these plaines he afterwardes remoued, and turned his course, not to Nassiuan, as still hitherto he had constantly kept the speech he would doo, but now to Tauris.

Assoone as the Souldiers of Greece and Constantinople heard this sodein alteration of the Iourney, they were in a great rage, and comming again before the Generall; spake thus vnto him. And what are we, thou villaine, thou Turk, thou dolt, whom thou handlestin this sort? 'We are neither oxen nor sheepe of the mountains, for the leading of whom thou thinkest thou art come out: neither can we brooke these thy lyes and deceiptes. If thou hast publikely professed to leade vs to Nassiuan, and by that speech hast trained vs from the furdest bounds of Grecia: to what end now, after thou hast wearied vs so much, doest thou deceiue vs with such vanities, and prolong our iourney, and set before vs such strange and important dangers, as our minds neuer once thought on? But if this was thy first purpose and intent, & that now not foolishly nor by chaunce, but vpon premeditation and good aduise, thou changest thine opinion, why diddest thou dismisse so manie souldiers, that might haue made the Armie more terrible and the stronger for thy enterprise of Tauris? Doest thou think, that by suffering others to redeme their liberties, and so to encrease thy riches, thou shalt set our lyues to sale, and so make vs slaues to the Persians?' At these arrogant speeches Osman was in a great confusion, & when he saw his good meaning, and the earnest desire he had to satisfie the Maiestie and honour of his King, to be taken in so euill part, and these men so highly offended at him, he was sore troubled, and began to reuolue many & sundrie cogitations within himself, what he were best to do. And although he could in deede haue readily vsed the sharpest and the hardest prouisions and remedies for it, that in such occasions

The wisedom of Osman Bassa.

The speech of Osman to pacifie the souldiers, that were in an vprore.

are ordinarily applied, yet verie prudently and vpon good aduise he forbare so to doo, and instead of rigor & punishment, he resolued to work by entreatie, by admonition, by lenitie, and by guiftes: and by reùealing to the Captaines and Chiefe of the rest, that were so readie to rage, the necessitie of the rumour that was giuen out for Nassiuan, myldlie and featlie to pacifie them all. Whereupon hauing caused manie of the said seditious persons to come before him, he first perswaded them, 'That the former speech for Nassiuan was not raysed at all by him, Nor that he was minded at that time to go to Tauris, but all that was done, he had done to fulfill the commaundement of the Sultan, who had charged him so to doo, to the end they might lessen, yea, and peraduenture wholie frustrate the sharpe forces & conflicts, which otherwise they might haue found on the Persians side, if the speech had bin giuen out at the first for Tauris, and so leasure and time giuen to their enemies to prepare themselues, and to come and encounter with them in order and well appointed. For the auoyding whereof, and that all glorious successe and ioyfull victorie might happen vnto them, euen with the least inconuenience to the Armie that might be imagined, the King so commaunded, and so would he haue it: who, of his Princely nature did not onely not delight in the harmes and troubles of his vassals, but also thought nothing to be more greeuous, or ignominious to him, then their losse and hinderance. And therefore they for their partes also ought willingly to accomplish his good pleasure: for so should they stil preserue that great opinion, which both the King, and all the Nations of the world had conceaued of their valour, and fidelitie. Neither needed they to feare, that the souldiers, which were dismissed, might enfeeble or weaken the Armie:' for that they were not onely sufficient to pierce into Tauris, and to open the way euen vpon their enemies, but also the Persians would not endure theyr lookes: and that those, which were discharged, had purged the hoast of all cowardise, and left nothing in it, but vertue and courage. By this mild aunswere of the Visier, the tumultuous souldiers were sufficiently pacified: but much better appayed and contented they were, assoone as he put his hand to the common purse, and bestowed among them all a certain small quantitie of Moneis; for by this gentlenesse of nature, all their stomakes were ouercome, and they became so willing, & so couragious, that now they durst venture, not onely to Tauris, but also to Casbin, yea, euen to the farthest partes of all the kingdome of the Persians.

 These importunate & inconsiderate outrages being thus appeased and quenched, the Generall turned himselfe with all his armie towardes Coy, being a citty situate beyond Van, and in the middest betweene Tauris and the Martian More, subiect to the Turkes, where the appetites both of the souldiers and also of their cattell were satisfied with all thinges which they could desire. From Coy he passed to Marant, a city subiect to the Persians, very plentifull and fruitfull also in all things, that are wont to be acceptable to man and beast. From thence he leaned downe towardes Soffian, a little ground, subiect likewise to the Persians, but in all kind of fruites most aboundant and fertile: and from this place they began to discouer Tauris. Great was the ioy of the whole Campe, but principally the souldiers of Greece & Constantinople, when they saw themselues to haue passed so farre, without feeling any annoiance of

The souldiers well quieted.

Osman distributeth a certain litle quātitie of money among them.

Osman turneth towards Coy.

Osman arriueth at Merant.

Osman leaneth towards Soffian.

They discouer Tauris.

the enemy, did highly commend the aduise of the Captaine, or rather of the king, in chaunging the rumour of Nassiuan for Tauris, and did thinke verily, that this their great quyet did happen vnto them, because the Persians were wholly occupied about Nassiuan: in somuch that euery man now being waxen more couragious, and replenished with ioye, without any feare at all, proudly plotted to themselues, nothing but sackings, pillings, taking of prisoners, rauishments, robberies, and all those insolent and dishonest actions, that vse rashly to proceed from the greedie affections of these barbarous victors. But the chiefe of these were those of the Vauward, who being desirous of a bootye, and to discouer the enemies countrey rounde about them, descended downe towardes certain gardens, full of all sorts of trees, springes and fruites, and hauing refreshed their appetites with the water and other meates, they withdrew themselues to a certaine little riuer, neere to a bridge called The bridge of salt water, and there stayed with pleasure, attending the arriuall of their fellow-army. But euen whiles they were thus enioying the water, the fruites, the shade, and the greene grasse, besides all their expectation, they were suddenly assaulted and very shrewdly handled by the Persians.

The Turkish souldiers make accompt of sackinges and robberies &c.

The Vauward of the Turkes.

The Vauward at the bridge of Saltwater assaulted by the Persians.

This was Emir Hamze, the eldest sonne of king Mahamet, who being accompanied with ten thousand souldiers, had craftely hidden himselfe, watching till some of the ennemies bands should come downe to those resting places, that he might set vppon them. For hee was thus come forth against the Turkes, whiles his blinde father was encāped about twelue miles beyond the city of Tauris, with a fifty thousand persons or thereaboutes. In Tauris was Alyculi-Chan the Gouernour of it, and with him foure thousand souldiers. A greater Army then this the Persian king could not possibly leauie, and the principall occasion thereof was, the death of Emir-Chan; for which all the nation of the Turcomannes being waxen rebellious and disobedient, would not by any meanes bee brought to defend that Citty, which was now committed to the gouernement of Alyculi-Chan their capitall enemy. From Gheilan and from Hery there came not somuch as one souldier, to relieue the necessities of Persia. So that the King could scarsely gather together these threescore and foure thousand men, who by reason of the vncertainety of the Turkes rumour for Nassiuan and for Tauris, were plonged into a thousand disquiets, and scant had leasure enough to be ready all at Tauris at the arriuall of their enemies. With these forces the Persian had no stomack, so suddenly to go and set vpon the Turkish Army in open battell, and to aduenture themselues vpon their Artillary: but sought in deed by all the meanes he could, first to annoy him with as little losse to himselfe as possibly hee might, and so by attempting his forces, to make triall of euery way, how he might in dyuerse and sundry sortes

Emirhamze Mirize, the Persian Prince, with 10000. souldiers.

The Persian King beyond Tauris with 50000. souldiers.

Aliculi-Chan in Tauris with 4000.

The occasion why the Persians could not gather a greater armie against the Turkes.

64000. souldiers the whole force of the Persians.

weaken and endamage him. And yet afterward hee wished, that he had beene assaulted, when being certified of the infirmitie of Generall Osman, and aduertised of the sundry losses that hee had receaued at his arriuall to Tauris, and in other conflictes, which shalbe told you hereafter, he thought he might haue recouered the spoiles that had beene taken in the sacked and desolate Citty. But the Bersian Prince, thus at vnawares set vpon the Vauwarde of the Turkes, who being greedy of their victuailes, and desirous to discouer their enemies countrey, had turned themselues vpon the gardens of Soffian. This assault, & the discomfiture of the said Vauward was done at once: for such was the speed, so haughty was the courage of the Prince, and so great the astonishment and strangenes of the case, that as it had beene a lightning, and (as a man might well say) without any resistanee, he ouerran all the said band of the Turkes, and dispersed them, putting to the sworde about seuen thousande persons of all sortes. Which being done, he withdrew himselfe back towards his fathers Tentes, leading away with him, horses, slaues, and much apparrell, besides sundry standerdes & Turkish drommes, that were brought after him.

The Persian Prince assayleth and discomfiteth the Turkish Vauward at once.

7000. Turks slaine.

Osman had intelligence of this discomfiture, & fourth-with caused his Armie to be raised, and dispatched Sinan Bassa sonne to the late Cicala, and Mahamet the Bassa of Caraemet, with diuers other Aduenturers, in all to the nomber of fourteene thousande, to the end they should follow the prince abouementioned. These then ranne amaine to pursue the kings sonne, who had already sent newes to his father of this his first action by certaine swift horsemen, and so quick they were in their marching, that they ouertooke the yongman, who like a ioyfull victor was iournying towardes his fathers Campe. Assoone as the Prince saw the Turkes so neere him, and knew that without a daungerous and shamfull flight, hee could not auoid the battell, couragiously hee tourned his face vpon them, and ioyned a most bloudy conflict with them. It was as yet two houres before night, when these sharp and cruell skirmishes began, from which they ceased not, vntill night with her darknes did bereaue them of the vse of their swordes, and enforce both the one side and the other to retire, which was doon with the notable losse of the Turkes, who being farre fewer in nomber then they were, and also shrewdly beaten and discomfited, returned to their pauilions from whence they came. The like did the Persians also, who were stayned and imbrued much more with the bloud of their enemies, then with the spilling of their owne. It is a common speech that in this second battell, (which notwithstanding together with the first exploitis reckoned but for one onely) there wanted six thousand Turkes, and that there would haue followed a generall slaughter of them all, if night had not interrupted so vncouth

Osman maketh a new expedition against the Persian Prince.

A bloody battell.

The night ceasseth the battell.

6000. Turks slaine.

an action, well worthie (in truth) of a thousand day-lightes. So that hitherto the Turkes haue sustained the losse of more then ten thousand souldiers, & yet scarce haue discouered or seene the Citty, which so greedely they longed for.

The next morning the Turkish Campe remoued, and approched within two miles of Tauris where they encamped. But whiles they were about the setting vp of their pauilions, Aliculy-Chan issuing out of the City with all his guard aboue mentioned, and with all the inhabitantes that were able to fight and manage weapons, he set vpon the face of the Vauward, being now renued, and with cunning tourninges and windinges so charged and seised vpon them, that with great shedding of bloud hee made them to retire, euen to the Visiers warde, from whence when he espied the artillarie, he withdrew himselfe againe to the Citty, before he was annoyed or offended by any of them. The nomber of the slaine, and the confusion of the Turkes was notable. For in a very small space of time, the Vauward was put in a disaray, & almost three thousand slaine. But Alyculi being not contented with this, assoone as the darkenes of the night was come, issued out the second tyme closely and couertly, & swiftly ran along all the side of the enemies Army, that lay towards Tauris, and besides the death of the Bassa of Maras, put all that band to great damage and destruction. And when he had so doone, without any stay hee fled to the Kinges Campe, and forsooke the defence of the sorrowfull City. In this sort was the Turkish Captaine welcomed by the Taurisians, who gathering themselues to the gates as many of them as remayned within the Citty, well armed & consederate together, were now prepared to make it a bloody entrance for the Turks, whensoeuer they came. All the whole night was spent in watching both on the one side and on the other, neither could the flattering entisement of sleeep procure any quiet or rest to the poore soules either of the Cittizens or of the enemies: and yet there was no motion of war on either side. But vpon the breake of day, a great bande of the seruile sort of Turkes, and of the rascall common rout, without any leaue asked of the Captain, armed with corslets, with speares and with swordes, went to the towne, with resolute mindes to sacke it, and to enrich their owne priuate estate with the spoiles and pillage of that welthie City. And now were they come to the guarded gates, where contrary to their expectation they found a terrible rescue, and were enforced to ioyne a hard and mortall medley, wherein the walles, the entrance, yea all the ground thereabout was bathed with blood, & (as it were) paued with weapons and carcases. And yet for all that, though the Persians stood firme & stout at the arriuall of this insolent and seruile troupe, at the last they were constrained to yeeld the entrance, being ouercome by the multitude of them, that flowed

---

Aliculy-Chan assayleth the Turkesh army, whiles they were encamping themselues.

Alyculy-Chan retireth again into the citty.

3000. Turkes slaine.

Aliculy in the night issueth out of the Citty & assaulteth the Turkes.

The Bassa of Maras slaine by Aliculy. Aliculy abandoneth the citty of Tauris.

The Persians garde the gates of Tauris.

The seruile people first go to the city to sack it.

Slaughter in the gates.

in vpon them lyke a floud, and retiring thēselues into the cittie, which was now astonied & amased on euery side, they fortified themselues in their houses vnder the grounde, and in the corners and winding tourninges of the streetes: from whence, by their arrowes, & some few Arcubuscs, they did great scath to the Turkes that entred. Howbet the Persians were not able to kill & destroy so many of their enimy people, but that at the last they were too mighty for them, and wrought many grieuous mischiefes and calamities in the wofull City. And so a great number of this rascall people, which remayned aliue, returned to the Turkish Campe, enriched with booties and slaues, leading away with them both virgins and children, and shewing too manifest tokens of the poore oppressed City, wherein the miserable wemen & impotent soules embracing and strayning their domesticall doores, and kissing their natiue soyle, with prayers, with mourninges, with complaints, bewayled their present misery, and feared also worse & more deadly euents. Osman, who was now made acquainted with these calamities, and with this particular misaduenture, caused proclamation to be published, that no man should be so hardy as to molest the Taurisians, those I meane, which were naturally there borne: and in the meane time he himselfe went round about the saide City, viewing thoroughly the situation of it, and surueighing the place, wherein he might both incampe himselfe safely, and also with the better foundation and greater security erect a Castell or Forte of defence of that conquered countrey.

Tauris is seated at the roote of the hill Orontes, which standeth (as it were) ouer it vpon the North side, distant from the shore of the sea of Bachu, eight dayes iourney or thereaboutes. It hath Persia vppon the Southside, which leauing the Caspian mountains on the West, reacheth out to Great Media: and therefore the City is subiect to windes, cold, and full of snow, but of a very holesome ayre: It aboundeth in all manner of thinges necessary for mans life. It is enriched, aswell by the perpetuall concourse of merchandises, that are brought thether from the countryes of the Leuant, to be conueighed into Soria and into the countries of Europe, as also of those that come thither out of the Westerne partes, to be distributed ouer all the East. It is verie populous, so that it feedeth almost two hundred thousand persons: but yet open to the furie of euery Armie, without strength of walles, and without bulwarkes. It hath a great number of houses vnder the ground: The buyldinges, after the fashion of those that are buylt in the East, are of burnt clay, & rather low then high. It hath Springs, Gardens, and running waters. And for all things it caried the name, as also of their Kings residence. Tamas was the man that remoued his seat from this Citie, and translated it to Casbin: but still for all that, both before and sithence, although it hath bene molested by the inroades and spoyles of

The Taurisians yeeld the gates to the Turkish peole.

The Taurisians fortifie themselues in their vaultes, and in the corners of their streets.

The Turkes returne to the Campe with diuers praies and booties.

Osman vieweth the place where to encampe himselfe, and build a forte.

The description of the citty of Tauris.

the Turkish Emperours, yet it hath alwayes maintayned it selfe in great estimation and renowme.

Now of this City, Osman did diligently view the situation, and at the last caused his Pauilions to be pitched vpon the side that looketh towardes the South, commanding that all the rest of this Souldiers should do the like, & that all the Workemen and Ditchers should repaire thether to beginne the building of a Castell. On the same side of Tauris, there was a garden, all flourishing & beautyfull, replenished with a thousand sundry kindes of graftes, trees, and sweete-smelling plantes, among which the Lilly, the Hyacinth, the Gillyflower, the Rose, the Violet, the Flower gentle, and a thousand other odoriferous flowers did yeeld a most pleasaunt and delectable sight both to the Inhabitantes and to Straungers. There were a thousand Fountaines, and a thousand brookes, & among them all, as the Father of them all, a prettie Riuer, which with his milde course and delight some noyse, deuided the Garden from the ground of Tauris, and one onely bridge for those to passe ouer it, which for pleasure repayred out of Tauris to recreate themselues in the shadowes and walkes of those greenes: whose beauty was so great, being also made famous by reason of antiquity, that it was also called by the countrey Inhabitantes Sechis-Genet, which in our language is as much to say, as Eight Paradises. This was in times past the standing house of their kinges, whiles they kept their residence in this Citty: and after they had withdrawne themselues from thence, and translated their seate to Casbin, it became the habitation and place of aboade for the Gouernours of Tauris, and namely Emir-Chan kept altogether there, whiles hee had the gouernement of it. These gardens and places Osman did choose to builde his Castle in, whereof hee gaue the modell himselfe, and commaunded that all the whole circuite of those Greenes should bee enuyroned with walles, and trenches digged round about them, to conueigh the water from the foresayd Riuer. And so the fabricke was begunne, with the greatest care that possibly might be, the foundation of the embattelled walles layd, the ditche digged, foureteene foote broade, and a mans heigth in depth, and in the space of sixe and thirty wholy finished and brought to an ende. The first day of building the Visier fell sicke of a feuer with a bloudy flixe (as it was told me in Constantinople, by one of the Phisitions, that was alwayes assistant at the cure) which infirmity peraduenture was the cause of the slownesse in building, and of many other losses that afterwardes happened, as shall be declared vnto you. In the saide space also of sixe and thirty dayes, there was distributed vppon the walles great store of Artillery, and within the Forte there were built diuers bathes, lodginges, and such other housing necessary for Turkish vses.

The tentes pitched on the south side.

The most pleasant and beautifull garden of Tauris.

The garden called the eight Paradises

Osman chooseth the gardens to build his fort in.

dayes In 36. daies the fabrick finished.

The sicknesse of the Visier Osman.

Whiles this Fabricke was in hande, there wanted not sondry Accidentes, and straunge newes, to fill the eares and mindes of all men: which it shalbe necessarie to report in order as they fell out. Fiue daies after the buylding of the Fort was begon, there came newes into the Turkish campe, that within the Citie of Tauris, in a certain baine, there were eight Iannizzaries, and diuerse Spaoglanj seen strangled: wherof the Zaini, Spahini, and Iannizzaries being certified, went presently before the Visier, declaring vnto him, that although hee had ouer mildlie giuen order, that the Taurisians should not be molested or hurt, and that according to his pleasure, euery man had vsed modestie towards them, and obedience to him, yet the Taurisians themselues, who should haue remayned in quiet and in awe, had most audaciously strangled in one of their baynes eight Iannizzaries, and certain Spaoglanj, and that in their iudgement these iniuries and insolencies were not to be suffered. The Captain was exceeding wroth at this most cruell and impious action, and without any further delay commaunded, that the whole Citie should be sacked, and that euery man should do the worst, that possibly he could, or might do to it. Heere a man had need of a verie learned and eloquent penne, to describe the fierce and cruel execution of these men, who handled the matter, not as though they would requite an iniurie, but rather exercise an vtter vengeance vpon them, insomuch, as it would require great force of witt, and readinesse of toung to declare it. For in trouth, who is hable either by writing, or by speech sufficiently and liuely to set foorth the treachery, the couetousnesse, the wrath, the crueltie, the impiety, the wickednesse of these triumphing Turkes? And on the other side, who can expresse the criyng of Infants, the complaintes and howlings of weomen, the groanings of the woūded, the teares of parents, the praiers of old men, the feares, the griefes, and to be briefe, the miserie of the Taurisians? There was nothing but slaughter, pilling, rauishing, spoiling, and murdering: Virgins deflowred, men-children defyled with horrible and vnspeakable sinnes, yonglings snatched out of their parents armes, houses laied euen with the ground, and burnt: riches and money caried away, and to be short, all things wasted and ruynated. Neither were these mischiefes committed once onely, but the second followed worse then the first, and the third vpon that, worse then the second: so that it was a miserie almost vnexplicable, to behold that Citie, which was so populous and so riche, sometimes the Court and Palace of the Crowne, and the honor of the Persian Empire, now subiect to the furie, to the rauine, to the crueltie of the Turkes, plonged in calamitie, and vtterly destroied. With the spoyle that was taken, there were many thousands of Camels loaden, and euery man,

Turkes strangled in a bath within Tauris.

Osman commandeth that the Citie of Tauris should be sacked in the vilest maner.

The villanies of the Turkes in Tauris, while they sack it.

The misery of the Citie of Tauris.

besides the thinges of greatest value, which they kept secretly, caried away with him some boy or some wench for his captiue.

> Boies & girles caried away captiues by the Turkes.

The lamentable and sorowfull aduertisement hereof was brought to the King of Persia, who bewayled the miserie of himselfe, and the destruction of others: But the Persian prince beyond all the rest felt rising inwardly within himself the most ardent affections of griefe, of disdain, and of desperation, & being vtterly resolued to put any thing in execution, whereby he might be reuenged of so great a crueltie, and recouer the pray that was taken away, he exhorted his whole Armie to put on the same resolution. And hauing grounded and confirmed himselfe therein, he commaunded, that fiue hundred of his souldiers should ryde out on hors-back, euen to the verie sight of their enemies Tentes, and prouoke the Turkes to battell. These souldiers so appointed went accordingly, and made a gallant show of themselues, at the discouery wherof, the Turks imagining, that the Persians were come in great number to assault their Armie: Order was giuen by the Visier to Bassa Cicala, and the Bassa of Caraemit, (the same two which were at first in the former blouddie conflict,) that with the people of Grecia, and all the rest of their whole power, they should go to encounter the enemie. They presently gaue warning with the sound of their Trompets, and straight way their standerdes were displaied: Vnder which there were assembled about fower and thirtie thousand Souldiers stronge, partlie stipendiaries, and partlie voluntaries, and besides them a number of seruile people, men exercised in labour and perills, so that there were gathered together in all well neere fortie thousand men. The fiue hundred Persians, with a meruailous cunning kind of skirmishing, dallied with the Turkish souldiers, and drew them forward, for the space of eight miles and more. And when they were brought to that point, being now fore-wearied with the skirmish, they were lustely assaulted by the Persian Prince, who with part of his Armie, which might be to the number of about twentie thousand persons, couragiously & valiantly seised vpon the two Bassaes, betweene whom there was ioyned the deadliest and cruellest battell, that euer was written of. Wherein the Persians hauing giuen a most perillous onset vpon the Turkes, it was thought, that they would haue been contented with so luckie an encounter, and so to haue retyred. Which the Turkes foreseeing, and beeing not minded to returne this second time, but with victorie, and a notable great conquest, they hardilie followed vpon the Persians, hoping to put them to flight, and to giue them a blouddie and deadlie ouerthrow: But the Persians hauing quietly and easilie endured their charge, for a reasonable space, at the last made head vpon them a fresh, and began a new conflict with them. By the vehemence of this assault, the Bassa of Caraemit aboue

> The Persian Prince commandeth 500. souldiers, to go and prouoke the Turkes to fight.

> Osman appointeth two Bassaes, to encounter and fight with the Persians.

> 40000. Turkes go to encounter the Persians, and to fight with them.

> A mortal and cruel battell.

named, was put to flight, who beeing wholie dismaied and difcomfited, fled back to his Tentes, with a manifest token of the vnhappie issue in the battell. The Bassa Cicala notwithstanding, sustained the furie of the Persians, and valorously with great cunning & skill went about to harten the Armie to fight, and to doo their best endeauours, shewing his notable courage in euery respect. But when he perceaued that in both the winges of his people there was still great harme done in euery moment of an hower, he aduised with himselfe to retyre with the least danger that possibly he might. Wherein he could not so warily carie himself, but that his Squadrons were shrewdlie beaten and discomfited, and in the end, he was enforced in the sight of euery man to withdraw himselfe to the Armie, and openly betake himself to flight. So that he also arriued at the campe, altogether discomfited, without any Ensigne, bereaued of three yong men, whom he loued verie deerely, and without any of his horses which he had caused to be lead with him, to haue serued his turne in time of neede: and so speak all in a woord, he was quite ouerthrowen, and (about) eight thousand of his souldiers slaine. Great was the cowardise of the one, and great was the courage of the other: whereby it may manifestly appeare, how much more the Persians are exercised and acquainted with the doubtful conflicts & perils of warre, then the Turkes are.

With this so fortunate and happie euent, the Persian Prince being somewhat encouraged, he sent speedie Herauldes to the sick Visier, (whom he thought notwithstanding to haue been in health) giuing him to vnderstand, that if it pleased him to fight with him, he was readie for him, and in what sort soeuer he would accept of battell, he would make him good accompt of his valour, & cause him to know, not onely that Amurath had most iniuriouslie and vniustly raised this warre, but also that it had been good for him not to haue withstood his force and valiance. Osman accepted his offer, but being not hable himself to go and aunswer the Prince in person, hand to hand, by reason of his sicknesse, which euery hower encreased more mortally vpon him, he sent out all the Captaines of his armie. The Persian Prince remained ten miles of there aboutes, distant from the Campe of Osman, and that vpon verie good consideration, least peraduenture in the heate and furie of the battel, he might haue been spoiled by the Artillarie: so that of necessitie the Turkish armie must needes ryde to encounter with him.

The Turkish Captaines marched in this maner; The middest of the battel was guided by the Bassa of Caraemit, and Sinan Cicala, with all the Souldiers of Assiria and Babylon: The left hand was lead by the Bassa of Natolia, with the band of Graecia: And the right hand was conducted by Amurath the Bassa of Caramania, with the people

The Bassa of Caraemit put to flight.

Cicala Bassa flyeth also.

8000. Turkes slaine.

Heraulds sent by the Persian Prince to Osman.

Osman accepteth the offer, but his sicknesse encreaseth mortally vpon him.

The array and order of the Turkish souldiers.

of Soria: to the number in all of three score thousand, besides all those that were slaine in the two former conflicts, and besides a great multitude of seruile people, & diuerse voluntarie, and sundrie waged souldiers also, that were stil within the Citie, busied about their new pillages, and searching for hidden treasures, and other rich booties, euen in places vnder the ground, and in their Churches: and besides the trustie guard of the Iannizzaries of Constantinople, with all the Artillarie, which was left behind for the safegard of the sick Visier, and all the Tentes.

Being thus ordered and deuided, they confronted the Persian Prince, who was himselfe in the middest of his Army, and had placed all his people in very good order on all sides, hauing on his one side, the souldiers of Persia and Hircania, and on his other side the souldiers of Parthia and Atropatia, in all to the nomber of forty thousand. I do not belieue, that Ida the mountaine, or Xanthus the riuer by Troy, did euer see so terrible and bloudy battels, as these were, that were fought neere to the Riuers and mountaines of Tauris, by these nations, who, though they be all in deed of Asia, yet (as Aristotle saith) are not very martiall. The Turkes were in a feare least the Persians would haue fetched a great compasse, and with all celerity and fury would haue runne to set vpon their tentes, & the riches which they had layed vp together in their pauillions: and therefore at euery motion of theirs they continually feared this suddain outroade. Whereof they had such speciall care, that retiring themselues asmuch as they might, and faining that they yeelded and gaue place to the Persians, they withdrew so neere to their Army, that they wanted but a little from being brought euen within the iust leuill and marke of their artillarie. Which when the Persians had espyed, and perfectly discouered the cunning and craft of the Turkes, without any further dallying they began to seise vpon the maine body of the battell. And the Prince himselfe being entred among the souldiers of the Bassa of Caraemit, who (as wee tould you a little before) as Generall sustayned the place of Osman, & pressing into the middest of the battel, dispatched euery man that came in his way, and hauing drawen out the Bassa from among the rest, he smote of his head, and gaue it to one that waited vpon him, to carrie about vpon the top of his launce. The speechles head being openly discried, wrought a terrour to the Turks, and a courage in the Persians, who being imbrued with blood in the battell, and remembring also the crueltie vsed vpon the Taurisians, accounted it an impiety to shew any pitty to their enemies, and a great point of cowardise to foreslow the victory ouer them. Whereupon they entermingled themselues more and more, & made a most confused, and generall slaughter: wherein besides the Bassa aboue named, there died also the Bassa of Trabizonda,

---

60000. in the Turks armie.

The order of the Persians.

40000. in the Persians army.

Terrible and bloudy battels about Tauris.

The Persian Prince cutteth of the head of Mahamet the Bassa of Caraemit.

The Bassa of Trebisonda, the Sangiacco of Bursia, & 5. other Sangiacchi slaine.

the Sangiacco of Bursia, with fiue other Sangiacchi, and many other Chiaus, and diuers common souldiers taken prisoners. It fell to the lot also of Amurath the Bassa of Caramania to be taken prisoner, being (as they say) fallen into a Well or ditch, whiles hee was fighting: and to be shorte it is the common report, that the number of those that were slain in this battell, amounted to twentie thousande Turkes. The night came vpon them, and the Persians were now somewhat too nigh to the Turkish Artillerie, and therefore they resolued to leaue fighting, and as they were occasioned by the darkenes of the night, to withdraw themselues backe to the pauilions of the king, the Princes father.

Amurath the Bassa of Caramania taken aliue in the fight.

20000. Turks. slaine.

But now there were many daies spent, wherein (as we told you afore) the fabricke of the Fortresse was fully finished. And after so many victories, and so many losses, that fell out on both sides, the souldiers of Grecia and Constantinople, being nowe wearied with seeing their frendes and louing fellowes thus slaine before their faces, hauing also layed vp safely in their owne custody those praies and booties, which they had gotten in the sack of the Cittie, resolued with themselues to procure their owne departure, being partly moued thereunto by the violent and sharpe season of the winter, which was nowe comming vpon them. And for that purpose they came to the Visier, who being already brought into a most dangerous estate of his health, and waxen very faint through the aboundant issue of blood, that mortally flowed out of his bellie, was (as a man might say) in despaire with himselfe to liue any longer, and quite abandoned of all hope by his Phisitians. And therefore they were faine by the mouth of such as were trustie about him to represent vnto him the necessity of their returne: and withall after many frendly and reuerent entreaties, they caused also to be signified vnto him, that if he stoode obstinate & vnwilling to yeeld to their request, and wold needes stay dallying and spending the tyme in those quarters, where there was no such need, they should be inforced to withdraw themselues & forsake him. Osman, who had nothing els to do in those countries, but onely to leaue at Tauris within the new fort for the custody thereof, some cōuenent garrisō of soldiers, did liberally promis to gratify thē in their suit, & to yeeld them al satisfactiō, as they desired, by departing from thence the next morning. And there fore for asmuch as he was now to remoue, & before his remoue to leaue such a garrison in the new fort, as might be sufficient to maintaine and defende it, vntill the next spring, wherein there should be some new captaine and fresh supplies sent thether for their succor, he concluded, that Giaffer the Eunuch, being thē the Bassa of Tripoli, who (as we told you in the last booke) would not follow the warres of Ebrain the Visier, should bee the keeper and gouernour of the said Forte. And the rather to encourage him that he would take the charge vppon him, he gaue

The people of Gseece and Constantinople procure their returne home into their cuntries.

Osman through sicknesse desperate to liue any longer.

Giaffer the Bassa of Tripoli in Soria, chosen Gouernour of Tauris.

him freely, for the space of three whole yeares, not onely the office and authority, but also the rentes and reuenues of the Bassa of Caraemit, in the place of him, whose head (we told you lately) the Persian Prince had cut of: and withall honoured him with the title of the Bassa of the Court, where hauing finished his three yeares office of Caraemit, he was to go & sit among the soueraigne seates in the order and ranke of the Visiers. The Eunuch, seeing so faire and so nigh a way for him to mount to those high honours, readily obeyed his pleasure, and presently dispatching his Lieutenaunt, (whom the Turkes call Checaia) for Caraemit, to the gouernement of those countries in his absence, with a hundred of his owne subiectes, hee setled himselfe in the said Fort, and afterwardes, besides his said subiectes, there were deliuered vnto him twelue thousand souldiers, some voluntaries and some stipendiaries, furnished with all necessarie prouision, and sufficient for the warre till the new spring. And when the custody of this Fortresse was thus ordered, and safely prouided for, the Visier departed according to his promisse made to the souldiers of Grecia and Constantinople, & the same morning, which was the fourescore and seuenth day after his departure from Erzirum, hee went to a place called Sancazan, seuen miles distant from Tauris, with an entent in this his returne, to take another course, then he tooke when he came to that Citty.

12000 souldiers appointed to Giaffer the Eunuche to guard the fort.

Osman Bassa at Sancazan.

They were now vpon the point of their encamping (as the maner is) in a confused disorder & hurley-burley, when those that were hindermost in the armie heard the neighing of horses, and the noise of drommes and trumpettes, which when all the whole Campe vnderstoode (by the report of the first hearers vnto them that were formost) they ranne all headlong and disordered (as they were) to the rescue on that side, where the report was that the noise of horses and warlike instrumentes was heard. But while the Turks were thus intentiuely busied on that side, to expect the arriuall of their enemies, on the other side without any signe or token of battell was the Persian Prince ready vpon them with eight & twenty thousande persons in his company, who, (hauing discouered the Camelles, the horses, the Mules, & other cariages, wherevpon their booties, their spoiles, and their riches were loaden which they had taken in Tauris, besides their corne and much of their prouision for victuaile, necessarie for the sustenaunce of the armie,) had turned vpon them, & with a prouident and safe conuoy had taken for a praye eighteene thousand of the Cammelles and Mules, well loaden with the said booties and other victuailes. The Prince sent away presently six thousand of his souldiers for the safegard of the cariages, that they might lead them away in safety: and he himselfe with his two and twenty thousand Persians entred into the Turkishe Army, who now to withstand his assault, had conuerted their anger

The Persian Prince assaileth the Turkes, with 28000. persons.

18000. Camelles, and mules laden with spoile, reskued by the Persians from the Turkes.

and fiercenes against him. It was a gallant thing, & a terrible withall, to see what a mortall battell and what singular prowesse was shewed, presently euen in the forefront of the army. For in a moment you might haue seene the Tentes and Pauillions turned vp side downe, and their encamping lodgings replenished with carcases & blood, and victorious death ranging in euerie corner. The Turkes themselues, through vnwonted astonishment, became more attentiue beholders of this affray, then their enemies were, and to this day with great meruaile doo recounte the vertue and valour of the Persians, who although they were so few in nomber, and intermingled among so populous an army of warlick people, yet it seemed that they couched their speares & brandished their swords ouer them, as though it had thundred & lightned vpon them, and were in deed rather like fatall ministers, then humaine executioners of so generall a slaughter. But these mischeefes being already foreseene and too much feared by the trusty guard of the Ianizzaries, & all of them doubting greatly least the Persians would forcibly inuade the very lodginges of the Visier, it was commanded, not by himself, (for he was now at the last gasp) but by him who at that time had authority to command in his name, that without any delay the artillary should be vnbarred, & by that means the valorous conflict of these fierce souldiers was vnequally parted. For the Artillary wrought perchance greatter harme among the Turkes themselues, then it did among the Persians. For the medley and mingling of the two nations which fought together, being all in a confusion and a hurley-burley, the artillary entring among them without any exception or distinction of persons, ouerthrewe both frendes and foes. At the first thondering noise whereof, the Prince was most ready & swift to flie, & all that were with him, followed presently after him, so that the Turks which remained behind were moreshrewdly afflicted then the Persians were, who by flying away could not feele any dammage, but the Turkes must first bee well payed for their labour. The Graecians, the Constantinopolitanes, and those that were of Natolia, pursued these fugitiues, making a shewe as though they would gladly haue ouertaken the stollen carriages, and recouered them againe: but they being already arriued in safety, and the night come vpon them, they feared to proceede any further, then they might easily returne with the safegarde of their liues. And therefore the Persians, though greatly wearied and weakened, thus saued themselues, and the Turks also retourned into their Tentes, wholly dismaied and discomfited, leauing too manifest a token of the sondrie calamities which hapned in these broiles, and the maruellous ouerthrowe of their whole armie. So that there is no man but confesseth, that in the battell of Sancazan there were slaine twentie thousand of the Ottoman souldiers, and that in this enterprise

The Visier at the last gaspe.

The artillary workeh happely more harme among the Turkes, then among the Persians.

20000. Turks slaine in fight at Sancazan.

of Tauris, there died by this time threescore thousande Turkes with that small losse of the Persian forces, which we haue before described.

Among the rest, in the same place died also the Visier Osman, Generall of the late dreadfull, but now desolate Armie, not by wouuds, (as some write) nor by any such like means, but being vtterly consumed by the mortall & vncurable disease of an Ague and a Flix, (as wee haue told you before, and doo now againe testifie vnto you, by the certain and vndoubted report of those faithull Phisitians, which were about him,) whose death notwithstandinge was kept secreate from the whole Armie, and euery man thought verily, that it was but onely the continuance of his sicknes, because the charriottes wherein he lay, were still kept close, and in his name Cicala Bassa, (for so he had appointed by his will) gaue out aunsweres and commandementes to all the Armie. But although it was thus concealed from the Turkes, yet was it disclosed to the Persians, by the meanes of three youngmen, who in the life of Osman had the charge of his precious stones, of his iewels, and of his gold, and now hauing gathered together, the best, the cheefest, and the fairest of them, and also the goodliest and the fairest horses that the Visier had, were fled to the King of Persia, and reuealed vnto him the death of the Generall. The comming of these youngmen was most acceptable both to the king & also to the prince, aswell for the iewels & gold, as also for the aduertisement of Osmans death: who reasoned among themselues, that it was not possible for so great cowardise, and so dishonorable a kind of fighting and ordering of an Army to proceede from the vertue and valour of Osman, of whome they had had too manifest a triall and experience in times past: and therefore they were thereby encouraged to put in practise some new and strange kindes of exploytes, and by attempting the vtter ouerthrow of the Turkish remnant, to giue them an honorable Farewell. And therevppon the Persian Prince, hauing gotten together fourteene thousand men, went to follow the Turkes, who had now raised their Campe, and were remoued to pitch their Tentes neere to a certain streame of salt-water, not farre from Sancazan: where also the said Prince caused certain fewe Tentes to be pitched, about fower or fiue miles distant from the Turkish Campe, the foresaid brooke running in the middest betweene the two Enemies armies. Now it was the purpose of the Sofian Prince to haue assayled the Turks in the morning, whiles they were loading their cariages, hoping in that confusion to haue wrought them some notable mischiefe: but the Turkes had caught a certain spye of his, who reuealed all vnto them. And therefore they did neither arise so earely in the morning ás their maner was, nor load their stuffe, vntill such time as they were all armed and on hors-backe, trusting by that means to rebate and to quaile their enemies assaults. The Persians were greatly discontented,

Osman the Visier and Generall dieth at Sancazan.

The death of Osman disclosed to the Persians by three youngmen.

The Persians encouraged to giue the Turkes a famous farewel.

A brooke betweene the two armies.

when they saw this warie and vnvsuall maner of the Turkes raysing of their Tentes, and perceaued that some inkling had been giuen them of the purpose which they had intended: And yet considering, that if they should loose this occasion, they could not haue any other good oportunitie to annoy them, vntill the next Spring: they vtterly resolued to venture the assault: and hauing obserued, that the Rankes of their Artillarie were on the right side of the Armie, they began to enter (in the sight of euery man) vpon the left hand. But the Turkes made a wing presently on that side, and so vncouered and vnbarred their Artillarie against the assaylants, to their great losse and danger. Howbeit they were so nymble and quick to shrowde themselues vnder their Enemies armie, & to auoid this mischieuous tempest, that being now come verie neere to the Turkish Squadrons, they must needes send out people to encounter them, and ioyne present battel with them. They were purposed before, assoone as they saw the Turkes begin to stirre, to haue brought them towards their side, into a verie filthy and deepe Moore, which being then drie, yet breathed fourth a most stinking and foggie ayre, neyther was it doubted of, or feared by any, but onely by those that were acquainted withall, and borne there aboutes: and so verie boldly they went towards that place, entycing their enemies to follow after them. But the Rebell Maxut-Chan, and with him that other Traitor Daut-Chan, who had knowledge of this treacherie, as being well acquainted with those places, perceaued the policie of the Enemie, and particularlie gaue notice thereof to Cicala Bassa, who presently caused a great compassing wing to be made, commaunding them to set vpon the Persians, and to giue them a continuall charge. The commaundement of the Captaine was put in execution, and so their fore-front opened it selfe wyth verie large and spacious Cornets vpon the Prince: who no sooner saw this kind of order, but by and by he perceaued, that his intended Stratageme was discouered. Whereupon without any stay he began to retyre, and called all his people after him. But they could not be so readie and quick to flye, but that three thousand of them remayned behind, all miserably styfled and ouer-trodden in the myre, with verie little dammage or losse of the Turkes. And this onely battell, among the fiue that were fought vnder Tauris, and in those quarters, was it that was lesse hurtfull to the Ottomans, then to the Persians.

  The Prince returned to the pauilions of the King his father, and told him the whole action how it had fallen out, together wyth the departure of the Enemie: And so the Turkes came to Salmas, where the death of their Visier was published. From Salmas they went afterwardes to Van, where they took a surueigh of their Armie, & found wanting therin about fower score and fiue thousand persons: and some say, more.

The Persians begin to assault the Turks on the leftside, to auoide their Artillarie.

The purpose of the Persians, which afterwards came to no good issue.

3000. Persians ouerwhelmed in the myre.

The only battell among fiue, most hurtfull to the Persians.

A surueigh of the Armie in Van.

At Van all the souldiers were dismissed into their owne countries, and Cicala gaue notice to the King at Constantinople of all that had happened. I my self also was in Constantinople at the same time, when the postes arryued, that brought word of these great aduentures. First was published the death of Osman, for whom there were many signes of verie great sorrow: and together with his death were blazed the blouddie and mortall actions that were performed, so that it seemed all the whole Citie was greatly discomforted: and diuerse times, in those few dayes, by sundry persons in many places, and particularly in the house of Mahamet Bey, one of the San-Giacchi of Cairo, my verie great friend, I heard much rayling vpon the King, many curses of this warre, and infolent maledictions of these many mischiefes. Then was dispersed the great fame of the new Fortresse erected in Tauris, of the sacking of that Citie, and of all the losse that hapned therein. And lastly there was a general Edict published in the Kings name, that through all the Cities of his Empire, they should make solemne feastes, & shew other expresse tokens of mirth and reioysing, which the Turkes call Zine: And therupon all the Artificers in Constantinople, with diuerse goodly and sumptuous shewes, with musicall instruments, and bountifull banketting performed the Kings royall commaundements. There was also woord sent to the Embassadours of Hungarie, of Fraunce, of Venice, and of other countries, that they should doo the like: But they all aunswered with one accord, that it was neuer the custome of Embassadours to make anie signe of reioysing, but onely when the King himself in person returned from the like victories.

In the mean time, great consultation was at Van, how they might attempt to send succours to Teflis in Georgia, whereof there was a rumour spread abroad, that it was yelded to the Georgians: which in deed was a lye, as at an other time the like report was also. And while they were thus in consideration of many matters, Daut-Chan, who to deserue some reward at Amurathes hand, neuer ceassed to remember and vrge, whatsoeuer might set forward the conceits of the Ottomans, offered himself to performe this so important seruice, & could so well discourse vpon the maner how to bring it to passe, and to make the enterprise certaine and secure, that at the last, Cicala Bassa deliuered vnto him thirtie thousand Cecchini to cary to the Fort at Teflis. Daut-Chan went and returned, and releeued those souldiers, without any thing hapning vnto him in his voyage worthie the writing. And yet was this seruice so well accepted by Amurath, that he honoured the Rinegate with the dignitie of the Bassa of Maras, a Citie seated in the confines of Cappadocia and Armenia, neere to the riuer Euphrates, where also the same Daut gouerneth, euen at this present day: although there was a speech deliuered out by the same, that King Amurath had

Marginalia:
- At Van the souldiers discharged.
- The Authour at Constantinople.
- Newes published in Constantinople.
- Feasting in Constantinople.
- The Christian Embassadors refuse to reioice for these victories.
- Consultation in Van how to send succour to Teflis.
- Succours appointed for Teflis, and deliuered to Daut-Chan the Rinegare.
- Daut-Chan named by the king the Bassa of Maras.

caused him to be strangled, which was not true. Maxut-Chan also, he that was the guide of the Turkish Armie to Reiuan, and to Tauris, was honoured by the same King with the great rich Office of the Bassa of Aleppo. Of whom, as also of his children, and of his vassals, I haue had verie many particulars, both touching this warre, and matters of peace, wherein this man was a dealer. So that I haue not written (to my knowledge) any thing herein, which hath not been certified vnto me, from persons of credite and auctoritie, euen of their owne sight, for that they were present and Agents themselues in these enterprises. Whereunto, that such credite may be giuen, as an Historie deserueth, I haue thought good in this place to translate a certain Letter, sent from the Sangiaccho of Aman, to Aly the Bassa of Aleppa, who was with Ebrain, and so could not be at the actions of Tauris. A Copie whereof was also sent to the Senate of Venice, by Giouanni Michele, at that time Consul for that most honourable Common wealth, of whom we haue a little before made mention. It was written in the Arabike, and beeing translated into our toung, it was word for word in this maner.

Maxut-Chan nominated by the King the Bassa of Aleppo.

'To the rich and mightie among the rich and mightie, the noble Lord of Lordes, among honourable and great persons the honourable and great person, the Lord Aly Bassa, Humble salutations, and long prosperitie. 'Your Lordship hath giuen me to vnderstand, that you desire to be aduertised of all that hath hapned this yeare betweene vs and the Cheselbas: and I, now I haue good leasure to doo it, will not fayle readily so to do. So you shal vnderstand, that from Erzirum we came to Tauris in forty dayes: and the day before wee arriued at Tauris, at the Bridge of salt-water, our Vanigard was assaulted by the Sonne of the King of Persia, who quite discomfited it, and gaue vs a great ouerthrow, with the death of almost fiue thousand of our men, among whom Aly the Bey of Grecia was one. And because you would know the very day, that we entred into Tauris: I do let you vnderstand, that two dayes before our feast, we entred into it in great number. Two daies the Citie was kept locked, because the Persians had gotten the gates, and in that time there was a great fight both within and without the Citie, with the slaughter of our men more then eight thousand, and little losse to the Persians. For Alycull-Chan the Gouernour of the Citie, with the best of his people were readie to flie, and abandon the defence of the Citie, who as he went out, met with the Bassa of Maras, and flew him with many of our men. But afterward being scarred with the Artillarie, that was set right vpon him, he fled away, and all the rest of the Cheselbas-Captaines, who vpon that occasion also at the last retyred with him. You desire to know, how those of Tauris were entreated: and I tell you, that three dayes after we were entred into it, and Alyculi-Chan fled with those aboue named, order was giuen for the

A Letter written to Aly the Bassa of Aleppo.

buylding of a Fortresse in the middest of the Citie, which was then all sacked, in such sort, as it was great pitie to see, and yet without any direction or commaundement from the Visier, although in deed they haue giuen out speeches, that it was by his appointment. The Iannizaries and the Spahini of the Porta, tooke away all their goods and houshold stuffe, and twice afterwards sacked it againe: and the second time they slew many of the inhabitants of Tauris, and found a great quantitie of stuffe hidden vnder the ground, and sold their children for ten and twelue Ducates apeece. The buylding of the Fort was finished in six and thirtie dayes, and twelue dayes before this Fabrik was finished, newes came to the Visier, that the Persians, were comming to assault him: Wherevpon he sent out the sonne of Cicala, and Mahamet the Bassa of Caraemit, who from the topp of an hill discouered the Persians that were comming, and so they descended into the plaine and ioyned battell with them. Wherein it seemed at the first that the Persians would haue taken their heeles, but they returned vpon our men, and pursued them with slaughter to the number of fower thousand Turkes; and took prisoners Sinan the Checaia or Lieutenant of Cicala, Chenan the Kings Chiaus or Embassadour, and the Clerk of the Spahinj of the Porta. A few dayes before the Fort was finished, the Visier was certified againe, that the Persians were comming in a verie great number to assault him, whereupon he began to set all his Armie in an order? but while he was busied there abouts, the Persians arriued about noone, and setting vpon our men, they faught such a battell from that time till two howers within night, that it cannot be expressed, either with toung or pen. But as farre as mens iudgments can reach, it is verily thought, that there may be about fortie thousand of our men slaine, with great losse also of the Enemie. Among our men, the Bassa of Caraemit had his head stroken off; Murat the Bassa of Caramania was taken aliue in fight, being fallen into a water, whiles he was in fighting: Mustaffa the Sangiaccho of Bursia; and Schender the Bey of Grecia, and fiue other Sangiacchi were hewen in peeces, and the Bassa of Trebisonda also left his carcase in the field. In verie trueth the battell was so great, that it cannot well and sufficiently be described. Afterwards, the Visier being departed from Tauris, and arriued at Sancazan, would needes stay there and pitch: But whiles they were drawing out their Tents, and euery man busie to encampe, the Prince of Persia was discouered with a great number of souldiers: who seeing vs in this plight, hastened his pace, and betweene our Rereward and the Visier, began battell vpon vs. It was then an hower after day-light, and we had trauailed all that night. From that hower euen vntill euening did this fight last, with such effusion of bloud, as is not credible, and the common opinion is, that we felt the losse of more then twentie thousand persons: among whom there is slaine poore Vstref the Checaia, so well knowen vnto you. Heere also died the Visier of his infirmitie. In the first battell the Spahini of the Porta, with certaine of the Kinges Chiaus brought to the Visier three hundred heads of Persians: but in the second they made no great boast, for in deed both the one and the other was not without great losse vnto them. We remoued from Sancazan, and were againe pursued by our enemies the Cheselbas, and yet without any fight between them and vs: sauing onely, two dayes after we were departed from them, they took away from the tayle of our Armie, a great number of Camels and Mules, loaden with stuffe, slaues, and munition, which although they were followed, yet could not be recouered: but that Mahamet the Bassa of Siuas, with the souldiers of the Porta, and of Caraemit, brought vs a thousand heads of Persians, fiue Drummes, and one Ensigne, besides that with our Artillarie, they were hardly entreated, and two of their Chans slaine. We came afterwards in a direct course to Erzirum, without hearing any word at all of the Persians. And to the end you may know how we haue left Erzirum, I do further aduertise you, that there are remaining in it certaine Spahini of the Porta, with certaine Sardari and Vlu-Bassi, and two Sangiacchi, the one of Bir, the other of Marra, who afterwards fled away both. There is least for the Sardar or Generall and Capteine of these in the Fort, Giaffer the Eunuche Bassa of Tripoli, to whom the Visier hath also graunted, that for three whole yeares together he shall be Bassa of Caraemit, and afterwardes one of the Visiers of the Porta. There is least also for them victuaile, and munition, and great store of Artillary. But I may not omit to tell you, that in our Armie wee haue indured such a dearth, as wee haue beene enforced to giue our Camelles Biscot and Ryse: and when that failed vs we gaue them Packsaddles to eate, and after that peeces of wood beaten into poulder, and at last me gaue them the verie earth. And this great dearth endured euen vntill we arriued at Van. And at Tauris wee were of necessitie constrained, while the fortresse was in building, to giue our horses their doung in very drie poulder, by reason whereof there followed a greeuous mortallitie of horses, Camelles, mules and men: and the stinke, which grew of this mortallitie was so great, that we were faine alwaies euerie one of vs to carrie halfe an Onion vnder our nose to auoyde it. Yet at last we are now arryued at Erzirum, from whence we hope also shortly to be deliuered, for that euery bodie had licence to depart euen from Van. God be with you. From Erzirum the first day of the Moone of Mucaren.'

By this Letter it may manifestly be perceaued, that the number of Turkes which perished in this enterprise of Tauris, is peraduenture greater then that which we haue written. And although there be therein discouered some kind of diuersitie in the actions, otherwise then we haue deliuered them: yet ought no man greatly to maruaile thereat: for that it is a verie easie matter to varie in such a point, because the maner how, and the occasions why, yea, the verie proceedings of battels are many times not knowen to all men alike, especially in so huge an Armie, wherein the effectes and issues can verie hardlie be throughly knowen, much lesse the causes and occasions thereof.

The end of the eight Booke.

The Ninth Booke

The Argument.
The Occasion of the Persians perplexed cogitations.
The Persians resolution to assault the Forte.
The Persians seeke to be reconcyled with the Turcomannes.
The Turcomannes do deceitfully promise to helpe the Persians in their common miseries.
The Persian king deliuereth his sonne Tamas to the Turcomannes.
The Turcomannes fly from the assault of the Forte, and call Tamas their king.
The Persian Prince pursueth the fugitiue Turcomannes.
The Persian Prince putteth to death Mahamet-Chan, and Calife the Sultan: He committeth his owne brother Tamas to prison, and withdraweth himselfe to Casbin, to gather a new Army.
Saitan-Chalasi abandoned by the Souldiers that were in it.
The Inhabitantes of Chiulfall giue tribute to the Bassa of Reiuan, and also to Alyculs, whereby they preserue themselues in peace.
Cicala the Bassa at the request of Giaffer the Bassa mindeth to succour the Forte.
Cicala feareth the comming of the Persian king, and retyreth to Van.
King Amurath at Constantinople chooseth Ferat the Bassa to bee his Generall, who had once already bene Generall before Osman the Bassa.
Ferat goeth to Siuas and so to Erzirum, where he meeteth with a very great Army, which was in great distresse by reason of a dearth.
Ferat passeth-on to Van, and there findeth the Souldiers of Soria, Palestina, Iury, and Mesopotamia.
The mustering of the whole Army.
The Turkish Generall hath intelligence with certaine trayterous and rebellious Persians
The Persian Prince commeth to Tauris
The causes, why the Prince would not attempt to assault the Forte.

The Persian Prince ouerthroweth Zeinello, sacketh the Cittie of Salmas, and discomfiteth the Bassa of Reiuan.

A treaty for the exchange of the two Prisoners Ebrain-Chan and Amurath the Bassa, but nothing concluded by it.

The subiectes of Manogli do great harme in Soria.

Aly the Bassa is sent from Constantinople to Soria against the Drusians.

The Prince setteth his Army in array, and goeth to meete and endommage Ferat.

The Prince discouereth the treason of the Rebelles, and so retyreth.

The Forte is succoured by Ferat, without any speech or word of any battell from his enimies.

The Stratageme of Simon commeth to no good issue.

Teflis is relieued with succours.

The Persian Prince commeth to Genge, and is thrust through the body by one of his owne keepers.

THE NINTH BOOKE

The troublesome cogitations of the the Persians.

But the Persians in the meane time, were all full of wrath and indignation for the Fort that was builded by their enemies. For on the one side they found themselues not onely disfurnished of artillarie, and of other engines to batter the walles downe to the ground, but also to be much fewer in nomber, then were sufficient and requisite to resist the tempest of fires, which they knew they must endure in assaulting those that should be enuironed within the Castell. And on the other side, they reconed it too great a shame vnto them, that the enemie hauing made a Fort within their owne naturall Cittie, should quietly rest there, and insolently threaten them with daily oppression, and mischeeuous calamities in time to come. And therefore being pricked on by glory, by vertue, and by very necessity, they determined euen in the sharpenes of winter, to gather fresh souldiers, and reducing the forces of their armie into a cōuenient order, with trenches of earth, to approach the ditch, and to trie if they could aduaunce a countermure as high as their walls, and so attain to the conquest thereof. But in the gathering together of their new men they discouered new difficulties. For then they perceaued manifestly, that to hire souldiers either from Heri, or from Gheilan, it was denied them by Abas and Amet-Chan: and that the Turcoman nation, which might haue been the readiest and neerest at such a neede, for the late death of Emir-Chan, and for the succession of Aliculi, were growen very contumacious: so that neither the King nor the Prince, nor the presidents and gouernours of the kingdome could

The determination of the Persians.

tell on which side to tourne them. At the last, foreseeing the safegarde of the Common wealth, they determined to draw the Turcomani to a reconciliation, hoping that if they should promise them any honest satisfaction for the wrong, wherewith they challenged themselues greeued for the death of their captaine, they would become more tractable to do them seruice in their common necessities. And therefore the king sent letters to the heades & captaines of those nations, & principally, to Mahamet-Chan, and to Calife the Sultan, wherein declaring plainely vnto them the perill of his honour, and the libertie of that whole kingdom, he shewed vnto them that all his hope of ridding Persia from that yoke, and setting free all those people, which in all ages heretofore had beene so faithfull and frendly vnto them, was reposed onely in their aide and assistance: and that their onelie Armes was hable not onely to mainetaine, but also to encrease the renown of valour in the Persian nation: which estate, as in yeares forepassed it wrought enuie and terrour euen in the farthest and most remote peoples of all Asia, so at this present, if it bee not succoured and releeued, standeth in termes to become a most miserable spectacle to all the world. And that therefore, forgetting all thinges that are past, as being doone not to worke any shame or scorne to their nation, but onely for zeale and loue to the kingdome, they wold demand such satisfaction as they would require: for hee would bee ready to agree to any iust request they should make. With these and perhaps with more affectionate and passionate letters were the wrothfull Turcomani inticed to the reuenge of the iniuries which they had receaued by the Ottoman forces. To which Letters they were not a whit slacke in framing an aunswere, but readily wrote back, that they would come vnto hym, and put in execution, whatsoeuer for the common necessitie he should command.

The Persian king by letters solliciteth the Turcomans. The tenor of the kinges Letters.

The aunswere of the Turcomanni, and their craftie deuises.

Now they had already craftely concluded among themselues, that they wold not suffer any other to sit in the ranke of their Captaines in the rowme of Emir-Chan lately deceased, but onely the young Tamas the Kinges thirde sonne. Which conclusion they had plotted to themselues, with a resolute mind, to cause him to bee accepted for King at Casbin, in dispight of the king himselfe and of the Prince Hamze, nothing regarding, that by this action farre greater seditions would arise in Persia, then euerwere yet heard of, but onely being wholly bent to reuenge the sole death of one onely Emir-Chan. So vile and so base an account did they make of the honour of their naturall King, and of their auncient religion, that before such matters of so great respect and importance, very audaciously (I will not say temerariously) they preferred their owne priuate reuenge: and chose rather to become most bloody and cruell against those, to whome they were allied in religion, in blood and in countrie, then against their common enemies.

Ten thousand Turcomans go to the Persian king.

With this malitious and fraudulent reasolution, to the number of tenne thousand, vnder the conduct of two Captaines Mahamet, and Calife, they went to the king in all reuerence, and offred all readinesse to bee employed in the enterpryse, whereunto they were called. The old credulous king, not suspecting any mischeefe plotted by these rebelles, was greatly comforted at their comming. And although by some of his Sultanes, that had felt some inkling of this conspiracie, he was aduised to deale circumspectlie and warilie with them, and especially not to trust them with any secret, or to let any matter of importance to be in their defence: yet did he thinke euerie hour to be a thousand, till he had made them satisfaction, hoping thereby that if they had conceaued any mischeefe in their mindes, they wold lay it aside, and being pacified by his amiable and courteous entertainement, yeeld themselues in very truth faithfull and obedient vnto him. And therevpon being more constant then hee was in this his imagination, whiles hee bestowed good wordes and giftes among them, at the last hee demanded of them what Captaine they wold nominate in the rowme of Emir-Chan: promising vnto them, and peraduenture (as some say) with an oath, that whomsoeuer they desired, if possibly it might be, they stould be satisfied. Herevntoo the dissembling Mahamet-Chan made answeare, that their desire was principally to doo him pleasure and seruice: of whose bounty and good inclination they did so well hope, as that he wold not appoint any person but such a one, as should be valourous, noble, and deere and acceptable vnto them. The King stayed not from giuing them presently to vnderstand, that so hee had determined to doo, and frankly declared vnto them, that finding Tamas his thirde sonne to bee without any charge, and being desirous to geeue them a Captaine that might please them, to the end they might rest more assured of the good will which hee bare vnto them, and haue a good ostage in pawne thereof, hee had made choise of his childe Tamas to be the successour of Emir-Chan: and that if it so pleased them, they might accept of him, and with one accord endeauour themselues to conquer those odious walles of the Forte, which with so great ignominy and reproach of all the Persian Nation was there erected by the Turkes. As soone as Mahamet-Chan heard the resolution of the king, who beesides all expectation offered thus to gratify them, and voluntarily of himselfe, without any suspicion at all, yeelded them the meanes whereby they might put in execution the worke which they had maliciously contriued against the peace and liberty of the kingdome: hee became more ioconde then he was wont to be, and outwardly shewed himselfe readie, for whatsoeuer the King would commaund him: and yeelded also in the names of all the rest, large promises of fidelity and obedience, so that the matter might be perfourmed, for which he had now giuen his word.

The king, who longed to see the houre, wherein this assault should be begunne, as a matter no lesse desired by euery man, then necessary for all; the more he was aduised and counselled by his Sultans and the Prince, not to deliuer his sonne Tamas into their handes: and the lesse they feared that the king would haue committed such an errour, but rather beleeued verily, that the king would haue made the conspiracy, which they had reuealed vnto him, to bee capitall and matter of treason in the Turcomanni:) the more resolute and vnwise hee was, and therevppon very secretely, and (as it were) by stealth, aswell to maintayne hys promise made vnto them, as also to sett his Sonne in such security, as hee might not so easely bee made away by hys brother Hamze, or hys brother Ahas, he gaue him into the handes of Mahamet-Chan, as chiefe of all the Turcomanni, who to nourish the good opinion and credulitie of the King, and to secure the Prince and the Sultans, gaue a lustie beginning, by the helpe of all his followers, with trenches and Rampires to approch the Fort. Neither was there any greate time consumed therein: For they had nowe almost made the farther side of their ditch euen with the enemies wall, and the ditch it selfe was also almost filled vp with earth, so that there wanted but little more labour to begin the desired assault.

The king deliuereth his son ramas to Mahamet-Chan.

Great hopes that mooue the Turcomans to assault the fort.

And nowe was there a great fame published ouer all the East, in what daungers the newe Fortresse was vpon these occasions, yea and aduertisementes were nowe sent into Italie, that it was quite demolished, ouerthrowne to the ground, and burnt by the Persians: when as contrarie to the common opinion, and contrarie to the publique expectation, wherewith al the world was nowe replenished, that false and wicked Traitor Mahamet-Chan, with all his Turcomanni, leading away with them the child Tamas, departed in the night time and vpon a sudden from so noble and honourable an enterprise: and being vtterlie blinded with ardent desire to put in execution his ill-hatched purpose, couertly and without any noyse remooued from the besieged walles, and put himselfe on his way towards Casbin, still terming Tamas, by the name of the king of Persia, and sundrie wayes abusing and mocking the poor olde king, and the Prince. Great was the astonishment of the subiect Cities, when they hard the new publication of this vnripe & vnexpected yong King. Great was the griefe, that the olde king conceaued of this daungerous rebellion. But verie greate was the sorrowe that afflicted the Prince, for these alterations of so great importance. Whereby not onlie so honourable and so necessarie an enterprise was quite abandoned, but also ther was put in hazard the preseruation of his own dignitie, the honour of that Scepter, the peace and quiet of the Kingdom, and his succession to the Crowne which was due and appoynted to him. Wherupon being wholly incensed with

Aduertisements sent into Italie.

The Rebellion of the Turcomanni.

The Doubtes of the Persian Prince.

griefe and anguish, hee began to tosse and retosse a thousand deuises in his heade, that he might resolue what he were best to attempt. To abandon the siege of the Forte, it grieued him aboue measure, and to suffer so pernicious a rebellion to go forward it semed also to be too dangerous for the state of Persia. To prouide for both these inconueniences at one time, it was altogether impossible. And therefore for certaine daies he stoode wauering in a huge tempest of contrarie thoughts: but at the last being inwardlie prouoked with the pricke of glorie, and encouraged by the chiefe Sultans of the Kingdome, hee resolued to turne himselfe against the Turcomanni, and by rooting out first these newe springing daungers, that might haue bene able, alone of themselues, to haue impeached euerie enterprise against the Turkes to make the way more open for him to compasse the siege, and to begin the preparation of his Armie for the next Spring. And so hauing gotten togegether twelue thousande Souldiers, and raysing also a part euen of the Kings ordinarie Guarde to go with him, all couragious and hardie, hee sette himselfe to followe the rebellious and fugitiue Turcomannes, and marching in a direct course towardes Casbin, all the way as hee passed, hee had always notice of the iourney which they helde. And being arriued at a place called Califteza, a dayes iourney on this side Casbin, hee ouertooke them, and ioyned battell vvith them. Wherein manie: of them being sorie for their vvicked reuenge, woulde not so much as stirre their swordes against the Prince and manie other also fledde away for feare, and so hee obtayned his vvished victorie ouer them. The sedicious Mahamet-Chan was taken prisoner, and by the commaundement of Emirhamze presentlie beheaded: the like also was done to Calife the Sultan, and to diuers other Captaines of this pestilent conspiracie. Young Tamas also was taken prisoner, and by the direction of the Prince himselfe, sent aliue to the Castle of Cahaca. Fiue thousande Turcomanni there were, that being nowe the followers of Mahamet, fledde out of this battell towardes Babylon by the vvay of Siras: touching whome, the opinion of manie was, that they shoulde goe to yeeld themselues to Solyman beeing then the Bassa of that Citie, vvhich also was done, although repenting themselues afterwardes of their follie, they sought to returne into the fauour of their king: But all in vaine: so that being become Rebelles to the one, and suspected to the other, they did at one time loose their Countrey, their Libertie, their honour, and the fauour of all men, as well friendes as foes. The Persian Prince passed to Casbin, and staying there, hee laboured to gather together the dispersed Turcomanni, those especiallie, that beeing mooued with the honestie of the cause, woulde not beare Armes in so vniust an action: And afterwardes to make an Armie as greate as was possible, whereby he might be the better able, at his returne to Tauris,

The determination of the Prince.

The Prince, with 12000 pursueth the Turcomans.

The turcomans discomfited by the, Prince.
Mahamet-chan & Califo the Sultan beheaded.
Tamas imprisoned.

The Prince at Casbin.

THE NINTH BOOKE

to attende the besieging and conquest of the Forte. And this was the ende of the Turcomanne stirres.

But the Turkes in this meane time were busie about diuers matters. At Constantinople, Amurath was busie about the election of his Generall▪ and the Souldiers of those Garrisons, that were placed in the Fortes vpon the frontiers, they were also attempting many thinges. Those of Saitan Chalasi, by the Kinges direction relinquished their Forte, because the King thought, that Lory a Fortresse verie neere thereunto, was sufficient for the defence of that quarter: and now that there was a newe charge for maintenance of Souldiers in the Forte of Tauris, added to his other expences, this might be very well spared. And hereupon there was a lying rumour spread at Aleppo, that Lory was recouered by the Georgians.

Saitan Chalasi relinquished by the garrison ther.

The Bassa of Reiuan, more for couetousnes then for any glory, being very angry that the nation of the Chiulfalini did bring no presentes vnto him, seeing that Leuentogli had sent very rich gifts to the Bassas of Van and of Teflis, setled himself against the Country of Chiulfal, and made an inroad vpon them to annoy thē, with a thousand fiue hundred Harquebusiers. The Chiulfalini being aduertised hereof, shut vp their gates, and stayed wayting for the comming of the Bassa, with purpose to pacifie him, by sending him some bountifull presents. Now Chiulfal is a place of some ten thousand soules or thereabouts, situate in the frontiers between the Armenians and the Atropatians, and yet within Armenia, three dayes iourney distant from Tauris, inhabited by Christians partly Armenians, partly Georgians: a people rather giuen to the trafique of silkes, and other sortes of wares, whereby it waxeth rich and full of money, than instructed in weapons and matters of war. It was always subiect and tributarie to the Scepters of Persia, and contrariwise, both by nature and affection great enemie to the Turkes. The Bassa thus went against them, and being arriued at Chiulfal, hee founde it defended with good store of armed souldiers, and the gates well and safely locked. Notwithstanding the Bassa was entertayned by their Embassadors, who were already gone out to meete him with their liberall presents, and to entreat him that he would accept of the peoples good wils: Who if they had not heretofore brought vnto him their voluntarie tributes, it was done for feare least they should haue fallen into the displeasure of their King: who no doubt if hee should haue vnderstood any such matter, would haue bene ready to destroy their countrey, and depriue them of their liberries and liues. The Bassa who rather to make a booty, then for any other cause had that inroad, receauing his presents, was well pleased with their intertainment, allowed the excuses of the Chiulfalini, and returned again to Reiuan.

The Bassa of Reiuan at Chiulfal.

The situation of Chiulfal.

The Bassa of Reiuan returneth from Chiulfal wel pleased.

Aduertisement hereof did flie in all hast to the Persian King, who imagining that besides the paimente of these voluntarie tributes some worse thinge had happened, dispatched away Alyculi Chan with three thousande Souldiers, and with this direction, that if the Countrey were subdued by the Turkes, hee should fight against it: And if it had voluntarily yeelded it selfe vnto them, hee should not onlie recouer it, but also burne it, and bring away all the chiefe men of the Countrey for prisoners and slaues. Alyculi went to Chiulfal, and finding the matter to haue passed as before is described, without vsing either sword or force, hee perwaded them, that in signe of their obedience still continued towardes the Persian Prince, they woulde present him with greater and more liberall giftes, then they did their enemie Bassa. The Chiulfalini were verie readie to perfourme what hee required, and pleased him in fuch sort, that hee caried backe verie good tydinges of their fidelity and obedience to the King. Whereby this miserable people in middest of Armes and Squadrons of the Enemie, what with presentes and what vvith lies, preserued their liberties and their liues in safetie.

Aliculi chan at Chiulfal.

Aliculi returneth from Chiulfal wel pleased.

Giaffer the Bassa in a great feare.

Whiles the Chiulfalini were in this sorte molested, Giaffer the Bassa of the Forte, fearing leaste the Persian Prince would returne with the Turcomanne forces, and with a mightie Armie for the siege, perceiuing himselfe euerie day to vvaxe weaker and weaker, by reason that manie did secretelie and priuilie flie from him, determined to sende aduertisement thereof to the Bassa Cicala at Van: signifying to him by writing, that hee feared greatly least if the Prince should returne with Souldiers to assault the Forte, he should of necessitie be inforced to yeeled it vp vnto him, because manie were fled out of the Fortresse, manie perished by sicknesse, and many also slaine, whiles too boldlie and rashlie they aduentured to goe abroad to prouide victuals. And that therfore he would take care, as he tendered the honour of his Sultan, to send him succour, to the end that at the return of the Prince he might be able to resist him and maintaine himselfe. Adding moreouer, that now at this time, especiallie, this designment might easilie be performed, because there were no forces of the enemies in those quarters, sauing only a few which remained about the king, being twelue miles distant from Tauris. The Bassa Cicala, although he had a great zeale and loue to his owne Cittie, which is indeede the greatest and moste noble frontier towne in all those countries, notwithstanding being deeplie mooued by the importunitie of the enterprise that was propounded vnto him, and verie desirous to gaine some credite of glorie and renowne with his King, entertained and accepted the aduices of Giaffer, and getting him to Horse, with a traine of three thousand Harquebufiers, and good store of munition, he trauelled towardes Tauris. The Persian King being aduertised of this stirre, sent out certaine Spies to learne vvhat vvay they helde, meaning to meet them, and to set vpon them: But the Spies comming neere vnto Salmas, were apprehended by the

Cicala the Bassa of Van goeth to succour Tauris.

fore-runners of Cicala, and being put to torture, they reuealed at the last, how their King was in Armes, and on his way towardes Sancazan. At this newes Cicala was greatlie astonied, as vvell for the daunger, vvhereinto the sorces and munition, which hee had with him, were likelie to fall, as also for that by any losse, which his troupes should sustaine in this stirre, the Fortresse of Van must needes bee in great hazarde to bee lost, because hee had left in it but a verie fewe persons, neither was there any Captaine to commaund them but onelie the Checaia his Lieutenant. And thereupon hee determined to relinquish this daungerous enterprise, and to withdrawe himselfe backe, to the defence and preseruation of the Cittie, that was committed to his truste and gouernement. But although these expected and desired succours, were not conueighed to the Fort accordinglie, yet had Giaffer as good fortune as hee coulde vvish. For the preparations of the Prince were so long and troublesome, and his returne so much prolonged, that there was time ynough yeelded vnto the Turkish Generall, now newlie chosen, (as by and by shal bee tolde you) to goe into those quarters, and to preserue all that, which the onlie expedition and celeritie of the enemie might haue put in great hazard, and almoste haue brought to a desperate case.

Cicala the Bassa in a great feare.

Cicala the Bassa retireth to Van.

In the meane time, at the Citie of Constantinople, the King was in a greate doubt within himselfe, what hee were best to resolue for the choyce of a newe Captaine. On the one side Osman the Bassa hauing by his last will and testament left Sinan Cicala to be his successour, the manie dangers he had runne through in the quarrelles about Tauris, and besides these his desertes, the greate fauours that Cicala had in the Serraglio, did make the King greatly incline to this his election. On the other side he heard of a certaine publike rumour spread among the Souldiers, that they coulde not by any meanes endure, to haue so yoong a Captaine appointed ouer them, giuing out in plaine tearmes, that euery man might knowe it, that they would not obey him, and that some daungerous disorder would ensue vpon it in matters touching the Armie. Then was there also Ferat the Bassa, the same man which once already had had that charge, before Osman had it: and hee shewed himselfe verie ambicious and desirous of this honour, and had of late performed some honest and conuenient office in the Serraglio, whereby the King might take some liking of his person. Any other to make choice of, he had none, so that in this consultation with himselfe, hee was vtterly vnresolued what to doe. Yet in the end, because he was to prouide in good time for his businesse, he determined to make choyce of Ferat, a man of great fidelitie, of honourable valour, and already throughly instructed in all such points, as were necessarie for the brideling of such an Armie. Him therefore he chose to be Captaine

K. Amurath busied about the election of a new Generall.

Ferat the Bassa chosen Generall.

for the conducting of his succours to Tauris, and to him hee graunted the ordinarie authoritie to manage at his pleasure such affayres of the Empire, as concerned this his iorurney.

Vppon this resolution, generall preceptes were sent out to all Citties within the Kingdome, and to the Bassas, the Sangiacchi, and other Gouernours and Officers thereof, with speciall commandement, that all their souldiers, together with their taxes, tenthes, munitions, victualles, Armour, Artificers, and to bee short all their necessarie furniture and prouision should be readie and in order vpon the firste warning that should bee sent vnto them at the next Spring. And direction was geuen to Ali-Vcchiali the Captaine of the sea, that hee should arme fourteene Gallies for conduct of the Ianizzaries to Trebisonda, and such other garrisons as were to bee transported to Erzirum, and from thence to bee employed where the Generall should commaund. Great prouision of money was made, and in Soria (besides the ordinarie somme that is bestowed vpon the yearely pay of Souldiers in Reiuan, in Erzirum, in Aggiachalasi, in Lory, in Tomanis, in Teflis, and in Chars, which swallowe vp all the reuenue of that Countrey, and also of the Cittie of Tripoli, and amounteth to the summe of sixe hundred thousande Duckatets) there was taken vp in prest, of priuate Merchantes in the Cittie of Aleppo onely, the summe of three score thousand Cecchini, to bee repayed vnto them with the firste moneyes that should bee receiued by the Officers of the Custome houses. A matter that mooued an extraordinarie grudging among the people, for that it seemed a verie strange and intollerable exaction to euerie man, besides so manie grieuances and impositions laid vpon them for corne, for carriages, for Pioners, and for workmen, to endure this burthen also of lending their money without any hope of restitution thereof. Yea and in deed euery man did greatly woonder, how they were thus ill aduised, by this meanes to make it knowne to the Christian Princes, what scarsitie and want of money they had. Generall had also with him foure hundred peeces of Artillery: and did besides so worke the matter, that Maxut-Chan, who was now appointed the Bassa of Aleppo, vvas graunted vnto him to bee the guide of his Armie, and that Cicala the Bassa of Van, beeing scarse his good friend was remooued from thence, and sent as Bassa to Babylon.

And thus hee departed from Constantinople in the moneth of Aprill, and by the way of Chalcedon passing ouer the Sea into Asia, hee came to Siuas, in trueth, something later than hee should haue done, by reason of the greate plague, which at that time did generally afflict and grieuouslie vexe the Citie of Constantinople, besides manie other occasions and executions that hindered his iorney. Neuer was there so greate a number of Souldiers sent out of Grece and Hungarie, as was

The reuenue of Soria 600000. duckats.

A loane of 60000. Cecchini lent to the King by the Merchāts of Aleppo.

The 400. peeces of artillerie with the Generall.

Maxut-chan, Guide of the Armie.

Ferat departeth from Constantinople.

The plague at Constantinople.

this yeare: And yet had he gathered them altogether, and mustered them before hee departed from Siuas, where hee stayed so long, that it was nowe the latter ende of the moneth of Iulie, before hee went thence. Neither was it the plague onely that caused this his stay (for the most parte of the Turkes make no more dayntie to auoyde the plague, then wee vse to eschewe any gentle disease:) but another greate cause of it was the exceeding dearth of victuals in Erzirum, where there was neither graine nor corne sufficient for the necessitie of their Cattell and men: which dearth was also so great in Aleppo, that a Venice-bushel of wheat was fold for a dozen Checchini. *Exceeding dearth at Erzirum and Aleppo.*

At the latter ende of those dayes, wherein Ferat made his abode in Siuas, and was nowe readie to depart from thence, there came vnto him certaine postes sente from Giaffer the Bassa of Tauris, by whome hee was aduertised, how the Persian Prince was hourelie expected with a populous Armie following him, and that if hee should foreslowe to send succours, and to preuent the comming of the Prince, and so giue him time and leasure to assaulte the Fortresse, hee was in exceeding greate feare, least the Prince might surprise the same. Vpon this aduertisement Ferat presentlie remooued, and hastened his iourney in such sorte, that hee was in Erzirum about the beginning of August: where hee was scarslie arriued, but suddenlie being prouoked thereunto by the reporte of the Princes comming, which was daylie more and more confirmed, hee set himselfe towardes Van. To which place all the Souldiers of Aleppo, of Tripoli, of Damasco, of Iurie, and of Palestina were alreadie gone by the way of Caraemit: for so they were commaunded to do, because they might auoyde the Cittie of Erzirum, from whence, by reason of the great dearth Hassan the Bassa, gonernour thereof was remooued, and coulde not keepe residence there, but withdrewe himselfe to Chars, where hee lay at greater ease and lesse charges. Ferat therefore made haste to Van, where hauing gathered all his Souldiers together, and made a reuision and newe surueigh of all his Armie, hee departed thence, and being presentlie come into the open and large Champaynes, hee marshalled them in such sorte, as though hee shoulde haue bene prepared to fight the Battell. Wherein hee did imitate olde Sinan the Bassa, vvho although hee reaped small commendations for these his fained battels, whereof he made shew in the Champeynes of Chielder, yet notwithstanding hee shewed greate cunning and experience in matter of warre, for that hee woulde bee assured of the Arte and discipline of his Souldiers: without which, manie Armies in numbers infinite and in Armes terrible, haue bene defeated by few squadrons in number far fewer, and in Armes lesse fearfull, though in matter of Warre, and skill in fighting more cunning and experienced.

Aduertisement from Giaffer the Bassa of Tauris, to Generall Ferat.

Ferat in Erzirum.

Ferat at Van.

The marshalling of Generall Ferat Armie.

His Vauward.	And therefore for the Vaunt-garde of his Armie hee appointed the Bassa of Mesopotamia, with all his souldiers: a people watered on the one side with Tigris, and on the other side with Euphrates, partlie infected with the fearfulnesse of the Arabians, and partly endued with the constancie of the Armenians: And of these, to the number of twelue thousande. In the Rereward hee set the Bassa of Damasco, Captaine of a Nation more famous than valiant, to the number of eight thousand: in which reckoning were all the people of Soria, of Palaestina, and of Iudaea, watered with Iordan and Orontes. In the bodie of the battell he placed himselfe with the souldiers of Grecia, of Peloponnesus, and of Bithynia to the number of eighteene thousande. In the right Cornet there were marshalled the Bassaes of Cilicia, of Pontus, and of Cappadocia, and of all those places that are comprised vnder the name of Caramania, and Natolia, with all those peoples that are dwelling vpon the coast of Pontus Euxinus, vpon Sangario and vppon Maeander, to the number of twelue thousande. In the left Cornet the Bassas of Maras, of Erzirum and of Van made the Wing, with the Souldiers of both the Armeniaes, and the Sangiacchi of the Curdi: watered with the Lakes Tospite and Martiano, dwelling in the middle betweene the Iberians and the Mesopotanians, on the one side frozen with the colde of Taurus, and on the other side warmed with the prospecte of the South, in all to the number of twelue thousande. This last Cornette was kept with a perpetuall watch by the Knight Marshall of the fielde, and the other was defended with a continuall trench of artillery: And in them both were mustered the voluntarie Souldiers, that after so longwarre being greedy of spoyle, and ambitious of glorie, were equallie diuided betweene them, to the number of twenty thousande. The Vaunt garde went alwayes a mile before the Armie, with two thousande Horse, and foure companies of the readiest light Horsmen to the number of three thousande: and before all these, foure or six Fore-runners or Spies on horsebacke. After the Auauntgarde rode the Master of the Kinges Horse, called the Imbrahur Bassi, with foure hundred Ianizzaries. Nexte after them followed foure hundred Solacchi, and then foure thousande Ianizzaries more, and presently after them, the Long-shot wrought in Algier and called Sciemete, being the ordinarie and perpetuall Guarde of the Generall, who without any company by his side, sauing onely his twelue footmen, came next vpon them. And behinde him his Standerdes, his Drummes, his Trumpettes, and the whole bodie of his Battell: betweene vvhich and the Rere-vvarde follovved his huge carriages for the necessarie vse of his Armie, and on both sides the two greate and large Cornettes before described. The watch of the night, whether the Armie were martching or lodged, was committed to the truste of the Bassaes of Cilicia, and Natolia
The Rereward.	
The bodie of the battel.	
The right Cornet.	
The left Cornet.	
The Marshall of the field.	
Voluntarie souldiers 20000 Master of the Horse.	
The Ianizzaries and the Solacchi.	
The Sciemete. The place of the Generall.	
The carriages.	
The night-watch committed to the Bassas of Cilicia and Caramania.	

aboue named. And thus had the Generall Ferat marshalled his Armie, with further direction that they shoulde not hazarde battell with the enemie, but vppon certaine hope that they might shunne and auoyde such cruell and memorable slaughters, as the laste yeare vnder the vnhappie gouernement of Osman, had left heapes of deade Carcasses almoste euen and leuell vvith the tops of hilles: And vvithall hee failed not to comforte and encourage all such, as quaked in their heartes at the remembraunce of those mischances that they had seene or heard.

The Generall was greatlie perplexed in his minde with continuall feare, least his enemies shoulde come vpon him with some sudden assaulte: and the fame also that was spread before in Amasia and after confirmed in Erzirum, of the arriuall of the Prince Amze at Tauris, with such an Armie, as was publikelie reported, did euerie moment encrease his irksome cogitations. But on the other side, hee reposed great confidence in the conspiracy that was plotted against the life of the Prince, with the priuitie of Alyculi-Chan the Protector and Champion of Abas the Mirze of Heri: Who vnder collour of accompanying the Prince to assist his forces, had resolutelie concluded with himselfe, and absolutely promised Abas (hauing also giuen intelligence thereof to the Turkish Generall) that hee would rid the Prince Amze of his life, or at least (which he thought might more easilie be brought to passe) in the sundrie reuolutions and variable chances of the battell at some time or other, to make him fall aliue into the handes of Ferat, and so to settle his Lord and Master Abas, in his estate. Vpon these treacheries Ferat grounding himselfe, began with greater confidence to dispose his designementes, and somewhat lesse to feare the reportes of the Fame, that blazed abroad the huge preparations of Persia against him: which preparations in trueth, as by moste wicked deuices and malicious conspiracies they were turned quite contrarie from that end, whereunto the Prince Amze had continuallie appointed them, so if they had bene employd with such saith and fidelitie, as so righteous a cause required: without all doubt the writers of our time shoulde haue had in this four-skore and sixth yeare, matter ynough to shewe, and represent to the vvhole worlde such accidentes as shoulde be nothing inferiour to those of the yeare before going. And Persia should haue seene some reuenge at the least, of those most mischieuous iniuries that it hath receaued. But forasmuch as rebellion and discorde, those two infernall Ministers of the Deuill, haue for the vtter vndoing and ouerthrowe of the glorie of Persia, continually fauoured the Turkish Armies. No maruell it is, that the Persian Nation cannot vaunt of any reuenge, that they haue taken of anie one indignity offered vnto them by their enemies: and that our Writers cannot choose but write of the true and vndoubted victories of the Turks, and the bare shadowes of

The General Ferat made acquainted with treacheries in Persia.

the Persian exploytes. Which notwithstanding (but all in vaine) our Christian Nations, euen vntill this day, although they doe see the manifest prospering, and euident conquestes, which the Turkes haue had in diuers States and Countreyes, yet doe they easilie beleeue, because they doe moste earnestlie desire them to bee true. But wee vvill not fayle as trulie as possiblie wee may, to reporte, whatsoeuer wee vnderstande to haue happened: that out of our writinges the Readers may take such aduise, as out of such aduertisementes may bee gathered.

The Persian Prince arriued at Tauris with the greatest parte of his Armie, about the twentie eighth of the Moone Regeb, which may bee about the latter ende of Iulie: In which place euery body thought verily he would haue stayed, and attended the conquest of the Forte: which now hee might haue vtterlie destroyed with more ease than before he coulde haue done, because the souldiers that were in it were reduced to a very small number, and those that did remayne were greatly impayred by sundrie inconueniences, and withall shrewdlie terrified with the expectation of the Princes arriuall. Notwithstanding this common opinion, and publike conceite was vtterlie frustrated. For Amze did not onelie forbeare to attempt this expugnation, but hee scarse taried any while in the Citie of Tauris. The cause of this his so doing, is diuerslie, yea and vainlie reported. The Persians and all their adherentes say, that Prince tooke this course, not because hee was not able immediately to besiege the Forte, and easilie to haue gotten the victorie ouer it, (for they did not sticke verie gloriouslie to vaunt, that it was in his power so to doe,) but onelie because if hee had taken and destroyed the Forte, then woulde the Turkes haue for borne to come to Tauris, and so the Prince should haue loste the opportunitie of ioyning battell with them, and plaguing the Turkish Armie with such losses and discomfitures, as hee earnestly desired to afflict them withall: meaning notwithstanding to destroy the Forte, after hee should haue satisfied his longing to bee reuenged on his enemies Campe. Others cannot beleeue that the Prince woulde relinquish so necessarie and honourable enterprise for any such respect: for they were of opinion, that Amze could not haue had a more glorious reuenge, nor more grieuouslie endommaged his enemies, then by ouerthrowing that Forte, which to the greate daunger and perill of the Persians was erected euen in the middest of them: yea that Forte, for the building and accomplishment whereof, they had compassed all those mischiefes the laste yeare. Another cause also there is yeelded of this his so doing: And that is, the infirmitie which the Prince knew to be in himselfe, as a man vnacquainted with the daungerous attemptes of a siege, verie fearefull of Artillery, and more corragious in anie other kinde of battell, then these that are vsed to be foughten vnder

The Persian Prince at Tauris.

The cause why the Prince attempteth not the winning of the Fort.

the walles of any place. But let it be that he was lead by eyther of these two respectes, it maketh no greate matter: The trueth is, that Amze with all the troupes, which hee brought with him (the number and order whereof shall bee shortly hereafter declared vnto you) did scarse make any stay in Tauris. For he had vnderstood, that before the Cittie of Salmas Zeinel the Bey, by nation a Curdo, and by office the Bassa of that Cittie, had encamped himselfe: whome hee determined suddenly to set vppon, and chastise, not onely for his rebellion, whereby of a Persian hee became a Turke, but also for many other his insolent behauiours, which hee had diuers times vsed against the liberties and priuiledges of the Citties of Persia. This determination hee put in execution, and being accompanied with twelue thousande Souldiers, hee rode to Salmas, where finding Zeinell with all his people, hee gaue him the assault. Zeinell was more readie to flie and make escape, then minded to fight or make rescues: and his Forces also as ready to followe his example: who beeing more intentiue to saue themselues, with their housholde stuffe and other implementes to resist their enemies, the more they sought by all meanes to preserue their liues, and slippe out of the Persians handes, the more they fell into the spoyle, and were woonderfully ill entreated, so that the Bassa himselfe with a fewe other fugitiues, coulde hardly saue themselues in the cloasest and darkest corners thereaboutes. And in this sorte was Zeinello and the Cittie of Salmas, that was committed to his charge, and defence, endommaged and left for a praie to the Conquerours: Who entring into their streetes, houses, and Temples, sacked and spoyled the same, exercising thereon such cruelties and indignities, as partlie the naturall desires of souldiers doe vse to practise, and partely such as the Turkes themselues shewed vpon them (as it were for an example howe to doe in the like case) in that miserable and most vnfortunate sacking of Tauris the laste yeare. The like spoyles did the Persian Armie make in all those quarters rounde aboute: and so woulde peraduenture haue returned to Tauris, but that certaine Spies arriued vpon them, who brought aduertisement, howe the Bassa of Reiuan, being issued out of his Fortresse with fifteene hundred Harquebusiers, had committed the like outrages in the villages and fieldes thereaboutes, as the Prince had done about Salmas. With this newes Amze was greatlie mooued, and immediatlie raising all his Armie, he iourneyed euen vntill night, towardes Reiuan, and not farre from the Cittie encountred the Bassa: who discouering his enemies forces a farre off, beganne in great disorder to flie and retire into his Fort, leauing the greatest parte of his Souldies, being nothing so speedie in flight as himselfe, to the fury of the Prince, who slewe them all, and exercised all mischiefe, that might be deuised, and al terrible maner of crueltie in those quarters.

Zeinello the Bassa discomfited by the persian Prince.

The citie of Salmas also sacked by him.

The Bassa of Reiuan put to flight & discomfited by the Prince.

But notwithstanding all these wrathfull conflictes and broyles of warre, the two famous Prisoners, Ebrain-Chan and Amurat the Bassa, of whom we haue made mention in the former books of this historie, ceassed not, by peaceable enter course and treatie about their own liberties, to procure that they might interchangeably be inlarged and restored to their owne Lordes. This practise continued verie hote for manie dayes together, and at the laste the Turkes were contented to enlarge Ebram-Chan, vppon condition that Amurat also might be set at libertie. But the offer was thought to be verie vnequall: For (say the Persians) Ebrain-Chan, was emprisoned against all right, by the dishonourable treacherie and infidelitie of Amurath, to the great contempt and vtter subuersion of al lawes, which towardes Embassadours ought most sacredlie and religiously to bee maintayned in any cause whatsoeuer: and Ebrain-Chan ought not in any respect to be kept in prison, but with most manifest iniustice and iniquitie. Whereas on the other side Amurath the Bassa was lawfully taken captiue, and brought into thraldome, not by deceite of wordes, nor breach of faith, but in plaine battell, euen with the daunger of those that tooke him prisoner, and to bee shorte, agreeablie, and according to the lawes of warre, and Enemy-Nations. And therefore so vnequall and vnproportionable an exchaunge was not onelie vtterlie to bee denyed and reiected, but also vnreasonable on the Turkes behalfe to be offered. These sounde and effectuall reasons of the Persians coulde not be answered, but eyther by money or by some other meanes that mighte supplie the defeates of the Turkes inaequalitie: Whereunto they woulde neuer agree to yeelde, and so the two Captaines remanyned still in prison as thy did before.

A treatie to exchange the two prisoners Ebrain and Amurat.

The treatie of inlarging the two prisoners is in vaine.

At the verie same time, in the confines of Tripolie, certaine Drusians of the territorie of Manogli, who after the departure of Ebrain the Bassa were quietlie and peaceablie retired to their owne homes, beganne to raise new stirres and troubles. Whereuppon the Drusian Captaines, that were carried prisoners to Constantinople by Ebrain the Bassa, and were nowe vpon the poynt to bee set at libertie, and to returne to their woonted habitations; at the reporte of these fresh troubles and tumultes, were againe restrayned, and clapt vp in close custodie, and in great daunger also to haue lost their liues. Nowe the rumour of these stirres was this: that Manogli perceauing all the Souldiers and garrisons to bee now departed, for the warre of Persia, as wee haue tolde you, and none other prouision sent for the defence of those places, hee determined to issue out into the fielde, and not onelie to reuenge the death of his people, which vniustlie, and by treacherie they had suffered, but also to licke himselfe whole, and by a kinde of violent restitution to bee recompensed for all those bribes and presentes, which with so manie shiftes and subtilties, as before is declared, were extorted from him by the Messengers and Stratagemes of Ebrain the Bassa. For which purpose, beeing issued out into the playnes and Champeignes of Tripoli and hauing first wasted and sacked all the territorie of Ebnemansur and of his other enemies, hee forced all that Countrey with sudden inuasions and inroades, euen verie neere to the Citties of Balbecke and Tripolie. As for the defence and rescue of Balbech, Acra woulde not stirre a foote, fearing belike least hee might bee endaungered by the valour and resolution of Manogli, wherewith hee was verie well acquainted. But for Tripoli, there were diuerse Souldiers, that remayned in that Cittie, and liued as it were in Idlenesse, which with a greate sum of money they had purchased at the handes of the couetous Officers of the Sultan Emperour. And these souldiers beganne to bestirre themselues lustelie. In this number of idle mates was one Mamut Bey, sometime a Sangiaccho, but nowe cassiered and put out of Office, who by meanes of his bribes hauing auoyded to serue in these warres of Persia, imagined with himselfe, that such a fitte occasion, whereby hee might shewe himselfe willing and readie to represse the insolent inuasions of the Drusian, might make him deserue so well at the Sultans handes, that hee woulde bestowe vpon him the office of Customer in that Cittie, which so greatlie he desired. And therefore hee before any of the rest, displaying his Standerd, and mustering all his bandes of Souldiers, in so much that hee did not spare the verie Caddi and the Deftardar (that is to say, the Iudge and Chamberlaine of the Gittie) but made them to ride out with him, he roade to encounter the Drusians and to ioyne battell with them, hoping eyther to destroy them, or honourablie to put them to flight: Or els (as others doe discourse of the matter) in deede not to meete with them at all, but onelie to beare away the commendation, that he was readie with his weapons in his hande for the publike defence of the Cittie, and custodie of his Lordes Countreyes. These Souldiers of Tripolie were not farre departed from their Cittie, but the Drusians presentlie confronted them, and with continuall shot of Harquebusies began to disorder and diuide them. But the people of Tripolie, although indeede somewhat negligentlie, yet did they continue the skirmish a great while, and would peraduenture also haue endured the battell a longer time, but that in the sight of all the Armie, to the generall astonishment of them all, the Caddi or Iudge of their Cittie was shot starke deade with a Peece, and fallen from his horse: Who as among all other men that came out of the Cittie should haue bene the last man that should haue entermedled in such like actions, so was he the first man that was slain in the sight. At this spectacle there arose such a confused feare among the Turkes, that the Deftardar or Chamberlaine of the Cittie, without any longer stay fled as fast as hee could into Tripolie, and all the rest after him.

The subiectes of Manogli do great harme in Soria.

The Caddi of Tripoli slaine by the Drusians.

The Drusians bereaue the Sangiacco of his Standerd, and kill his standerd-bearer.

The Sangiaccho also, who was the chiefest and busiest instrument of raysing these stirres, had his Standerde bearer slaine, and his Ensigne taken away, with manie other losses that happened besides among the baser sorte. Aduertisementes hereof was sent to Constantinople, and presentlie thereupon, the Drusian Captaines (as wee tolde you before,) were againe restrayned: Mendel, as a great confederate with Manogli, that had raised all these troubles, and Mansurogli with his complices, as friendes vnto Acra, that woulde yeelde no defence in so greate a necessitie. Howbeit the Turkish King dispatched away Aly Bassa borne at Aleppo, with the title of the Bassa of Damasco, and with authoritie to muster fresh Souldiers, and so vvhollie to attende the vtter subuersion of Manogli. But comming thither, hee founde no innouation at all, but his presence in that Countrey serued rather for a reconciliation and peace making amongst them, then for moouing any vvarre againste them. And in trueth, if euer at anie time there vvere good cause to auoyde newe vvarre, at this time of all other it vvas moste necessarie to auoyde it: because neither the common treasure, nor aboundance of victualles, nor the desire or readinesse of the Souldier did yeelde anie courage to enterprise such troubles: Besides, the huge number of Locustes, vvhich vvere in such aboundance ouer all the Countrey of Soria, that in the memorie of all the oldest men there liuing, neuer vvas there seene so greate a multitude of those Excrementes in those Quarters, did as a moste horrible specctacle mightilie encrease the vniuersall feare of grieuous calamities to ensue thereupon.

Nowe the Persian Prince hauing made an ende of those outroades and spoyles, vvhich before wee haue mentioned, retyred himselfe to Tauris, and towardes his Fathers Campe, gathered together all the reste of his Armye, that vvas novve arriued. The Order, Number, and Condition vvhereof it is not amisse to describe, in such manner and sorte as I hearde it reported at Aleppo, vvhen I made diligent and due enquirie of these nevves there. They reported, that vvhat vvith the Souldiers of Heri, the Turcomannes, and the bandes of Gheilan, and vvhat vvith all the reste of the Armie, sent from the Cities that vvere subiecte and obedient to the King of Persia: The Prince had gathered fourtie thousande Souldiers: whereof, notwithstanding that I and others had some doubt and suspition, yet was it commonlie maintained by conferences among the Turkes and Persians, and by letters among the Persian Merchantes, and afterwardes it was confirmed also to bee true in deede. From Heri, vnder the conduct of Alyeuli Chan, they say there came an Armie of eight thousande: From Ghetlan, vnder the gouernment of a sonne of Amet-Chans, they say there came feuen thousande Horsemen: Of the Turcomannes there were gathered together about sixe thousand: And all the rest leauied by the subiect

Aly the Bassa sent from Constantinople into Soria against the Drusians.

The Army of the Persian prince.

The ordering of the Army of Persia.

and obedient Citties of Persia, whereof wee haue often made mention before. And besides all this multitude, the King was guarded by his ordinary Guarde of Churehi and Esahul, whose number and necessarie prouisions we haue already described in the second booke. The companie of Heri, with some part of the Turcomannes were dispatched by the Prince vnder the conduct of Alyculi-Chan, to encounter the Turkish Generall: And the like order giuen to Emanguli-Chan, who had the Souldiers of Media, and the borderers of Armenia, vnder his gouernement. Both these Captaines had in speciall charge, that in the moste narrowe and most deceitfull places by the way they should meete and receiue their enemies Armie, and worke them the gretest mischiefe and losse that possibly they coulde. All which, Amze did thus order and appoint, because hee thought by this meanes to weaken his enemies Forces, and then being so weakened, to come vpon them with a fresh bartell, and vtterlie to destroy them at their arriual to Tauris.

The order of the Persian prince to annoy the Armie of Ferat.

Both the Captaines departed accordinglie, making shewe that they woulde with all affection obey and accomplish the commaundementes of their Prince: But neuer was there heard any seruice of moment put in execution by them. For Alyculi went about to alleage reasons and excuses, why they shoulde surcease from meeting with the Turkes: and Emanguli being as yet vtterly ignorant of the wicked purposes and mischieuous treacheries of Alyculi, followed also his example. But these excuses and delayes of these two Persian Captaines, the Turkish Generall tooke leisure, without any losse or hindrance at all, to arriue at Tauris, and to place the expected succours within the Fort. At what time, by good hap, but by what meanes I knowe not, the Prince was certified of the malignant intent of Aliculi, and of the designementes, which many of the Sultans had lately contriued together, to betray the Prince aliue into the handes of the Turkish Captaine. Of which suspition Amze being greatlie affraide, hee durst not onely not trust himselfe to perfourme those battelles that hee had detremined to perfourme, but quite abandoning all this noble and honourable enterprise, hee wholly employed all his care and studie, for the safe custodie of his owne person, and so left the triumph of the matter in the power of the Turks And thus those great hopes and expectations, which the Persians had conceaued of compassing verie famous exployetes against their enemies, did not onely prooue vaine and come to no good issue, but contrariwise by this discouerie they were conuerted into moste daungerous disturbances, and all Persia thereby endured sundrie alterations and reuolutions of most important consequences. For both Aliculi-Chan and his Complices were pursued by the Prince as Rebelles and Traytors, and also Abas Merize of Heri was manifestlie discouered for a wicked and treacherous contriuer of his brothers death. Whereupon the

Prince Amze retireth for suspition of rebellion.

common mischiefes were encreased more then euer they were before, and the publike calamities yeelded greater hopes to the Turkes, then they had euer conceaued and fostered in all this warre.

Besides these designementes, there were others also, that contrarie to all expectation came to the like infortunate issue, laide and plotted by Simon in Georgia, who by the direction of the Persian Prince had vnited together his Neighbours the Georgians, for the accomplishing of most noble and honourable enterprises. And the designements of Simon were these: That at such time, as he thought most conuenient for sending fresh succours vnto Teflis in Georgia, he meant himselfe in person, with the companie of seuen or eight thousand Georgians, and with a number of horse-loades of money (if not true loades indeed, yet seeming in apparance so to bee) to present himselfe vnder the Fort of Teflis: and to the Turkish Bassa, Gouernour of that Castle, to deliuer a counterfeit commaundement wherein it should appeare, that King Amurath did giue the Bassa to vnderstand, that by Simon being now conuerted to the Turkish Religion, hee had sent fiftie thousande Chechini, and other muntion for the Souldiers: and that he had also giuen vnto Simon full commission and authoritie at his pleasure to manage and dispose of that Fort: and therefore that hee should entertaine Simon and giue him credence therein. This his defignement Simon put in execution, hoping thereby without force of Armes and without any other inconuenience to make himselfe Lord and Maister of that Castle. But the Turkish Bassa, although both the forme, and the tenour, and the Seale of the commaundement were verie like to the ordinarie maner of the Court (wherein Simon had vsed greate care and diligence:) and although he thought it also verie likelie to bee true, because he was reuolted to the Turkish religion, as hee had fayned in the counterfect commandement, and that for all these causes he ought to receaue and entertaine Simon into the Fort: Yet Simon wanting one speciall thing, which in such like cases is a matter of greatest importance, he was deceaued in his expectation, and with great shame and derision forced to retire, and so to auovde the Artillery, that by the direction of the Bassa rayned like a Tempest vppon his Souldiers. Nowe the thing which Simon wanted, was a certaine token deliuered to the Turkish Bassa, when hee was first appointed Gouernour of that Castle: For to euerie one that is left as Lieutenant in such Fortes, ordinarilie in this warre, with all secrecie, and straitest conditions of allegiance and fidelitie, there is deliuered a Counterfect of the Marke, which shall be vsed by him, that the next yeare following shall be receiued with succours into the Fort. Which beeing required of Simon by the Turkish Bassa, Simon knewe not what answere to make, and because he could not so doe, he was disconered to be a treacherous deceauer and for

The plot of Simon the Georgian.

Simon when his plot came to no good issue, retireth with losse and shame.

such a one was he presentlie pursued in such and so eager maner as people included within a castle wall, could in so sudden an occasion vse against him. And in this sort, did all the designementes and hopes of the Persians vanish to nothing, and the reporte published in Italie, and particularlie in Rome of the taking of this Fotte was quite dashed and found to be false, for that the fortunate Turkes remained in quiet possession of the Countreyes which they had conquered.

Whē the Turkish General had placed his succors in the Castle of Tauris, leauing for the custody thereof Giafter the Bassa with his former companies, hee returned towardes Erzirum, hauing first caused a Fort to be erected at Chucchiue Tauris, a place neere vnto Tauris: another at Coy, and a thirde at Cum, which sometimes belonged to Ebrain-Chan now prisoner at Erzirum as we tolde you before. And in euerie one of the saide Fortes he left a necessarie number of Souldiers, with sufficient munition and maintenance for them. Hee sent also afterwardes to Teflis in Georgia the succours, which they there had long expected and desired, and without any hinderance or difficultie verie willinglie receiued, because the counterfeyt of the Marke was well knowne vnto them, which before to Simon was both vtterlie vnknowne, and also greatly hurtfull. *General Ferat hauing succoured the fort, returneth toward Erzirum.*

Succours sent to Teflis.

But the Persian Prince hauing hunted Alyouli-Chan out of the quarters of Tauris, thought himselfe wholly deliuered from the greate feare of treason and rebellion, wherein he liued; and therefore in as great haste as hee could, he put himselfe on his iourney towardes Genge. In which place hauing gathered together a good number of Souldiers, hee determined to remooue thence, and to stop the succours for Teflis, and so to procure the vtter ouerthrowe of the conductors thereof. Hee had always found Emanguli-Chan to be both faithfull and wise, and in him he reposed an assured confidence for perfourming of any enterprise that he had in his hand, and communicated with him euery deuise that he had conceaued in these warres. And therefore hee made heade and ioyned with him, and lodging most familiarlie within his Citty, hee stayed there for the setting in order, and disposing of his foresaide designment, being verie desirous not to suffer this season to slip, without signification to the world of some notable noueltie which might be correspondent to the fame, that of matters passed and perfourmed the yeare before, was now spread and published abroad ouer all the world. But when he was euen at the verie fayrest to put this his desire in execution, and when least of all hee feared any treacherie or treason, vppon a sudden in the night time, he was miserablie stricken through the bodie by an Eunuch of his, that guarded him: and so the most resplendent and bright shining lampe that euer was in Persia, was vtterly extinguished. *The Persian Prince slaine by the treason of one of his Eunuches*

What was the occasion therof and who procured his death, diuers & sundry are the opinions of men. Some think that his brother Abas Mirize of Heri, who had before conspired to cause him to bee betrayed into the handes of the Turkish Generall, had now by force of money and giftes perswaded the wicked Eunuch thereunto. Others deeme, that his owne Father, being become verie desirous to see Abas setled in the kingdome, did procure his death: which notwithstanding in mine opinion hath no poynt of probability. Diuers others do reason the matter diuerslie. But wee, not onelie are not able to affirme the certen trueth of this accident, but also haue scarse any heart to testifie to the world, that thus or thus in trueth his death was procured. For we are not minded to set downe any discourse for a trueth, in such matters as haue happened in these warres, since wee returned and haue remayned in Italy: to the ende that wee woulde not diminish that credite and good opinion, which we know our Readers haue iustly giuen to all thinges hetherto written by vs, as vnto things that wee were most desirous to vnderstand for certenties, by such good meanes, as we haue already named in our Epistle to the Readers. And we in the meane time wil expect that some other Writer will pursue these aduentures in such sort as shall seeme best vnto him. For touching our selues: being wearie of the many diuersities which wee daylie heare by aduertisementes out of the East countrey, we haue had no hart at all, to describe, what hath happened therein, in the yeare fourscore and seuenth. But by the fauour of the Readers here we haue thought good to make a full point.

A LETTER TO THE VVORSHIPFUL SIGNOR MARIO CORRADO

Wherein is prooued, that Tauris is not Terua, as Iouius writeth: nor Tigranoama, as Negro taketh it: nor Tigranocerta, as others doe thinke: but Ecbathana, as Ortelius and Anania doe iudge.

Worshipfull Sir, I haue always made that reckoning of your Worships counsels and aduises, which your vertue deserueth, and especially touching those matters whereof it pleased you to aduertise mee, at such time as I was resident in this Citie, and so kindlie entertained therein with all curteous and bountifull entertainment. For whatsoeuer I could possiblie obserue in the Historie of the Warres betweene the Turkes and Persians, both concerning words and also concerning matters, I haue endeuoured by all meanes to reduce vnto that note which you deliuered vnto mee, and haue not fayled asmuch as my skill could reach, to put in execution all your good preceptes and aduertisementes. Only there remayneth in this historie one thing which as yet is not throughlie iustified: and that is, mine opinion touching the Citie of Tauris, which your Worship by reason of your douhting thereof, made mee suspect at the first, but afterwards it pleased you to allow and confirme to be the best and soundest. And although I haue freely and boldly set downe, that Tauris is not Terua, as Iouius writeth, but Ecbathana, as manie others both before and after Iouius do take it: and although I find manie reasons wherby I haue bene perswaded so freely to auow it: Notwithstanding, when I considered that this was a matter of great importance in this Historie, to entrreat of the true finding out and acknowledgment of a Cittie, for the conquest whereof, almost all these troubles of warres were principally raised: to the end that all things might the more plainlie appeare, I resolued to publish these my reasons, and particularly to send thē to your W. not only because you first encouraged me with liuely arguments to approue this particularity, being of it self a very important matter, yea & the more importāt in regard of the authority of such men as are of the contrarie opinion: but also because you were a great helper vnto me with your owne priuate study to furnish mee with so goodly a number of reasons for the same. By twelue arguments therfore, me thinks I may certainely and demonstratiuely reason, that Tauris cannot be the Terua of Ptolomey, but ought indeed to be called the ancient Ecbathana.

My first reason is, because Strabo teacheth vs, that the Poole Mantian, or Martian, or Margian (call it as yee will) that which is now tearmed the Poole Actamar, is situate in the confines of great Armenia, and stretcheth euen as far as the cōfines of Media Atropatia. And in the twelfth book of his Geographie, it is manifestlie seene, that there is either verie little or no quantitie of countrie or people at all betweene the Mantian Poole, and Media the greater. The same may be collected out of Ptolomie, who (as it seemeth) doth place the forenamed Poole, rather in the entrance of Media the greater, than in the latter end of great Armenia. Out of this certaine trueth I gather this foundation. The Martian Poole is in the confines of the Medes and of the Armenians: and therefore it must needes followe, that if Tauris should be Terua, it must either be in the West, or in the. West Southwest, or in the West Northwest, or els in the verie Northwest of the saide Poole: for in the South or in the North I doo not beleeue that any man doth place it, and if hee should so doe, hee should commit an errour, not onely worthy of correction but also of chastisement. But if Tauris bee Ecbathana, it must either bee in the East, or in the East Southeast, or in the Southeast, or in the East Northeast, or els in the very Northeast. For much lesse will any man be so bolde as to place it in the South, or in the North of the saide Poole, and whosoeuer shoulde so place it, hee shoulde commit a double errour. Terua indeede according to Iouius, and according to that which the discription of Ptolomey doeth inferre, is (as a man may say) in the verie center and middest of great Armenia, and consequentlie it muste bee in the West, or West Southwest, or West Northwest of the said pool.

Wherevpon, if Tauris should be Terua, then should Tauris haue the very selfe same situation. But both sence and reason, yea & Iouius himselfe, & all other doo with one accorde confesse, that Tauris is in the East of the forenamed Poole, and by a good quantitie of grounde distant from it. And therefore it remaineth, that Tauris is not Terua: but Ecbathana being a good way distant in the East of the saide poole,

The first reason.

a man may conclude, that the verie situation and auncient ruines of Ecbathana haue yeelded matter and stuffe to this new Tauris.

And somuch the more likely, because all the Marchantes and souldiers that vse the viage from Van to Tauris, and from Tauris to Van (being a place situate as it were on the easterne banks of the Martian poole) doo vniformly testifie, that in their trauelling from Van to Tauris they haue their faces looking towards the East: and in their returne from Tauris to Van they haue their faces turned towardes the West: and that they passe through certaine vallies between certain mountaines which peraduenture may be the toppes of the Caspian mountaine. *The second reason.*

The like testimonie is geuen by many of the souldiers that went to Tauris with Osman. Besides whose testimony, we may also make a sound coniecture by the iourney which that army made. For the said armie being gathered together at the city of Erzirū, (which out of all doubt wee must hold to be Simbra or Sinibra in Ptolomee) and by the way of Hassan-Chalasi and Chars, passing by Euphrates, and leauing Araxis on the leaft hand, it arriued at Van vpon the Martian Poole. And from Van it came to the champaines of Caldaran, and thence to Coy. From which place it passed afterwarde to Merent, to Soffian (which peraduenture may be the auncient Soffia of the Medes) and so to Tauris. After that Tauris was sacked, and the Forte erected there, the armie retourned to Van, & from Van by the wonted way to Erzirum. Now doo not I know, to what end all this people should go to Van and to Coy, if Tauris were in the sight of Terua, which is on this side of Van, fiue degrees or there abouts. For it had beene much better for them by a direct course to haue passed from Chars to Terua, then first to go to Van, & then to come to Chars, and so to Erzirum. Neither can Iouius be excused, in saying, that in those dayes they had no such way. For he himselfe in the three and thirtith booke of his histories, (reciting the viage which Soliman made, at such time as retiring from Tauris, which he had sacked, he iourneyed toward Mesopotamia,) doth expressly write, that Soliman in his returne first arriued at Coy, and to the Champaines of Caldaran. And a little after he addeth, that Tamas pursuing Soliman came to Tauris, and from Tauris to Coy and to the Caldaran Champaines. By which voyages Iouius might easily perceaue, that Tauris, (which in his fourtinth booke he situateth more toward the East then Coy is, by the space of foure score miles or thereabouts) by this means must be in Media the Greater, where Ecbathana is: and that consequently it could not bee thought to bee Terua, which by Ptolomee himselfe is placed on the west not onely of Coy, but also of the Margian Poole. *The third reason.*

This opinion is also fortified and made manifest by the authoritie of Ptolomee, who placeth Terua for latitude in 78. degrees, and the *The fourth reason.*

Martian Poole, 83. degrees. and so setteth Terua more towards the west, then that poole is, by foure whole degrees. Howbeit if this Terua should be Tauris, as Iouius will haue it, then should it bee on the east side of the said Poole, not onely 4. degrees but fiue or six degrees. By these selfe same reasons me thinketh that Negro is likewise conuinced, who in his Geographie doth resolutely write, that Tauris is Tigranoama. And with Negro are those also confuted, which say that Tauris is Tigranocerta. For Tigranocerta is by Ptolomee situated on the West of Tigranoama, and Tigranoama on the west of the Martian Poole, by the space of three whole degrees. Besides that Strabo writeth, that Tigranocerta was aboue the riuer of Euphrates, from which riuer Tauris is distant more then twentie daies iourney of sumpter-horses.

The errour of Negro and others.

Moreouer another argument may be framed in this manner. From Tauris to Casbin at this day it is no more then nine daies iourny: & euey daies iourney may be reconed after fiue and twenty miles or thereabouts: which besides that I can iustifie it with the greatest certainety, that may be (next to a mans owne sight) is also confirmed by Barbaro, and by others according to Ramusius. Howbeit this iourney could not be finished in so few daies, if Tauris were in the situation of Terua, considering that from Terua onelie to the verie entraunce of the Martian Lake there fall out three degrees, much more to Casbin which is in the middest of Media the Greater. For vnto Casbin the way wold fall out to bee far greater for number of miles, of daies-iournies, and of degrees.

The fift reason.

Those also that going from Tauris doo trauell in a direct line towardes the North, do cleere this for a manifest truth. For they report, that after a long iourney, hauing first passed ouer certain mountaines, they doo arriue vpon the Southerne side of the Caspian sea, euen directly wherethose hauens of the sea of Tauris are, whereof Barbaro speaketh. A thing that was neuer read to haue happened vnto those, that trauelling from Terua doo go in a directlyne towards the North: for they alwaies leaft the saide sea on their right hande, and went into the verie middest of the Isthmus, which is a narrowe peece of land situate betweene the Caspian and Euxine seas: as it may sensibly bee iudged, by the right measure of Ptolomees Table, without any further reading of other wryters or information of trauelling straungers.

The sixt reason

The custome also, which the kinges of Media obserued in spending the Sommer season at Ecbathana, as a Cittie more cold, more northerne, and more subiect to the winds, seemeth to me to be no small argument for maintenaunce of myne opinion. For by that custome I doo coniecture, that Terua being one of the midland Citties of Armenia must needes be lesse cold, and lesse subiect to snowes and windes then

The seuenth reason.

Tauris is at this day. Whereof all men do with one consent agree, that it is a cold, and a snowie Cittie, and euen in the sommer time subiect to the continuall blastes of the windes.

Next hereunto may bee added the situation of Terua, which in Ptolomee is placed betweene Euphrates & Araxis, and yet somewhat distant from both the saide riuers towardes the South: which doth manifestly declare that Terua cannot be Tauris, because Tauris is not onely at this day beyond Araxis, but is also beyond the Caspian Sea, whereintoo Araxis doth discharge it selfe. The eight reason.

A man may also drawe no sclender argument, from those that goe from Tauris to Ormus or Armuza, which we now call, the Island in the Persian sea, from whence they fetch their pearles and other precious things, although in deed it be otherwise somewhat vnhappely seated by reason of the excessiue heate that raigneth therein. These trauellers leauing the Caspian mountaines on their right hand, and not troubling themselues either with climing ouer them, or with ferrying ouer Euphrates or Tigris, and without touching either of Mesopotamia, or Babylonia, or tourning to Van or to the Mantian Marish, do ascend vpwardes towardes Siras in Persia, & going as it were southward, they come at last to the Persian sea. So that if Tauris were Terua, and so in the middle region of the greater Armenia, then should they not need to go towards Siras, but they must of necessity passe ouer rhe Caspian mountaines, or ferrie ouer Euphrates or Tigris, or els trauell the rough Mesopotamia, or tourne themselues towardes the Mantian Marish, or towards Babylonia. The ninth reason.

With the like reason may a man confirme this to bee true, by those that passe from Bitlis, (a famous Cittie in Armenia) to go to Tauris. For they must of necessity trauell ouer the Caspian mountaines, and still to iourney eastward, leauing behind them the Mantian marish, the Cittie of Coy, and the Caldaran champaines: which whether they be the Champaines of Araxis, or some other neere vnto them, let other men vse their owne iudgment: for wee can hardly certify the truth of that particularitie. But if Tauris were Terua, which is in the middest of Great Armenia, then should they not neede to make this iourney. For neither should they trauell so much towards the east, neither should they leaue behind them either Coy, or the Mantian Marish, or the Caldarane Champaines. The tenth reason.

This opinion of mine is no lesse confirmed to be true, by others also, that comming from the furthest partes of the East Indies, doo first arriue at Cassan a famous City of the Persian kings, and then trauell to Tauris, & from Tauris to Coy and to Van, making alwaies about eight or nyne daies iourney towardes the west: which could not be so, if Tauris were either Terua, or Tigranoama, or Tigranocerta. The leauenth reason.

The twelft reason.	Like vnto these reasons is that also which may be drawn from the iourney that is vsually made from Tauris to Babylonia. For as euerie man doth testifie, and namely Angiolello in his viage lately made into Persia, they trauell by south southweast. Which is a manifest token, that Tauris is iust in the situation of Ecbathana & not of Terua. For whosoeuer trauelleth from Terua to Babylonia, hee must of force trauell not by south southweast, but by southeast.

These are the reasons, whereby I haue beene perswaded not to leaue this parcell of my history to remaine in such doubt, but haue taken vpon mee resolutely to decide the same. Which although they be very pregnant and strong, yet shall I account the better of them, if your W. will willingly accept of them, and vouchsafe to continue the reading of this my letter, vntill you vnderstande also in what sorte Iouius and his followers haue on the other side confirmed their opinion.

The first argument of Iouius and his followers.

For three causes doo they belieue, that Tauris should bee Terua. The first Argument is drawn from a verie subtile consideration, which they haue, touching the similitude & likenes of the names of all those places, whereof they doo find that many auncient Citties doo yet at this day retaine the first nomination, although by the alteration of speeche it bee somewhat different from the same. As for example, the Turkes call Constantinople by the name of Stambul, which is a terme borrowed from the Grecians, who call this Cittie Stimboli. And this terme which the Graecians do vse, was first brought in whiles their Emperours raigned at what time the City of Constantinople was called by excellencie ὡόλίς, that is to say, the Cittie: and such as went thither, or came from thence, vsed to say (euen as we vse also at this day to say of Rome) We go to the Cittie, we come from the Cittie, alwaies vsing the terme ὡόλεί. Which Greek worde, being corrupted by the common people of Graecia, began first to bee Stimpoli, and afterwardes being more deformed and depraued by the Turkes, it came to be Stanbul. The like may bee said of the Cittie of Charsa, which Ptolomee calleth Corsa: of Anguri, which in old time was called Ancyra: of Euphrates and Araxis, the one being now called Frat, and the other Arais: of Cesarea, which still is called Caisarie: of Alexandria, which yet is called Schenderie: of Ioppa, which is called Iaffa: of Antiochia, which is called Tachie: & of many others, among whom Terua may also be nombred, which afterwarde with a small alteration of the worde came to be called Taruis, Teruis, and Tauris.

The second argument.

To this first argument, they added also a second. For they say, that those which trauell from Amida, beeing at this day called Caramita, the cheefe Cittie of Mesopotamia, & go to Teruis, do passe ouer the riuer Tigris: which riuer runeth from the one side of the Mantian Marish vnto the other side thereof with such swiftnes, that it is likened to an arrow, and thereof it purchased the name of Tigris which it hath at this day, (as Strabo teacheth vs). Neither doo they passe ouer any other Riuer of fame there. And that is a manifest token, that Tauris is in Armenia, euen in the very situation of Terua.

Besides these two reasons, they haue also a third argument, fortified vpon the relation and report of those Armenians, that come to Venice, to Rome, and to other partes of Christendome: from whom, it may be peraduenture, that Iouius tooke his information. For all these haue geuen, and at this day doo giue vndoubted testimony, that Taruis is in truth in Armenia. Which testimonie, if it bee true, then must it needes bee concluded (say they) that Taruis can be no other but Terua. *The third argument.*

These three argumentes I haue not deemed to bee so pregnant & sure, as that they do deserue or enforce, that I should commit the truth of mine opinion to the authority of Iouius. And therefore rather then I wold yeeld vnto them, I haue founde out a most easie way to resolue them, and to aunswere them most sufficiently.

Wherevpon, concerning their first argument, I say, that although the similitude of wordes do fall out well in many matters, yet in many other it doth greatly erre, & may easily deceaue vs. For whosoeuer should go about to recon vp all the Cities, and all the Riuers, and all the Mountaines, and all the Prouinces, hee should finde a great want and errour in the most parte of them. And therefore wee will alledge some fewe of them, by whose example a man may know the slender force of the reason that is drawē from this similitude of words. And in truth what similitude hath Damasco with Siam? Ierusalem with Godz? Arsacia with Casbin? Persepolis with Siras? Bithinia with Bursia? Calcedon with Scutar? Tyrus with Sur? Ptolemaida with Acri? Derbent with Alexandria? Albania with Zuiria? Iberia with Gurgistan? Atropatia with Siruan? Mesopotamia with Diarbech? Appamea with Aman? Seleucia Pieria with Soldin? Anazarbo with Acsara? Arabia Faelix with Giamen? Cilicia with Caramania? and many others the recitall whereof wold bee troublesome and tedious. And in deed, with great reason ought we to hold this for an vncertaine kind of argument, which is taken from the liknes of wordes. For those nations, that haue gouerned these regions haue not alwaies had one and the selfesame regard in naming the places which they had subdued. But as in some of them they haue still retained their verie proper names, although their language hath made them somwhat to differ: (as in some aforenamed may be seen, and as now of late we haue obserued in Cipris, which yet they call Cupros.) So in some others altogether forgetting their former names, they haue called them by diuers names, according to diuers occasiōs, & in diuers respects. Yea and Iouius himselfe saith, that Amida was called by the Turkes Caramita, for the blacknes of *The answere to the first argument.*

the earth: and we also, besides the obseruation of Iouius, doo know that Alexandria vpon the Caspian Sea is now termed by the Turkes Schenderia, (as it shold bee called by the aunciant name:) but because it is longe and straite, it came to be called Derbent, and because it hath Iron Gates Demir-Capi. Likewise for Casbin, or as the Persians terme it Casuin, (let it bee which of the aunciant Citties you will haue it to be) it is notoriously knowen, that it was so called because it was at the first a place, whereintoo they were wont to banish or confine such persons, as for their offences and misdemeanours had deserued that chastisement. Which for that it was a place of punishment, it was called by the Persians Casuin & Casbin, which in the Persian language signifieth Chastisement. The like I might say of the city of Aleppo, by the Moors called Halip, which in our tongue signifieth Milke (for the same Arabians do say, that it was so called for the aboundaunce of milke, which in the time of the Patriarches was yeelded by the heardes and flockes of cattell in those champaines). But because I haue not that certaine testimony hereof, which I haue of mine other examples, I will not make account to build any foundation therevpon. And therefore next after those thinges that I haue already noted, I will set down also what I haue obserued touching the riuer, that entreth into the sea betweene Beryto and Tripoli. Which riuer, because it runneth neere vnto a Church, which was sometimes dedicated to Sainte Iacob, is by the inhabitantes there called Mar Iacut, which is to say, the Riuer of Iacob. Likewise the riuer Orontes, which is nombred amonge the famous Riuers of Soria, (whose bankes I haue viewed, euen from his springing head to his maine channell, which is neere to Seleucia Pieria,) hath among the Arabians and the Turks quite lost his ancient name. And because it is very swift in his course, & hath many turninges and windings, (so that those which swim in it are oftentimes drowned therein,) as though the poore riuer had in that respect the nature of a murderer, therefore the Turkes and the Moores haue geuen it a name, that signifieth expresly, a murderer or traitor. And to the end that the truth hereof may likewise be knowen in mountains also, I will not conceale that which cometh to my memory touching the mountain Bacras, which is also called Beilun. This is a mountain, lying in the ranke of the mountains that deuideth Soria from Cilicia, (which how it was termed by aunciant writers, I leaue to other men to iudge). But by the Inhabitants there, it hath been alwaies, & is at this day called Bacras, for none other reason or cause, but for that it is so ragged, so eaten as it were, and in some partes, euen in the grassie plottes of it, so bald and so bare, that it resembleth the head of one that is scuruie, which by the Turkes is called Bacras, and by the Moores Beilun: for so do the Moors also call that mountaine. Hereby then it doth manifestly appeere, that it is no sound argument which is drawen from the likenes or similitude, that aunciet names haue with the names of later times. For all places haue not reserued, & retained among the diuersity of sundry languages their auncient denominations: and so it seemeth to mee that this first argument remayneth sufficiently confuted. As also the second, which hauing no good and sound roote, may easily bee ouerthrowne.

Vtterly false is that foundation, which the followers of Iouius do vse in that place where they say, that the riuer Tigris passeth from the one side of the Mantian Lake vnto the other side thereof. For it woorketh not that effect, which they speake of, in the Mantian Marish, but in the Marish, that by Strabo is called Tospite, and Topiti, and Arassena. I will not here alleadge the testimonies of later liuers, as namely of Cicala himselfe (the Bassa of Van) nor of a thousand and a thousand marchantes and souldiers, but onely the testimony of Strabo, whose authority cannot be refuted as a lyer. Hee, in the eleuenth booke of his Geography, thus writeth. Armenia hath also great Lakes. One is the Mantian Lake, that is to say, Blacke and Greene like the Sea Water: & (as they say) it is the greatest Lake next to Mwotis. It arriueth euen vnto Atropatia, and hath diuers salt-springes. The other is the Arassen Lake, called likewise Topiti: (for so it should be read, and not Toeti, as some translate it.) This hath Nitrum in it: and teareth & renteth a mans apparell, and for that cause the water of it is not good to drinke. The riuer Tigris, departing from the mountaine neere vnto Nifates, passeth through this Lake, without mingling of it selfe with the water thereof, by reason of his swiftnes, whereof it hath taken his name: for the Medians call an arrow Tigris. It hath fishes of many and diuers kindes, whereas the fishes of the lakes are but of one kinde onely. Neere to the vtmost corner or Gulfe of the Lake, this riuer falling into a great deep, and running for a great space vnder the ground, riseth againe neere to Colonitis, and from thence courseth towards Opis, and the walles of Semiramis, leauing the Cordiq [...]ns on the right hand. All this did Strabo write, by the authoritie of Eratosthenes in his sixteenth booke: where he saith also most plainely, that the saide Riuer Tigris doth not passe through the Mantian Marish, but through the Topiti. But no maruell it is, that Iouius hath conceaued this errour, cō sidering how greatly hee is also deceaued, when he will needs call Siras, Ciropolis: when likewise he saith, that in Cassan there is trafficke for silkes, and that this Cittie standeth in Sultania, betweene the South and the West: and lastly, when hee putteth no distinction or difference betweene the Zogdiani, the Bactrini, the Ariani, the Margiani, & the Aracosi, but maketh them all one. And therefore leauing these considerations, it shall be sufficient for me to answere to their last argument,

Aunswere to the second argument.

which is drawn from the report of the Armenians, who say that Tauris is situated in Armenia the great.

Aunswere to the third argument.
A reason (in verie truth) verie daungerous, verie slipperie, and verie deceitfull. And it seemeth to me to bee altogether like to the reason of those, who going about to proue, that the Amomū of Dioscorides, is none other thing, but the Pes Columbinus (that is to say, the Pigeon Foot) of Mount Libanon, do vse the common word of the Sorians, which call that Plant Hamana being in very deed nothing els but a kind of Pigeon foot. And in troth what assured credit may bee reposed in those Armenians, and in such kinde of people as are vtterlie vnskilfull in Geographie, who neuer read any authour, that had taught them the proper Termes of those prouinces? Doo wee not see what a confusion and mingle-mangle they make of the same regions? Doo they not precisely call one part of great Armenia, by the name of Gurgistan, onely because many Georgians inhabite there? And likewise on the other side, doo they not call one part of the great Media by the name of Armeni, because many Armenians do at this day dwell dispersed here and there in diuers villages of that country? But vnder the word Rumeli, which in our language signifieth Greece, how many places doo the Turkes entertertaine, which are quite out of Greece? And with their Natolia and C […]ramania doo they not likewise confound & (as it were) murder so many prouinces, that it seemeth a matter impossible to find out their ancient names? what man is hee then, that if hee had many other meanes, and many other reasons to proue the truth for the certaine acknowledgement of sundrye places, would reporte himselfe wholly and absolutely to the relation of that people?

The conclusion.
This is as much as I thought sufficient to aunswere the reasons of Iouius, & to confirme mine owne opinion. All which notwithstanding, I doo refer to your worshippes iudgement, who as a most gentle person, and a speciall frend to the truth, will make that accoumpt of my reasons as they deserue. Which that you will doo, I humbly beseeche you, and so hartely recommend my selfe vnto you.

From Rouigo the 17. of August. 1587.

Your worships most affectionate seruitor, Iohn-Thomas Minadoi.

A TABLE, CONTEYNING THE DECLARATION OF THE NAMES AND WORDES, *VSED* IN THIS HISTORIE, ASWELL AUNCIENT, AS BARBAROUS

Wherein the letter A. signifieth the Auncient: B. the Barbarous: P. The Persian: and T. the Turkish name or word.

A.

- ACca and Acri, B. a Sea-coast Citie in Soria. Ptolomaida. A. according to Ortelius and Anania.
- Adena and Adana, B. a Citie in the confines of Cilicia, Adana, and it may be, Nicopolis, A.
- Aga, B. a Capitayne, or Chiefe of his companie.
- Aggia-Chala, B. the Castell Deregrine, or the Castell of Strangers.
- Aggiami, Look for Cheselbas, and the Persians.
- Aleppo, B. and Halep, B. look for Halip.
- Alger, B. by Iouius is thought to be Iulia Cesarea, A. and by Castaldo and others, to be the Citie of Cirtha in Africa.

- Altun-Chala, T. the golden Castell, or Castell of gold: A place in the confines of great Armenia, and Georgia.
- Amadan, B. a Citie of the Persians in Parthia.
- Aman, B. a Citie in Soria, watred with the riuer Orontes. Apamea, A.
- Amasia, B. Castaldo thinketh it to be Cappadocia, A. and others take it to be in aunciect times called Amasia, A.
- Andera, or Andara, a Towne in Drusia, where most exquisite Silkes are made.
- Andrinopoli, B. a principall Citie in Thracia, Adrianopolis, A.
- Angori, B. a Citie in Cappadocia, which is a Region in Asia the lesser, and by Bellonius thought to be Encyra, and Ancyra, A. in the peregrination of Sainct Paul.
- Antachie, B. a Citie in Soria, now decayed, but yet worth the sight, both in respect of the situation and walles thereof, as also for the Riuer that runneth by it. Antiochia, A.
- Arasse, B. a Riuer that watreth the South part of great Armenia, & almost diuideth it from Georgia. Araxis, A. Achlar, and Ares, T.
- Arbella, B. a Citie in Assyria, according to Strabo, and Q. Curtius, and by the error of some thought to be Taruis.
- Arcipelago, B. but in old time called Mare Egaeum, A. a part of the Sea Mediterraneum, that seperateth Europe from Asia.
- Ardachan, B. a Citie of the Turkes in great Armenia.
- Ardouil, P. a Citie in Media, the first Seat of the Persian Sect, wherein Giunet, Sederdin, and other their successors, that were authors of the Persian superstition, did reside and reigne.
- Arz, T. a Supplication, a Request, or an Information.
- At-Maidan, B. the high Street, or chiefe Market place in Constantinople.

B.

- BAgdat, B. Laonicus calleth it Bogdatis, and the Italians call it Baldacco, in old time Babylon, A.
- Balbech, B. a Citie in Palaestina, which Bellonius taketh to be Caesarea Philippi, A. and so is it accompted in the peregrination of Sainct Paul.

- Balsara, and as Frederico writeth it, Bassora, B. a Citie in the channell of Euphrates, called by Castaldo, and others, Teredon, A.
- Bassa, T. a Capitaine, a Gouernour, a chiefe Lord.
- Beglerbey, T. a great Lord.
- Bestan, P. a Citie in Hircania.
- Bey, or Beg, or Bech, T. a chiefe man, or a Lord.
- Bir, which some call Birta, B. a Citie vpon Euphrates, in the confines of Soria.
- Bruz, B. a Hill in Armenia; the creast of the Periardj Mountaines.
- Brusia and Bursa, B. in old time the chiefe Palace of Bithynia, and called in the old time Prusia, A. But Ortelius vnaduisedly thinketh, that Bursa and Brusia is not a Citie, but a whole Region. And herein also is Castaldo deceiued, if our owne sense haue not shewed vnto vs one Citie in steed of another, or if we be not deceiued in deed in the verie names of them.

C.

- CAddi, T. a Iudge.
- Cafe, B. a place within two dayes iourney of Babylon, where Aly and his children are buried.
- Caffa, B. Anania vset h no other name: although in deed Caffa now was in old time called Theodosia, A.
- Cahaca, B. a Towne so called, situate betweene Casbin and Tauris.
- Cairo, B. a huge Citie in Aegypt, neere whereunto are the famous Pyramides: whereby a man may easily iudge, that there was the most renowmed citie of Memphis.
- Ortelius thinketh that it is Babylon: but Ortelius himself setteth downe another Babylon in another table of his, and placeth it in Assiria. So that he maketh two Cities of one name. Whereof notwithstanding it is no time now to dispute.
- Caissar, B. a place in Cilicia, of no great reckoning, and without any note of antiquitie.
- Calaus, T. a Guide.

- Caldaran, B. the name of certain famous Champeynes. Perhaps they may be the same Champeynes which Strabo called the Champeynes of Araxis.
- Calife, P. a Priest, or Prelate.
- Canac, B. a Riuer that diuideth a part of Atropatia from Armenia.
- Candahar, P. a certaine Kingdome. In old time Peripaniso, A.
- Capigi, T. a gentleman Vsher.
- Capigi-Bassi, T. the chiefe gentleman Vsher.
- Capigi-Larchecaiasi, T. the Lieutenant or chiefe Lord of the gentlemen Vshers.
- Caracach, P. a Territorie of the Persians in Media.
- Carachala, T. the black Castell, it is in Armenia, but it belongeth to the Georgians.
- Caraemit, T. the black Citie. It is now the Metropoliticall Citie of the Mesopotamians. Iouius and others call it Amida, A.
- Caramania and Caraman, B. the black Region: It is commonly deemed to be Cilicia, A.
- Casbin and Casuin, P. we may well interpret it: The place of punishment. And it is the Citie, whether the palace of the Persian Empire was translated by Tamas, and called Casbin, because those that for their punishment had deserued banishment, were at the first banished thither. It is yet in Media the great, a little more South then Tauris: So that a man may verie well think it to be Arsacia, A. in Strabo.
- Casenda, T. the common Treasure. Look Hasna.
- Cassachi, T. Robbers by the high way.
- Cassan, B. a Citie in Parthia, verie famous and rich. Ortelius and the rest make no mention of it.
- Cassangic, B. a place belonging to Maxut-Chan in Armenia.
- Cecchino, or Zecchino, a Venetian Duckate.
- Chala, and Chalasi, B. a Towne or a Castell.
- Chan, P. and also vsed in Tartaria, and is the same that the Turkes call a Bassa.
- Chars, B. peraduenture it is that which Ptolomie calleth Corsa, A.
- Checaia, T. a Deputie or Agent.

A TABLE, CONTEYNING THE *DECLARATION OF THE NAMES AND WORDES*

- Cheiserie, B. we think it to be Caesarea in Palaestina, A. a litle from Ioppa. Ptolomie saieth it is Caesarea, wherof Strabo maketh mention. It hath many notes of antiquitie.
- Cheselbas, B. a Red-Capp. It is a title giuen to the Persians: who are also called the Soffians, the Cheselbas, the Persians, and the Aggiami. Look Persians.
- Chianichie, B. a place neere to Ragusa, verie famous, because it was the natiue Countrie of Ebrain Bassa, sonne in law to Amurath.
- Chiaus, T. a Nuntio, or an Embassadour.
- Chielder-Giol, B. the Lake of Chielder: for Giol signifieth a lake: and it may be thought without any error to be the Poole of Euphrates, A.
- Chielder Monte, B. the hilles of Periardo.
- Chielebi, B. a Gentleman.
- Chiulfal, B, a Towne in Armenia, yet inhabited at this day by the Georgians.
- Chiuri-Chala, B. a new Territorie in Georgia, that is to say, inhabited of old by the Georgians, but yet comprehended vnder Armenia.
- Clisca, a Territorie in Armenia, and in old time possessed by the Georgians, though now in the handes of the Turkes.
- Codabanda, P. Blind or weak of sight. Hodabanda signifieth the selfe same thing, but other writers erroniously pronounce it Hodabende.
- Coran, B. a Citie in Parthia.
- Corfu, a late word: a famous Island, called in old time Corcyra, A. and according to Ortelius, Corfinio, A.
- Coy, B. a Citie in the borders of Armenia, and Media, betweene Van and Tauris.
- Culbat, B. a Citie in Parthia.
- Cur, B. a Citie in Parthia.
- Curchi-Bassi, P. Captain of the Curchi, who are the souldiers, that are appointed for the guard of the Persian Kings Court.
- Curdi, B. a people which many think to be the Parthians, A. But we cannot possiblie thinke them to be so. wherein we agree with Castaldo.

- Curzolari, B. in old time called the Echinades, A. which are certain Rockes, verie famous by reason of the victorie by Sea obtayned by the most happie and fortunate League of the Chatholikes, against the Turkish fleet.
- Cussestan, B. a part of Assyria.

D.

- DAgmat, B. a Citie in the confines of Parthia, and of Media the great.
- Damasco, A. a Citie in Soria. Look Sciam.
- Deftardar, T. a Treasourer or Chamberlein.
- Demir-Capi, T. the Iron-Gates. Demir-Capi is also called Derbent. It is a Citie sometimes called Alessandria, A. neere to the Hircanian Sea. It is called Derbent, because it is in figure narrow and long: and Demir-Capi, because there were the Iron-gates, that were sometimes the entrance into Scythia.
- Demotica, B. a Citie in Thracia, famous in regard of the banishment of Sinan-Bassa into that place, wherof mention is made in the Historie, Lib. 5.
- Derbent, B. a Citie called Demir-Capi. Derbent signifieth streit or narrow.
- Diarbech, B. the Countrie of Mesopotamia.
- Diuano, B. a place of audience, or a Counsaile-house. It is sometimes taken for the audience it selfe, and sometimes for the Counsaile it selfe.
- Don, B. the Riuer sometimes called Tanais, A. in Sarmatia.
- Dreuis and Deruis, B. a Religious person, an Heremite.

E.

- EDel, B. sometimes called Volga, A. a famous Riuer in Sarmatia within Europe.
- Emir, B. a common name among the Arabians, and the Drusians, vsed for a Prince, a Duke, a chief Noble man.
- Eres, B. a Citie in Atropatia.
- Erzirum, B. we think it to be Simbra in Ptolomie.

- Essahul, P. a troupe of Souldiers beionging to the Guard of the Persian King.

F.

- FAchi, B. a Master of Ceremonies, a Master of Religion.
  Famagosta, B. a new word corrupted from the vulgar Greeke, which calleth it Famausta, in old time it was Salamina in Cyprus, A.
- Farssi, P. the Region of Persia.

G.

- GAngiara, B. a sharpe crooked dagger.
- Gaza, A. a Citie in the confines of Iudea, and in the way that leadeth towards Pelusium, A.
- Genge, B. a Citie of the Persians in Armenia the greater.
- Gheilan, B. a Citie in the Region of Gilan, which Castaldo calleth Geli.
- Giamen, B. a Prouince in Asia, where Arabia Felice is situated.
- Gianizaro, B. a degree of Turkish Souldiers so called.
- Giauat, B. a Citie of Atropatia, in the confines of Media the greater.
- Gien, B. a Citie of the Parthians.
- Giol, T. a lake or a poole.
- Giurgi-Chala, T. the Georgian-Castell, now possessed by the Turkes. It is in the confines of Georgia and Armenia.
- Godz, B. the Citie of Ierusalem.
- Gogna, and Conia, B. a Citie so called, and in old time Iconium, A. the chiefe Citie of the Lycaonians.
- Goletta, B. a famous Island.
- Gori, and Gorides, B. a Territorie in Georgia.
- Grin, B. a Territorie inhabited by the Georgians, situated on the hither side of Araxis.
- Gurgistan and Georgia, B. the Region that contayneth all the auncient Iberia, and part also of Armenia the great.

The inhabitants of the Countrey do call all that Territorie Gurgistan, which is inhabited by the Georgians. In which point, Negro, Anania, and Pius secundus are not well aduised, because they think that Georgia is onely Iberia.

- Guuergi-Chalasi, B. a Castell situate in the middest of a little lake towards Tauris.

H.

- HAlip, an Arabian word, and signifieth Milke. It is a verie famous Citie in Soria, which Iouius calleth Alapia, Bellonius calleth it Hierapolis, and Qillanoua being in a notorious error for this point, calleth it Antiochia. For Antiochia is two dayes iourney distant from Aleppo, more toward the Sea, as we our selues haue seen with our eyes.
- Hasna, T. It signifieth Treasure, Store, Money collected aswell for publike, as for priuate vses, although properly it is onely taken for the publike Treasure, or for the Kinges monyes.
- Hassan-Chalasi, T. The Castell of Hassan. It is also called by the Turkes, Passin. It is a new erected thing betweene Erzirum and Chars, situate vpon the bankes of the riuer Euphrates.
- Heri, B. a Citie in Aria.
- Hispahan, B. a Citie sometimes in Parthia.

I.

- IEsselbas, B. a greene-Cap. A certain people betweene the Bactrians and the Sogdians, so called, because they did weare Greene-Capps on their heads.
- Imammadulasis, B. a Citie in Parthia.
- Imbrahur-Bassi, T. Master of the Kings horse.
- Isnic, B. a Citie in old times called Nicea, A. in Bithynia, neere to the Moore Ascania, A.
- Istigelu, and Sagialu, B. a Renowmed familie, both at Casbin, and also ouer all the kingdome of Persia.

L.

- LAke-Actamar, in old time called the Moore or marish Martiana, or Margiana, or Mantiana, A. and according to Strabo, it is in Armenia the greater.
- Lake of Esseecchia, in old time called the Marish Lychnitis, A. in Georgia.
- Lake of Isnic, in old time the Marish Ascania, A. in Bithynia.
- Lake Tospite, or Toeti, it is in great Armenia.
- Lizza, B. a Citie by the Sea-coast in Soria, called in old time Laodicea, A.
- Lori, B. a Fortresse in Armenia, sometimes belonging to the Georgians, but now possessed by the Turkes.

M.

- MAcadems, B. a word vsed among the Drusiani for a Deputie, an Agent, or a chief Factor. For an Emir or Lord in Drusia. Look the 7. Booke.
- Macuco, B. a Measure in Soria, wherewith they measure Corne. It is a little bigger then the bushell of Padua, that is fower bushels and a halfe, Venetian measure.
- Malan, B. a Citie in Parthia.
- Mar delle Zabacche, B. in old time called Palus Moeotica, A. the Fennes of Moeotis.
- Mar di Bachu, B. in tymes passed Mare Caspium, and Mare Hircanum, A. It is also at this day called the Sea of Corazum.
- Mar Maggiore, the great Sea. And Mar Nero, the black Sea, sometimes called Pontus Euxinus, A.
- Mar Morto, the dead Sea, sometimes called the Lake Asphaltitis, A.
- Marant, B. a Citie neere to Armenia in the confines of the Medians, or rather within Media.
- Maras, B. a Citie in Cilicia, called by Bellonius and Ortelius, Maronia, A.
- Marmara, B. a Citie vpon the Sea-coast of Thracia.
- Masandran, B. a Citie in Hircania.

- Massiat, B. a Citie in Parthia.
- Masul, T. a man cassiered, or depriued of his Office: in English, lack out of office.
- Mecca, B. a Citie in Arabia Foelix, where some think Mahamet was borne, and where he is also buried.
- Mengrellia, B. sometimes the Region of Colchos, A. famous for the golden Fleece.
- Meschita, B. the place where the Barbarians do meete together, to say their prophane prayers: in English a Temple, or a Church.
- Miana, B. a Citie situate in the borders of Media the greater, of Persia, and of Parthia. It is peraduenture so called, by the Riuer that is neer vnto it, whose name is Miana.
- Miriza, and Mirize, P. the title of a Prince in Persia. The Kings chiefe Lieutenant.
- Moldauia, a Region in Dacia.
- Mordar, P. a Chaunceller. The Turks call him Tescheregi.
- Mucaren: the first moneth of the Turkish yeare: much agreeing with our Ianuary.
- Mufti, T. the chiefe Priest.
- Mustaed-Dini, P. the same which the Turkes call Mufti. The chiefe Priest.

N.

- NAplos, B. in old time called Napoli, A. in Samaria: peraduenture it was in time past Nephthalim, A.
- Nassiuan, B. a Citie in Media the greater, or els in the confines of Media, and Armenia. Some think it to be Nasuana, and others take it to be Artaxata, A.
- Natolia, in the opinion of Bellonius, comprehendeth all the Regions of Phrygia, Galatia, Bithynia, Pontus, Lydia, Caria, Paphlagonia, Lycia, Magnesia, Cappadocia, and Comagena.
- Neneruan, B. a place in Armenia bordering vpon Georgia.
- Nisabul, B. a Citie in Aria.
- Nisaur, B. a Citie in the confines of Parthia and Hircania.
- Nosul, T. a Taxe or collection of Corne.

O.

- OLti, T. a place belonging to the Turkes, betwene Erzirum and Ardachan.

P.

- PAngiazar, B. a Citie bordering vpon Hircania and Media the greater.
- Passin. Look Hassan-Chalasi.
- Persiani, The Persians. They are also called Aggiami, Cheselbas, & Sofiani. Persiani, of the Prouince of Persia: Aggiami, of the Region Azemia, or Aggiamia: Cheselbas, of the Redd-marke which these people weare in their Turbantes: and Soffians, of the Sofi, who is their chiefe Gouernour.
- Peruana-Giol, T. the lake of Sclaues. It is in Armenia.
- Phasis, A. a Citie in Colchis, called yet at this day Phasis and Fas.
- Porta, a Gate: but principally in this Historie it is taken for the Court of the Turkish Sultan: because all his Counsailors, and chiefe Gouernours of his kingdome do vse to sit in the Gate of the Emperours Court, to heare and dispatch causes aswell priuate as publike.
- Portugall, in old time called Lusitania, A.

R.

- RAfadi, B. a man of a false Religion, of a false faith.
- Rama, a Towne in Palaestina, which Castaldo calleth Lidda. Peraduenture it was that Rama, A. which mourned and wept for the great slaughter of the holie Innocents, Math. 2.
- Ramadan, T. one of the solemne feastes of the Turkes. It is also the proper name of a man, and the name of a Moone. For as we haue twelue Monethes, with their seuerall proper names: so haue the Turkes their xij. Moones with their seuerall proper names also.
- Reiuan, B. a Citie in Armenia. It may be, it is Terua in Ptolomie. But I do not altogether agree with him in that point.

S.

- SAffetto, B. a Citie in Galilie, inhabited by the Iewes.
- Saha, or Shah, P. the great King or Sofi of Persia.
- Saitan-Chalasi, B. the Castell of Satan, or the Deuils Castell, in the confines of Armenia and Georgia.
- Salmas, B. a Citie betwixt Tauris and Van, but Southward to them both.
- Sancazan, B. a place neer to Tauris, famous in this Historie, aswell in respect of some battells there foughten, as also of the death of Generall Osman, who died there.
- Sangiacco, B. a Lord, or a kind of Captaine.
- Sardar, T. Captaine of the Iannizzaries, Captaine of the Armie, and properly the Generall.
- Saru, B. a Citie in Media the greater.
- Sasuar, B. a Citie in Parthia.
- Sciam, B. the Citie of Damasco. Look Damasco.
- Scutar, and Scutari, B. sometimes called Chalcedon, A. a Citie in Asia, right ouer against Constantinople. Some do erroniously call it Chrysopolis, A.
- Sechi, B. a Citie in Atropatia bordering vpon Georgia.
- Seida, and Seit, B. in old time called Sidonia, A. a Citie on the Sea cost in Drusia.
- Sembran, B. a Citie in Parthia.
- Semitarra, B. a Scimitarre, a long crooked Sword. A Faulchon.
- Ser, B. a Riuer sometimes called Cirus, A. that watreth the South part of Georgia.
- Sessa. Look Tocca and Turbante.
- Siec, B. an old, wise, Religious, learned, and prudent man. A man of good, and holie life.
- Siliurea, a Citie in Thracia called Selymbria: Which the Persian calleth Selimbria, and Nicolo Nicolio, Seliurie.
- Sinibra, or Simbra In Ptolomie A. It is now called Erzirum, fower daies iourney distant from Trabisonda.
- Siras, B. some call it Persepolis, A. and some Ciropolis. A. It is the chiefe palace of the Region of Persia.

- Siruan, and Siruania, B. sometimes called Media Atropatia. The Hebrewes called it Madian, A.
- Siuas, B. in old time Sebastapolis, A. a Citie in Natolia.
- Soffi, and Sofito, P. an aunciet word signifying a wise man, learned and skilfull in Magike Naturall. It is growen to be the common name of the Emperour of Persia.
- Soffian, B. a place neer vnto Tauris. It may be perhaps the aunciet Soffia.
- Soldin, B. a Citie vpon the Sea-coast of Soria, destroyed long ago. It was called in old time Seleucia Pieria, A. within fiue miles whereof the Riuer Orontes dischargeth it self into the Sea: But Castaldo in his description of Asia, doeth not describe it in deed, as it standeth.
- Soria, B. in times past the Region of Syria, A.
- Spahini, T. a companie of Turkish Souldiers so called.
- Spaoglani, B. a companie of foote-men, inferiour in degree to the Iannizzaries.
- Stambul, by the Turkes and Arabians so called, in steed of Constantinople.
- Subassi, B. The Lieutenant or Captaine of a Garrison or Guard.
- Sultania, a Citie in great Media.
- Sultano, or Sultan, B. a Captain. A great Lord. It is verie often vsed for the Emperour of Turkie: as Sultan Amurath, the great Turk Amurath.
- Sumachi, and Sumachia, B. the chiefe Palace of Atropatia.
- Sunni, B. a man of sound faith, and sincere opinion in matter of Religion.
- Sur, B. a Citie vpon the Sea-coast of Soria, in old time called Tyrus, A.

T.

- TArtari, and Tatar, B. the Tartarians, inhabiting Scythia and Sarmatia.
- Tatar-Chan, B. the chiefe Lord or Gouernour of the Tartarians. He is called the great Chan of Tartaria.

- Tauris, and Taruis, Read the Letter to S. Mario Corrado in the end of this booke.
- Techisnandan, B. Certain Mountaines in Caramania Deserta.
- Teflis, and Tiflis, a Citie in Armenia, but belonging to the Georgians.
- Teftis, T. a Processe or Bill of complaint, put vp by the Plaintife.
- Teracan, B. a Citie in Parthia.
- Tocca, B. the round Roll, which the Barbarians vse to weare on their heades. It is also called Sessa and Turbante.
- Tomanis, a Citie in Armenia, but belonging to the Georgians, verie famous for the notorious & treacherous straites that are neer it.
- Trabisondo, B. a Sea-coast Citie vpon Pontus Euxinus, called in old time Trapezuntium, A.
- Triala, B. a place in Armenia, renowmed for a number of Churches there, which held of the Romish Religion.
- Triala, B. a Sea-coast Citie in Asia and in Africa.
- Triala, B. a white Roll, which the Barbarians were
- vpon their heades. Look Tocca.
- Turbat, B. a Citie in Parthia.
- Turcoman, a Citie betwixt Tauris and Casbin.
- Turcomanni, a people mingled among the Turkes and Persians.
- Turcomania the greater, of old called Great Armenia, A.
- Tursis, B. a Citie in Parthia.

V.

- UAn, B. a Citie in the Martian Marish.
- Visier, B. a chiefe Counsailour, or Gouernour generall of the State of Turkie.
- Vlac, and Volacchi, T. Postes, or Currors to run of a message in hast.
- Vlu-Bassi, B. the Captain of a certain number of Souldiers, but not so high in degree as an Aga is.

Z.

- ZAffo, and Giaffa, B. a Citie by the Sea-side, in old times called Ioppa, A.
- Zagatai, B. certain Tartarians, comprehended vnder the name of the Sogdiani.
- Zaghen, B. a City in Armenia, inhabited by the Georgians.
- Zaini, T. a noble companie of valiant Souldiers.
- Zanga, B. a Citie in great Armenia.
- Zante, B. an Island in the Ionian Sea, called in old time Zacynthus, A.
- Zine, B, certain festiual signes and shewes of publike ioy.
- Zuiria, B. a Region lying at the rootes of Mount Caucasus, towards the Hircanian Sea, and was called in old time, Albania, A.

FINIS

www.ingramcontent.com/pod-product-compliance
Lightning Source LLC
Chambersburg PA
CBHW082032300426
44117CB00015B/2455